MORAL LEADERSHIP
IN BUSINESS

MORAL LEADERSHIP IN BUSINESS

LaRue Tone Hosmer
University of Michigan

IRWIN
Burr Ridge, Illinois
Boston, Massachusetts
Sydney, Australia

© RICHARD D. IRWIN, INC., 1994

Senior sponsoring editor: Kurt L. Strand
Editorial assistant: Michele Dooley
Marketing manager: Kurt Messersmith
Project editor: Rebecca Dodson
Production manager: Laurie Kersch
Designer: Larry Cope
Art coordinator: Heather Burbridge
Art studio: Graphics Plus
Compositor: J.M. Post Graphics, division Cardinal Communications
        Group, Inc.
Typeface: 10/12 Palatino
Printer: R. R. Donnelley & Sons Company

Library of Congress Cataloging-in-Publication Data

Hosmer, LaRue T.
    Moral leadership in business/LaRue Tone Hosmer.
        p.   cm.
    Includes index.
    ISBN 0-256-14325-0
        1. Business ethics.   2. Leadership—Moral and ethical aspects.
    3. Social responsibility of business.   I. Title.
    HF5387.H675   1994
    174'.4—dc20   93–5058

Printed in the United States of America
    2 3 4 5 6 7 8 9 0 DOC 0 9 8 7 6 5 4

PREFACE

Many good books are now available in the field of business ethics from a number of distinguished authors. Why then did I write this one? It was not to simply add one more to that group. Instead, I believe strongly that ethical reasoning—the means by which we deal with moral problems—is so different from the quantitative and comparative reasoning methods used in the other disciplines of management education that it is necessary for those of us who teach in business ethics to be much more direct and explicit in the way we describe and discuss our reasoning methodology. Consequently, I have attempted to achieve five goals:

A direct and explicit definition of moral problems. Moral problems are those in which some individuals or groups are hurt or harmed in some way outside their own control. Moral problems are not "moral" because they contravene generally accepted moral standards. They are "moral" because of the hurt or harm caused to other people, and clear recognition of this fact seems to quickly gain the attention and the interest of the students.

A direct and explicit description of moral or ethical reasoning. Moral problems in management are particularly complex because some individuals or groups are going to be hurt or harmed while others are to be benefited or helped. We cannot simply average harms to others and benefits to ourselves, and then make the decision. Instead, we need a different reasoning method based upon ethical principles that will eliminate our self-interest.

A direct and explicit explanation of ethical principles. Ethical principles are the first rules for a "good" society; they are the basic postulates that, if everyone adopted, would ensure a society in which people willingly cooperated for the benefit of all. Obviously, everyone will not adopt these rules, but they do provide a means for managers to eliminate self-interests from their decisions. What is "best" for society is the appropriate question, not what is "best" for us and our company.

A direct and explicit discussion of organizational precepts. Ten ethical principles are described in historical sequence in the text. They enable managers to make decisions in the moral problems where some are to be harmed while others are to be benefited by eliminating self-interest. What is "right"? What is "just"? What is "fair"? But the use of ethical principles in management decisions is not enough. The spirit or intent of these decisions has to be infused throughout the organization.

A direct and explicit listing of managerial responsibilities. Why should a manager be "right" and "just" and "fair"? Why should a manager worry about harm to others? The argument of this text is that managers are now so dependent upon the cooperation and innovation of others that they must be moral, they must treat others in ways they consider to be "right" and "just" and "fair" to build trust, commitment, and effort.

Treating the other stakeholders—both those within and those outside the firm—in ways that they consider to be "right" and "just" and "fair" in order to build trust, commitment, and effort among those stakeholders, is moral leadership in business. It is the subject—as well as the title—of this book.

Let me say in closing that the ideas in this book are not entirely my own. I have learned greatly from others who have long been active in managerial ethics, and I should like to acknowledge my debt to Richard DeGeorge (Kansas), Manual Velasquez (Santa Clara), Thomas Donaldson (Georgetown), Patricia Werhane (Loyola of Chicago), Gerald Cavanagh (Detroit), William Frederick (Pittsburgh), Edwin Epstein (Berkeley), Oliver Williams (Notre Dame), Lisa Newton (Fairfield), Kirk Hanson (Stanford), and Nicholas Steneck (Michigan). I thank you all.

LaRue T. Hosmer

TABLE OF CONTENTS

CHAPTER 1

The Nature of Moral Problems

Moral problems are those that result in hurt or harm to others. Moral problems are not "moral" because a widely respected moral authority says that they are, and they are not "moral" because they go against generally accepted moral standards. They are "moral" because they result in hurt or harm to other people in ways that are outside their own control.

Moral problems in management are particularly complex because they usually result in benefits to some individuals along with the harms to others, and it is this mix of benefits and harms, of positive and negative outcomes, that makes them so difficult to resolve. How do you decide when one group of people will be substantially better off as a result of a managerial decision or action for which you are responsible and another group will be substantially worse off? It is not easy to make that decision, and there is little in the functional and technical training of business men and women that helps in sorting out the major considerations and understanding the different choices. Let us start with an example in which the benefits are obviously very substantial, the harms seem minimal by comparison, and yet those harms will be devastating to the very few people who may be forced to bear them.

FIRST EXAMPLE OF A MORAL PROBLEM

Hydro-Quebec, a large public utility owned by the Province of Quebec, has proposed building a huge hydroelectric generating station in the remote wilderness of northern Canada. The company plans to construct a dam 17 miles long across the valley of the Great Whale River, close to the mouth of that river where it empties into Hudson Bay. The dam will create a lake covering 9,100 square miles, leaving only isolated peaks and upland areas as islands in a forested and tundra region stretching 300 miles to the east, almost to the border to Newfoundland, and 200 miles to the north, nearly to the Arctic Circle.

The dam would serve a hydroelectric generating station that will produce 14,000 megawatts of electric power, equivalent to the total power output of 14 modern coal-fired or nuclear generating plants, but of course without the acid emissions or nuclear wastes that are associated with those energy sources. The power would be sold to the six New England states and New York City; it would eliminate any need for the electric utilities in that geographic

1

EXHIBIT 1–1   Map of the Hydro-Quebec Great Whale Generating Project

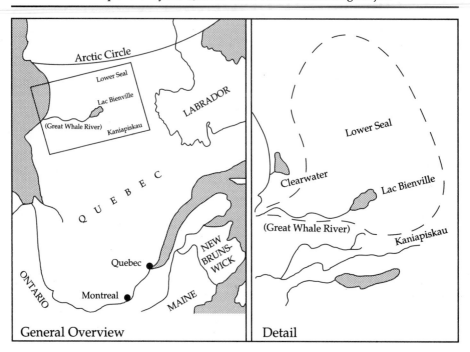

General Overview   Detail

area to build additional capacity for the next 10 years. Profits from the sale of the power will be used to fund improvements in education for the children of Quebec.

The electric power is needed in a region of the United States that for years has been dependent upon the importation of foreign oil for both home heating and industrial expansion. The profits are needed in an area of Canada that for years has suffered from insufficient funding for primary and secondary education. The only possible problem with the project is the opposition of the Cree Indians and Inuit Eskimos who live in the area to be flooded, a total of 750 families. The chief of the Cree has refused to sell the land (which had never been formally deeded to his people by treaty) saying, "It is hard to explain to white people what we mean when we say our land is part of our life. We are like rocks and trees, beaver and caribou. We belong here. We will not leave."

How do you decide when faced with this issue? Millions of people will benefit. Only 750 families will be harmed. Certainly you can pay the 750 families a fair price for their land. But how do you establish a "fair" price for scrub forests and tundra that has no commercial value? And how do you compensate those families for their native culture which will be totally destroyed? There is no equivalent land in Canada that is not currently occupied either by native peoples or by recent settlers, so that you cannot simply ask the Cree Indians and Inuit Eskimos to move farther east into Newfoundland or farther west into Manitoba without disrupting the lives of other people. Lastly, the Indians and Eskimos say that they do not want your money; they want to stay where they are, living their lives the way they have for hundreds of years on land they consider to be their own.

If you were to compute the net present value of the project, discounting the projected cash flows firstly for the investment amounts and then for the revenues less expenses, you would find an exceedingly high rate of return because hydroelectric generating plants have no fuel costs. If you were to arrange a special election in the province, you could expect the approval percentage to be overwhelming because the educational benefits will go to the vast majority of the population. Economically, the project makes sense. Politically, it is feasible. Legally, there are no obstacles. Still, is it "right" to force a small number of native people to move from their ancestral land?

Is it "right"? That is the basic question that you have to answer when you encounter a moral problem in management. The basic question is not, "Is it profitable?" Often the financial returns are very high, as they will be with the Great Whale dam and generating station. Further, the basic question is not, "Is it legal?" Often the legality is not an issue, as it would not be in Quebec were an election held to approve the project, or were a court asked to rule on the issue of the province taking the land by eminent domain (right of a government agency to expropriate private land for a public use, such as a highway or an airport). Instead, the basic question in the ethics of corporate management is, "Is it right to harm one group of people in order to benefit others?"

In private business firms, a group of "other" people who always have to be considered are the stockholders. They own the company. Legally, business managers serve as representatives of the stockholders and are expected to act in their interests to increase the long-term value of the firm. But the question here is whether there are moral limits on managerial actions to increase the long-term value of the firm. Is it "right" to harm one group of people in order to benefit the shareholders? Let us look at another example where the harms to a specific group of people are very real, yet the benefits to the stockholders would be very great.

SECOND EXAMPLE OF A MORAL PROBLEM

Medical costs within the United States are escalating rapidly. Medical costs for older people are escalating particularly rapidly because the elderly are susceptible to the types of health care problems that can be alleviated if not cured by modern medical technologies. These modern medical technologies can be very expensive. Heart transplants are one example of an expensive medical technology that is particularly applicable to older people; joint replacements of the knee or hip are another example.

Companies that promised their workers medical insurance when they retired have become burdened with costs that have risen to be five to seven times higher than were expected at the time of retirement. General Motors, for example, has 84,000 middle level management retirees who receive an estimated $252,000,000 per year in health care benefits. Health care benefits for older retirees is the most rapidly growing expense classification in the domestic auto industry. As General Motors has encountered intense global competition from foreign firms that do not provide health care benefits to retirees (generally those benefits are provided by the governments in Japan and Germany), there have been numerous efforts to control or reduce these costs.

General Motors has attempted to negotiate special rates for its retirees at hospitals and health centers. That has not worked because the retirees are spread throughout the country and are not concentrated in any one region. General Motors has attempted to limit payments to physicians and clinics. That has not worked as the doctors and clinics have simply refused to serve non-emergency patients from that company.

Now there is a proposal, seriously being considered by the senior executives at General Motors, that the health care benefits for middle and lower level management retirees be "capped" at an average cost of $2,000 per person per year. Any amounts above that figure would have to be paid by the retiree or his or her family. Health care benefits for worker (hourly paid) retirees are not an issue; they were capped earlier and cannot now be cut further because they are the subject of a union contract. Health care benefits for middle and lower level management retirees can be cut because those people never were represented by a union, and consequently they lack the protection of a written contract. The middle and lower level management personnel received a verbal promise when they retired, not a formal contract, and there is even a question as to how many actually received that promise. Many of them simply "always assumed" that their medical expenses would continue to be covered when they retired. Only the upper level management retirees received a formal contract that specifically included the full coverage of medical costs following retirement.

What is "right" in this instance? What is "fair"? Medical costs above the $2,000 limit can easily wipe out a family's total savings. Before you say that obviously General Motors has to keep its verbal promise to its management retirees and continue the program, realize that medical costs for the elderly segment of the population are escalating at over 20 percent per year. The total costs if General Motors decides to continue the program "as is" are expected to grow to $627 million in five years, and to $1.56 billion in 10 years.

Those large amounts of money, in the range of $627 million to $1.56 billion per year, could be distributed to the stockholders as dividends if they were saved by the proposed cap. Or they could be used to design new products (perhaps alternative fuel vehicles) which would lead to improved competitiveness in the automobile industry and greater benefits for the current workers, managers, suppliers, creditors, distributors, and customers as well as the stockholders of the company. A successful alternative fuel vehicle would also lead to

---

EXHIBIT 1–2
Two Forms of the Basic Moral Question

Form I is consequential; it focuses on the outcomes of managerial decisions and actions.

> Who will be hurt, and how badly?
>
> Who will be benefited, and how much?

Form II is obligational; it focuses on the duties and responsibilities of the persons holding managerial positions.

> What, if anything, do you owe to others?
>
> What, if anything, do others owe to you?

Both forms ask the same set of questions: "Is it right?" "Is it just?" "Is it fair?"

---

greater benefits for local residents in the community where the car was built; they would have more jobs in the supporting retail and service companies. A successful alternative fuel vehicle would even lead to greater benefits for the citizens of the country where it was designed; they would have better air quality in the cities where commuting creates smog, and they would have a better trade balance with the nations that export oil. How do you balance the very real benefits for that wide range of individuals against the very obvious harms for the middle and lower level management retirees?

TWO FORMS OF THE MORAL QUESTION

"Who will be hurt, and how badly?" is one form of the moral question that you will face as a member of corporate management. Another form is, "What do you as a corporate manager owe to others associated with the organization?" What, if anything, do you owe to an industrial customer who has purchased your product but now finds that it doesn't perform quite as well as the customer expected? What, if anything, do you owe to an employee who has worked for your company for 37 years but now can't quite keep up with the current pace of business? What, if anything, do you owe to a resident of the local community who objects to your plan to establish a toxic waste dump that meets all federal, state, and local laws close to her backyard?

The "Who will be hurt?" form of the moral question focuses on the outcomes or consequences of managerial decisions and actions. It asks, in brief, whether the proposed distribution of the benefits and the expected allocation of the harms generated by the firm can be considered to be "right" and "just" and "fair."

EXHIBIT 1–3
Stakeholders in a Business Firm

Plant workers	Retail distributors
Functional managers	Industrial customers
Technical staff	Retail consumers
Senior executives	Credit sources
Material suppliers	Company owners
Component suppliers	Local residents
Equipment suppliers	National citizens
Wholesale distributors	Global inhabitants

The "What do you owe?" form of the moral question focuses on the duties and responsibilities of corporate managers to the other people associated with the firm. This is the *stakeholder* approach to management. The name was obviously chosen to contrast with the more familiar *stockholder* approach to management.

Stockholders are owners. They own stock in the company and elect the board members who appoint the managers. The stockholder approach to management is the belief that managers have duties and responsibilities solely to those owners and that those duties and responsibilities primarily focus on increasing the long-term value of the firm through the maximization of profits.

Stakeholders, on the other hand, are people associated with the company. They can be said to have a "stake" in the company because of that association, and they include such groups as workers, managers, technical personnel, senior executives, suppliers, distributors, and customers. The stakeholder approach to management is the belief that managers have identifiable duties and responsibilities to the full range of people associated with the firm, not just to the stockholders.

The "Who will be hurt?" and the "What do we owe?" forms of the moral question are obviously related. They are different ways of looking at the same moral problem. One focuses on the distribution of benefits and the allocation of harms brought about by managerial decisions and actions; the other concentrates on the duties and responsibilities of the managerial personnel to the people who will be affected by those decisions and actions. The two forms of the moral question provide different perspectives of the same moral problem and help managers in first recognizing and then understanding those problems.

SIMPLE VS. COMPLEX MORAL PROBLEMS

Some moral problems are very easy to recognize and simple to understand. Usually, these are the problems where the benefits are concentrated upon a single person or a small group, and the harms are diffused throughout the

---

EXHIBIT 1–4
Simple vs. Complex Types of Moral Problems

Type I. Simple moral problem with concentrated benefits and dispersed harms. The benefits can usually be expressed in financial terms ($), and they often seem to come to the manager who will decide and his or her associates.

"Will I do the right thing?"

Organizational pressures to perform.

Type II. Complex moral problem with dispersed benefits and concentrated harms. Neither the benefits nor the harms can usually be expressed in financial terms ($), and the harms often seem to come to people who are relatively powerless.

"What is the right thing to do?"

Organizational pressures to conform.

---

organization or the society. Often in these simple problems, the person who will benefit the most is the manager who will make the decision or take the action.

Many sales managers know at least one purchasing agent who will be glad to specify products from a given company if that company will provide free vacation trips or home electronic equipment. Obviously, the yearly bonus will be much higher for the sales manager who provides those gifts. Most production managers know at least one manufacturing operation where costs could be cut at the expense of product quality or process safety. Obviously, the annual evaluation will be much more favorable for the production manager who makes those cuts. Most active consultants learn at least one piece of inside information about their clients that would enable them to buy or sell stock in that firm profitably. Obviously, the capital gains will be much higher for the consultant who does make those trades.

These simple moral problems are easy to recognize because the benefits come to a single person or to a small group of people who share the benefits, while the harms are widely distributed. These simple moral problems are also easy to understand. The people who are involved know what they should do. The only question they face is, "Will I do the right thing?" They know that they should not pay bribes to increase sales, cut corners to decrease costs, or trade on inside information to make profits.

Organizational pressures, of course, may make it more difficult for managers to answer that question as they know they should. The incentive system may so heavily emphasize commissions that it is difficult for a sales manager to earn an adequate income without paying bribes. The control system may so heavily emphasize costs that it is difficult for a production manager to survive without cutting corners. Or the corporate culture of the consulting firm may so openly tolerate insider trading that a new person feels, "Everyone else is doing it; why shouldn't I?" However, organizational pressures do not excuse the managerial decisions or actions that are so clearly "wrong" in these simple moral problems; all they do is make those decisions or actions more understandable.

The more complex moral problems are not so easily recognized because the benefits are widespread, distributed throughout the organization or even the society, and the harms are often focused on groups that are geographically far away, or not very influential in the decision process, or both. Neither the Inuit Indians nor the General Motors retirees will have much say in the decisions that will affect them so severely.

The complex moral problems concern plant closings, employee layoffs, workplace dangers, tax rebates, political contributions, advertising claims, salary differentials, pharmaceutical prices, foreign payments, oil spills, waste exports, and junk bonds. Complex moral problems mix benefits and harms, duties and responsibilities. They are not quickly recognized. They are not easily solved. Here the question you face is, "What is the right thing to do?"

Complex moral problems are often made particularly difficult to resolve because of organizational pressures to conform for the alleged good of the firm. Here it is not a question of individual managers losing a bonus or a chance for promotion if they don't take an action that they know to be "wrong," such as paying a foreign bribe or taking a production short-cut. Here it is a question of individual managers losing their jobs and even perhaps their careers if they *do* take an action that they believe to be "right," such as reporting unsafe conditions or challenging improper practices.

"Whistle-blowers" are not popular in most organizations. They report situations which either have harmed people or have the definite potential to harm people such as unsafe working conditions or improper marketing practices, and they force changes in those conditions or practices. They are not popular because those conditions and practices have usually been in place for some time and have often been fully accepted by other members of the organization. Organizational pressures to conform create what is probably the most difficult of all moral problems because they force a manager to choose between his or her career and his or her duty.

THIRD EXAMPLE OF A MORAL PROBLEM

Lincoln Savings & Loan was a large financial institution based in Phoenix, Arizona, that accepted customer deposits and provided real estate loans in both Arizona and California. It declared bankruptcy in 1979. It is famous chiefly because its majority owner and senior executive, Mr. Charles Keating, made substantial political contributions to five U.S. senators who subsequently intervened with federal regulators on his behalf.

Lincoln Savings & Loan became bankrupt, at a cost to the U.S. taxpayers of more than $2 billion, because it made investments in real estate projects in Southern California and Arizona that were subsequently found to have been greatly overvalued. Members of the Keating family, and other favored insiders, would buy and sell land, condominiums, and shopping centers at continually increasing prices. All of the transactions would be financed, without down payments, by Lincoln Savings & Loan. In the defense of Mr. Keating and the others, it has to be admitted that Arizona and Southern California were in the midst of a real estate boom and that real estate prices within the area were continually increasing. It also has to be admitted, however, that the prices recorded for the real estate projects owned by Mr. Keating and others and financed by Lincoln Savings & Loan were considerably above those for equivalent properties in the area. Profits, as the properties were traded back and forth at continually increasing prices, went to the Lincoln Savings & Loan insiders. Risks on the financing of the properties went to the Lincoln Savings & Loan depositors.

Let us assume that you were working for one of the major public accounting firms in Phoenix, Arizona. You have been assigned to work on the annual audit of Lincoln Savings & Loan. You have specifically been asked to validate its portfolio of real estate projects. You know that investment projects of that nature should be valued at the lower of cost or market. The purchase cost is no problem; that is clearly reported for each loan and supported in the files by copies of the bills of sale.

The market value, however, is far more difficult. Each loan file contains a copy of a recent report by a qualified real estate appraiser giving an estimated market value that, inevitably, is higher than the purchase cost. You are, however, troubled by the method of obtaining those estimated market values. All real estate appraisers within the area are asked to provide an estimate of the value of each of the projects; the highest of those estimates is then accepted, and the appraiser who provided that estimate is paid for his or her work. The other appraisers who submitted lower estimates are not paid for their work. It is a process called "bidding for the appraisal contract," but it is far different from any other bidding process with which you are familiar. In this, the person who submits the highest value for the property receives the contract, not the lowest cost for doing the appraisal.

You ask to see the other appraisals submitted by those who did not win the bidding process. You are told that they were not retained in the files and are unavailable. You happen to be a personal friend of an employee in one of the appraisal firms. You ask, and your friend looks in the firm's files and gives you a figure for one of the projects you are validating that is far below the recorded estimate. It is even below the reported cost.

Now you have a problem. You have a market estimate that was obtained informally (if not illegally). It contradicts the recorded estimate. It obsoletes the reported cost. You go to see the partner who is supervising this audit, and he or she reprimands you for going outside the standard auditing procedures. He or she impresses upon you the need for public accounting firms to maintain confidentiality for their clients.

What do you do? You go back to your friend at the appraisal office, and that person looks up the estimates of all of the real estate projects you are charged with validating. All are lower than the recorded estimates, and most are lower than the reported costs. You know that if you insist, through an appeal to the managing partner in New York City, that the property will be recorded at more realistic estimates and that your firm will certainly lose the auditing assignment and the fee of over $1 million that goes with that assignment. Lincoln Savings & Loan will simply change public accounting firms. You know that you will not be a very popular person in the Phoenix office if that occurs. You know that if you report your suspicions to the federal government, you will be fired for failing to maintain confidentiality for the client.

What do you do? Where do you draw the line? This last is the most basic moral question of all. How do you decide "where to draw the line"? You will find that there are no absolutes, no firm ways of deciding that are exact and precise, but that there are principles and means of applying those principles through moral reasoning. That is what the next chapter will be about.

ASSIGNMENT QUESTIONS

1. What do you think are the duties and responsibilities of management? You know the functions (marketing, production, and finance), and you know the techniques (financial and managerial accounting, planning and control systems, organizational behavior and design), but what are the duties?

2. The boxed exhibit on page 6 lists the "stakeholders" in a business firm. Who are the "stakeholders" in a college or university? List the groups that have some association with your university and consequently may feel that they have some "rights." You are a student. What rights do you have?

3. The text described three moral problems in which people associated with a public agency (Hydro-Quebec) or a business firm (General Motors and Lincoln Savings & Loan) were going to be hurt or harmed in some way that was outside their own control. What would you do in each of those instances?

Case 1–1

WHEN IS IT PERMISSIBLE TO PAY A BRIBE?

The term "bribe" in the context of this series of examples of cash or benefit payments made to influence managerial or political decisions is really an overstatement. A bribe technically is an *illegal* cash or benefit payment made to influence the decision of an individual or a group, and none of the following examples is illegal under current U.S. law.

These payments of cash or benefits may not be illegal under current U.S. law, but that does not automatically mean that they are "right." Some of these payments are uncommon, and apparently many people do object to them. "I know that sort of thing happens occasionally in our industry, but we don't do it" is a typical comment. Other payments are so common that they are considered to be an accepted practice. "Everybody does it, and I for one see nothing wrong with it," is often the explanation here.

Decide which of the following *legal* cash or benefit payments are "right" and which are "wrong" in your opinion. And be prepared to say why you think that they are "right" or "wrong."

1. Many large U.S. manufacturers now operate abroad in sections of the world where cash payments to government officials in return for purchase contracts, import privileges, or tax concessions may be illegal under local law but are still either acknowledged or tolerated by local custom. The U.S. firms are forbidden to make those payments, under terms of the Foreign Corrupt Practices Act. European and Japanese companies are not under similar constraints, and it is said that their ability to follow those local customs has enabled them to receive many of the contracts, privileges, and concessions that formerly went to the U.S. firms. It is also now said that many of the U.S. firms have adopted the practice of hiring local consultants who claim to be able to obtain the contracts, etc. "legitimately." The invoices from the local consultants, however, are generally 20 percent above the amounts of the requested bribes, which has led to the suspicion that the consultants are simply paying the bribes in lieu of the U.S. firms. Is it permissible to hire those consultants?

2. It is illegal within the United States to make direct cash payments to government officials, except to members of the legislative branches at the national and state levels where the payments are often considered to be "honoraria" in return for speeches at conventions or attendance at meetings. It is not illegal, however, to provide noncash benefits to members of the executive branch, again at the national and state levels. For example, almost all of the large defense contractors maintain hunting lodges along the Maryland shore (hunting for ducks and geese) and in South Carolina (hunting for quail, woodcock, or wood doves). It is felt that many of the senior officers in the military like to hunt and that inviting them to participate, along with company officials, in the often rustic conditions of a hunting lodge is an inexpensive but effective means of "building future relationships."

3. Noncash benefits are also provided to corporate executives for the purpose of building future relationships or expressing gratitude for past orders. The upper levels of most modern sports stadiums are now occupied by "boxes" rented by corporations, law firms, and in-

vestment banks to entertain their clients. Tables at expensive restaurants, seats at popular plays, and rooms at exclusive clubs are also reserved for similar purposes. It is said that a senior executive at a large corporation can—if he or she wishes—visit New York, London, Paris, Tokyo, or any other major city and pay for nothing during that visit except incidentals.

4. A combination of cash payments and noncash benefits may be provided by American companies to members of the legislative branches at both national and state levels. State legislators are often paid to attend dinners or other meetings, generally within the capital city and not at a vacation resort, at which possible changes in state laws are discussed. For example, 3M Corporation admitted in August 1988 that it had paid an honorarium of $250 each to members of the Michigan state legislature to attend an evening meeting to discuss a bill that would mandate reflectorized license plates. 3M makes the special paint required for reflectorized license plates.

5. A combination of cash payments and noncash benefits may also be provided by American companies to professionals in such fields as law or medicine. It is felt to be difficult for salespeople to meet with active lawyers or physicians in their offices, due to their time constraints, and so all-expense-paid trips to a central meeting place at a pleasant vacation resort are frequently arranged. For example, Merck and Company admitted in August 1988 that it made a practice of offering all-expense-paid weekend trips to physicians and their spouses to the Monterey Peninsula in California to hear company scientists discuss research advances in prescription drugs. The "all-expense-paid trips" included first-class air fares, hotel accommodations, and meals at the Lodge (a four-star resort) and guest memberships at the Pebble Beach Golf Club (a championship course directly on the Pacific Ocean). Merck, of course, manufactures and markets prescription drugs.

Class Assignment

Decide which of these actions are "right" and which are "wrong." Use your own judgment, but be prepared to support that judgment. Don't just give your answer in class and stop; instead be ready to say why you think they are "right" or why you think they are "wrong."

Case 1–2

FIVE MORAL PROBLEMS ENCOUNTERED BY MEMBERS OF ONE UNDERGRADUATE CLASS

Students in an undergraduate class on the ethics of management at the University of Michigan were asked to submit a written description of a moral problem they had encountered at work over the previous summer. This was a voluntary assignment. Obviously, if they had not encountered a moral problem, or if they had encountered one that they felt they could not describe without violating the implied confidence of their prior employers, they did not have to participate. Nineteen problems were submitted. The following five were selected by members of the class for discussion at one of the subsequent meetings:

1. Reporting inaccurate income. "I didn't get the job I wanted, so I worked as a waitress at a restaurant in a vacation resort. We got room and board, the absolute minimum wage (with a charge deducted for the room and board), and tips. Tip income was very good because it was a popular restaurant, right on the shore, with really good food and above-average prices. The owner told us that it was our responsibility to report our tip income to the IRS when we filled out our income tax forms for the year, but he also said that he had to provide the government with an estimate at the end of the summer, based upon credit card charges, and then he gave us a figure for that estimate that was less than half of what I actually made. Now I have to file the return, and I need the money. What figure should I put down?"

2. Misleading retail customers. "I spent the summer working as a telephone sales representative at a travel agency. Customers would call and say where they wanted to go. We would look up flights and times and fares on the computer and help the customer pick the one that seemed best. That part was all right. But often they asked us to reserve a rental car or find a hotel room. Here the problem was that there generally was a contest for the sales representative who could reserve the most cars from a particular rental firm or send the most clients to a specific hotel chain. All of those companies run contests like that, and the prizes they offer are not cheap. If I booked just 25 clients for (name of a car rental firm) during one month, my name would be put in a drawing for $2,500. If I booked 100 clients, the drawing was for $10,000. If I booked 200, I received a three-day Florida vacation free; there was no drawing. All of the other clerks participated in the contests, and the owner didn't seem to mind. The problem, of course, was that the rates to the customers were higher than they would have been had we

searched for the best deal for them rather than the best prize for us. The other clerks said I was crazy not to participate. Should I have participated?''

3. Misleading industrial customers. ''I worked in the office of a company that distributed repair parts for heavy machinery throughout northern Michigan. When somebody would call in for a part, we would look up the number and price and inventory level on the computer. The boss told us always to say that we had the part in stock, even if the inventory level showed that we were out, that we didn't have any left. His argument was that we could always get the part from Chicago in a day or two, and that a day or two was not going to hurt anyone. I didn't like it because it meant that I had to lie to somebody about once a day. What do you think I should have done?''

4. Reporting employee theft. ''I worked in the shipping bay of a company that manufactured house paint. House paint in one gallon cans is a product you can sell easily in your neighborhood if you can get it out the factory door; everyone needs paint. House paint in one gallon cans is also an easy product to get out the factory door; it's a big volume product, and no one seems to keep exact track of the numbers of cans. When we were making up the pallets to load a truck—the cans of paint were put in cartons that held four cans, and then 20 cartons were strapped onto a wooden pallet that could be handled by a forklift—you could easily set aside a

couple of cans. Then, when the foreman was on break and the office people were all working in the front of the building, you could just carry it out and put it in the trunk of your car. Most of the shipping crew did that once or twice a week. They felt the company owed it to them. I didn't because I didn't want to run the risk of being caught and having that put on my record. But I didn't object when they gave me a couple of cans to use on my mother's home. And, I didn't tell the management of the company about it either. What should I have done?''

5. Misusing employee time. ''This did not happen last summer. It happened a couple of summers ago. I was part of the maintenance crew for the parks and recreation department in the town where I lived. We mowed the grass on the parks and athletic fields and picked up the trash and did some painting and repair work. The problem was that we not only did the parks and athletic fields, we also did the lawns and gardens of some of the people in the city government, the school system, and the athletic department. I mowed the lawn of the football coach every week until practice started. He used to tell me I'd never make the team unless I could move faster on the football field than I did on his front lawn, but he always gave me a glass of lemonade and a $5 tip when I was finished. I never thought about it until I took this course, but maybe it wasn't right to use city employees to work on private property.''

Class Assignment

What, in your opinion, would have been the "right" action to take in each of these instances? It is suggested strongly that you use the moral reasoning framework, starting in each instance with a clear definition of exactly who is hurt or harmed in ways outside their own control.

Case 1–3

FIVE MORAL PROBLEMS ENCOUNTERED BY ONE MBA CLASS

Students in an MBA class on the ethics of management at the University of Michigan were asked to submit a written description of a moral problem they had encountered at work over the previous summer. This was a voluntary assignment. Obviously, if they had not encountered a moral problem, or if they had encountered one that they felt they could not describe without violating the implied confidence of their prior employers, they did not have to participate. Twenty-three problems were submitted. The following five were selected by members of the class for discussion at one of the subsequent meetings.

1. Telling lies at a market research firm. "I was working for a market research firm in Chicago over the summer. We had an assignment to gather information from companies that used a line of industrial products. This was confidential data, on usage rate, price sensitivity, etc., and people won't fill out written questionnaires on that type of information. We had to use a telephone survey, for people will generally say much more than they intend to over the telephone if you can get them talking about the topic. We still weren't getting the information the project director wanted, so he told all of us who were doing the survey to say that we were college students, gathering the information for a term paper."

2. Providing gifts at a wholesale distributor. "I was working for a company that supplied packaging materials throughout Ohio. It was just a sales job, but there was a good commission structure so that I could make a lot of money if I was successful. Packaging materials are close to a commodity. You can buy the same boxes and fillers and tape from just about anyone, at just about the same price. The suppliers tend to compete on service to the customer, and on gifts to the purchasing agent. Not all of the purchasing agents are like that, but many of them will tell you exactly what they want: a new TV for their rec room, a pair of tickets to a ball game, a new set of tires for their

car. You either give them what they want, or you don't get the order."

3. Falsifying reports at a consulting firm. "Much of managerial consulting is not done for the purpose of helping one company compete against other companies within the same industry. Much of it is done for the purpose of helping one group within a company compete against other groups within the same company. You have one group within a company who wants to use a particular technology or to develop a specific product, and you are hired to provide support for their project. It is clearly understood at the start what the conclusions of the report will be. If you develop some information during the study that contradicts that conclusion, you explain it to the group that arranged to have you hired, but you don't put that information in the final report to the company without the permission of the people from your group."

4. Firing employees at a chain store. "I was working for a discount chain store that was expanding very rapidly. I was the assistant manager for a new store that was opening in the suburbs of Richmond, Virginia. There is an awful lot of work to be done in opening a new store: you have to order the merchandise, and when it comes in you have to check it off against the right orders, put it in the right racks and on the right shelves, add the right price tags, and generally keep things organized despite the chaos of last-minute construction and cleaning.

I was helped by five really good people, who had been convinced to move from other stores in the chain because this was billed as a "training program" for management. We worked long hours. We got the job done. One week after the store opened, I was told to find a reason and fire three of them because 'we only have room for two trainees'. When I objected I was told, 'Hey, there's no problem. They can go back to the jobs they came from.' "

5. Taking company property at an accounting firm. "I spent the summer working at the office of a Big Six accounting firm in Denver. The attitude of the people in that office was "anything goes." Expense accounts were a joke. Nobody expected you to submit a receipt, and the result was that half of the employees cheated. People used company telephones for personal long-distance calls, not just occasionally but all the time. Pencils, pens, magic markers, and writing paper disappeared continually. When we left at the end of the summer to come back to school, two of the other summer interns took enough office supplies to last for the rest of the year. I never took anything, but I never told any of the senior partners either. I didn't know what I should do."

Class Assignment

Decide if the situations described in these five short cases are "right" or "wrong" in your opinion, and be prepared to support your conclusions. It is strongly suggested that you apply the conceptual framework for moral reasoning described in the text, and start by clearly identifying the individuals or groups in each case that may be hurt or harmed in ways outside their own control.

1. Then start thinking about how these situations developed. Do the senior executives at each firm know what is happening?

2. What, if anything, could you do about these situations (if you were the person involved) beyond saying "I quit"?

Case 1-4

NEW ALTERNATIVES, INC.

Southwest Detroit is a section of the inner city that fully exhibits all of the characteristics, both physical and personal, of urban blight. Statistics on ethnic composition, income level, employment rate, etc. are said to be unreliable, due to the difficulty of gathering the original data. General observations, however, would seem to support the following conclusions:

1. High ethnic diversity. The population is approximately 45 percent Hispanic (primarily from Mexico, Puerto Rico, and Cuba), 25 percent black (primarily from other portions of the city of Detroit), 15 percent white (including both recent emigrants from southern Europe and native born from the Appalachian states), 10 percent Arab (from Lebanon, Jordan, and Syria), and 5 percent Asian (primarily from southeast Asia).

2. High unemployment rate and consequently low per capita income. The basic income sources are government assistance programs and neighborhood retail operations. Neighborhood retail operations are locally owned, not parts of chains.

3. Low educational level. Few of the younger residents complete high school, and less than half of the adult population is able to read and write English. Other, more technical job skills are also lacking among adult members of the population.

4. Rampant drug use, particularly of crack cocaine. Drug trafficking is a dominant activity along many of the streets in the area.

5. High crime rate, with occasional property losses experienced by almost all residents. Personal assaults are not uncommon, caused by both the drug trade and domestic strife.

6. Damaged or decaying housing, with many vacant homes and deteriorating apartment buildings. Little maintenance is done by the owners, who tend to live outside the area.

New Alternatives, Inc. (a business

venture formed by three socially committed individuals who at the time of the case were living in a home they had renovated within the area) have prepared a proposal to provide high-quality, affordable housing for residents of Southwest Detroit, following a new and very different "shared community" pattern.

The company planned to purchase, renovate, rent, and manage small apartment buildings. These buildings, constructed in the 1920s, are exceedingly numerous in the region. They tend to have brick walls and concrete floors and consequently are structurally in better shape than many of the wooden frame single-family and two-family homes. A two- to five-story brick structure housing 20 to 60 apartments in some combination of one-bedroom, two-bedroom, and convenience units is typical. The buildings have few amenities, such as laundry facilities or common rooms, and—as was described previously—they tend to be in superficially poor condition, unpainted, with dirty hallways, broken light fixtures, leaky roofs, old kitchen appliances, and limited or nonexistent security. They can, however, be repaired.

At present, there is little economic reason for this repair. Residents within the area tend to move frequently. Tenants often move into larger quarters after acquiring a new job or after forming a new relationship. They move into smaller quarters after losing an existing job or to escape from a previous relationship. Others move to avoid drug dealers, angry neighbors, rental agents, or the police. The lack of permanency destroys any sense of belonging among the residents, and the lack of maintenance destroys any sense of respect for the building. Tenant damage to the units can be severe. Tenant nonpayment of rent can be common.

New Alternatives, Inc., planned to avoid these and other problems by forming a much more permanent *community* within each building. Central to the plan for the permanent community was the proposal to employ a full-time, on-site resident manager for each apartment building. The resident manager would be a paid Christian ministry worker who would build a sense of a shared community commitment through seven very specific activities:

1. Screen prospective tenants for willingness to follow community rules and contribute to community activities. Community rules would be very simple: no alcohol or drugs on the premises, no loud noises or physical disputes in the buildings, and a commitment to maintain a job so that the rent could be paid. Prospective tenants would *not* be screened for religious affiliation, belief, or interest; the intent was to offer membership in the shared community to all, regardless of background.

2. Conduct monthly community meetings to vote on new group members and discuss new community activities. Examples of community activities would be shared child care, group meals, religious services, educational programs, teenage activities, job searches, etc. Participation in the community activities would be voluntary.

3. Supervise cleaning and mainte-

nance of the public areas and maintain security of the building. It was planned that the apartment of the manager would be directly adjacent to the main entrance and that the other entrances would be sealed except for fire emergencies. It was also planned to have a voluntary security watch by members of the community.

4. Discern and deal sensitively yet firmly with tenant problems and violations. Prospective tenants would be asked to join the community only after declaring obedience to the rules; existing members could be asked to leave in the event of continual violations of those rules. Help and counseling would be offered, however, prior to the request to leave.

5. Support community members in obtaining needed public services. One of the problems faced by residents in the area was the difficulty they encountered in registering for and receiving public services such as health care, job placement, or welfare assistance. The manager could help in filling out forms, giving references, or interceding with authorities.

6. Assist community members in maintaining employment through providing group transportation. Another of the problems faced by residents in the area was the lack of public transportation. The desirable jobs were in the northern suburbs, not in the southwestern city. The community would have a van to transport workers to one or two of those major job locations.

7. Help community members with

spiritual discovery and growth. The exact wording of the proposal by New Alternatives, Inc., was that "the resident manager will provide opportunities to interested tenants for discussion, counsel, teaching, and participation in establishing and cultivating a personal relationship with Jesus Christ."

Obviously, the position of the resident manager was critical in the success of the apartment building. In the proposal submitted by New Alternatives, Inc., it was stated that candidates for the position must have "a demonstrated concern for people in inner city neighborhoods, and a willingness to live and work in the inner city for a minimum of two years in addition to Christian training and orientation."

One of the candidates for the position of the first resident manager was a veteran of seven year's service with a Marine Corps infantry battalion who had returned to pursue graduate studies in the Bible and Mission Service at the Wheaton Graduate School (part of a religiously oriented university, 25 miles west of Chicago). The proposal prepared by New Alternatives continued with a description of the character of this individual as follows: "Mike's strong perseverance and discipline add to his viability for the job. Ranked in the top 20 male marathoners in Michigan in 1988, Mike has qualified for and twice competed in Hawaii's Iron Man Triathlon. The cross-country ski team on which Mike competed in 1987 finished second in the state."

The founders of New Alternatives, Inc., felt that strong candidates such as

"Mike" would not be lacking. A surprising number of middle-aged men and women, many with extensive military or industrial leadership experience, attended the Wheaton Graduate School and majored in the Bible and Mission Service. Many looked for challenging positions where they could "make a difference" before joining the more pastoral ministry at a church. They tended to be active, committed men and women who emphatically rejected the view that Christian service meant taking a kindly but ineffectual approach to the problems of the world.

The founders of New Alternatives, Inc., exhibited many of the characteristics of the potential resident managers. They were two men and one woman, all in their late 20s or early 30s. All were committed to helping others in Christian faith and service. Two had undergraduate degrees in engineering; one in computer science and economics. Two of the three had (or were working towards) a master's degree in business. All had extensive experience in construction and maintenance. All felt competent to evaluate the structural integrity of a deteriorated apartment building, estimate the cost of repairs, and then supervise the performance of those repairs.

The founders expected to continue working full-time at their regular jobs to locate, evaluate, and renovate apartment buildings, and to assist in the development of the "shared community" attitudes and beliefs among the residents of those apartment houses, in the evenings and over weekends. They anticipated three potential problems:

1. Possible resident opposition to the concept of Evangelical Christianity. Southwest Detroit is not an area of "storefront" churches, as are some of the black sections of the city where religion remains an important part of the lives of many of the citizens. There was no guarantee that the residents of the area would accept the shared community values of the founders, even in return for safe, clean, decent housing at affordable (and competitive) rates.

2. Possible legal opposition to the restrictions on "membership" in the communities. Potential members would be screened by the manager and then accepted by a vote of the other residents of the building, but legally the community still remained based upon a landlord-tenant relationship, and landlords are forbidden to discriminate. "Discrimination" seems an unusual concept in the circumstances of a decayed inner city neighborhood, but legally it could be applied with a disastrous impact upon the plans of New Alternatives, Inc.

3. Possible financial opposition to the loans needed for the purchase and renovation of the apartment buildings. The buildings to be purchased are located in a section of the city where banks and other financial institutions are exceedingly hesitant to make loans. In their defense, it must be admitted that the prior experience of lenders in this area has not been good. Many owners, after their building has decayed so completely that rental is no longer possible, simply walk away, leaving loans (and taxes) unpaid. Building

fires are so common that fire insurance is either unobtainable or unaffordable.

The founders of New Alternatives had prepared pro forma financial statements that showed that the concept of a "shared community" apartment building was financially viable *provided* the necessary down payment ($40,000) could be supplied by a group of suburban churches as a charitable gift, *provided* the city of Detroit was willing to negotiate taxes based upon the present value (not renovated value) of the building, *and provided* the essential mortgage loan could be offered by a commercial bank at a below-market interest rate.

The down payment created no problem. Numerous suburban churches said they would be pleased to help financially, and to bring members to assist in the cleaning, painting, and simple carpentry jobs associated with the renovation. (Complex carpentry, masonry, plumbing, wiring, and roofing tasks, of course, would have to be done by professional contractors.) The negotiated taxes would be no problem; numerous precedents existed, and city officials were known to be sympathetic to the concept. The subsidized interest rates, however, could be a problem.

The total capital expenditure for purchase ($80,000) and renovation ($220,000) of a 40-unit apartment building would total $300,000. The renovation would be complete: new roof, new furnace, new electrical and plumbing systems, new appliances, rebuilt interior walls, rebuilt stairways. Fireproof (masonry and tile) construction would be used through-

out to reduce the cost of insurance.

Rental charges would be typical of those charged within the area. It was believed that many residents would be willing to pay a premium to live in safe, clean "shared community" housing but that they simply did not have the income to support that willingness.

The first apartment building to be considered for purchase had 40 units, divided among studio, one bedroom, and two bedrooms. Rates for those apartments were set as shown in the financial statements in Exhibit 1. The .95 adjustment factor refers to an accepted inability to collect all of the rent for all of the periods, even in carefully maintained structures with screened tenants.

The problem was that the gross margin was not sufficient to repay the principal of the mortgage, provided a market rate (at the time 10.5 percent) of interest was charged. The amount of the mortgage required was $260,000, and a 10.5 percent interest rate resulted in payments of $27,300 per year. Repayment of principal with only $5,700 per year available for that purpose ($33,000 minus $27,300) would take over 40 years.

If the bank would subsidize the mortgage by charging 7.5 percent, the principal could be repaid in just slightly over 12 years. The repayment schedule is shown in Exhibit 2; note that the interest for the current year is always figured on the "new principal amount" at the end of the prior year.

The plan of the founders of New Alternatives, Inc., was to buy and renovate as many apartment buildings in the inner city as they could staff with committed Christian managers, fill

EXHIBIT 1   Estimated Income and Expenses, per Month, for New Alternatives, Inc.

	Per Month			Per Year
Rental income				
10 convenience units	$2,250			
20 single bedroom	5,100			
10 two bedroom	2,850			
Total	10,200	x	.95	116,300
Manager's expenses				
Salary	1,832			
Benefits, at 27%	500			
Apartment provided	285			
General expenses	167			
Total	2,784			34,000
Janitor—½ time				
Salary	465			
Benefits, at 24%	113			
Average performance bonus	56			
Total	634			7,600
Building expenses				
Mechanical and major repairs	211			
Painting and minor repairs	240			
Gas for heating	1,067			
Electricity for lighting	516			
Taxes—negotiated w/city	400			
Insurance	600			
Total	3,034			36,400
Van expenses				
Gas, oil, and maintenance	267			
Insurance	175			
Total	442			5,300
Gross margin, before depreciation and interest				$ 33,000

SOURCE: Company records.

with "shared community" members, and finance with subsidized bank mortgages. The founders did not wish to profit from the venture; the intent was that the ownership of the apartments would be "vested" in the ten- ants over time. That is, a tenant who stayed for the full 12 years of repayment would own his or her apartment and could continue to live in the apartment "rent free" (by paying expenses only, as in a condominium) or

EXHIBIT 2   Repayment Schedule for New Alternatives, Inc.

	Interest Paid	Principal Repaid	New Principal Amount
1st year	$19,500	$13,500	$246,500
2nd year	18,480	14,510	231,390
3rd year	17,400	15,600	216,390
4th year	16,230	16,770	199,620
5th year	14,970	18,030	181,590
6th year	13,620	19,380	162,210
7th year	12,160	20,840	141,370
8th year	10,600	22,400	118,970
9th year	8,920	24,080	94,890
10th year	7,120	25,880	69,020
11th year	5,170	27,830	41,190
12th year	3,090	29,190	11,280

SOURCE: Company records.

could sell the apartment back to the membership at a fixed amount and use the proceeds as a down payment on a house within the area (which would lead to further revitalization). As one of the founders stated:

> We're excited about this idea. It is a way to revitalize the inner city through faith in Jesus Christ and the love and truth of the Gospel, and to treat people justly who have never been treated justly before. The commercial banks *owe* the people of this city that opportunity.

Class Assignment

You are a senior executive in a large commercial bank headquartered in the city of Detroit. What, if anything, do you think that you owe to the people of Detroit? Will you agree to provide a series of subsidized mortgages to New Alternatives, Inc., if the founders can establish the number of "shared community" apartment houses they propose?

Case 1–5

INTERCOLLEGIATE ATHLETICS AND THE NCAA

Intercollegiate athletics started in the late 19th century. The teams were organized by student clubs, not by athletic departments or university administrators. These clubs bought the uniforms, hired the coaches, arranged the games, and occasionally employed a few large, strong individuals from the local farms and factories to ensure a winning season. It is said that the name for the Purdue University athletic teams—the Boilermakers—came from the early practice of ensuring victory by recruiting football players from the locomotive repair shops in town. Purdue was not alone in this deception. The Harvard football team of 1879—the first to wear the crimson jerseys which later became the official color of the university—included three members of the Boston Police Department.

Intercollegiate athletics soon became so popular that wooden stands were built to accommodate all those—students, alumni, and members of the general public—who wished to attend. The results of the games were reported in local newspapers. The rules for the games were codified by national agencies. And the responsibilities for the games and the management of the teams were taken over by the colleges and universities about 1900.

The popularity of intercollegiate athletics continued to increase throughout the 20th century. Concrete stadiums were built to replace the wooden stands. Full-time coaching staffs were hired to replace the part-time advisers. Athletic scholarships were offered to replace the paid players. The advent of television just prior to 1960 expanded the appeal of the two primary sports—football and basketball—and brought greatly increased revenues for the teams that won and that were invited to the bowl games (in football) or asked to participate in the NCAA tournament (in basketball). Television ushered in the era of "big-time" college athletics.

The amounts of money involved in "big-time" college athletics are astonishing, particularly when the payments for the bowls and tournaments—both heavily sponsored by television—are included. The University of Michigan in 1989 received $8,500,000 from football ticket sales, $2,100,000 for basketball ticket sales, $2,000,000 from its share of television and radio broadcasts of regular season games, $1,300,000 from concession sales and parking fees, $6,000,000 for going to the Rose Bowl (which it won), and $3,800,000 for playing in the NCAA basketball tournament (which it also won). Receipts from the Rose Bowl and the NCAA tournament were shared with other members of the Big Ten conference, but the monies gathered by these two "revenue-producing" sports financed all of the other intercollegiate athletic teams at that university and many of the intramural recreational activities on that campus.

There are numerous advantages to being one of the successful participants in "big-time" college athletics beyond the direct payments for ticket sales, television licenses, and bowl game or tournament invitations. Everyone seems to love a winner, and consequently the benefits extend to many nonathletic aspects of the university:

1. Increased contributions from the state government. Legislators have traditionally been found to be much more generous in allocating funds from their state budgets to public universities that field winning teams rather than to those that participate in intercollegiate athlet-

ics on an "also-ran" basis. State funding for Michigan State University, for example, expanded dramatically in 1958 after MSU joined the Big Ten conference and began playing the University of Michigan and Ohio State University on equal terms.

2. Increased donations from the college alumni. Graduates of colleges and universities respond with generosity as well as pride to winning teams. At the University of Missouri, alumni contributions jumped by 95 percent in 1989 when the Tigers went from a 6 and 5 season to a 10 and 1 record in football. Donations at Ohio State in that same year dropped by 23 percent when the Buckeyes fell to a 4 and 5 conference record from a 7 and 2 finish the year before.

3. Increased applications from potential students. Winning records in football and basketball seem to bring sharply higher student interest in both undergraduate and graduate programs. At the undergraduate level, the reasons probably are the desire to be part of a winner and to share in the spirit that often goes with winning. At the graduate level, the reasons seem less clear. It may just be a result of the widespread publicity that goes with winning. In 1984 Doug Flutie led Boston College close to a national championship with a famous win over the University of Miami that featured a last-second "Hail Mary" touchdown pass; the next year applications at both undergraduate and graduate programs were up more than 30 percent.

4. Increased sense of community among students, faculty, alumni, and staff. Sports have long served as a rallying point for colleges and universities, and many students, faculty, alumni, and staff psychologically associate themselves more with their teams than with their schools. Allen Guttmann, sports historian at Amherst College, explained this phenomena by saying, "In a society that views scholarly and scientific achievements as arcane and mysterious, athletic achievements serve as a visible symbol of the Alma Mater to which everyone can identify" (*Chronicle of Higher Education*, September 14, 1988, p. B2). Paul "Bear" Bryant, football coach at the University of Alabama, expressed the same thought somewhat more simply: "It's kind of hard to rally around a math class" (*Newsweek*, September 15, 1986, p. 84).

Winning teams in intercollegiate athletics bring increased ticket sales, television contracts, bowl game payments, tournament invitations, state government contributions, college alumni donations, graduate and undergraduate student applications, and a general sense of pride in the institution. Losing teams bring none of those advantages. The result has been an emphasis upon winning that seems prevalent among many of the nation's colleges and universities and the adoption of a number of practices that seem contrary to the avowed mission and purpose of most of those colleges and universities:

1. Improper payments to potential

team members. Skilled athletes in high school are heavily recruited by the coaches of football and basketball teams at colleges and universities that participate in "big-time" athletics. It is acknowledged that this recruiting sometimes includes the offer of cash or other material incentives (such as clothing, a car, or a job) either directly to the athlete or indirectly to the family of the athlete.

Those offers are contrary to the rules of the NCAA. Colleges and universities that can be shown to have made them are penalized heavily by the NCAA with the loss of television revenues and the denial of the right to participate in post-season bowl games or tournaments. It is even possible, in the event of repeated violations, for the college or university to be excluded from the right to participate in intercollegiate athletics at all, as happened in the so-called "death penalty" imposed on Southern Methodist University in 1985.

Recruiting violations continue, however, despite the best efforts of the NCAA, which has issued a thick booklet of rules that attempt to define what is permissible and what is not. The problem with policing these rules, of course, is that it is often very difficult to prove that illicit offers and/or payments have been made. It is obviously to the self-interest of both the coach and the athlete to remain quiet, and it is only when a member of the team becomes disgruntled, perhaps at not playing as much as was promised, that revelations occur.

These revelations receive extensive publicity, both in local newspapers and in national sports magazines, and the publicity tends to give the impression that recruiting violations are much more widespread than in fact they probably are. Many colleges and universities run intercollegiate athletic programs that are reputed to be "squeaky clean." The majority of coaches have never been accused of wrongdoing. Despite this record, however, there is felt by the critics of the present system of intercollegiate athletics to be a growing "crisis of confidence" about the integrity of higher education.

Some of the critics are concerned with the continual revelations about the violations of the rules. Others are more concerned with the rules themselves. The rules are thought, through unqualified student admissions, poor preparation levels, excessive time demands, restricted scholarship benefits, marginal course selections, and limited career options, to exploit the athletes for the benefit of the institutions:

> The worst scandal does not involve cash or convertibles. It involves slipping academically unqualified young men in the back doors of academic institutions, insulating them from academic expectations, wringing them dry of their athletic-commercial usefulness, then slinging them out the back door even less suited because they spent four years acquiring the idea that they are exempt from normal standards [George Will, quoted in *Newsweek*, September 15, 1986, p. 84].

2. Unqualified admissions of potential team members. It seems incredulous, but it has to be admitted that functionally illiterate students, those who can neither read nor write, have been admitted to col-

leges and universities. One of the most pathetic instances is that of Kevin Ross, a star basketball player at Creighton University. He attended that university for three years without either knowing or learning how to read or write and then resigned his scholarship and enrolled in the second grade of a private elementary school in Chicago to acquire those basic skills. "Kevin couldn't even figure out what the score of a game was. He just knew if they were ahead or behind" [Daniel Wolff, attorney for Kevin Ross, quoted in *Newsweek*, January 30, 1990, p. 58].

The most famous example of a functionally illiterate student admitted to a major college or university is Dexter Manley, an All-Pro defensive end for the Washington Redskins football team before he was banned from that sport for repeated drug violations. Dexter had graduated from Oklahoma State University, where he had also played football for four years, but he was unable to read his first professional contract. Dr. John Campbell, president of the university, defended his institution by saying that the opportunity to learn to read had certainly been made available but had been rejected because Dexter did not attend many classes. Dr. Campbell went on to say that this particular football player had profited from being at Oklahoma State University, just as Oklahoma State University had profited from having him there (from success on the football field) and that consequently whatever bargain existed between them had been "fair":

There would be those who argue that Dexter Manley got exactly what he wanted out of Oklahoma State University. He was able to develop his athletic skills and ability, he was noticed by the pros, he got a contract. So maybe we did him a favor by letting him go through the program [John Campbell, president of Oklahoma State University, quoted in Louis Barbash, *The Washington Monthly*, July/August 1990, p. 40].

That explanation, together with a subsequent quip that "We're just trying to build a university our football team can be proud of" (Dr. Campbell, quoted in *Newsweek*, September 15, 1986, p. 84) infuriated at least one critic of the current recruiting process:

It's appalling that an accredited state university would admit a functional illiterate, even recruit him, and leave him illiterate after four years as a student. It's shocking that it would do all this in order to make money from his unpaid performance as an athlete. And it's a little short of grotesque that an educator . . . would seriously argue that this cynical arrangement between an institution of higher learning and an uneducated high school boy was, after all, a fair bargain [Louis Barbash, *The Washington Monthly*, July/August 1990, p. 40].

3. Poor preparation for potential team members. Total functional illiteracy is certainly not common among the members of football and basketball teams at major colleges and universities, but critics of the present system say that many of the members of those teams have been poorly prepared for college work. One study revealed that in the early 1980s more than 25 percent of all major college basketball players

were unable to read above a sixth grade level (Moyers, "Sports for Sale," *Public Affairs Television,* March 19, 1991).

In order to ensure adequate preparation for college work and to avoid the adverse publicity associated with college students reading at a sixth grade level, the NCAA in 1986 instituted a set of minimum requirements for athletic scholarships. These minimal requirements, which were voted upon and approved under the term "Proposition 48," included the need to achieve both a 2.0 scholastic average in 11 basic high school courses (English, math, science, history, etc.) and a score of 700 or better on the Scholastic Aptitude Test.

Originally, an athlete who failed one of those requirements but passed the other could still attend the college or university and keep his or her scholarship but could not participate in team sports until after the successful completion of all courses in the freshman year. That rule, however, was modified in 1989 by the introduction of "Proposition 42," which eliminated the partial qualifiers. Now a student who does not meet *both* the grade and the test standards is denied an athletic scholarship.

John Thompson, the head basketball coach at Georgetown University and a person whose teams are frequent participants in the "final four" of the NCAA basketball tournaments, immediately objected to the modification of the original rule. He stated that its intent was "obviously racist" and that its result would "clearly be to exclude a disproportionate share of black athletes"

[*Chronicle of Higher Education*, January 3, 1990, p. A32].

Coach Thompson felt that the Scholastic Aptitude Test was both culturally and economically biased and that a black student from a poor neighborhood had a limited chance of passing that test. He pointed to the experience of the NCAA institutions in the 1986/87 academic year: 500 freshmen had been declared ineligible for athletic competition, and blacks made up 85 percent of those affected by the ruling [*Fortune*, October 12, 1987, p. 235].

Some of the critics of the present system of competitive intercollegiate athletics claim that there has to be a better way to ensure the adequate preparation of the members of football and basketball teams than to apply standards that primarily affect members of one racial group.

> If you were a member of a math class in an inner city school, poorly taught, overcrowded, and filled with disruptive kids, you would find it difficult to achieve exactly the same score on whatever admission test your college or university used as students from the better schools out in the suburbs. There is nothing wrong with waiving admission requirements to give somebody from the inner city a chance to attend college. Most of them do pretty well when they get here [Statement of first admissions officer at the University of Michigan].

Other critics of the existing system say that it is inherently unfair to waive admission standards for one group of minority students who happen to have good athletic skills while not waiving those requirements for other groups from exactly the same backgrounds who do not possess those skills:

If you're 6'8" tall and can dunk a basketball or if you're 230 pounds and can run 40 yards in 4.5 seconds, but happen to be poor, black, and so poorly educated that you can't pass the admissions tests, many of our colleges and universities will still say to you, "Come along; we'll help you get through college." But, if you're short, dumpy, uncoordinated, or—worst of all—female from exactly the same background conditions, then those same colleges and universities have a much shorter message, "Get lost" [Statement of second admissions officer at the University of Michigan].

4. Excessive time demands upon current team members. It is estimated that a member of the football team at a major college or university must devote 35 hours per week to practice, to training, and to preparation for home games during the season. Basketball players devote only slightly less time, 28 hours per week. The amount of time taken away from studying is compounded, of course, by the amount of energy that has been drained off by the strenuous physical activity:

It's really hard to study because you put in such a long day. You know, the first thing you want to do is climb into your bed and watch a little TV and then turn off the lights. I mean a normal student can take a nap. If they're lazy they can take a nap for three or four hours, then get up and study and do whatever they want. With us, our time's so filled, it's hard to get going at the end of the day because you're so exhausted. . . . It's year-round. Even in the off-season, you're putting in three or four hours a day: lifting weights, running, trying to stay in condition, you know, gaining strength [Kyle

Carroll, football player at Southern Methodist University, quoted in "Sports for Sale," a television program produced by Bill Moyers and shown on *Public Affairs Television* on March 19, 1991].

Traveling to "away" games takes additional time away from studying and from classes. Football players at Division I colleges and universities normally play 11 games during the season, and 5 to 6 will be at other schools. The squad will leave on Friday and return on Sunday, for a total of 15 to 18 days away from campus during the season. Basketball teams, which often play on Tuesday or Thursday nights to accommodate television schedules and have many more games during their season, will be away 30 to 40 days over the late fall and early winter semesters.

Many of the football and basketball coaches at major colleges and universities institute two-hour study halls in the evening and provide tutors in order to help their players prepare for classes. It's almost impossible, though. The players are physically exhausted, and they are away so much of the time. How many of us can study on an airplane or a bus? [Statement of a tutor assigned to the football team at the University of Michigan]

5. Inadequate scholarship benefits for current team members. Athletic scholarships at major colleges and universities are limited to the payment of charges for tuition, room and board, books, and miscellaneous fees. Recipients of these scholarships receive no "walking around" money. They are forbidden by the NCAA to work at part-time jobs during the school year; this rule was instituted in order to

prevent indirect payments to team members by local "boosters." The result is that team members have little or no spending money beyond that provided by their families unless they accept underhanded gifts from wealthy alumni, which, of course, brings up once again the issue of the integrity of higher education:

If a guy, an alumni, comes to you and offers you money, you're going to take it. It's happening everywhere. You can't stop it. You do it until you get caught [Statement of a football player, quoted in *Time*, January 9, 1989, p. 43].

Most recipients of athletic scholarships feel that they are poorly paid for their efforts. They receive full tuition, which averages $8,000 at most colleges and universities, plus room, board, books, and fees, which easily push the total to $12,000 for the 9-month scholastic year. They claim, however, that the 35-hour week extends almost throughout the calendar year, instead of just during the active season, and that consequently they receive only about $8 per hour.

A survey of active and retired National Football League players in 1989 revealed that more than 70 percent felt that the financial aid packages they received while in college were inadequate. Seventy-eight percent of all respondents and 85 percent of those still in their 20s (i.e., those who were recent graduates) said that college athletes ought to be paid on a "semipro" basis. The reason was that they were unable to participate in college activities—other than sports—on an equal basis and unable to associate with their campus peers [*Business Week*, January 8, 1990, p. 45].

We take a player out of a ghetto and put him in a college atmosphere. Often the youngsters are unable to dress like the other students. It is certainly embarrassing to him, and to me [Statement of the basketball coach at Tulane University, quoted in J.F. Rooney, *The Recruiting Game*, 1990, p. 143].

6. Inappropriate course selections for current team members. Due to the lack of preparation on the part of some athletes prior to attending college and due to the lack of time and energy on the part of almost all athletes during the seasons for their sports, many members of varsity teams take courses that are not recommended for, or even open to, students who are not participating in intercollegiate athletics. At the University of Michigan, for example, a special major termed "Sports Management and Communication" is open only to members of varsity teams; it includes such three-credit courses as Personal Exercise, Organized Camping, and History of Athletics. At the University of Iowa, a well-known football player boasted that he had majored in Computer Science, but he had only three courses in computers or mathematics on his transcript; the balance was listed in such nonmath or science topics as Beginning Billiards, Ancient Athletics, Advanced Bowling, Watercolor Painting, and Recreational Leisure. Ohio State University put together a special four-credit course with the respectable title of Comparative Social and Economic Systems; it was available only to members of the

basketball team during a five-country tour of Europe during the 1986 summer vacation [*Time*, April 3, 1989, p. 56].

Critics of the current system of intercollegiate athletics object strongly to these special courses. They believe that they leave students unprepared for their future careers:

> Quite often, coming out of high school these kids don't know anything but basketball. . . . Once they're in college, they're directed to take basket weaving and play-and-games, or whatever the hell it is. Tell me what they're going to do in our society. I know quite often college coaches think they're doing these kids a favor. The reality is that they're doing them a disservice, and I resent it [Wayne Embry, General Manager of the Cleveland Cavaliers, a professional basketball team, quoted in *Time*, April 3, 1989, p. 56].

Defenders of the system say that the special courses may not meet the career needs of the vast majority of students at a particular college or university, but that they should not be rejected for that reason alone. They may meet very well the career needs of students from disadvantaged backgrounds who happen to have good athletic skills:

> It is somewhat trite to say that people get out of their college experience what they put into it, but it also may be somewhat snobbish to say that athletes don't get very much because they don't put very much into the "classic" courses. They may get a very good return in the sense of discipline, skill, and self-confidence from their investments in competitive sports [Statement of admissions officer at the University of Michigan].

If you come into a school, you may not be on an academic par with the general population at that school, but if you as an individual can sit there and learn something and better yourself, that's an education. I always ask my mother, "If I hadn't played basketball what would have happened?" Ninety percent of the people I grew up with are dead or in jail, and I would have been the same way [Fred Brown, former basketball player at Georgetown University, quoted in *Time*, April 3, 1989, p. 60].

7. Limited future options for current team members. Only 42 percent of football players attending Division I colleges and universities graduate within five years. Only 39 percent of the basketball players at those schools ever graduate. Division I colleges and universities, of course, are those that have the largest and most successful athletic programs.

The graduation rates for athletes vary tremendously among Division I schools. At Harvard, it is 97 percent. At Michigan, 77 percent. UCLA, 63 percent. Michigan State, 58 percent. Western Michigan, 41 percent. University of Louisville, 16 percent. Memphis, 0 percent. The issue for critics of the present system of intercollegiate athletics, however, is not the graduation rate. They point out that the graduation rate for nonathletes is not that much higher, at 57 percent, for the same set of schools. The issue, in their opinion, is the lack of career options that follow the overemphasis upon team sports and the underemphasis upon meaningful courses.

Well-paid participation in professional sports is often felt to be the major option, and the major attraction, for college athletes. The probability of a college athlete actually playing for a professional team is very low, however. In professional basketball, there are only 27 National Basketball Association (NBA) teams. Each team is limited to only 12 players. That means that there is a total of 324 places in professional basketball for the 20,000 players in college. Robert Minnix, a member of the NBA staff, claims that more college basketball players go on to become brain surgeons than to become NBA players. This "brain surgeon" claim does seem exaggerated, but it is known that fewer than 1 percent of all college athletes go on to play professional sports in the major leagues for basketball, football, baseball, or hockey.

The large potential payments for professional football and basketball players provide an almost irresistible attraction, but the high probabilities against success lead to almost continual disappointments:

Like so many high school athletes, Sammy Drummer was poorly prepared for college, yet he was heavily recruited because of his basketball skills. He quit academically demanding Georgia Tech two years short of a degree to play for the Houston Rockets of the NBA. Let go in training camp, he latched on for a time with the Harlem Globetrotters. Today [in 1986] he earns $13,228 a year as a cleaning staff supervisor at Ball State University near his home in Muncie, Indiana. "I sit back and think about the way things turned out, and at times tears pop into my eyes," he says [U.S. News and World Report, September 15, 1986, p. 62].

8. Excessive salary payments to the coaches of Division I teams. The salaries paid to successful football and basketball coaches at the Division I level are much higher than those paid to the faculty or even to the presidents of colleges and universities. As one example, Bo Schembechler, the former head football coach and athletic director at the University of Michigan, was paid $275,000 in salary during 1989; in that same year, James Duderstadt, the president of the university, received only $163,000.

In addition to the high salaries from their respective institutions, coaches of successful teams are able to earn additional income from product endorsements, television programs, and summer camps, etc. As an example of this indirect income, John Thompson, the head basketball coach at Georgetown University whose statements about racial inequality were quoted earlier in this case, received more than $700,000 in 1988. His compensation consisted of $318,000 from Georgetown for being both the coach and a member of the faculty; $200,000 from Nike for adopting its brand of athletic shoes for his basketball team; $100,000 from Fox Television for appearing on a weekly sports show during the basketball season, and $100,000 for conducting a summer basketball camp. Coach Thompson stated during an NCAA convention, "I'm a capitalist. I'm in this for the money. Who in this room isn't?" [Dealy, Win at Any Cost, Carol Publishing Group, 1990, p. 166].

Both Bo Schembechler and John Thompson were poorly paid in comparison to Jackie Sherrill, the former head football coach at Texas A&M University. Coach Sherrill moved to

Texas A&M from the University of Pittsburgh, where he had won a national championship, for a salary that was reported to be $1,600,000. He became the highest paid educator in the country in that year, exceeding the salaries of all five of the Nobel Prize winners put together [*Time*, January 1989, p. 43].

Class Assignment

You are an influential member of the NCAA Presidents Commission, a 44-member group composed of the presidents of representative colleges and universities that participate in intercollegiate sports. What do you think should be done? At your first meeting, you received two conflicting bits of advice:

The athletic scandals are perhaps more serious than the crimes of Washington or Wall Street because they infect the institution, the university, which exists to provide the one indispensable resource for the future—the human resource. The university is the guardian of our social values and the institution most responsible for realizing those values in our professions, our institutions, and our public life [Dr. Thomas Hearn, president of Wake Forest University, in a speech titled "Sports and Ethics: The University Response," delivered to the 1988 College Football Association Conference, and quoted in Vital Speeches of the Day, June 5, 1988].

College presidents ought to stay out of the NCAA. They know nothing about college athletics, and always screw them up [Bo Schembechler, former football coach and athletic director at the University of Michigan, in an informal statement at the same 1988 College Football Association Conference, and quoted in Dealy, *Win at Any Cost*, Carol Publishing, 1990].

CHAPTER 2

The Method of Moral Reasoning

Moral problems involve harm to other people, and moral problems in management involve a mixture of harms to some stakeholders and benefits to others, which makes these moral problems particularly hard to resolve. The harms can be fairly minor as in the case of consumers who may purchase products they don't really need due to exaggerated advertising claims, or they can be truly substantial as in the instance of management retirees who may lose their health care benefits due to cost reduction programs.

"Who will be hurt and how badly?" is the first, most familiar form of the basic moral question. It focuses on the consequences of managerial decisions and actions. "What, if anything, do we owe to others?" is the second, less familiar form. This addresses the duties and responsibilities of managerial personnel. Both forms are concerned with issues of what is "right," what is "just," what is "fair" in corporate management.

MORAL STANDARDS OF BEHAVIOR

Most people, when they first encounter a moral problem in which some individuals or some groups are going to be hurt or harmed in some way, or in which some of the duties and responsibilities of management are going to be compromised in some other way, turn to their moral standards of behavior. Moral standards of behavior are gauges of individual actions. They are the means we all use to decide whether our actions and those of the other people with whom we are associated are "right" or "wrong," "just" or "unjust," "fair" or "unfair."

The problem is that moral standards of behavior are subjective. They are personal. They are the way each of us intuitively feels about our actions and those of our neighbors, friends, and peers, but we can't really justify those feelings. You may feel that lying is wrong under any and all circumstances. I may feel that lying to avoid causing embarrassment or anguish to a close associate is perfectly all right. We can't or at least we generally don't resolve those differences, and so we usually just agree to disagree on the issue. Such an agreement is perfectly acceptable when we are dealing with a minor moral problem such as lying to avoid causing discomfort to a friend. Such an agreement—to agree to disagree—is not acceptable when we are concerned with a substantial moral problem such as discontinuing health care benefits for company retirees.

EXHIBIT 2–1   The Determination of Moral Standards

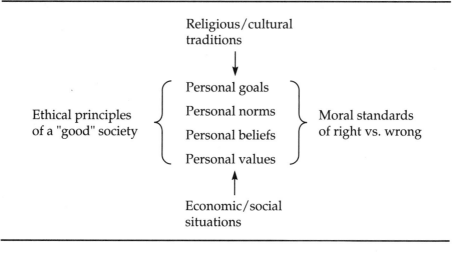

Moral standards are variable as well as personal. They vary by individual, by group, by region, by country, by culture, and by time. We all have evidence of that variation. Business managers in South and Central America and large parts of Africa and Asia think that it is perfectly acceptable to make small payments to government officials to facilitate needed documents and permits. That is termed *bribery* in the United States. Government officials in the United States feel that it is perfectly acceptable to work for foreign firms that have business with the government after their retirement. That is termed *treason* in South and Central America and large parts of Africa and Asia.

DIFFERENCES IN MORAL STANDARDS OF BEHAVIOR

Moral standards of behavior differ between peoples because the goals, norms, beliefs, and values upon which they depend also differ, and those goals, norms, beliefs, and values in turn differ because of variations in the religious and cultural traditions and the economic and social situations of the individuals involved. This complex set of relationships is shown graphically in Exhibit 2–1.

"Goals" are expectations of outcomes. They are the things we want out of life and the things we expect others probably want out of life as well. They include material possessions (cars, homes, boats, money), nonmaterial lifestyles (position, vacations, associations, power), personal goods (family, friends, respect, reputation), and social aims (justice, equality, a clean environment, a world at peace).

"Norms" are expectations of behavior. They are the ways we expect to act and the ways in which we expect others to act in given situations. Norms differ from moral standards in that they have no close association with issues of "right" and "wrong." Norms are expectations of behavior; morals are gauges of behavior. I expect you to drive on the right-hand side of the road; that is a norm. If you persist on driving on the left-hand side (in the United States), I will say that you are "wrong"; that is a moral standard.

"Beliefs" are expectations of thought. They are the ways we expect to think, and the ways in which we expect others to think, about given situations. Our beliefs generally support our norms, and our norms usually lead towards our goals. For example, I believe that cigarette smoke causes cancer, and consequently I expect you not to smoke in my presence because one of my goals is good health. If you persist in smoking, despite my repeated (and heated) objections, I am going to say that you are "wrong," for you have acted against my moral standard derived from those goals, norms, and beliefs.

"Values" are priorities between goals, norms, and beliefs. They are the ways we judge the relative importance of what we want to achieve, how we want to act, and why we have adopted those goals and norms. Most people do not consider that all of their goals, norms, and beliefs are of equal importance; generally there are some that seem more important, more "valued" than others. I may value personal wealth very highly; you may value a clean environment equally highly. We will be in continual conflict on such wealth versus environment issues as disposing of toxic wastes and logging in national forests.

REASONS FOR DIFFERENCES IN MORAL STANDARDS OF BEHAVIOR

The goals, norms, beliefs, and values of a person will vary, depending upon the cultural and religious traditions and the economic and social situations of that individual. The economic situation of a person includes the relative income and financial security of that person. The social situation is not the social status or standing of that person; instead it is his or her membership in different organizations whose members can influence his or her goals, norms, beliefs, and values.

It is possible to give a very brief example of the way in which the economic and social situations of different people will affect their goals, norms, beliefs, and values and consequently will determine their moral standards. An attorney in San Francisco, who is well paid, financially secure, and a member of the Sierra Club (an association of active environmentalists) will almost inevitably feel that it is "wrong" to cut old growth timber in the national forests of the west coast. He would say that he values preservation of the environment. An unemployed sawmill worker in Oregon, getting by on welfare and associated with others in her union, church, and community who are also just barely getting by on welfare, will almost inevitably feel that it is "right" to cut old growth timber in the national forests of the west coast. She would say that she values the right to work, and that the attorney is putting "trees in front of people."

Moral standards of behavior and value judgments of priority are both subjective. They vary with the cultural and religious traditions and with the

---

EXHIBIT 2–2
Summary of *The Nature of Human Values*

Milton Rokeach, in *The Nature of Human Values* (New York: Free Press, 1973) proposes that everyone has a set of values that is important to him or her; these values can be divided into those that are goals (end-states of existence) and those that are norms (modes of behavior):

1. "Terminal value" is an enduring belief that a specific end-state of existence is preferable to an opposite or converse end-state of existence. There are two types of terminal values:

   Personal values, which are self-centered and include such goals as wealth, health, and friendship.

   Social terminal values, which are society-centered and include such goals as peace, equality, and justice.

2. "Instrumental value" is an enduring belief that a specific mode of conduct is preferable to an opposite or converse method of conduct. There are two types of instrumental values:

   Moral instrumental values which have an interpersonal focus, that is, to behave honestly and responsibly.

   Competence instrumental values which have a personal focus, that is, to behave logically or intelligently.

---

economic and social situations of the individual. Other well-known explanations of this variation in moral standards and value judgments (by Milton Rokeach in *The Nature of Human Values* and Lawrence Kohlberg in *Moral Development and Behavior*) are summarized in Exhibits 2–2 and 2–3.

ETHICAL PRINCIPLES OF ANALYSIS

Moral standards of behavior and *value judgments of priority* are both subjective. They vary by person, by group, by region, by country, by culture, etc. *Ethical principles of analysis*, however, are not subjective. They do not vary. They remain constant across individuals, groups, regions, countries, cultures, and times. Moral standards and value judgments look at what is "right" from the point of view of the individual; ethical principles look at what is "right" from the point of view of the society.

Ethical principles of analysis are often termed "first principles" because they are explicit statements of what makes a "good" society. They are the primary or the most basic requirements for that society. Even more specifically, an ethical principle is the single rule that can logically lead to all the other rules within a complete system of belief, and that, if everyone followed it, would guarantee a society that was "better" in some sense than all other societies that can or could be conceived.

EXHIBIT 2–3
Summary of *Moral Stages and Moralization*

Lawrence Kohlberg, in *Moral Stages and Moralization,* proposes that moral standards of behavior are developed over time, as children mature into adults. There are six stages, grouped into three major levels termed "preconventional," "conventional," and "postconventional."

Level 1—Preconventional.   This is the level of most children under 9 years old, some adolescents up to age 20, and many adolescent and adult criminal offenders. Individuals at this level do not understand or accept societal rules.

Stage 1—Individual benefits. Avoid breaking rules backed by punishments. Think only in terms of your own interests. Do not recognize the interests of others. Morality, in short, is doing what's right for you.

Stage 2—Interpersonal exchanges. Avoid breaking rules backed by rewards. Still focus on your own interests, but recognize that others have interests too. Morality is an exchange, a deal, an agreement on what's right for both.

Level 2—Conventional.   This is the level of most adolescents and adults within our society and within other societies as well. Individuals at this stage accept societal rules just because they are society's rules, conventions, expectations.

Stage 3—Interpersonal expectations. Live up to what is expected of you in a small family group; follow the roles as a son or daughter that make the family function. Morality is behaving as expected by others close to you.

Stage 4—Social expectations. Live up to what is expected of you in larger social groups to keep those institutions going. Obey the law as a set of written social rules. Morality is behaving as expected by others similar to you.

Level 3—Postconventional.   This is the level that is reached by only a minority of adults. Individuals at this stage accept societal rules, but acceptance is based upon recognizing the general ethical principles that underlie those rules.

Stage 5—Social contract. Follow the law which is a reciprocal agreement to protect the rights and welfare of all citizens. Recognize that others have different morals and values, but that you have all agreed to honor such basic goals as the right to life, liberty, and property.

Stage 6—Social principles. Follow self-chosen ethical principles. Obey the law only when it does not violate those principles. Believe in the validity of rational ethical principles on such issues as justice, equality, and respect for the worth of individual human beings.

What are these ethical principles of analysis? There are 10 of them in a generally accepted listing. These are summarized briefly below; they will be described in much greater detail in the succeeding three chapters.

1. Self-interests. The argument here is that if we would all look after our own self-interests, without forcefully interfering with the rights of others, then society as a whole will be better off for it will be as free and productive as possible. Over the short term this seems to be a simple recipe for selfishness; over the long term, however, it creates a much more meaningful guide for action, for our long-term interests are usually very different from our short-term desires. The principle, then, can be expressed as "never take any action that is not in the *long-term* self-interests of yourself and/or of the organization to which you belong."

2. Personal virtues. The argument in this instance is that the lack of forceful interference is not enough. As we each pursue our own self-interests, even those that are good only over the long term, we have to adopt a set of standards for our "fair" and courteous treatment of one another. We have to be honest, open, and truthful, for example, to eliminate distrust, and we should live temperately so as not to incite envy. In short, we should be proud of our actions and of our lives. The principle, then, can be expressed as "never take any action which is not honest, open, and truthful, and which you would not be proud to see reported widely in national newspapers and on network television."

3. Religious injunctions. Honesty, truthfulness, and temperance are not enough; we also have to have some degree of compassion and kindness towards others to form a truly "good" society. Compassion and kindness are best expressed in the Golden Rule, which is not limited to the Judeo-Christian tradition but is part of almost all of the world's religions. Reciprocity—do unto others as you would have them do unto you—and compassion together build a sense of community. The principle, then, can be expressed as "never take any action that is not kind, and that does not build a sense of community, a sense of all of us working together for a commonly accepted goal."

4. Government requirements. Compassion and kindness would be ideal if everyone would be compassionate and kind, but everyone won't be. People compete for property and for position, and some people will always take advantage of others. In order to restrain that competition and maintain peace within our society, we all have to obey some basic rules from a central authority that has the power to enforce those rules. In a democratic nation, we think of that authority as the government, and of those rules as the law. The principle, then, can be expressed as "never take any action that violates the law, for the law represents the minimal moral standards of our society."

5. Utilitarian benefits. Common obedience to basic rules would

work if the people associated with the central authority did not have self-interests of their own. They do. Consequently, we need a means of evaluating the laws of the government, and that same means can be used to evaluate the justice of our own actions. A law or an act is "right" if it leads to greater net social benefits than social harms. This is the principle that is often summarized as *the greatest good for the greatest number.* A more accurate way of expressing the principle is, "never take any action that does not result in greater good than harm for the society of which you are a part."

6. Universal rules. Net social benefit is elegant in theory, but the theory does not say anything about how we should measure either the benefits or the harms—what is your life or health or well-being worth?— nor how we should distribute those benefits and allocate those harms. What we need is a rule to eliminate the self-interest of the person who decides, and that rule has to be applicable to everyone. This principle, then, can be expressed as "never take any action that you would not be willing to see others, faced with the same or a closely similar situation, also be free to take."

7. Individual rights. Eliminating self-interest on the part of the decision maker isn't really possible, given what people actually are like. They are self-interested. Consequently, we need a list of agreed-upon rights for everyone that will be upheld by everyone. These rights would certainly include guarantees against arbitrary actions of the government and would ensure freedom of speech, of assembly, of religion, etc. and would provide security against seizure of property, interference with privacy, or deprivation of liberty without due process. The principle, then, can be expressed as "never take any action that abridges the agreed-upon and accepted rights of others."

8. Economic efficiency. Basic rights are meaningless without the essentials of food, clothing, and shelter. Therefore, we should maximize the output of the needed goods and services by setting marginal revenues equal to marginal costs. At this point, the economic system will be operating as efficiently as possible, and we can reach a condition known as Pareto Optimality in which it is impossible to make any one person better off without harming someone else. The principle, then, is "always act to maximize profits subject to legal and market constraints, for maximum profits are the sign of the most efficient production."

9. Distributive justice. The problem with the economic efficiency argument is that the market distributes the output of needed goods and services unjustly, for it excludes those who are poor, uneducated, or unemployed. We need a rule to ensure that those people are not left out. If we did not know who among us would be rich and who poor, who educated and who uneducated, then any rule that we made for the distribution of the output goods and services could be considered just. It can be argued that under those conditions—known as the Social Contract—the only agree-

ment we could make would be that the poor and uneducated and unemployed should not be made worse off. The principle, then, is "never take any action in which the least among us are harmed in some way."

10. Contributive liberty. Perhaps liberty—the freedom to follow one's own self-interests within the constraints of the law and the market—is more important than justice—the right to be included in the overall distribution of goods and services. If so, then the only agreement that would be made under the conditions of the Social Contract—in which people do not know who would be rich and poor, who active and slothful—would be that no law should interfere with the right of self-development, for self-development will eventually contribute to society. The principle, then, is "never take any action that will interfere with the right of all of us for self-development and self-fulfillment."

These 10 ethical principles of analysis provide a different perspective, a different way of looking at managerial decisions and actions. The usual perspective is that of economic return on investment analysis. Will the proposed action contribute to company profits?.

The ethical principles add other perspectives. What will be the long-term impact of this action? Have I been open and honest about it? Can I be proud of my part in it? Will it add to the sense of community, to the belief that "all of us are working together for a mutually beneficial outcome," or will it detract from that sense of unity? Is it legal; does it fit within the minimal moral standards of our society? Is it beneficial; will it help more than harm our society? Is it universal; would we be willing to see other people take the same action in similar circumstances? Does it harm anyone's rights, particularly those to life, liberty, or property? Does it follow market forces, or does it manipulate those forces? Does it help the least among us, or does it at the least refrain from harming those people? Does it improve everyone's opportunities for self-development and self-fulfillment, or does it lessen those opportunities?

Each of these ethical principles taken singly seems to be a weak means of deciding upon the basic moral question whether a given decision or action that will harm others or abridge their rights is "right" and "just" and "fair." Taken together, however, most people find that these principles do form a powerful argument and do help to determine whether a given decision or action is "right" or "wrong," "just" or "unjust," "fair" or "unfair."

METHODS OF MORAL REASONING

How can these ethical principles be applied to moral problems? The method is termed *moral reasoning*. There are six steps. Remember as you go through these steps that as a manager you want two outcomes: (1) you want to arrive at a decision that you believe to be "right" and "just" and "fair" so that you feel justified in taking the proposed decision or action; and (2) you want to use a process that you can clearly explain and that will logically convince others of the "rightness," "justness," and "fairness" of your proposal.

EXHIBIT 2–4   The Method of Moral Reasoning

Personal moral
standards

Apparent moral
problem
• Harms to others
• Rights of others

⟩ State moral
problem

Develop other
answers

Resolve factual
issues

Consider personal
impacts

Apply ethical
principles

⟩ Reach moral
solution

---

1. Start by defining the moral problem, and explain why you believe this to be a moral problem. Once again, a moral problem is one in which some people are going to be hurt or harmed in some way through interference either with their welfare (the benefits and harms allocated to them) or with their rights (the duties and obligations owed to them). It is a moral problem to you because it conflicts with your moral standards and value judgments. It may not appear to be a moral problem to others because they have different moral standards and value judgments. Consequently, you want to explain your concerns fully yet concisely:

> Is it "right" that I (we, you, they) should (the decision or action that is being considered), given that this may result in (the adverse impact upon the welfare or the rights of others that you foresee)?

2. Then, develop possible alternatives. Many of the simple moral problems (the type where the moral question can be expressed as "Will I do the right thing?") are dichotomous and have only two alternative answers: "Yes, I will" or "No, I won't." Most of the complex moral problems (the type where the moral question can be expressed as "What is the right thing to do?") are not dichotomous. They have multiple possible answers. If you don't include in your analysis the alternatives that intuitively appeal to others, you will be unable to convince them of the "rightness" of your proposed action.

> What are the midpoints or the major compromises that are available? You will find that it becomes overly complex to include all of the alternatives in moral reasoning, but (as explained above) you do want to include the major ones.

3. Next, sort out the factual issues. Factual issues are those that can be resolved if you can get enough reliable data. Ask yourself, "Is it a fact that (the issue that is in dispute), and what evidence do you have that this indeed is true?" Is it a fact that all of the Cree Indians and Inuit Eskimos refuse to leave their ancestral lands in northern Quebec to make way for the giant electric power plant, or is it only the chief who objects? Is it a fact that the valuations for the property carried as security for the commercial mortgages from Lincoln Savings & Loan have been artificially inflated, and what evidence can you show that supports this view?

> In many instances you will find that it is not possible to get enough clearly reliable data to resolve the issue, or (more commonly) you will find that much of the data you do get will be conflicting. Attempt to show how the final solution would change under the different scenarios.

4. Now, start to think about the personal impacts. Personal impacts are not the consequences to the people in the moral problem whose welfare will be harmed or whose rights will be infringed. Personal impacts are the consequences to you, to the person making the decision. Ask yourself the question, "What will happen to me if I report this action or make this decision?" Remember, whistle-blowers tend not be appreciated by members of their organizations because they call into question policies and practices that have been accepted for years and that often work for the benefit of the members of those organizations.

> Many complex moral problems arise from a conflict between the economic performance of the organization (measured by sales, costs, and profits) and the social performance of the same organization (measured by the benefits and harms for the stakeholders). Many managers receive commissions and bonus payments based upon the economic performance, and resent people who bring about decreases in those commissions and payments by focusing on the social performance.

5. Lastly, apply the ethical principles in sequence. Apply all of the ethical principles, not just one or two. Ask yourself a series of questions. If I think in terms of ethical egoism (my self-interests and those of my organization over the long term), what would I decide? If I think in terms of personal virtues (openness and honesty, and pride in the resulting action), what would I decide? If I think in terms of the religious injunctions (compassion and kindness, and the creation of a sense of community among the stakeholders), what would I decide?

> Don't just apply the ethical principles that support your intuitive point of view. Remember, your task is not only to convince yourself that your decision or action is "right"; it is also to convince others. To do so you really have to include all of the different perspectives.

6. End up with a moral solution that you believe you can support, explain, and (if necessary) defend. Express that solution clearly. "I recommend that I (we, you, they) should take this action (your proposed

solution, because (the ethical principles that led to your solution)." For example, "I recommend that the auditor at the Lincoln Savings & Loan should report his or her concerns regarding the overvaluation of the property serving as collateral for commercial loans at that institution to the managing partner of the public accounting firm. I make this recommendation because (1) I believe that the benefits to the depositors of making that report far outweigh the harms to the owners (utilitarian benefits) and because (2) I would be willing that everyone, faced with an equivalent situation, should be free to take the same action (universal duties)."

People differ in their moral standards of behavior and in their value judgments of purpose. Consequently, you will find that most moral solutions—even those based upon the ethical principles of analysis—will not find universal support. Everyone may not agree that your proposed solution is "right" and "just" and "fair." Everyone can agree, however, that your proposed solution is "thoughtful" and "logical" and "reasonable." Perhaps in complex moral problems, where there are no absolutes, that is the best you can expect.

ASSIGNMENT QUESTIONS

1. Understanding the differences between (1) moral standards of behavior, (2) value judgments of importance, and (3) ethical principles of analysis is important in understanding the process of moral reasoning. Here are five statements about lying that are examples of those three concepts, and each is clearly labeled. Why is the first a moral standard? Why is the second a value judgment? Why are the third, fourth, and fifth ethical principles? Now, what ethical principles do the third, fourth, and fifth statements represent?

> Lying to avoid causing discomfort or anguish to a friend is perfectly all right. (moral standard)
> No one expects you to tell the truth all the time in business, and you have to be willing to lie occasionally in order to get ahead quickly. (value judgment)
> Lying is right if, and only if, you can agree that greater social benefits than social harms will result from the lie. (ethical principle)
> Lying is right if, and only if, you can agree that everyone, faced with an equivalent situation, should be free to lie. (ethical principle).
> Lying is right if, and only if, you can agree that the lie will protect someone's basic rights to life, liberty, etc. (ethical principle)

2. The text in Chapter 1 described three moral problems in which people associated either with a public agency (Hydro-Quebec) or with two business firms (General Motors and Lincoln Savings & Loan) were going to be hurt or harmed in some way that was outside their own control. An assignment question at the end of Chapter 1 asked you what you would do in each of those instances.

a. Now, apply the ethical principles in sequence. What is in the long-term interests of Hydro-Quebec? Would you be proud of building the dam? Does that act show compassion and kindness, and create a sense of community?

b. Has your opinion changed as a result of using the ethical principles, or does it remain exactly the same? If it is exactly the same, do you feel more confident in being able to explain your opinion to others? To convince others?

3. The last sentence in Chapter 2 contains the phrase "in complex moral problems where there are no absolutes" (see page 44). What does the term "no absolutes" mean to you?

Case 2–1

WHEN IS IT PERMISSIBLE TO BREAK THE LAW?

The phrase "to break the law" doubtless is overly dramatic as a title for this series of short cases. Only two of the situations described below actually involve people acting in ways that are directly contrary to existing U.S. laws. The others involve situations where there seems to be a conflict between the applicable U.S. and foreign laws, or where the relevant U.S. laws have never been tested in the courts.

1. Painting billboards in New York City. It is, of course, illegal to deface private property, and doubtless a claim could be made that it is especially illegal to deface advertising billboards because that act would interface with the freedom of speech of the advertising firms. Despite that illegality, a group of church members from Harlem in New York City have begun whitewashing billboards advertising cigarettes, liquor, and beer in the inner

city. Armed with ladders, long-handled rollers, and buckets of white paint, they have simply painted over advertisements for the offending products. One of the leaders of the group has been quoted as saying. "We have to stop these efforts to market unhealthy products to neighborhoods already overcome by poverty, disease, and despair" (*The New York Times*, April 10, 1989, p. 3). In your opinion, is it right to break the law against defacing private property, given that the products being advertised do harm the health of the individuals who buy them?

2. Reporting improper practices by an auditing client. Federal law, AICPA rules, and generally accepted accounting principles all prohibit disclosing confidential information gained during the performance of an audit. In the event that accounting irregularities are

discovered, it is expected that the auditing firm will either resign from the assignment or issue an adverse opinion. In the event that nonaccounting irregularities are discovered, such as lax safety practices, self-serving managerial decisions, or illegal political contributions, it has never been determined exactly what actions are required by the auditing firm, beyond the overriding prohibition against public disclosure. In your opinion, is it right to break this law against public disclosure of confidential information, given let us say that an auditing firm does discover evidence of very hazardous chemical wastes being buried close to a populated area?

3. Selling banned products in foreign countries. Locusts are exceedingly destructive pests. They gather in swarms, some of which are as large as 5 miles wide by 50 miles long and contain 5 billion insects. These huge swarms have plagued North and East Africa on a regular cycle for centuries, destroying food crops and natural vegetation and causing famine, disease, and death. Dieldrin, a pesticide once manufactured by the Shell Oil Company, is known to be highly effective in controlling locusts. Only a small amount is needed—approximately 2 ounces per acre—and it kills locusts in their crawling stage before they can take flight and infest new areas. It is therefore very cost effective. The problem is that Dieldrin is also very toxic and persistent. Many environmental scientists believe that it poses significant risks to the long-term food chain. It has

been banned for manufacture and use in both the United States and Europe.

In the winter of 1990, many of the countries of North and East Africa asked the Shell Oil Company to manufacture the pesticide for use within their own borders. The leaders of those nations explained that they expected very large swarms of locusts in the coming spring due to the hot, dry weather that had produced nearly ideal hatching conditions, and they wanted to head off the widespread destruction and famine that were sure to follow. In your opinion, is it "right" for the Shell Oil Company to produce this product, given that it could be manufactured in a plant outside Europe and the United States so that there would be no violation of any applicable law?

4. Rewarding company employees for "whistle-blowing" against their employer. A very large manufacturer of aircraft bolts and fasteners on the West Coast recently paid an $18 million fine for the falsification of test results. Aircraft bolts and fasteners have to be exceedingly high quality: lightweight yet strong and very resistant to corrosion and metal fatigue. The metallurgical tests that confirm these qualities are destructive in nature—that is, they destroy the part that is being tested—and consequently they generally are not repeated by the purchasers of the fasteners, who instead rely upon a written certification of testing. The company admitted in this instance that many of the certified tests had never been performed. The prosecuting attor-

ney admitted in return that no accidents had been traced to the untested fasteners and that "most" of the company's bolts and fasteners still in inventory or now in use did meet "most" of the original specifications.

The two employees who had reported the test falsifications to the federal government, and who had provided secretly videotaped proof of those falsifications, received an award of 25 percent of the fine under the provisions of a 1988 federal law that was designed to encourage "whistle-blowing." An aircraft industry executive described his concerns verbally as follows: "No one is defending the practice of falsifying quality checks on critical aircraft components, but the federal government is paying two employees $2.25 million each for spying on their employer. The federal government is bribing the employees of private companies." In your opinion, is it right for the federal government to pay company employees very substantial amounts of money to report company wrongdoing, given that in the past (without the payments) many similar wrongdoings did go unreported?

Class Assignment

Decide which of these actions are "right" and which are "wrong." Use your own judgment, but be prepared to support that judgment. Don't just give your answer in class, and stop; instead be prepared to say why you think that they are "right" or why you think that they are "wrong."

Case 2–2

VARIATIONS IN THE MORAL STANDARDS OF INDIVIDUALS

The text in Chapter 2 made the argument that the moral standards of an individual are dependent upon that person's specific set of goals, norms, beliefs, and values. The text made the further argument that those goals, norms, beliefs, and values in turn are dependent upon that person's cultural and religious traditions, and economic and social situations. This view of the development of moral standards may be shown graphically.

Perhaps it would be well to review very briefly the definitions of each of these terms so that all members of the class will be talking about exactly the same concept when they answer the questions at the end of this assignment.

Moral standards are the criteria we use to determine whether an act that impacts others is "right" or "wrong." Moral standards differ

EXHIBIT 1   Variations in the Moral Standards of Individuals

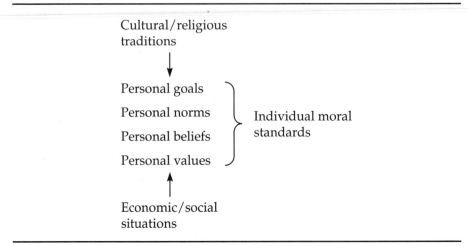

between individuals; it is easy to find evidence of those differences by just asking people about their standards.

Personal norms are our expectations of behavior; they are the way we expect people to act in a given situation. For example, we expect drivers in the United States to drive on the right-hand side of the road and to stop at red lights.

Personal beliefs are our expectations of thought; they are the way we expect people to think about given concepts. For example, we expect citizens in the United States to respect the ideas of racial equality and environmental preservation.

Personal values are the priorities or rankings that a person establishes between his or her goals, norms, and beliefs. For example, a person may "value" his or her belief in environmental preservation higher than his or her goal of financial success.

It seems intuitively clear that a person's set of goals, norms, beliefs, and values will determine that person's choice of moral standards. A person who strongly believes in the preservation of the environment probably will also believe that actions that harm the environment are "wrong." It also seems intuitively clear that a person's cultural and religious traditions and economic and social situations will influence that person's set of goals, norms, beliefs, and values. A person who is currently employed and financially secure probably will be more likely to be active in environmental preservation than a person who is currently unemployed and increasingly desperate. The purpose of this assignment is to test whether those two propositions, which seem "intuitively clear," really are true.

Class Assignment

Start to think about your own goals, norms, beliefs, and values. What do you want to achieve? What is important to you? Select your personal goals in money, lifestyle, position, performance, reputation, family, and church from the list below. Add your social values on independence, interdependence, protection of the door, equality among races and sexes, preservation of the environment, and peace between nations.

Determine your goals and values by ranking each category from 1 (lowest in your priority) to 6 (highest in your priority). You may have as many "3"s and "4"s as you want, but limit yourself to one "6," which is then your most important goal or value, and to two "5"s, which are your next most important goals and values. Pick at least one "1," which is your least important goal or value, and two "2"s, which are also far down in your opinion. Enter your choice for each question on a computer program in your computer center (which will automatically and anonymously calculate the number of choices and the weighted average of those choices for all of the members of the class), or hand in your choices on an unsigned copy of this listing before class for your instructor to manually summarize the entries and calculate the means.

Remember, "1" is the lowest in importance in your opinion, "6" is the highest, and you are limited to one "1" and one "6":

1. Increases in my wealth and the power, possessions, and life style that go with money, are important to me.

   1   2   3   4   5   6

2. Promotions in my company, and the authority and privileges that go with advancement, are important to me.

   1   2   3   4   5   6

3. Performance in my job, and the security and respect that go with achievement, are important to me.

   1   2   3   4   5   6

4. Reputation within my community, and the political offices and social activities that go with prominence, are important to me.

   1   2   3   4   5   6

5. Attention to my family, and the affection and companionship that go with family life, are important to me.

   1   2   3   4   5   6

6. Devotion to my church, and the sense of community and sharing that are part of most religions, are important to me.

   1   2   3   4   5   6

7. Independence in my personal life, and the ability to achieve my own goals and follow my own rules (as long as I do not directly interfere with others), are important to me.

   1   2   3   4   5   6

8. Interdependence with my fellow citizens, and the opportunity to set social goals and adopt mutual rules (through representative government), are important to me.

   1   2   3   4   5   6

9. Protection of the poor, and the need to help others within our society who have been less fortunate than I

have been, are both important to me.

| 1 | 2 | 3 | 4 | 5 | 6 |

10. Equality among races, sexes, and ethnic groups, and the need to achieve courtesy/respect/opportunity for all peoples, are both important to me.

| 1 | 2 | 3 | 4 | 5 | 6 |

11. Preservation of the environment, and a lack of exploitation of the earth's resources, are both important to me.

| 1 | 2 | 3 | 4 | 5 | 6 |

12. Peace between nations, and a lack of oppression of the earth's peoples, are both important to me.

| 1 | 2 | 3 | 4 | 5 | 6 |

Case 2–3

THE GOOD LIFE
AT RJR NABISCO

RJR Nabisco was formed June 1, 1985, as a result of a merger between R. J. Reynolds Tobacco Company and National Brands Corporation. National Brands was itself the result of an earlier merger between National Biscuit Company (crackers and cereals) and Standard Brands (packaged foods).

The products of RJR Nabisco are generally well known. They include Camel, Doral, Salem, Vantage, and Winston cigarettes; Ritz, Premium, and Triscuit crackers; Oreo, Chips Ahoy, and Fig Newtons cookies; Fleischmann's and Blue Bonnet margarines; Shredded Wheat and Cream of Wheat cereals; Planters peanuts, Life Savers mints, Baby Ruth candy bars, Royal gelatines, Del Monte canned fruits, Grey Poupon mustard, and Milk-Bone dog food.

The sales of RJR Nabisco have steadily increased since the merger, helped by the strong cash flows from the tobacco products. It is said that cigarettes and pipe tobacco are ideal "cash cows"; that is, they have high margins and steady sales in a mature market, and consequently provide excess cash which can be used for other corporate purposes. The excess cash provided by the cigarettes was used at RJR Nabisco to promote the food products, which in turn achieved high margins but expanding sales in a growth market.

The profits of RJR Nabisco expanded even more rapidly than did sales. The simplified income statement below shows this growth in million of dollars:

	1985	1986	1987	1988
Sales revenues	$11,622	$15,102	$15,766	$16,956
Cost of goods sold	6,024	7,920	8,221	16,956
S & A expenses	3,646	4,842	4,991	5,322
Financial costs	380	660	848	577
Income taxes	662	718	527	893
	$ 910	$ 962	$ 1,179	$ 1,393

The steady tobacco cash flows and the expanding corporate profits funded a lifestyle at the corporate headquarters of RJR Nabisco that was described in *The Wall Street Journal* as "a monument of free-spending, nouveau-riche excess" (*The Wall Street Journal*, January 4, 1990, p B1).

Executives were very well paid. Mr. F. Ross Johnson, the chairman and chief executive officer, received $3,500,000 in 1988. The next 31 persons (whose salaries were published in total, not individually, in the 10K annual report for that year) received an average of $458,000 each.

Executives also received numerous "perks." All of the senior managers at corporate headquarters, and many of the functional and technical people at the divisional offices, were given an allowance of $10,000 a year for estate planning, tax assistance, and investment counseling. Everyone at the managerial rank received at least one country club membership and was given at least one company car. Executives could select their own country club and their own car model. Some managers received multiple club memberships; Mr. Johnson held the record with over 24 club memberships spread across the country. Some man

agers selected very luxurious cars; the record here was a special Mercedes Benz said to have cost over $200,000.

Office decorations at the corporate headquarters matched the managerial salaries, perks, and cars. *The Wall Street Journal* reported that Mr. Johnson's office included a $51,000 vase, a $36,000 table, and a $100,000 rug (Ibid.). Expensive furnishings even extended to the corporate jet hangar at the Atlanta airport.

The RJR Nabisco jet hangar was not a sheet metal building of the type that is commonly seen at airports. Instead, it was a three-story building of tinted glass, surrounded by $250,000 in landscaping. A visitor entered through a tall open "atrium", with a roof made of glass panels, floors laid in Italian marble, and walls paneled with Dominican mahogany. $600,000 in furniture was spread through the pilots' lounge and control room, which were also decorated with $100,000 in paintings and statuary.

RJR Nabisco employed 36 pilots and co-pilots and maintained 10 corporate jets in a fleet commonly known as either the RJR Air Force or Air Johnson. The pilots and planes were used to carry managers to workday meetings and inspection tours, of course, but they were also used to bring sports figures, entertainment stars, and elected officials to Atlanta for weekend outings. The sports figures and entertainment stars were paid to be representatives for the company but spent much of their time playing golf and socializing with the senior executives.

> [Mr. Johnson] took excellent care of them, paying more for occasional public appearances than for an average senior vice president: [Don] Meredith got $500,000 a year, [Frank] Gifford $413,000 plus a New York office and apartment, golfer Ben Crenshaw $400,000 and golfer Fuzzy Zoeller $300,000. The king was Jack Nicklaus, who commanded $1 million a year [Bryan Burrough and John Helyar, *Barbarians at the Gate: The Fall of RJR Nabisco* (New York: Harper & Row, 1990, p. 95)].

It was said that many of the representatives for RJR Nabisco did very little "representing." Jack Nicklaus, for example, refused to make more than six appearances a year, and he didn't like to play golf with RJR Nabisco's largest customers or meet with them at the evening cocktail parties and dinners.

> Then there was the O. J. Simpson problem. Simpson, the football star and sports announcer, was being paid

$250,000 a year but was a perennial no-show at RJR events. So was Don Mattingly of the New York Yankees who also pulled down a quarter million. Johnson didn't care. Subordinates took care of those and other problems. He was having a grand time. "A few million dollars," he always said, "are lost in the sands of time" [Ibid.].

Class Assignment

Is this lifestyle of the senior executive officers at a major U.S. corporation "right" or "just" or "fair" in your opinion? Be prepared to support your belief; don't just say "yes" or "no" in class, and stop. Why is it "right," or why is it "wrong"?

1. What was the responsibility of the board of directors of RJR Nabisco relative to the expenditures of corporate funds for the management salaries and perquisites, for the airport building, for the professional athletes?

2. What was the responsibility of Ernst & Whinney, public accountant for RJR Nabisco, relative to the expenditures of corporate funds for management salaries and perquisites, for the airport building, for the professional athletes?

Case 2–4

THE LEVERAGED BUYOUT OF RJR NABISCO

On October 15, 1988, the stock of RJR Nabisco was selling at $56 per share. The company was a conglomerate, put together during the period 1978 to 1985 by means of mergers of R. J. Reynolds (cigarettes and other tobacco products), Standard Brands (coffee, tea, margarine, candy, wine, and liquor), the National Biscuit Company (cookies, crackers, and breakfast cereals), and Del Monte Corporation (canned goods).

On October 20, Ross Johnson, the chairman and chief executive officer of RJR Nabisco, announced an offer to "take the company private" at $75 per share. Taking the company private meant that RJR Nabisco, supported by the investment banking firm Shearson Lehman Brothers, was offering to buy back, from the existing shareholders, all of the common stock of the company. The assets of the company were to be pledged as security for the bank loans and corporate bonds needed to pay for that common stock, in a process known as a "leveraged buyback." The company would then be "restructured," which meant that new common stock would be sold to the members of the management and the partners in the investment banking firm who had arranged the buyback. The new common stock would not be publicly traded on one of the stock exchanges but would be privately held by the investors. Consequently, the complete process was termed "taking a

company private through a leveraged buyout or leveraged buyback."

How exactly does a "leveraged buyout" (an offer to purchase all of the stock by an outside group of "raiders") or a "leveraged buyback" (an offer to purchase all of the stock by an inside group of managers) work? It is easiest to explain the complete process as a series of steps:

1. The investor group, whether outside raiders or inside managers, puts up approximately 10 percent of the purchase price in cash, using either their own resources or those of an investment bank. Investment banks have traditionally been willing to commit their capital to facilitate a buyout or buyback because they receive substantial fees for advising on the transaction, substantial commissions for the eventual sale of the corporate bonds, and a substantial portion of the equity of the "restructured" firm.

2. Then, the investor group, relying on the assets of the company as collateral, borrows 30 percent to 40 percent of the purchase price from a syndicate of commercial banks. Commercial banks have traditionally been willing to commit their capital to finance a buyout or buyback because they hold allegedly secure collateral for the loan amounts, and they receive substantial fees for the loan commitments.

3. Finally, the investment bank, acting either by itself or as a member of a syndicate of other investment banks, raises the balance of 50 percent to 60 percent of the purchase price through the sale of high-risk "junk" bonds to savings and loan institutions, mutual bond funds, and investment pension trusts. The savings and loans, mutual funds, and investment trusts have traditionally been willing to invest their capital in these bonds because they receive much higher interest rates than could be obtained in more normal investments.

4. The existing stockholders, including arbitrageurs who buy in anticipation of the price rise that almost inevitably follows a buyout or buyback offer, are paid the bid price of the stock. The stockholders are not forced to sell. They "tender" their stock, or promise to make it available in the event that the buyback or buyout is completed. The buyback or buyout is completed when a substantial majority of the stockholders (the actual percentage required by law varies from state to state) have tendered their shares.

5. After the buyout or buyback is completed, selected portions of the company are sold in order to repay the bank loans (known as "bridge" loans due to the short amount of time they are expected to be in effect). The company is then owned by the members of the investor group and the partners of the investment bank and is financed by the junk bonds. The high interest charges of the junk bonds continue,

of course, and usually no dividends are paid on the common stock in order to use all of the available cash flow to service the debt and repay the bonds. The available cash flow is usually increased by eliminating the luxuries and "perks" of management, and frequently, though not inevitably, by cutting employment, reducing R&D, closing plants, and halting capital improvements. Once the junk bonds have been repaid, the company can be "taken public" again through a public issuance and sale of the stock on one of the major stock exchanges. Very large profits can be made by the members of the investor group and the partners of the investment bank when (and if) the company can be successfully taken public.

The actual buyout or buyback process is usually not as direct or as simple or as straightforward as has been described. Once the first offer has been made, the company is considered to be "in play." Other investor groups make higher offers. Other investment banks propose different terms. Arbitrageurs and private investors buy and sell legally on the public rumors (or illegally on the "inside" information) of higher bids and/or unavailable financing. "Unavailable financing," of course, means that a prior bid that had been considered legitimate must be taken off the market, and the next lower bid becomes the probable price for the buyout or buyback.

In the particular case of RJR Nabisco, Ross Johnson made the initial offer of $75 per share on October 20, 1988. Mr. Johnson said that despite the best efforts of his management team, the price of the stock had remained depressed at $56 per share for a number of years, and he wanted to "increase value for the shareholders."

On October 24, Kohlberg Kravis Roberts (a private banking firm and "buyout" specialist) bid $90 per share. The firm said that the stock of RJR Nabisco was obviously worth much more than the $75 per share offered by Mr. Johnson and questioned his motives in making the original offer at "such an unrealistic figure."

On November 4, Mr. Johnson and Shearson Lehman Brothers increased their bid to $92 per share. They claimed, in making the new offer, that Kohlberg Kravis Roberts wanted only to "break up" the company (divide it into its basic product divisions of tobacco, coffee, tea, etc.) and sell off those pieces to the highest bidder, which often meant a foreign firm wishing to enter the U.S. market. Mr. Johnson, on the other hand, said that only "poorly performing" divisions would be sold under his restructuring plan.

On November 5, a spokesperson for Kohlberg Kravis Roberts released to the press an internal document from RJR Nabisco that detailed the agreement between that company and Shearson Lehman Brothers. It was not explained how Kohlberg Kravis Roberts had obtained the copy.

The document stated that Ross Johnson and "six to nine other executives" (the other executives were not named, and it was unclear why the number might vary) would receive 8.5 percent of the stock in the new company at the successful completion of the buyback. The balance of the stock was to go to the partners at Shearson Lehman Brothers and to a series of wealthy private investors and university endowment funds who were providing the original 10 percent of the purchase price and (in small amounts, as a "sweetener") to some of the savings and loans, mutual funds, and pension trusts that were expected to purchase the junk bonds.

The stock percentage allocated to Mr. Johnson and his fellow executives was to increase to 20 percent, provided "certain conditions were met." These conditions involved the sale of over 50 percent of the divisions of the company, both those that were classified as "poorly performing" and others that were operating profitably, by certain times and at certain figures, in order to rapidly repay all of the bridge loans and some of the junk bonds.

The 8.5 percent of the stock in the company allocated to Mr. Johnson and his fellow executives was to be purchased for $20 million in total (not $20 million from each executive). The company was to provide an interest-free loan of $20 million to the group in order to facilitate that purchase. The additional stock, if the certain conditions were met, was to be provided as a "bonus."

The amounts of stock, which were to go to the Shearson Lehman Brothers partners, wealthy private investors, university endowment funds, and junk bond purchasers, were large and apparently promised a return of 35 percent to 50 percent per year upon their investments, but these amounts and returns were common in leveraged buyouts and buybacks and raised no concerns among members of the financial community.

The amounts of stock, which were to go to Mr. Johnson and the "six to nine other executives," were considered to be unprecedented by people within the financial community. If RJR Nabisco were valued at the most recent offer of $92 per share for all of the stock in the firm, then the company as it currently existed was worth $22 billion. Granted that the stock to be issued to Mr. Johnson and the small group of other executives would be in the restructured firm, after the issuance of junk bonds, but it had to be assumed that the $92 bid price represented Mr. Johnson's accurate valuation of the worth of the company's assets. Mr. Johnson and "six to nine other executives" were to be given stock worth $1.87 billion and were required to invest only $20 million in the form of a noninterest-paying loan from the company. If the "certain conditions" of the buyback were met, that small group would receive additional stock worth $2.53 billion as a "bonus," for a total of $4.40 billion. Members of Congress and representatives of the media expressed both shock and outrage.

On November 7, a spokesperson for Frostman Little, a private investment bank, said that the very large amounts of capital being used to compensate members of management indicated that the value being placed upon RJR Nabisco was still too low and announced a new offer of $97 per share. Frostman Little, a relatively small investment bank, said that it was financially supported by Procter & Gamble, Castle & Cook, and Ralston Purina, all large manufacturers and marketers of packaged consumer goods and food products. It seemed obvious to members of the financial community that arrangements had already been made by Frostman Little for the purchase of the nontobacco divisions of RJR Nabisco by those manufacturers and marketers and that consequently, the $97 bid approached an accurate valuation for the firm.

On November 16, Ross Johnson and Shearson Lehman Brothers raised their bid to $100 per share and announced that the package of compensation for the senior executives had been "misunderstood" and was being rescinded. It was not stated exactly what compensation arrangements would be made to replace that original "package." It was known that Kohlberg Kravis Roberts was planning to rebid before the final deadline of November 23, and it was thought that Frostman Little might do so also.

Ross Johnson and the partners at Shearson Lehman Brothers realized that they would have to submit another bid, higher than their current offer of $100 per share, to defeat the other contestants. They had invited Salomon Brothers, a very large investment banking firm with expertise in selling junk bonds, to participate in the bidding process. The participants in that process began to gather shortly after 9:00 in the morning of November 23 to set the price and terms of the final bid, which was due at the offices of Skadden Arps (attorneys for RJR Nabisco) at 5:00 that afternoon.

The problem was to select a number, above $100 per share, that would just barely exceed the final bids from the other competitors. Those final bids, of course, were unknown. Consequently, the selection process became a guessing game. No one wanted to name a specific figure, and become personally responsible for the eventual success or failure of the largest buyout in the history of the merger movement. Everyone wanted someone else to name that figure, and assume that responsibility.

For six hours, interrupted by telephone calls to and from friends, informants, and experts, the investment bankers and company executives alternatively considered and then avoided talking about the size of the final bid in an aura of increasing urgency and concern. *The Wall Street Journal* (January 4, 1990, p. B1) reported that these supposed sophisticated discussions of financial market economics were punctuated with cries of "Let's get on with it," "Christ, we need a *** number," "If you don't make up your minds soon, we'll have no bid at all," and "Can you believe this? I can't believe that this is happening."

Just after 3:00, a number was selected, apparently at random (no one ever claimed responsibility). The number was $114 per share. That figure had to be entered into the formal bid, a six-inch-thick package of cash flows, pro forma statements, repayment schedules, loan guarantees, and interest rates, all of which were influenced by this final price for the company. Across Manhattan, at commercial banks, law offices, and accounting firms, the numbers were computed and telephoned or faxed to the 87th floor office of Shearson Lehman Brothers where the bid package was being assembled. A 4:20, four attorneys were ordered into a cab with the incomplete bid package and a portable telephone; they were to write in final numbers during the trip to the law offices of Skadden Arps, where the bid was due precisely at 5:00.

Traffic in Manhattan is never light, and this was a Friday afternoon when it is traditionally very heavy. The cab was soon stopped in traffic. It was obvious that the bid would not be delivered to the law offices on time. The four attorneys bolted from the cab and sprinted along the sidewalks in a desperate effort to reach Skadden Arps before 5:00.

> When [the] breathless group reached Skadden Arps, their path was blocked by a throng of photographers and television cameras. The newsmen, spotting the portable phone, crowded around and began shouting questions. The attorneys plunged like fullbacks through the assemblage and into the lobby.
>
> . . . . .
>
> As Truesdell [leader of the group] and his three companions spilled from the elevator on the upper floor, their way was blocked by an enormous security guard. A minute later, Truesdell was escorted into the reception area where, exhausted, he handed over a binder containing the group's bid.
>
> [He] looked at his watch. It was 5:01. The largest takeover bid in corporate history was late. He prayed no one would notice [Bryan Burrough and John Helyar, *Barbarians at the Gate: The Fall of RJR Nabisco* (New York: Harper & Row, 1990), p. 401)].

On November 29, the board of directors of RJR Nabisco announced that it would recommend to the stockholders of the company that they accept the new bid from Kohlberg Kravis

Roberts at $109 per share. The bid from Ross Johnson and Shearson Lehman Brothers (the one that had arrived at 5:01 on November 23 at $114 was rejected. Complex tax reasons were given for the rejection of the higher offer, but it was widely believed that the original bid at $75 per share, which was now considered to have been far too low, and the compensation package, which had always been considered to have been far too excessive, were also at least partially responsible. Ross Johnson retired from the company he had tried to purchase with a "golden parachute" said to be worth $56 million.

Mr. Johnson obviously benefited from the leveraged buyout of RJR Nabisco, even though he had lost in the bidding process. Who else benefited, and who was harmed, and what were the extent of those benefits and harms? The balance of the case will discuss those two issues.

It is difficult to tell exactly the extent of benefits and harms in most leveraged buyouts because the published information is so limited. Once a company has been "taken private," the owners no longer have a requirement to file quarterly financial reports. And, the reports they do file are not truly comparable to the earlier firm because so many of the divisions have been sold. It is possible, however, to make some estimates of benefits and harms based upon "rules of thumb" that are generally accepted in the financial community. Using those rules of thumb, it can be said that the following groups probably will receive reasonably substantial benefits from the leveraged buyout of RJR Nabisco:

1. Members of investor groups can receive huge returns. The actual rate of return depends upon the ability of the investor group to quickly sell some of the divisions, cut many of the expenses, and repay much of the debt before they take the company public once again. The usual rule for a successful buyout is a compound return of 35 percent to 50 percent per year for the five years needed to prepare the company for the public sale. For RJR Nabisco, this would mean a profit of $11.2 billion to $18.9 billion, given an original investment by Kohlberg Kravis Roberts and others of $2.5 billion (10 percent of the total price).

2. Company stockholders also do very well. RJR Nabisco stockholders, including the arbitrageurs who purchased shares only after the first hint of the takeover attempt, were paid $109 per share for stock that had been selling on the open market at $56 per share just five weeks previously. It is said that more than 500 residents of Durham, North Carolina, where the original R. J. Reynolds Tobacco Company had been headquartered and run in paternalistic fashion until the merger with Nabisco, became instant millionaires as a result of stock they had received years earlier as employee benefits. Company stockholders in total received $12.15 billion above the prior market value of the stock as a result of the leveraged buyback.

3. The investment banks receive fees for providing take-over advice and commissions for arranging the sale

of corporate junk bonds. The usual rule is that 1.5 percent of the final price goes to the investment banks who are on the winning side. Kohlberg Kravis Roberts had retained Wasserstein Perella, Morgan Stanley, and Drexel Burnham Lambert to assist in the takeover. It is estimated that they received $375 million. The investment banks on the losing side receive far less; it is thought that Shearson and Salomon Brothers shared about $25 million.

4. Merger and acquisition attorneys receive fees both to assist and to fight takeovers. The usual rule is 1.0 percent of the final price. It is estimated that all of the law firms involved in the RJR leveraged buyout (including Davis Polk whose attorneys sprinted along the sidewalks of Third Avenue to reach the filing location on time) received $250 million.

5. Commercial banks receive fees to commit the funds needed for the secured loans in the buyout. The usual rule is 0.7 percent of the final price, even though the commercial banks finance only 30 percent to 40 percent of the cost, and the rest is raised through the sale of junk bonds. The purchasers of the junk bonds can be further compensated by receiving portions of the equity as "sweeteners." These sweeteners cannot be paid to commercial banks (who are forbidden to own the equity of corporate clients) and consequently they receive "commitment fees." The commitment fees from RJR Nabisco were estimated at $175 million.

Who loses when a company is "taken private" through either a leveraged buyout (outside raiders) or a leveraged buyback (inside management)? The accounting is even more difficult here, for it is difficult to express many of the harms or losses in dollar equivalents, but it is generally believed that three major groups share in the downside:

1. The U.S. government loses due to lower tax receipts. The capital gains of the stockholders are of course taxed when their shares are repurchased at the bid price. The interest payments of the company on the bonds and loans used to finance those repurchases, however, are all tax exempt. The interest payments normally are much larger than the capital gains, and consequently tax revenues to the government decline overall. It has been estimated that the federal government will receive $2.5 billion in capital gains taxes from the takeover of RJR Nabisco but will lose $7.5 billion through interest exemptions in the five years following that takeover, for a net loss of $5.0 billion.

2. The existing bondholders of the company lose due to lower bond rating. The ratings of the existing corporate bonds are downgraded following issuance of the high-risk "junk" debt needed to finance the buyback. The new debt does not take precedence over the existing bonds, but the very large increase in the total amount of debt decreases the "creditworthiness" of the firm and consequently the "credit rating" of the existing debt. At RJR Nabisco, the long-term debt

on the balance sheet increased from $3.88 billion before the buyout to $19.7 billion afterwards, and the market value of the earlier debt was reduced by over 30 percent. The State Employees Pension Fund of North Carolina, which had been a substantial investor in the bonds of the R. J. Reynolds Tobacco Company before it merged with the National Biscuit Company, lost $620 million. The close similarity of the loss to the pension fund ($620 million) and the gain to the investment banks ($400 million in total) and law firms ($250 million) did not go unnoticed. The state treasurer said in obvious exasperation, "We could have saved everyone a lot of trouble if they had just sent the bills for the bankers and lawyers directly to us, and forgotten about the buyout."

3. The current employees of the company lose due to company restructuring. It is hard to compare employment numbers and wage/salary payments before and after a leveraged buyout or buyback because so many of the divisions are sold and consequently are no longer included in the data base. It has always been assumed that most of the employees stay with those divisions under the new ownership, but recent evidence seems to indicate that this assumption about continued employment within the "disposed" divisions may not be warranted as duplicate offices and plants are consolidated and redundant positions are eliminated. It is usually estimated that 20 percent of the employees in the "retained" divisions are discharged or asked to

take early retirement as a result of the cost-saving moves. RJR Nabisco had 120,334 full-time employees prior to the leveraged buyout; if the 20 percent figure is applied to be retained and disposed divisions equally, the number of people adversely affected by the leveraged buyout would be 24,100.

Class Assignment

It has been claimed that leveraged buyouts and buybacks create value for the shareholders and for society. In the instance just described of the leveraged buyout of RJR Nabisco by Kohlberg Kravis Roberts, that claim would appear to be true. The benefits of the transaction have been estimated to total $24,175 million, the harms only $5,620 million:

Investor group benefits	$11,200 million
Company stockholders	12,140 million
Investment banks	400 million
Attorneys	250 million
Commercial banks, fees	175 million
Total benefits	24,175 million
Government tax losses, net	5,000 million
Existing bond holder losses	520 million
Total losses	5,620 million

Was this leveraged buyout of a major U.S. corporation "right" or was it "wrong" in your opinion? Be prepared to support your belief; don't just say "yes" or "no" in class, and pause. Why was it "right" or why was it "wrong"?

1. What was the responsibility of Ross Johnson, the chairman and chief executive officer of RJR Nabisco? As-

sume that he was invited to talk to the class. What would he say? What questions would you ask him? Try to think of questions that he could not answer with a simple "yes" or "no."

2. What were the responsibilities of the investment bankers involved in the leveraged buyout? Why did they act in such an apparently unprofessional manner when the final bid was being discussed? If Peter Cohen, the managing partner of Shearson Lehman Brothers, came and talked to the class, what questions would you ask him?

3. What were the responsibilities of the attorneys involved in the leveraged buyout? Put yourself in the position of the 26-year-old attorney, Richard Truesdell, who was one of those who sprinted along Third Avenue to reach the law offices of Skadden Arps on time. How would you respond to that question?

4. What are the responsibilities of Louis Gerstner, the person who was put in charge of RJR Nabisco after the leveraged buyout of that company by Kohlberg Kravis Roberts? If he came and talked to the class, what would he say? What questions would you ask him?

Case 2–5

THE MEXICAN MAQUILADORAS

Maquiladoras are manufacturing plants located in Mexico that process goods and services destined for the U.S. market. The goods tend to be high-volume industrial components and consumer products that require minimal job skills such as auto parts, textile items, and electronic units. The services tend to be high-volume information-processing tasks that also require minimal jobs skills, primarily in data entry. Most of the maquiladoras are owned by U.S. firms. They have been located in Mexico to take advantage of the low wage rates that are prevalent in that country.

The wage rates in Mexico are low in comparison to those in the United States, and that difference is particu-

larly noticeable in the maquiladora plants, which usually are located in areas with a large labor supply but a limited worker demand. In 1989, for example, the average wage paid to manufacturing employees in the United States was $13.85 per hour. In Mexico, the equivalent figure was $1.99, while in the maquiladoras it was half of that amount, at $0.99.

The term "maquiladora" is obviously Spanish. It originally referred to the toll a flour mill would charge for grinding the grain that belonged to farmers and land owners. The new industrial plants in Mexico operate on much the same basis. They do not own the products they produce. Instead, they receive under bond (that is, without paying import duties into Mexico) the sheet metal for auto parts or the cotton and synthetic fibers for textile items or the electronic components for television sets and recording units from their parent firms in the United States. They process the auto parts and textile items or assemble the television sets and recording units and then ship back the completed products. Export duties back to the United States for the completed products are charged only on the value added by the low-cost labor and consequently do little to raise the overall cost of the goods.

The maquiladora industry has expanded rapidly since its formation in 1970. The concept started as an agreement between the two countries to provide more factory jobs in Mexico and to lessen the illegal immigration into the United States. By 1990, there were 1,886 maquiladora plants operating in Mexico, and they employed more than 500,000 workers. Originally, most of these plants had been built along the border to reduce freight costs, but by 1990 they had expanded far into the interior. It is estimated that the number of maquiladora plants and their workers will double over the next five years and even triple if a free-trade agreement is signed with Mexico, which will further reduce the duties on the goods shipped back to the United States.

There are alleged to be a number of benefits to both Mexico and the United States of the present maquiladora program and the proposed North American Free Trade Agreement:

1. Mexican employment. The first benefit is also the most obvious one and probably the most critical one for the Mexican economy. Maquiladoras provide 500,000 jobs in a country that historically has suffered from very low industrialization and very high unemployment. Seventeen percent of all the manufacturing jobs in Mexico are now at the American-owned maquiladora plants. The supporters of the present system admit that most of these jobs pay very low wages, but they go on to say that those jobs and wages have to be compared to the alternatives that are available in Mexico.

Some critics of the industry argue that the maquiladoras pay poorly even by Mexican standards. They point to surveys such as one conducted by *Business Week* that showed that over a five-year period, the maquiladoras paid about half the average hourly manufacturing wage in Mexico. Supporters of the maquiladora industry, however, maintain that given the rudimentary type of work the maquiladora laborer typically performs, the maquiladora wages are quite respectable. They note that the average maquiladora worker's wages are about 20 percent higher than the Mexican minimum wage. "What you have to keep in mind is that in Mexico, that's a very good wage," said one of the supporters ["Maquiladora Operations," report prepared by the Investor Responsibility Research Center, Washington, D.C., dated February 8, 1991, p. H-9].

2. Mexican development. The maquiladora plants perform for the most part very low-level fabrication and assembly operations, but they perform them using mass manufacturing technologies under strict controls for both quality and cost.

Exposure to those technologies and gaining experience with those controls are felt to be the start of the critical movement for Mexico from a Third World to a Western-type economy.

The argument by maquiladora advocates that the industry teaches skills to substantial numbers of Mexican workers also should be noted. Although most of the maquiladora employees perform simple and routine tasks, a significant portion of them have jobs requiring some degree of skill. In recent years, almost one-fifth of the workers in the maquiladora industry have been classified as production technicians or administrative staff. These job categories may include some relatively unskilled positions, but most of them do provide the workers with technical or administrative experience ["Maquiladora Operations," report prepared by the Investor Responsibility Research Center, Washington D.C., dated February 8, 1991, p. H-7].

3. American competitiveness. The maquiladoras offer low-cost manufacturing to American firms and help to counter the current Japanese move to combine their capital, technology, and high-skilled assembly facilities with low-cost component manufacturing plants in southeast Asia for a distinct competitive advantage. Supporters of the present system admit that some low-skilled jobs will be lost in the United States, but they argue that overall, American companies will be much better able to meet their Japanese competitors and consequently will expand their employment in the skilled assembly operations.

With 36,000 maquiladora workers, General Motors is now Mexico's largest private employer. Ford, Chrysler, Honda, and Nissan also have Mexican plants. Mexico has 328 auto parts companies, which supply 13 percent of the parts for all U.S. built vehicles (both "Big-3" and foreign owned).

"It's useful politically to the UAW and to the AFL-CIO to complain about low wage labor," says Sean McAlinder, a University of Michigan researcher. "But, it's not like free trade with Mexico is going to make that any worse, and it's going to happen anyway."

Detroit automakers, McAlinder says, need a free trade deal as their "ace-in-the-hole" against the Japanese, who are farming out low-wage low-skill jobs to countries throughout Southeastern Asia [*Detroit Free Press*, March 12, 1991, p. 8B].

. . . . .

Carla Hills, the federal government's top trade negotiator [for the Bush administration], believes a U.S. and Mexico free-trade deal is a win-win proposition. "Reduced barriers will improve the efficiency and productivity of U.S. and Mexican industry and enhance their competitiveness in international markets," says Mrs. Hill [*Detroit Free Press*, March 12, 1991, p. 8B].

4. American markets. Lastly, the maquiladoras provide paying jobs and raise living standards in a nation of 90 million consumers who will eventually come to demand U.S. exports in both products and services. Supporters of the present system admit that the annual per capita income in Mexico is only $2,250, which is too low to support active import markets in automobiles, appliances, and other "big-ticket" items, but they believe that the increased Mexican prosperity

will lead to expanded American exports of consumer goods, industrial machinery, and financial services.

A three-way deal involving the United States, Canada, and Mexico would create the largest free-trade zone in the world, with 360 million people and annual trade of $6 trillion. . . . A study sponsored by U.S. companies with an interest in Mexico concluded that a free-trade agreement would stimulate growth across a broad range of U.S. industries, and thereby benefit thousands of U.S. workers [*Detroit Free Press*, March 1, 1991, p. 8B].

Opponents of the present maquiladora system and the proposed free-trade agreement suggest that in addition to the advantages listed above, there are an equal number of drawbacks, listed below:

1. American unemployment. Each new job created in Mexico by an American-owned maquiladora firm results in the loss of the equivalent job in the United States. Opponents of the present system admit that over time there will be trade adjustments as the Mexican markets for U.S. industrial goods and financial services expand, but in the short term they say that the displaced workers in the United States will suffer pain and hardship.

In a pro free-trade report, the U.S. International Trade Commission wrote "Unskilled workers in the United States would suffer a slight decline in real income, but skilled workers and owners of capital services would benefit more from lower prices and thus enjoy increased real income."

This statement was quickly pounced on by critics. "What's the moral calculus

here?" asked AFL-CIO official Mark Anderson. "Even if you accept that free trade is a little bit beneficial overall, you're still advantaging one-third of the people at the top who are already well off at the expense of the two-thirds of the work force at the bottom who aren't" [*Detroit Free Press*, March 1, 1991, p. 8B].

. . . . . .

I'm always amazed at the ease with which the government economists who can't be fired from their jobs write about the "slight decline in real income" of the industrial workers who just have been fired from their jobs. I think that every economist ought to be arbitrarily fired every three to five years, and left unemployed for a minimum of six months, just to teach them what it's like [Statement of union official, asked to comment on the report prepared by the U.S. International Trade Commission].

2. Nonrepresentative work force. The pay rates at the maquiladora plants in Mexico are admittedly low, only slightly above the minimum wage requirements in that country. The task assignments at those plants are admittedly rudimentary, requiring little skill and offering little interest. The supervisory practices at those plants are admittedly harsh, with constant pressures for faster performance. The result of the low wages, rudimentary tasks, and constant pressures is a work force that is not representative of the population. Eighty percent of the workers are women and another 10 percent are children between the ages of 12 and 16. Numerous reports have claimed that Mexican men will not accept the wages, perform the tasks, or tolerate the pressures without protest, and that consequently most of the

maquiladora plants have a hiring policy that deliberately discriminates against males.

If you walk through a maquiladora plant, you are immediately struck by the fact that the employees are almost all women, with some young children whom it would be illegal to hire in the United States. There are no men, except for the fork lift drivers and the machinery "set-up" mechanics. I don't think that it is unfairly stereotyping them to say that Mexican men are proud, and family oriented. There is something wrong with an economic arrangement that lessens pride and destroys families [Statement of union official, asked to comment on the work force composition at most maquiladora plants].

3. Working conditions. The American owners of the maquiladora factories are, of course, not required to meet U.S. standards for workplace safety. They are required to meet Mexican standards, but those rules and regulations are much less stringent and they tend to be poorly enforced. It has to be assumed that most of the maquiladora plants meet reasonable safety standards, but numerous reports have criticized the textile factories for "chronic asthma, conjunctivitis, bronchitis and brown lung as common occupational diseases caused by cotton dust and air-borne fibers," and the exposure of workers in electronics, film processing, and woodworking maquiladoras to toxic chemicals and hazardous materials is said to be "close to exploitation."

Questions about worker exploitation in a nation where unemployment is endemic draw ready rejoinders from maquila ("maquila" is the slang or street term for maquiladora) officials. "We're in a foreign country and it's a big mistake to impose U.S. values," says John Riley, vice president of Vertek, a Tijuana-based electronics company. Adds trade association chief Alfred Rich: "Are these people better off with me or without me? The small wage gives them the ability to enjoy a decent lifestyle. They may not be living in the lap of luxury, but they aren't starving."

Some, though, are getting sick. Interviews with dozens of employees in border communities turned up complaints of headaches, vision and respiratory problems, and skin diseases caused by soldering fumes, solvents, and other chemicals—particularly in the electronics assembly industry. Some plants provide protective gloves, but few women wear them because they hamper dexterity and prevent the workers from maintaining the fast-paced production schedules. "They take advantage of us because women are more docile," says electronics worker Alphonia Resendiz, 39. "The men complain, so they don't get hired" [*U.S. News and World Report*, May 6, 1991, p. 35].

4. Environmental deterioration. As with worker safety, the American-owned maquiladora factories are not required to meet U.S. standards for the protection of the environment, except in the instance of the disposal of toxic chemicals which should be shipped back to the United States for proper disposal. The result, it is said, has been a series of cost-saving shortcuts that have resulted in massive solid waste dumps and continual liquid waste discharges.

Environmentalists criticize the maquiladoras on the grounds that they have severely polluted the environment around the border region. Much of the border area is indeed polluted, especially the rivers that cut through the region. High levels of copper, selenium, mercury, fecal coliform, and bacteria have been found in the Rio Grande near Nuevo Laredo, and some sources have suggested a link between Rio Grande drinking water and the high rates of liver and gall bladder cancer found in the area. The New River is also severely polluted. One Environmental Protection Agency official was quoted in *The San Francisco Examiner* as saying that the New River "contains every disease known in the Western Hemisphere." The high level of pollution in these rivers and in the local groundwater threatens the water supplies not only of Mexico but of the United States ("Maquiladora Operations," report prepared by the Investor Responsibility Research Center, Washington D.C., dated February 8, 1991, p. H-10).

Beyond the water-borne discharges, other practices by some U.S. firms also degrade the environment. Adjacent to the Reynosa industrial park that is home to several major corporations is a massive open dump that contains acre after acre of industrial detritus: plastic, metal, rubber, resins, paint sludge. Foul-smelling slime leaks from drums marked "Zenith Plant #12." Zenith Electronics Corp. spokesman John Taylor acknowledged that the company, which employs as many as 10,000 workers at its Reynosa facility, dumps its bathroom, kitchen, office, and non-hazardous industrial trash here but says toxic wastes are returned to the United States. "This site is a SEDUE licensed disposal facility ["SEDUE" is the acronym for the Mexican federal agency charged with enforcing that nation's environmental regulations] and anything we do is in accordance with the laws," Taylor says. "We are a good corporate

citizen in Mexico." Both SEDUE and Reynosa municipal officials, however, say they have not authorized the area to be used as a dump [*U.S. News and World Report*, May 6, 1991, p. 40].

The inadequate supervision by SEDUE invites problems. Under a binational agreement, the maquiladoras are required to ship their hazardous wastes back to the United States for disposal and to notify the EPA. But transportation and EPA–approved disposal of a single 55-gallon drum of hazardous waste can cost anything from $150 to $1,000. As a result, most maquiladora wastes are stockpiled, buried, dumped, flushed, burned, or "donated" to charities for "recycling," an environmental charade permissible under a loophole in Mexican law. In 1989, reports the EPA's Kathleen Shimmin, the agency received just 12 notifications of hazardous-waste shipments being returned to the United States across the California and Arizona borders [*U.S. News and World Report*, May 6, 1991, p. 36].

Class Assignment

What do you think should be done relative to the maquiladora plants in Mexico? Should the proposed free-trade agreement with Mexico be signed, which will double or even triple the employment levels in those factories? More specifically, put yourself in the position of the president of Zenith Electronics Corporation; you have just read the claim printed in *U.S. News and World Report* that your company is dumping solid wastes in northern Mexico in contradiction to Mexican law and probably not shipping chemical wastes back across the border to the United States as required by U.S. law. What actions do you take?

CHAPTER 3

The Early Ethical Principles

Moral problems, to repeat the earlier definition from Chapter 1, are those in which some people are going to be hurt or harmed in some way outside of their own control. Moral problems in management add an additional layer of complexity. These are problems in which some people associated with an organization are going to be hurt or harmed, while others are going to be benefited or rewarded. These people associated with the organization are known as "stakeholders." The mixture of harms and benefits that will be distributed to the stakeholders and the blend of rights and duties that may be owed to the stakeholders make moral problems in management particularly difficult to resolve.

Most people, when they encounter a moral problem in management, turn first to their moral standards of behavior. Moral standards of behavior are what a person believes to be "right." They are the intuitive gauges we all use to evaluate our behavior and that of our neighbors. The problem is that moral standards are subjective, and vary depending upon the cultural and religious traditions to which we have been exposed, and the economic and social situations in which we find ourselves.

Moral standards of behavior are usually sufficient when we encounter a *simple* moral problem in management. These are the problems in which the benefits are concentrated upon a single person or a small group, while the harms are spread much more widely among most of the stakeholders. The benefits in these instances often can be expressed in financial terms, in dollars or dollar equivalents. These are the problems, such as insider trades, outright bribes, deliberate lies, in which it is clear what our reaction should be. The only question we face is, "Will I do the right thing?"

Moral standards of behavior are usually not sufficient when we encounter a *complex* moral problem in management. These are the problems in which the benefits are spread among most of the stakeholders, while the harms are concentrated upon a single person or (more likely) a small group. In these instances it is seldom possible to express both the benefits and the harms in purely financial terms; instead they involve trade-offs on such issues as profits versus jobs, environmental preservation versus needed goods and services, or global competitiveness versus domestic responsibility. Here it is not clear what our reaction should be. Here the question we face is, "What is the right thing to do?"

EXHIBIT 3–1 Morals, Values, and Beliefs

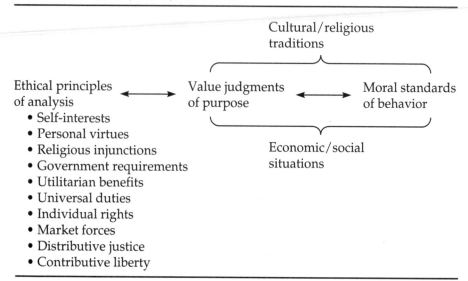

Most people, when their moral standards of behavior do not seem to lead to a convincing outcome in the worrisome trade-offs associated with a complex moral problem, turn next to their value judgments of purpose. Value judgments of purpose are what a person believes to be "important." They are the intuitive priorities we all set to guide and explain our behavior and that of our neighbors. The problem is that value judgments also are subjective, and vary once again depending upon the cultural and religious traditions to which we have been exposed, and the economic and social situations by which we are influenced.

When moral standards of behavior and value judgments of purpose both seem to be insufficient to deal with the worrisome trade-offs of complex moral problems, most people do not then automatically turn to their ethical principles of analysis. Most people do not know the ethical principles of analysis and the methods of moral reasoning. The reasons for this lack of knowledge about ethical principles and moral reasoning are not altogether clear, but they basically involve 50 years of industrial expansion and economic prosperity in the United States, Western Europe, and Japan. Private sector jobs were plentiful. Government social programs were widespread. Global environmental resources were thought to be limitless. It was not necessary to look at the harmful impacts of managerial decisions and actions; someone or some group or something would mitigate those impacts.

Now it is necessary to consider the harmful impacts of managerial actions, and a knowledge of the ethical principles of analysis is essential. Ethical principles are statements of the rules and conditions that would ensure a "good" society, and particularly they are statements of the first rules or single conditions within a complete system of belief from which all other statements can be derived. An example is utilitarian benefits: *Always act such that you maximize net social benefits, the balance of social gains over social costs.* Another example is universal rules: *Always act such that you would be willing that everyone else, faced with the same situation, would be free to take the same action.* There are 10 ethical principles. This chapter will look at the first three in greater detail.

SELF-INTERESTS

The principle of self-interests—also known as the principle of ethical egoism—can be summarized in the statement that everyone should rationally pursue their own long-term self-interests and rationally ignore the long-term self-interests of others. At first glance this principle would seem to be the epitome of outright yuppie selfishness. I should pursue what I believe will work out to my advantage over time, and you should pursue what you believe will work out to your advantage over time, and if you get hurt in the process, well, that is just too bad for you. I may feel momentarily saddened; I will not be overly concerned.

Some people add the proviso—in an attempt to somewhat ameliorate the apparent selfishness—that neither of us should forcefully interfere with the rights of others, but that merely complicates the outwardly simple prescription of the principle of self-interests. What is interference? What, even more to the point, is forceful interference? I obviously should not physically sabotage your car, but can I diplomatically sabotage your career?

You will find, however, that "first-glance" interpretations of ethical principles are often misleading. The principle of self-interests is not really a justification for outright selfishness. Remember that the principle states that we should each *rationally* pursue our *long-term* self-interests. "Long-term" eliminates all of the immediate gratifications that are often associated with egoism, and "rational" means that we should think through all of the alternatives that are open to us and the probable outcomes of each alternative. I might like to sabotage your career to gain a quick promotion, but according to the true principle of acting in my own self-interests I should realize that over the long term I might be found out which would destroy my own career, or you might suspect what had happened and return the favor.

Suddenly the principle of self-interests begins to make a great deal more sense. It states that I should not harm you, *not* because I owe you any duty of non-malfeasance (not doing harm), but because I owe myself the duty of beneficiency (actually doing good). I should not lie to you because then you would lie to me. I should not steal from you because then you will steal from me.

I should rationally look after my long-term self-interests because I know my self-interests better than you do. You should rationally look after your long-term self-interests because you know your self-interests better than I do. If I arrogantly appoint myself to look after your self-interests, you should object strongly because (1) I may accidentally misinterpret those interests and get you something you don't really want or—even worse—(2) I may

---

EXHIBIT 3-2
Excerpts from *Looking Out for Number One*
Robert Ringer

In deciding whether it's right to look out for Number One, I suggest that the first thing you do is eliminate from consideration all unsolicited moral opinions of others. Morality—the quality of character—is a very personal and private matter. No other living person has the right to decide what is moral (right or wrong) for you. I further suggest that you make a prompt and thorough effort to eliminate from your life all individuals who claim—by words or actions, directly or by inference—to possess such a right. You should concern yourself only with whether looking out for Number One is moral from your own rational, aware viewpoint.

Looking out for Number One means spending more time doing those things which give you pleasure. It does not, however, give you carte blanche to do whatever you please. It is not hedonistic in concept, because the looking-out-for-Number-One philosophy does not end with the hedonistic assertion that man's primary moral duty lies in the pursuit of pleasure.

Looking out for Number One adds a rational, civilized tag: man's primary moral duty lies in the pursuit of pleasure *so long as he does not forcibly interfere with the rights of others*. If you picked up this book in the hope that it might explain how to get ahead in life by trampling on the rights of your fellow man, I'm afraid you've made a bad choice. I suggest instead that you read *"Life and Death of Adolf Hitler,"* *"The Communist Manifesto,"* or the *"Internal Revenue Code."*

There is a rational reason why forcible interference with the rights of others has no place in the philosophy of looking out for Number One. It's simply not in your best interests. In the long run it will bring you more pain than pleasure—the exact opposite of what you wish to accomplish.

---

deliberately misinterpret your interests and get something for myself that you would much rather have for yourself. It has to be admitted that unfortunately these are both common results from a paternalistic—"I know what is good for you"—approach to either management, government, or life.

Why is it believed that this ethical principle of everyone looking after his or her own self-interests does work out to the betterment of society? The assumption is that as we compete for our self-interests, we will all get some of what we want, and that our society will be better under that condition than under the alternative, which is that some of us will get all of what we want and others will get none of what they want due to the dual errors of paternalism. The ethical principle of self-interests, similar to the political economy of Adam Smith, presumes an "invisible hand." Everyone competes, and society wins.

What is the problem with the ethical principle that everyone should rationally look after their own long-term self-interests? It certainly is simple. It certainly is direct. It certainly is easily applied. All I have to do is rationally

EXHIBIT 3–3
Lifeboat Ethics: The Case Against Helping the Poor
Garrett Hardin

If we divide the world crudely into rich nations and poor nations, two thirds are desperately poor, and only one third comparatively rich. Metaphorically each rich nation can be seen as a lifeboat full of comparatively rich people. In the ocean outside each lifeboat swim the poor of the world, who would like to get in, or at least to share some of the wealth. What should the lifeboat passengers do?

First we must recognize the limited capacity of any lifeboat. Here we sit, say 50 people in our lifeboat. To be generous, let us assume it has room for 10 more, making a total capacity of 60. Suppose the 50 of us in the lifeboat see 100 others swimming in the water outside, begging for admission to our boat. We have several options: we may be tempted to try to live by the Christian ideal of being "our brother's keeper," or by the Marxist ideal of "to each according to his needs." Since the needs of all in the water are the same, and since they can all be seen as "our brothers" we could take them into our boat, making a total of 150 in a boat designed for 60. The boat swamps, everyone drowns. Complete justice, complete catastrophe.

Since the boat has an unused excess capacity of 10 more passengers, we could admit just 10 more to it. But which 10 do we let in? How do we choose? Do we pick the best 10, the neediest 10, the first 10? If we do let an extra 10 into our lifeboat, we will have lost our "safety factor," an engineering principle of critical importance. For example, if we don't leave room for excess capacity as a safety factor in our country's agriculture, a new plant disease or a bad change in the weather could have disastrous consequences.

Suppose we decide to preserve our small safety factor and admit no more to the lifeboat. Our survival is then possible, although we shall have to be constantly on guard against boarding parties.

While this last solution clearly offers the only means of our survival, it is morally abhorrent to many people. Some say they feel guilty about their good luck. My reply is simple: "Get out and yield your place to another." This may solve the problem of the guilt-ridden person's conscience, but it does not change the ethics of the lifeboat. The needy person to whom the guilt-ridden man or woman yields his place will not himself feel guilty about his good luck. If he did, he would not climb aboard. The net result of conscience-stricken people giving up their unjustly held seats is the elimination of that sort of conscience from the lifeboat.

think through my own long-term self-interests, or those of the organization for which I am responsible. I don't have to consider any other duties or any other results or any other people. The problem, however, is that it obviously is biased by the position of the person considering his or her self-interests and those of the organization. I am a third-shift press operator at a metal stamping plant belonging to General Motors; you are the president of General Motors. Most people would agree that in the competition of self-interests, yours and those of the company you direct somehow are going to prevail. The "invisible hand" may not work that well when we move away from the ideal of free individuals who are equally able to negotiate the achievement of their own self-interests.

Despite the problems, the rational recognition of long-term self-interests is a legitimate ethical principle. It seems obvious that any moral answer that claims to be "right" and "just" and "fair" has to start with a recognition of the self-interests of the participants as determined by those participants. I know what I want. You know what you want. It is reasonably clear what is in the long-term interests of the organization in which we serve as stakeholders of one type or another. Now, let us see what additional ethical principles we can apply to resolve the differences between those interests.

PERSONAL VIRTUES

The principle of personal virtues can be summarized in the statement that people should act in ways that convey a sense of honor, pride, and self-worth. We don't necessarily have to be kind and compassionate to others. We don't necessarily have to be concerned about the rights or benefits of others who are in some way beneath us on the social or managerial scale. We do, however, have to be concerned with the character of our own actions. We have to be honest, truthful, courageous, temperate, generous, and high minded. Why? Because the goal of human existence is the active, rational pursuit of excellence, and excellence requires those personal virtues.

The active, rational pursuit of excellence—a goal also often termed "knowledge of the good"—is the basis of ancient Greek philosophy. If you commit those two phrases firmly to your memory, all of the rest of the teachings of Socrates, Plato, and Aristotle will be clear to you.

2,400 years ago in Athens those three men began to address questions of duties, rights, and justice and laid the foundation for the Western approach to both politics and ethics. Why in Athens, and why at that time? Greece is a mountainous peninsula, with limited agricultural land suitable for growing grain, but the climate is warm and mild, ideal for olives, grapes, and livestock. There were easy sea routes to Egypt, then the granary of the Eastern Mediterranean. Egypt had surplus wheat and barley for export but needed olive oil and wine. A very prosperous trade developed. The defeat of the invading Persian army at Marathon in 490 brought a period of peace that lasted for 140 years, a period that came to be known as the "Golden Age" of Athens.

Conflicts between the nobles (the ex-warriors) and the merchants (the ex-sailors) brought an interest in government within Athens. An interest in government brought schools to teach first rhetoric (how to talk to the assembled citizens) and then logic (how to convince the assembled citizens). An interest in logic led to questions of "What is the good life?"

Socrates (470–399 B.C.) addressed the question "What is the good life?" for

---

EXHIBIT 3–4
Excerpts from "The Apology"
Plato, one of the *Dialogues of Socrates*

Setting: Socrates has been accused and is being tried for corrupting the youth and disregarding the gods of Athens. He speaks in his own defense. It is not an "apology"; it is an explicit statement of his beliefs.

"I say again that daily to discourse about virtue, and of those other things about which you hear me examining myself and others, is the greatest good of man, and that *the unexamined life is not worth living.*"

---

individuals. He wrote nothing, yet Plato recorded Socrates' discussions with other Athenians in the form of "Dialogues" soon after the death of the older man, and they are assumed to be his thoughts if not his words. The teachings of Socrates can be very briefly summarized in six statements:

1. Socrates initiated the use of reason for practical inquiry, now termed the "Socratic method"; start with a statement or proposition, and then consider the logical consequences.
2. The goal of the Socratic method was to develop "first rule for a successful life." Successful then meant happy; it would probably now be translated as contented and prosperous.
3. There is no "happiness" in the pleasures of life or the ownership of property unless you know how to use them well. Knowledge of the "good" is then the objective of life.
4. Knowledge of the good comes from goodness/badness of the character, and wisdom/foolishness of the intellect. "Soul" (psyche) for the Greeks combined character and intellect.
5. Happiness is then care for the soul, or the development of both character and intellect so that you will recognize and can achieve the "good."
6. Ethics and politics are synonymous; both are concerned with recognition and achievement of the "good," in the first instance for yourself, in the second instance for society.

Plato (427–347 B.C.) is often termed a student of Socrates, yet he was probably more a younger contemporary than a disciple. Plato wrote the *Republic* still in the form of a dialogue by Socrates but now the content is assumed to be the thoughts of the younger man. It is outrageous to attempt to summarize the thoughts of Plato (all of Western philosophy has been termed "a footnote to Plato"), but for the purpose of explaining why the practice of personal virtues will lead to a good society, let me make that attempt:

EXHIBIT 3–5
Excerpts from "The Ring of Gyges"
Plato, one of the *Dialogues of Socrates*

Setting: Glauchon (an Athenian citizen) is challenging Socrates' praise of justice as a noble way of life. Glauchon recounts the following story to prove that justice is only a fear of being caught:

Glauchon: According to tradition, Gyges was a shepherd in the service of the reigning king of Lydia. There was a great storm, and an earthquake made an opening in the earth at the place where he was feeding his flock. Amazed at the sight, he descended into the opening, where he beheld a hollow brazen horse. He looked in and saw a dead body of a size and strength that was more than human. He took from the corpse a gold ring that was on the hand, but nothing else, and so reascended.

Now the shepherds met together, according to custom, that they might send their monthly report about the flocks to the king. Into their assembly Gyges came having the ring on his finger, and as he was sitting among them he chanced to turn the collet of the ring to the inside of his hand, when instantly he became invisible to the rest of the company and they began to speak of him as if he were no longer present. He was astonished at this, and again touching the ring he turned the collet outwards and reappeared. When he perceived this, he made several trials of the ring, and always with the same result—when he turned the collet inward he became invisible, when outwards he was visible. Whereupon he contrived to be chosen one of the messengers who were sent to the court; as soon as he arrived he seduced the queen, and with her help conspired against the king and slew him and took the kingdom.

Suppose now that there were two such magic rings, and that a just man put on one of them, and an unjust man the other. No man can be imagined to be of such an iron nature that he would stand fast in justice. No man would keep his hands off what was not his own when he could safely take what he liked out of the market, or go into houses and lie with anyone at his pleasure, or kill or release from prison who he would, and in all respects be like a god among men.

Then the actions of the just would be as the actions of the unjust; they would both tend to the same goal. And this we may truly affirm to be a great proof that a man is just, not willingly or because he thinks that justice is intrinsically good, but of necessity and fear of being caught. Any one who thinks that he can safely be unjust, will be unjust.

Socrates: Heavens, my dear Glauchon. How energetically you polish these images up for the discussion, first the one and then the other, as if they were two statues.

1. Central focus of the *Republic* is on the question, "What is justice?" The answer depends upon the nature of society, and the "lives" that are possible, each with different character:

Statesman	man of thought	wisdom
Warrior	man of action	courage
Merchant	man of property	temperance

2. "Justice" is the harmonious union of all three classes of citizens, with each class excelling at what it does best, and none interfering with the activities of the others.

   Justice is the equal treatment of equals, and the unequal treatment of unequals to the extent of their inequality. Justice leads to the ideal society.

3. It has to be remembered that "justice" and "republic" and "ideal society" are relative terms. Athens at the time was based upon slavery.

   Census around 307 B.C. lists 21,000 free citizens (males only), 10,000 metics (resident aliens), and 400,000 slaves. No one bothered to count the free women and children.

Aristotle (384–322 B.C.), the third moral philosopher in this remarkable sequence, was concerned more with individuals than with society, more with the "good" man or woman than with the "good" society. *Nicomachean Ethics* (named for Aristotle's son who collected the material as a sort of term paper or course pack) is on the actions of a "good" man. It is not easy to read. The argument can be summarized as a series of statements that describe the ultimate goal in life:

1. All activities aim at some goal, or "good," though there obviously has to be some ranking or hierarchy among those goals or goods.

2. Since governance of the state (politics) is the supreme art of man, the ultimate goal has to have some association with politics.

3. Since the aim of politics is happiness for the citizens, then happiness must be the ultimate goal. But what is happiness? Not pleasure, wealth, or fame.

4. Since man is a reasoning animal, happiness must be associated with reason: happiness, then, is living according to the active (not passive, or contemplative) use of reason.

5. Since the active use of reason leads to excellence, then happiness can be defined as the active, rational pursuit of personal excellence, or virtue.

6. Virtues are measures of personal excellence on a number of dimensions; reason always selects the mean between extremes, as courage is the mean between cowardice and foolhardiness. Then comes the famous list of 14 virtues:

   Courage, particularly in battle.

   Temperance, or moderation in eating and drinking.

EXHIBIT 3–6
Excerpts from "The Crito"
Plato, one of the *Dialogues of Socrates*

Setting: Crito, a friend of Socrates, has come to see him in prison, two days before the death sentence is to be carried out, and explains that he has bribed the guards so that Socrates is free to escape. Socrates refuses to do so, and explains that having benefited from the laws of the state he must now continue to obey the laws of the state.

Socrates: Ought a man do what he thinks to be right, or ought he betray the right?

Crito: He ought to do what he thinks to be right.

Socrates: Then, consider the matter in this way. Imagine that I am about to play truant (you may call the proceeding by any name which you like), and the laws and the government come and interrogate me: "Tell us, Socrates" they say; "what are you about? Are you not going by an act of yours to overturn us—the laws and the whole state? Do you imagine that a state can subsist and not be overthrown in which the decisions of law have no power, but are set aside and trampled upon by individuals?" What will be our answer, Crito, to these words? Any one, and especially a rhetorician, will have a good deal to say on behalf of the law which requires that a sentence be carried out. He will argue that this law should not be set aside, and shall I reply "Yes, but the state has injured me, and given me an unjust sentence." Suppose I say that?

Crito: Very good, Socrates.

Socrates: "And was that our agreement with you?" the law would answer, "or were you to abide by the sentence of the state?" And if I were to express my astonishment at their words, the law would probably add: "Answer, Socrates, instead of rolling your eyes—you are in the habit of asking and answering questions. Tell us: What complaint have you to make against us which justifies you in attempting to destroy us? Having nurtured and educated you, and given you a share in every good which we had to offer, we further proclaim to every Athenian that if he does not like us when he has become of age and has seen our ways, he may go where he pleases and take his goods with him. None of our laws will forbid him or interfere with him. Any one who does not like us and the city, and wants to emigrate to a colony or to any other city, may go where he likes, retaining his property. But he who has experience of the manner in which we order justice and administer the State, and still remains, has entered into an implied contract that he will do as we command him. Our commands are not rudely imposed. We give each person the alternative of obeying the laws or convincing us. That is what we offer, but you do neither." How shall I answer, Crito?

Liberality, or spending money "well."

Magnificence, or living "well."

Pride, or taking pleasure in accomplishments and stature.

High-handedness, or concern with the noble, not with the petty.

Unnamed virtue, midway between ambition and a total lack of effort.

Gentleness, or concern for others.

Truthfulness, or not being boastful about accomplishments and stature.

Wit, or pleasure in group discussions.

Friendliness, or pleasure in group associations.

Modesty, or pleasure in personal conduct.

Righteous indignation, or getting angry at the right things and in the right amounts.

Justice, which never is defined but probably is the result of the prior activities.

Socrates, Plato, and Aristotle together can be seen as an effort to make what was then considered to be a diverse society—composed of warriors, merchants, and statesmen, each with different goals, activities, and interests—work well. Cooperation between those groups of citizens was necessary to maintain independence from Persia and prosperity through trade. Socrates said that each citizen had a duty to the state, to obey the law. Plato said that the state had a duty to each citizen, to achieve justice. Aristotle, in an impressive sequence of logic, said that each citizen had a duty to himself (or herself) to achieve excellence.

What does this 2,400-year-old admonition to achieve personal excellence mean in current terms? Firstly, it is not a bad goal in life. Why not strive to be excellent? Secondly, you obviously are free to disagree on the dimensions Aristotle used to measure excellence, but a current summary might be expressed as, "Be honest, open, truthful, and proud of what you do."

The ethical principle that we should "be honest, open, truthful, and proud of what we do" can be translated into very modern terms. "Would you be willing to have your decisions and actions relative to a moral problem in which some people are going to be hurt or harmed in some way reported on the front page of a national newspaper, or during the evening portion of a national news broadcast?"

What is the problem with the ethical principle of personal virtues? Being "honest, open, truthful, and proud" really is not enough. Some people can be "honest, open, truthful, and proud" of decisions and actions that may seem to most of the rest of us to have been exploitive, mean, and self-centered. But, these very specific personal virtues do provide a different perspective from which to view complex moral problems, and they do seem to help in deciding when the question is, "What is the right thing to do?"

RELIGIOUS INJUNCTIONS

The ethical principle of religious injunctions can be summarized in the statement that people should act in ways that build a sense of community, a sense of people working together towards a common goal, a sense of "us" rather than "you versus me," or "your group versus my group."

All religious organizations have statements of ecclesiastical moral standards, of the ways in which members of that religion are to treat other members of the same religion. These codes of moral conduct have extra force and meaning for the membership because the rules are usually said to have come from their Supreme Being. It is difficult to use these codes in moral reasoning, however, because everyone is not a member of the same religious group and consequently does not accept the same set of moral rules, and because even within the same religious group different authorities can interpret the same set of moral rules in very different ways.

EXHIBIT 3–7
Examples of Compassion in the World's Religions

Buddhism (religious creed and ethical system of central and eastern Asia, founded about 560 B.C.). "Harm not others with that which pains yourself."

Christianity. "All things whatsoever you would that others should do unto you, do ye even so unto them, for this is the law and the prophets."

Confucianism (ethical system added to the existing Chinese religious creed about 510 B.C.). "Loving kindness is the one maxim which ought to be acted upon throughout one's life."

Hinduism (traditional religious creed and social system of the Indian subcontinent). "This is the sum of duty; do naught to others which if done to thee would cause thee pain."

Islam (religious creed of the Near East and Far Southeast, founded about 630 A.D.). "No one of you is a believer until you wish for everyone what you love for yourself."

Jainism (religious creed of the Indian subcontinent, founded about 500 B.C.). "In happiness and suffering, in joy and grief, we should regard all creates as we regard our own self."

Judaism. "What is hurtful to yourself, do not do to others. That is the whole of the Torah, and the remainder is but commentary. Go and learn it."

Sikhism (religious creed of northern India, founded about 1500 A.D.). "As thou deemest thyself, so deem others. Then shalt thou become a partner in heaven."

Taoism (religious creed and philosophic system of northern China, founded about 550 B.C.). "Regard your neighbor's gain as your gain, and regard your neighbor's loss as your loss."

EXHIBIT 3–8
Excerpts from *The City of God*
St. Augustine

God, desiring not only that the human race might be able by their similarity of nature to associate with one another, but also that they might be bound together in harmony and peace by the ties of that relationship, was pleased to derive all men from one individual, and created man with such a nature that the members of the race should not have died, had not the two first (of whom the one was created out of nothing, and the other out of him) merited this by their disobedience; for by them so great a sin was committed, that by it the human nature was altered for the worse, and was transmitted also to their posterity, liable to sin and subject to death. And the kingdom of death so reigned over men that the deserved penalty of sin would have hurled all headlong even into the second death, of which there is no end, had not the undeserved grace of God saved some therefrom. And thus it has come to pass, that though there are very many and great nations all over the earth, whose rites and customs, speech, arms, and dress, are distinguished by marked differences, yet there are not more than two kinds of human society, which we may justly call two cities, according to the language of our Scriptures. The one consists of those who wish to live after the flesh, the other of those who wish to live after the spirit.

Accordingly, two cities have been formed by two loves: the earthy by the love of self, even to the contempt of God; the heavenly the love of God, even to the contempt of self. The former, in a word glories in itself; the latter in the Lord. For the one seeks glory from men, but the greatest glory of the other is God, the witness of conscience. The one lifts up its head in its own glory; the other says to its God, "Thou are my glory, and the lifter up of mine head." In the one the princes and the nations it subdues are ruled by the love of ruling; in the other, the princes and the subjects serve one another in love, the latter obeying while the former take thought for all.

If you can't use the moral code of a specific religious group in moral reasoning, you can use the underlying concepts that seem to be part of all religious groups. These universal concepts include compassion, kindness, and a sense of community. It has been claimed, for example, that over 90 percent of the world's religions include a statement of compassion, kindness, and reciprocity closely similar to that in the Golden Rule.

Compassion, kindness, and reciprocity (treating others as you yourself would wish to be treated) form the basis for the sense of community. Three major Christian writers have addressed the critical importance of this sense of community, this sense of togetherness, in forming a "good" society in which people cooperate for the benefit of all. These three writers—St. Augustine, St. Thomas Aquinas, and Pope John XXIII—are included not because they are part of the Christian tradition but because what they are saying is universal and representative of all religions.

St. Augustine (354–415) was a bishop of the church in North Africa. Christianity was widespread throughout the Mediterranean at this time, but the power of the Roman Empire was rapidly declining. Rome had been sacked. North Africa was next. It was a period of chaos and conflict. St. Augustine in *The City of God* wrote of the need for faith rather than reason in establishing the means of living together in peace and justice: There are six major points:

1. God intended men and women to live together in harmony and peace. This follows much of early theology, trying to understand conflict given an omnipotent and omniscient God.

2. Original Sin destroyed that intention; men and women can choose—they have free will, or moral autonomy—and their choice can be wrong, leading to war and conflict.

3. There are two ways to search for harmony and peace, given free will. St. Augustine calls these cities, but they are really societies, or "cities" in the sense of Rome:

   City of Man. Nowhere does St. Augustine use this term, but this is what he meant. The City of Man is not a decadent society; it is one based upon reason. It is Athens.

   City of God. This is an ideal existence, but it is an ideal which can be realized. It is a society based upon faith, not upon reason.

4. The major argument is that you can't base your life upon reason and pursuit of happiness, for happiness is so problematical, so subject to illness, injury, death, and pain.

5. You must, then, base your life upon faith and pursuit of salvation, for salvation is certain. If you have faith, then you will have "rightly ordered love" for others.

6. If you have "rightly ordered love" then the important virtues of temperance, prudence, justice, and fortitude become inherent in your character, and the City of God can be realized.

St. Thomas Aquinas (1225–1274) may be said to join the two traditions of reason and faith. His argument in *Summa Theologica* is that you can reason through from the Will of God—the Eternal Law—to the natural inclinations of all creatures—the Natural Law—and then to the proper dispositions of a society—the Human Law. There are three major points in the argument:

1. Law is a rule by which one is led to action or restrained from action, and consequently must be based upon reason, and be concerned with the happiness of the community.

2. These universal characteristics "based upon reason" and "concerned with happiness of the community" must apply to all of the levels of law.

   Eternal Law. Law by itself is nothing else than a dictate of practical reason by a ruler who governs some community. Assuming that there is a

---

EXHIBIT 3–9
Excerpts from *Summa Theologica*
St. Thomas Aquinas

1. Is Law a Matter of Reason?

Law is a rule or measure of action by which one is led to action or restrained from acting. The word *law (lex)* is derived from *ligare*, to bind, because it binds one to act. The rule and measure of action is the reason, which is the first principle of human action. Reason has the power to move the will because whenever someone desires an end, reason commands what is to be done to reach it. In order for an act of will that something is to be done to have the character of law, it must be guided by reason.

2. Is Law Always Directed toward the Common Good?

Every part is ordered to the whole as the imperfect is to the perfect. The individual is part of a perfect whole that is the community. Therefore, law must concern itself in particular with the happiness of the community.

Divine Providence, then there has to be an Eternal Law for the governance of the physical world.

Natural Law. All creatures participate in the Eternal Law in that they have a natural inclination to their proper actions and ends within the physical world. This natural inclination is the Natural Law.

Human Law. Human reason must proceed from the precepts of the Natural Law to the rules and regulations needed for an orderly and peaceful human community. Those particular dispositions arrived at by reason are the Human Law.

3. A law that is unjust—that is, one that is not arrived at by reason from the precepts of the Natural Law—is no law at all. Remember, this was written in the 13th century when few people were concerned with what was "just" or "unjust."

Pope John XXIII (1881–1963) published the encyclical *Pacem im Terris* (Peace on Earth) in 1963. Again, there is an emphasis upon the value of the community. There are four major points:

1. Any human society, if it is to be well ordered and productive, must be based upon the recognition that every human being is a person with intelligence and free will, and consequently with rights and duties.

2. There is a reciprocity of rights and duties within each person. If a person has a right to life, then he or she has a duty to live it becomingly. If a person has a right to truth, then he or she has a duty to pursue it profoundly.

3. There is a reciprocity of rights and duties between persons. If one person has

a right to life, others have a duty to preserve it. If one person has a right to truth, others have a duty to ensure it.

4. Men and women are social by nature, and are meant to live with others and to work for the welfare of all. A recognition of the reciprocal duties leads to an understanding of spiritual values, and the meaning of truth, justice, charity, and freedom.

The ethical principle of religious injunctions is *not* based upon the moral codes—the "do's" and "don'ts"—of any specific religion. Instead, the ethical principle that we should take no action that might detract from a sense of community and cooperative effort is based upon the concepts of kindness, compassion, and reciprocity, which are part of nearly every religion. St. Augustine says that you cannot understand why "rightly ordered love" leads to personal well-being and community cooperation; it just does and you have to have faith in that outcome. St. Thomas Aquinas says that you can understand that connection for human law (the governance of the community) should be based upon natural law (the natural inclination of all creatures), which in turn has to be a reflection of Divine Law. Pope John XXIII says that well-being and cooperation come as a result of the recognition of the reciprocity of rights and duties within each person and between all people.

You obviously can accept whatever explanation of this relationship between compassion, community, and effort you prefer. The phenomena that a cooperative community is more productive, and does lead to the well-being of its members, is well established. The problem, of course, is that it is difficult to maintain such a community. The presence of short-term self-interests on the part of any of the members, and the consequent absence of kindness, compassion, and reciprocity between all of the members, can easily destroy the sense of community and the spirit of cooperation.

This chapter has looked at three ethical principles: self-interests, personal virtues, and religious injunctions. The three principles are partially supportive, and partially contradictory. Each provides a different perspective to judge the "rightness" of a managerial decision or action that will benefit some members of an organization or society, and harm some others. Each helps in deciding "What is the right thing to do?"

ASSIGNMENT QUESTIONS

1. Read "Lifeboat Ethics" once again, on page 70. This is the ethical principle of self-interests in its most uncompromising form. How would you answer it? Do you believe that people have an obligation to help others, or not?

2. It has been said that the brief quotation from *The Apology* of Socrates—"the unexamined life is not worth living"—is the most famous statement in moral philosophy. Why? What does it mean to you?

3. Read the Excerpts from *The Ring of Gyges* once again. The conclusion of Glauchon, the person who tells the story, is that people are good only from fear of being caught. Is that true? If it is not true, why are people "good?"

4. Read Excerpts from *The Crito* once again. Aristotle states that because he benefited from the laws of Athens in the past, he must obey those laws even now when it is not in his self-interest to do so. How would you respond if you were Crito?

5. It is claimed that 90 percent of the world's religions include a statement roughly similar to the Golden Rule: "Do unto others as you would have them do unto you." Why do you assume that this is such a universal concept?

6. The readings from St. Augustine and St. Thomas Aquinas can be viewed as their reasons why the Golden Rule is such a universal concept. What are those reasons? Does this question help you to understand why those readings were included?

Case 3–1

WHEN IS IT PERMISSIBLE TO TELL A LIE?

Lying can be defined as making a statement that the speaker knows to be false, with the intention of misleading other people. Knowledge and intention are both central to the concept of a lie. The speaker must know the relative truth/falsity of the assertion, and must intend to deceive, for most of us to brand the statement as a lie. Yet some deliberately deceptive statements are still considered to be "O.K." by people active in business. Which of the following deliberately deceptive statements do you consider to be permissible, given the circumstances?

1. You are an export manager for a U.S. steel company that provides heavy beams and prefabricated plates for large construction projects. You have a $20 million order for a project in a South American country. You need just one last approval from a government official. During a verbal discussion in that person's office, he requests a $20,000 bribe. You are surprised because the official policy in his country has changed recently, under a reformist regime, and bribes are now strongly forbidden. You say that it is against U.S. law and company rules for you to make that payment. He shrugs slightly and says, "Fine, we will give the order to the Japanese." It happens that you have a battery-powered tape recorder in your briefcase. You use it to dictate memos after meetings such as this one. It has not been turned on, but of course the government official does not know

that. Is it permissible for you to open your briefcase, take out the tape recorder, show it to the official, and say, "It is a policy of our company to record all conversations with government officials in Central and South America. Do you wish this tape to be given to the minister in charge of your agency, or do you wish to sign the necessary papers for our import permit?" (*Note*: I am indebted to Professor Joanne Ciulla of the University of Richmond for this true example.)

2. You are a senior manager at a large chemical company. You have just learned that some highly toxic by-products at one of your plants have been improperly dumped in steel drums. Fortunately, the director of safety at your company heard about this situation and was able to retrieve the barrels before "too much" leakage had occurred. She and others have assured you that there is no danger to public health, but local newspapers have heard of the situation and want to interview you. The corporate attorney has warned you that despite the prompt action the company doubtless will be sued and that you should not, under any circumstance, admit liability. Is it proper for you to say that there was no leakage, and consequently no danger?

3. You are a member of the human resources staff at a large consumer products firm. You have completed the annual series of interviews at colleges and universities, have arranged "flybacks" for a selected number of the people who were in-

terviewed, have summarized the comments of the managers who met the candidates during their plant visits, and have prioritized them according to those comments. You know that job offers have been made to the top five persons on that list. You also know that it is traditional, when a job offer is made by your company, for the candidate to be given two weeks in which to decide, and to be asked to treat the offer as confidential until he or she decides formally whether to accept or reject the offer. Lastly, you know that people who don't quite make the first cutoff tend to become defensive, if they hear of it, and quickly accept another offer. Now, the person who stands number seven on the list calls you and asks whether the decision has been made. Is it permissible for you to say that the final decision is still pending, but that you are certain that the person will hear something, either positively or negatively, within two weeks?

4. You are an assistant in the strategic planning department at a large manufacturing firm. One of the responsibilities of your department is to gather information about the production processes, cost structures, marketing policies, and research budgets of your competitors. Much of this information can be taken from published sources such as annual reports, local newspapers, trade journals, and business magazines. The really "good stuff," however, is said to be obtained most easily by talking to mid-level employees of the tar-

geted company. One way is simply to call them. A strategic planner who has done this frequently says, "People are generally proud of what they have accomplished, and they like to be asked. I call someone in marketing, for example, say that we are doing some bench marking (comparing our operations to those of well-regarded competitors) and ask a few questions. Inevitably they tell me much, much more than they should." Another way is to invite them to a job interview, and the same strategic planner says, "You don't have to lie to them. You don't have to mislead them. You don't even have to actually invite them to an interview. All you have to do is to call and say that your company has a job opening—it inevitably does—and ask if they are interested. Everybody wants to advance their own careers, so they are inter-ested. Then, you ask about their most recent accomplishments, and you generally get the information you want over the telephone. Before you hang up, you say that you are very glad that you called, that they do sound like the sort of person that your company needs in production or marketing or what-ever, and that you'll get back to them as soon as the position is con-firmed in the next budget." Is it permissible to make those calls?

Class Assignment

Decide which of these actions are "right" and which are "wrong." Use your own judgment, but be pre-pared to support that judgment. Don't just give your answer in class, and stop; instead be ready to say why you think they are "right" or why you think they are "wrong."

Case 3–2

PERSONAL VIRTUES FOR MODERN PROFESSIONALS

Following is the list of personal vir-tues (habits or customary modes of behavior) that Aristotle felt were re-quired for members of the ruling groups (soldiers, merchants, and statesmen) in Athens 2,400 years ago. Cross out those that you think are not applicable, and substitute others that you think are more applicable, for people in equivalent professional po-sitions today. That is, what 14 per-sonal characteristics do you think should describe a "good" man or woman currently employed as a man-ager, lawyer, engineer, or government official, in the industrialized societies of the world?

Courage, particularly in battle.

Temperance, or moderation in eating and drinking.

Liberality, or moderation in spending money.

Magnificence, or moderation in life-style.

Pride, or sense of accomplishment and stature.

High mindedness, or concern for the noble, not the petty.

Unnamed virtue, halfway between ambition and lethargy.

Gentleness, or never acting in a mean way.

Truthfulness, or not lying about accomplishments.

Wit, or pleasure in group discussions.

Friendliness, or pleasure in group associations.

Modesty, or pleasure in personal conduct.

Righteous indignation, or getting angry at the right things and in the right amounts.

Justice, which is never defined but probably is the result of all of the prior habits and customs.

Case 3–3

SARAH GOODWIN

Sarah Goodwin was a graduate of an MBA program on the West Coast. She had majored in marketing, was interested in retailing, and had been delighted to receive a job offer from a large and prestigious department store chain in northern California. The first year of employment at this chain was considered to be a training program, but formal instruction was very limited. Instead, after a quick tour of the facilities and a welcoming speech by the president, each of the new trainees was assigned to work as an assistant to a buyer in one of the departments. The intent was that the trainees would work with five or six buyers during the year, rotating assignments every two months, and would make themselves "useful" enough during those assignments so at least one buyer would ask to have that person join his or her department on a permanent basis.

Buyers are critical in the management of a department store. They select the goods to be offered, negotiate purchase terms, set retail prices, arrange displays, organize promotions, and are generally responsible for the operations of the departments within the store. Each buyer acts as a profit center, and sales figures and profit margins are reported monthly to the senior executives. In this particular chain, the sales and profits were calculated on a square foot basis (that is, per square foot of floor space occupied by the department), and the buyers contended, generally on a friendly basis, to outperform each other so that their square footage would be expanded. The buyers received substantial commissions based upon monthly profits.

Sarah's first assignment was to work for the buyer of the gourmet food department. This was a small unit at the main store that sold packaged food items such as jams and jellies, crackers and cookies, cheese and spreads, candies, etc., most of which were imported from Europe. The department also offered preserved foods, such as smoked fish and meats, and some expensive delicacies, such as caviar, truffles, and estate-bottled wines. Many of the items were packaged as gifts, in boxes or baskets with decorative wrapping and ties.

Sarah was originally disappointed to have been sent to such a small and specialized department, rather than to a larger one that dealt with more general fashion goods, but she soon found that this assignment was considered to be a "plum." The buyer, Maria Castellani, was a well-known personality throughout the store; witty, competent, and sarcastic, she served as a sounding board, consultant, and friend to the other buyers. She would evaluate fashions, forecast trends, chastise managers ("managers" in a department store are the people associated with finance, personnel, accounting, or planning, not merchandising), and discuss retailing events and changes in an amusing, informative way. Everybody in the store seemed to find a reason to stop by the gourmet food department at least once during each day to chat with Maria. Sarah was naturally included in these conversations, and consequently she found that she was getting to know all of the other buyers and could ask one of them to request her as an assistant at the next rotation of the assignment.

For the first five weeks of her employment, Sarah was exceptionally happy, pleased with her career and her life. She was living in a house, on one of the cable car lines, with three other professionally-employed women. She felt that she was performing well on her first job, and making sensible arrangements for her next assignment. Then, an event occurred that threatened to destroy all of her contentment:

> We had received a shipment of thin little wafers from England that had a creme filling flavored with fruit: strawberries and raspberries. They were very good. They were packaged in foil-covered boxes, but somehow they had become infested with insects.
>
> We did not think that all of the boxes were infested, because not all of the customers brought them back. But, some people did, and obviously we could not continue to sell them. We couldn't inspect the packages, and keep the ones that were not infested, because there were too many—about $9,000 worth—and because we would have had to tear the foil to open each box. Maria said that the manufacturer would not give us a refund because the infestation doubtless occurred during shipment, or even during storage at our own warehouse.
>
> Maria told me to get rid of them. I thought that she meant for me to arrange to have them taken to the dump, but she said, "Absolutely not. Call [name of an executive] at [name of a convenience store chain in southern California]. They operate down in the ghetto, and can sell anything. We've got to get our money back."

Class Assignment

What would you do in this situation? Make a set of specific recommendations for Sarah Goodwin.

Case 3–4

10 TOUGHEST BOSSES IN AMERICA

To come up with our list of the 10 toughest bosses in America, *Fortune* first asked for nominations from scores of management consultants, executive recruiters, investor relations specialists, public relations executives, organizational psychologists, lawyers, investors, business school professors, corporate chairmen, students of leadership, and psychiatrists who specialize in treating executive stress. We told them that we weren't necessarily looking for ogres— bosses who are demanding but fair would also qualify. Our only restriction was that the nominees had to be senior officers of major companies which meant leaving out hard-nosed types who were between jobs—Jack Tramiel, for example, who had left Commodore International but not yet bought Atari when we conducted our search. Only when a person garnered nominations from several quarters did he or she become a candidate.

We then interviewed people who report directly to the candidates or who had in the past, as well as those with firsthand knowledge of how candidates treat their subordinates. We sought out fans as well as detractors. In requesting interviews we asked for a candid appraisal; no one was asked to badmouth his boss. When employees requested anonymity in return for candor, we granted their requests. Only when a consensus emerged did a candidate become a finalist. All finalists were asked for interviews.

SOURCE: Reprinted from *Fortune*, August 6, 1984.

Using this method we selected the 10 toughest bosses in American business: in alphabetical order, Fred Ackman, chairman Superior Oil Co.; Martin Davis, chief executive, Gulf & Western Industries, Inc.; Andrew Grove, president, Intel Corp.; John Johnson, president, Johnson Publishing Co.; William Klopman, chairman, Burlington Industries, Inc.; Robert Malott, chairman FMC Corp.; Richard Rosenthal, chairman Citizens Utilities Co.; Joel Smilow, a senior executive with Beatrice Cos.; Richard Snyder, president Simon & Schuster Inc.; and John Welch Jr., chairman, General Electric Co.

While we threw our net widely, we may have overlooked some tough guys worthy of consideration. But we'll bet our bosses rival any of them. On occasion, each of the 10 carries toughness beyond the point where it's necessary or effective. The dramatic and sometimes bizarre ways in which they do this is what, finally, earns them a place among the 10 toughest.

In an era of Theory Z and one-minute praising, this kind of behavior is out of fashion. What does it accomplish? Making a case for it on economic grounds is hard—financial results from these bosses' companies vary from superb to pathetic. The median return on shareholders' equity over the past five years for the seven of the 10 companies for which data are available ranged from 7.3 percent (Burlington Industries) to 18.1 percent (General Electric). That compares with the median for the *Fortune* 500 of 13.8 percent.

On our list, John Welch Jr., 48, now

in his fourth year as chairman of General Electric Co., is the undisputed premier. Welch was the most-nominated tough boss in America, getting more than twice as many nods as the two who tied for second, Joel Smilow and Richard Rosenthal. According to Fred Adler, one of the top U.S. venture capitalists (and no pussycat himself), Welch is "the epitome of the effective, tough manager in America today."

Extraordinarily bright, penetrating in his questions, and determined to get results, Welch has carved out quite a reputation for abrasiveness since going to work for GE in 1960. According to former employees, Welch conducts meetings so aggressively that people tremble. He attacks almost physically with his intellect—criticizing, demeaning, ridiculing, humiliating. "Jack comes on you like a herd of elephants," says a GE employee. "If you have a contradictory idea, you have to be willing to take the guff to put it forward." Other subordinates think that he has mellowed a bit since becoming a top dog.

Managers at GE used to hide out-of-favor employees from Welch's gunsights so they could keep their jobs. At one division that Welch ran on his way up the ladder, these people were called "mummies." Since taking over, Welch has announced the closing of 25 plants. This has earned him the nickname "Neutron Jack." Employees joke that like the aftermath of a neutron bomb, after Welch visits a facility the building is left standing but a lot of the people are dead.

Welch denies that he behaves quite as badly as subordinates have charged. "Fair, fair, fair. That's what we're trying to do with this company," he says. "Our company expunges that sort of macho behavior." Others defend both Welch's methods and drive as necessary to rehabilitate GE. Reuben Gutoff, one of Welch's former bosses, now a man-agement consultant, says, "His attitude is, 'Look, you've got to know what you're talking about when you're talking to the boss.' There's nothing wrong with that." Gutoff maintains that large organizations tend to slow down, like an obese person. He credits Welch with bringing to GE the passion and dedication that characterize the best Silicon Valley start-ups.

Everyone agrees that Welch is a doer, and former staffers say that at GE there have traditionally been more reviewers than doers. "I'd present plans to 35 people," says a veteran of the system. "It was insane." And, at times, incredibly provoking. For example, while head of GE's consumer product sector, Welch instructed his general managers to cut inventories immediately. One month later he called a meeting to see what progress they had made. None had implemented his order. Sputtering with exasperation, Welch recessed the meeting, telling the participants that he wanted action before resuming deliberations that afternoon. He got it.

Welch says that as chairman he is trying to promote risk-taking by making heroes out of risk-takers in the company, even if they have failed. He cautions, though, that "the role for the mediocre is clearly short-lived." The mummies had better start donning protective entrepreneurial camouflage, or maybe just bury themselves deeper.

A boss who projects the same intense demand for performance on a smaller scale, is Richard Snyder, president of Simon & Schuster in New York. It is a subsidiary of Gulf & Western, where one of our other tough bosses rules. Snyder's efforts have helped make Simon & Schuster the most successful U.S. trade-book publisher. It is also a pressure cooker. "He's a genius at making the whole company sense that he's aware of every detail," says a former employee. "This conveys both incredible excitement and anxiety." During the Iranian hostage crisis the joke going around Simon & Schuster was: What's the difference between Ayatollah Khomeini and Dick Snyder?" Answer: the Ayatollah has only 52 hostages, Snyder has 700—the number of Simon & Schuster employees.

Employees are paid some of the highest salaries in publishing, but then they're expected to get a hit every time at bat. When Simon & Schuster had eight books on the list of the 30 best sellers a few years ago, Snyder grumped that they should have had more. This summer Simon & Schuster put 11 books on the list.

The results of Snyder's brooding omnipresence, and the ethic it has created, can occasionally be dramatic. For example, when early reviewers alerted company management to the potential of the book *Mayor* by [former] New York City Mayor Ed Koch, the head of production set up a cot next to the printing presses to ensure that the product hit the bookstalls in 72 hours rather than two weeks.

When performances aren't stellar, life can become exceedingly nasty. Snyder is renowned for a quick, flaring temper that has driven talented employees from the company, their self-respect in shreds. When asked about it, Snyder said, "Yes, I do yell at people, sometimes when I'm wrong to do so. I'm very direct and people don't like that." Those who know him point out that Snyder is also quick with an apology or a compliment. And he adds, "If you don't have somebody bitching about you, you're probably not really functioning as an authority figure. It's easy to be nice and never confront people; it's infinitely harder to win respect."

Andrew Grove, president of Intel Corp., approaches confrontation as a connoisseur. Grove has written a *Fortune* article on the subject (July 23, 1984)

and a no-nonsense book called *High Output Management*. Intel legend has it that he walked into a meeting carrying a walking stick, its handle carved as a hand whose third finger stuck out prominently. Grove began the meeting by slamming the stick down on the table and telling people what he'd do if they ever came late.

Histrionics aside, employees say that meetings with Grove can be withering. He puts all the intensity of his personality behind his analysis and refuses to accept anything less than well-thought-out, unembellished answers. But, former employees say, his greatest strength is his follow-through. "He is intensely persistent," says an Intel alumnus, "he tracks information and projects and doesn't let things fall through the cracks. He is merciless about making and keeping commitments."

Grove concedes that he's tough. "I consider it part of my job to be demanding," he says, with a nod to his competition in the semiconductor business. "We've had an onslaught from the Japanese. If we were any less demanding of ourselves, we would fall behind. Complacency is probably the biggest enemy anyone can have in this industry."

Only a bit less difficult to present proposals to is Robert Malott, chairman of FMC Corp., the big Chicago manufacturer of machinery and chemicals. Malott was only a member of the chorus in our 1980 article about tough bosses— he was quoted saying "Leadership is demonstrated when the ability to inflict pain is confirmed." This time around Malott made the first team, principally because of the grueling and sometimes abusive way he conducts management reviews. Employees say that he can grill subordinates mercilessly when there's no good reason. During meetings Malott has been known to grumpily show boredom, read his mail, or get up and leave the room.

"He often gets in an absolutely pissed-off-with-the-world" mood, says a subordinate. "Then there's no way of dealing with him rationally." Another FMC staffer adds, "One has to play a semi-Machiavellian game just to function with him. We spend an unconscionable amount of time trying to find out when he'll be least obnoxious."

Although Malott sees nothing wrong in being considered demanding, he harrumphs about being inconsiderate, moody, or bullying. When asked about reading his mail at meetings, he replied, "That's absolute nonsense. It's rude to read your mail when people are talking to you." Several of FMC's senior officers defended Malott as no more than normally hard-nosed. But one executive, in defending his boss, had to admit that Malott has read mail at meetings. "But he's listening all the time," he added.

The fallout from Superior Oil Chairman Fred Ackman's brand of toughness can be seen vividly in the figures on managerial turnover. "Ackman's staff has voted with their feet," says an oil analyst. In the year after Ackman joined Superior from Exxon, 9 of Superior's top 13 executives departed. Sour grapes about not getting the top job, say Ackman's supporters. But most of the executives didn't leave immediately; they waited to get acquainted with the boss.

Familiarity bred contempt. Employees say Ackman proved thoroughly autocratic, refusing even to discuss staff suggestions. He tended to treat disagreement as disloyalty. Many were put off by Ackman's abusive temper, which together with his stature (5 feet 8-1/2 inches) and red hair earned him the nickname "Little Red Fox." Says a former subordinate, "He couldn't stand it when somebody disagreed with him, even in private. He'd eat you up alive, calling you a dumb S.O.B. or asking if

you had your head up your ass. It happened all the time."

Others found it degrading to work for Ackman. He assigned one experienced executive the job of making sure Superior's executive urinals smelled better, more like those he was used to at Exxon.

More demoralizing, though, was Ackman's effect on decision-making. When he arrived, Superior's staff was proud that the company was finally on the move. Superior had improved its success rate on wildcat wells from about the industry average to three times that. "Ackman didn't recognize how that had been achieved—by delegating, by giving responsibility and freedom," says a former executive. "His concept of management was to get presentations, with no discussion, and then he would make a decision, even in areas where he wasn't qualified. It was a one-way street."

Ackman may not be in the driver's seat on that street for long. Company executives predict that when Mobil consummates its acquisition of Superior in the fall, Ackman will depart, reportedly with over $4 million in stock and what a company spokesman calls contractual obligations.

Former employees at Burlington Industries, the largest U.S. textile manufacturer, also criticize their chairman, William Klopman, for being autocratic and aloof. "He had the worst interpersonal skills of anyone I've ever known," says a subordinate who left the company. Ex-employees say that Klopman's mercurial temperament made him brutally arbitrary. "One could be a member of his ruling clique and do no wrong," says a former high-ranking executive. "Then one day, for no apparent reason, he treated you as the dumbest guy in the world." Says another employee who moved on, "He has seldom admitted a mistake, and he has never hesitated to make subordinates pay for them. Many of his executives, once proteges, were put in the pincers and discarded."

Such inconsistency has created an atmosphere thick with fear. As a result, the flow of useful information up through the company has decreased. "He has lost perspective because he has been cut off from good information from inside the company," says one of Klopman's former commanders.

The company may have suffered for it. Burlington's average return on sales and return on shareholders' equity have consistently been poorer than those of several competitors. Much of the over 1.2 billion the company has spent for capital improvements since 1977 hasn't paid off. When *Fortune* asked Klopman for an interview to discuss such matters, he said he wasn't interested.

There's no shortage of big egos among the toughest bosses, but the Legend-in-his-Own-Mind award may well go to Richard Rosenthal, chairman of Citizens Utilities Company of Stamford, Connecticut. Company insiders say that his specialty is making staffers feel they're employed only through his generosity. When flying on commercial airlines, he has been known to give a letter to the pilot instructing him how to take off and land the plane—Rosenthal doesn't want his sinus problems aggravated. In a recent annual report Rosenthal included pictures of his film making son, who is on the board, and shots of himself acting in one of the son's movies. Along with the pictures ran several column inches of text detailing Rosenthal's accomplishments in acting, teaching, business, and other pursuits.

All this might be merely amusing, except that sometimes Rosenthal's ego has worked against Citizens' interest. Once, while testifying in a rate case, he became so irritated by cross-examination that he began insulting the chief engineer of Vermont's utilities commission. Says an

investment broker, "If I had a marvelous acquisition for them, I wouldn't show it to him. It's just a constant struggle trying to do business with him."

This isn't to say Rosenthal doesn't have good qualities. Many associates say he's just about as smart as he thinks he is. "If he had a personality to go with his mind, he could be president of the United States," says one. Adds another, "Richard is an intellectual tyrant and I resent the need to constantly feed his ego. It gets demeaning." Rosenthal agreed to be interviewed for this article only when it was about to go to press, and then only in person at company headquarters. Result: no interview.

Some bosses achieve toughness on their own; others are tutored in it. Ask employees or business associates about Martin Davis, chief executive of Gulf and Western Industries Inc., and even before any charges are leveled, they jump to his defense. "Marty's not a bastard," goes a common retort, "he just had to do a lot of dirty work for Charlie"—Charles Bluhdorn, that is, Gulf & Western's late founder and chairman, whom Davis served as executive vice president. Other defenders say, "He's not the S.O.B. that he used to be."

Has the saber-toothed tiger changed his stripes since getting the top job? Most of our sources doubt it. "He exceeds all of the qualifications for the category of S.O.B.," says a business associate. Even Davis's supporters concede that he is a master of intimidation, using fear to "winnow out the cringing cowards from the upstanding types."

Since Davis took over and began reorganizing, the winnowing has been prodigious. According to Davis, close to 100 corporate staff members resigned or were dismissed. Resigned? "Nobody resigned voluntarily," he says. "We asked them to leave—their jobs didn't exist anymore." He continues, "If one has the responsibility of being a trouble-shooter ... I don't expect everyone to get up and applaud me." Davis's pruning at Gulf & Western has, admittedly, won applause from Wall Street. The company's stock has gone up 30 percent since he took over. Davis claims, without apparent sarcasm, that he's "thrilled" to be named one of the toughest bosses.

Joel Smilow doesn't go quite that far. "I think of myself as tough but very fair," he says. "I set a high standard of performance. I welcome dissent and discussion." The long-time chairman of the International Playtex division of Esmark will probably get a top consumer products job at Beatrice when that company completes its takeover of Esmark. If history repeats itself, Smilow's new subordinates may have quite a lot to learn about dissent.

In the early 1980s Playtex asked the Hay Associates consulting firm to conduct two surveys to determine the level of employee satisfaction at the Playtex division. Both times the firm got the same result: morale at Playtex was among the lowest it had ever encountered. Why? Smilow may have had something to do with it. Sources say he is uncannily effective at demoralizing subordinates. As a former staffer puts it, "He gives the impression that he thinks of employees as throwaways." Many have overheard him using his favorite phrase, "Stupid is forever," behind an employee's back; some suspect they are getting the same treatment.

Smilow fires people arbitrarily and unpredictably. Under the former head of Playtex's international division, Ralston H. Coffin, foreign sales and profits increased dramatically over four years. Smilow dumped him nonetheless. Once he fired an employee with over 15 years' service and then refused to extend the man's medical insurance while he sought a job, even though he had a heart condition. After some wrangling,

personnel executives got Smilow to relent on the insurance and even allow the man to use a company office in his job search. Soon, though, Smilow forced his personnel people to move the man's parking space. Smilow didn't like running into him in the parking lot.

This doesn't mean that there aren't some people who have been at Playtex a long time. Smilow says that just one or two people have left senior positions "on a basis that was not mutual" over the last 15 years. Yet a former personnel staffer in a position to know says that in fact annual management turnover has probably averaged somewhere in the high 30 percent range. Why? "Smilow has zero trust in people," says a former senior manager. "He's a very smart guy whose interpersonal skills didn't grow with his business acumen." When a former officer of Playtex was asked to characterize the boss's "people skills," he replied, "The guy is a train wreck."

In defense, Smilow says, "I am a strong believer in letting people know where they stand." And, he adds with unintentional understatement, "The respect I get would be totally on my ability and fairness and not from any popularity contest."

Perhaps none of the other bosses on our list enjoy the unfettered sway of John Johnson. As founder and owner of Johnson Publishing, the only private company on our list, he has unchallengeable authority over a broadcasting operation, Fashion Fair Cosmetics, and publications including *Ebony* and *Jet*. Johnson is probably worth well over $100 million.

Such hegemony often called forth the word "plantation" in interviews with Johnson's employees past and present. "He runs his business like a plantation," says one. "Just like on a plantation, he is lord and master," says another.

Others repeatedly used the term "slave master," partly in reference to the fact that, while salaries are now improving, Johnson could and did pay his staff inordinately low wages for years—where else was a black journalist to go?

Johnson dismisses all talk of involuntary servitude. "Nobody is in slavery here," he says. "Anybody who is unhappy can always leave. And all my top execs have company cars and they aren't small cars. I've been on a plantation and it was never like that."

Asked why so many employees chose the word, he replies, "I am a private company. Hell, Time Inc. (the publisher of *Fortune*) was a plantation when Henry Luce was there. I am like Henry Luce." Johnson points out that even low-level managers get TVs and stereos for their offices, and lunch in the cafeteria for $1.

Employees agree that Johnson does furnish lavish cars for some executives. But they say that while Johnson in public is witty and charming, he can be brutally hostile when displeased with someone inside the company. "He has wild temper tantrums. He threatens to fire his top people every other week," says a former staffer. A current employee adds, "It's like a crescendo with Johnson. First he puts you down with words. Then when you're down, he flattens you out. Then he walks on your face."

"Yes," Johnson says, "I am tough. I make no apologies. People from all over the world have come here to see the miracle of Johnson Publishing. It is something of a shrine. In the days of Alexander the Great and Napoleon, I am trying to be that kind of leader, riding ahead of the other horses. I must be doing something right, to be considered a legend in my time." At the very least, one of 10 tough legends.

Class Assignment

Pick 5 to 10 adjectives to describe these people. *Fortune* says that they are "tough," but what are some of the other words that could be used? Then, consider the following questions:

1. Is this style of leadership "right"? Are there any moral problems involved in how a senior manager treats other people within the company, or is it strictly a matter of personal character and choice?

2. Is this style of leadership effective? Robert Mallott, one of the 10 toughest bosses, says that "leadership is demonstrated when the ability to inflict pain is confirmed." Do you agree? How would you answer Mr. Mallott?

3. Richard Snyder, another of the 10 toughest bosses, says that "it's easy to be nice, and not confront people; it's infinitely harder to win respect." How, in your opinion, do you win respect? How would you answer Mr. Snyder?

4. "Neutron Jack" Welch, the toughest—in *Fortune*'s view—of the ten tough bosses, says that "the role for the mediocre is clearly short-lived." Do you agree? If so, how are you going to clearly identify people who are "mediocre"?

5. Apply the three ethical principles of Chapter 3 (self-interests, personal virtues, and religious injunctions) to this style of leadership. Particularly, should "compassion" or "concern for others" have any impact upon business decisions?

Case 3–5

VIOLENCE ON TELEVISION AND THE IMPACT UPON CHILDREN

By the age of 18, the typical child has seen 13,000 killings and 100,000 other assorted acts of violence on television. These "assorted acts of violence" are not cartoon cats being hit on the head by cartoon mice; they include rapes, beatings, assaults, explosions, fires, street robberies, home entries, gang confrontations, car crashes, and police arrogance if not police brutality. In 1989, 80 percent of all adult programs contained some violence, with an average of 9.5 violent events per hour. The adult programs containing violence originally are shown after 9:00 in the evening, when children's viewing is restricted to some extent, but the more popular—which often means the more violent—series generally are syndicated and eventually shown as reruns in the late afternoon, a period of high child exposure.

It is estimated that the average home has 1.8 television sets, and that the typical television set is turned on 52 hours per week. Everyone in the family, of course, does not watch during all of the 52 hours, and for much of the time no one is in the room or paying attention to the program and advertisements. Children, however, do watch a lot of television. Children between the ages of two and five typically watch 28 hours per week. Chil-

NOTE: References for this case appear on page 304.

dren between the ages of 6 and 11 watch 23 hours per week. Children between the ages of 12 and 17 watch 21 hours per week. This means that by age 18, children will have spent 19,500 hours watching television, which contrasts with the 14,000 hours they will have spent attending school.

Much of this watching is unsupervised. More and more families are single-parent households or households in which both parents work, so that in the afternoon no adult may be in the home to request that children change the channel. Those requests may not be common, even in the evening. A 1989 survey reported that 85 percent of all parents said that they gave their children no guidance in watching television either after school or during the evening (Singer, 1989).

In summary, children are exposed to extensive violence on television, and that exposure is almost continual throughout the periods (late afternoon and early evening) they are most likely to be watching. The question, of course, is whether this continual exposure to extensive violence influences their own behavior. That is, does violence on television lead to violence in real life?

There is no question but that violence in real life is present within the United States. In 1989 on a national basis, there was a murder every 24 minutes, a rape every 6 minutes, a robbery every 55 seconds, and an

	1950	1969	1970	1980	1988
Murders	5.1	9.0	16.0	23.0	20.7
Rapes	n.a	17.0	38.0	83.0	92.5
Robberies	50.0	107.0	350.0	566.0	543.0
Assaults	73.0	152.0	335.0	673.0	910.0

aggravated assault every 33 seconds. Moreover, it is believed that less than 50 percent of all nonlethal crimes are reported, so that the actual figures may be far higher.

There is also no question but that violence has increased within the United States since the middle of the century, a period of time that correlates almost exactly with the increase in the popularity of television. The figures above show the increase in violent crimes against individuals since 1950, and are expressed as the numbers of crimes per 100,000 citizens in order to index out the influence of the increase in total population (Statistical Abstract of the United States, Editions 73, 81, 91, 101, and 111):

The 12 fold increase in assaults is seen as the most telling statistic by those who believe that there is a direct relationship between violence on television and aggressiveness in real life. Assaults are physical confrontations that are not connected with the theft of money or property. Assaults are the result of disagreements over conduct that go beyond verbal abuse. They are ubiquitous. They occur in family homes, city streets, parking lots, suburban schools, college gyms, and softball diamonds. People disagree over who was first or who was right or who was responsible, and those disagreements seem to escalate into violence much more rapidly now than in the past.

It is easy to make the claim that the increases in murders, rapes and robberies are related to other changes within American society: the presence of drugs, the decay of neighborhoods, the repression of minorities, the lack of opportunities in housing, jobs and education. But, assaults are gratuitous violence. There is no sexual gratification. There is no monetary gain. There is just pain, humiliation, and defeat. Those are not related to the decline of neighborhoods; they are related to the decline in civility [Statement of proponent of television reform].

The question, then, is whether the very substantial increase in the amount of violence shown on television has led to the very substantial increase in the number of personal assaults reported to police. Again, bear in mind that because in a personal assault case there is generally no property loss that can be recovered through insurance if reported promptly to the police, the number of assaults that occur may be very much higher than the number that are reported.

There are two levels on which this question of whether violence on television is related to violence in real life can be answered. The first is the quantitative level: What do scientists have to say as the result of their empirical studies? The second is the qualitative level: What do law enforcement personnel, social workers, political figures, education experts, and industry executives have to say as a result of their personal experiences?

We will first look at the results of the scientific studies. There have been hundreds of these research projects, attempting to link the violence shown on television (and in other forms of entertainment, such as that portrayed in movies or advocated by rock groups) to violence in society. They have used a variety of study techniques and statistical tools. They have approached the issue from numerous perspectives. The purpose of this section of the case is not to be exhaustive and review every study, but to detail three of the best known as explanations of those techniques and perspectives, and then to summarize the conclusions and criticisms of the work thus far.

Bandura, Ross, and Ross; Stanford University, 1962

This is one of the earliest research projects in which the scholars were attempting to establish a correlation between television violence and aggressiveness in children, but it is also considered to be close to a classic. It is a laboratory study that is probably familiar to most students who have taken a college class in introductory psychology.

Description. Children watched a film clip of another child beating, punching, kicking, sitting on, and yelling at a Bobo doll (a big inflatable red-nosed clown, which was designed to bounce back to an upright position when hit). After seeing the film clip, individual children were put into a playroom with many toys, including a Bobo doll. Without any urging from the psychologists, who were observing behind a one-way mirror, the children would almost invariably start to beat upon the Bobo doll *exactly* as they had seen done in the film clip.

Conclusions. In general, this study firmly established learning theory in the field of psychology. It demonstrated that children do observe behavior and replicate it without being instructed to do so. In specific, this study also indicated that since children will imitate in a laboratory setting any filmed violence they view within the laboratory, then there is the *potential* for them to imitate in a natural setting the TV violence they view at home.

Criticisms. The study is not without its detractors. James Wilson, a professor of government at Harvard, pointed out many of its limitations:

> If it were in the public's interest to protect Bobo dolls from being hit by children, and if hitting Bobo dolls was a regular feature on TV, then admonishing the media to refrain from such features might be in order. But what evidence is there from Bandura's experiments that aggression against dolls is ever transferred into aggression against people, or even that children in the experiments define hitting a doll as aggressive? [Wilson, 1974, p. 297]

Other critics have pointed out that in a laboratory study with a Bobo doll the children have no fear of retaliation, so they can act without any "he or she may hit back" restraints upon them. Secondly, in a laboratory setting they are outside normal, real-life society, and can therefore act without any societal or parental constraints upon them. And thirdly, Bobo dolls were made to be beaten up; that was the function the toy makers designed them to fulfill. Most children in the study had encountered Bobo dolls before; they knew what they were supposed to do to them even before the film clips were shown. In short, it is hard to create a truly realistic replication of violence in a laboratory setting.

McLead, Atkin, and Chaffee; University of Wisconsin, 1972

This is another of the early works in which the researchers were attempting to establish a correlation between television violence and aggressiveness in children, but it was done through questionnaire administration, not through laboratory observation.

Description. Students were given two questionnaires. The first one asked them to indicate which TV shows and how many hours of each they were watching. All the television shows had been rated on their violence content by the researchers, and so it was possible to give each student a standardized score of overall violence viewing. The second questionnaire contained a broad range of questions asking the students how they would respond in various situations. For example, they were asked what they would do if someone were to cut into a line in front of them. Based on their responses to all questions, each student was given a standardized score of adolescent aggression. The researchers then compared the overall violence-viewing scores with the adolescent aggression scores and found a moderately positive association between the two.

Conclusions. The researchers concluded that the two variables were correlated and that the viewing of violent television was associated with more aggressive tendencies among adolescents.

Criticisms. With questionnaires, there is always the problem of whether the respondents fill them out correctly. In this instance, did the children respond truthfully about their television viewing at home and their probable behavior in confrontations? There was some independent verification; that is, the researchers asked the parents to validate the reported viewing habits but there was no way to check upon the probable behavior.

A more basic criticism is that—as the researchers themselves pointed out—the study had established *correlation*, not *causation*. The variables are correlated—that is, they move together—but that does not necessarily mean that one causes the other. Three conflicting theories could have accounted for the proven correlation:

1. Viewing a lot of violent TV causes children to act more aggressively.

2. Aggressiveness in children causes them to watch a lot of violent TV.

3. Some third, unknown factor causes children to both watch a lot of violent TV and act more aggressively.

Jonathan Freedman at the University of Toronto reviewed 10 similar studies done between 1972 and 1982 that established correlation but not causality, and then commented upon this problem:

It seems accurate to conclude that the evidence indicates a positive correlation between viewing television violence and aggressiveness. The importance of this finding should not be understated. The research has involved many thousands of subjects, of both sexes, ranging in age from young children to older teenagers, from a wide range of socioeconomic backgrounds and ethnic backgrounds, and from several countries. The relation between viewing television violence and aggressiveness is thus extremely well documented.

The existence of this correlation is absolutely central to the argument of whether television causes aggression. Without a consistent relation between viewing television violence and aggressiveness, there would be little reason to search further for causation. With this relation demonstrated, a causal relation must be considered a distinct possibility. However, it should be clear that demonstrating the correlation between aggressiveness and viewing television is only the first step in making the argument for causality [Freeman, 1984, p. 237].

Singer and Singer; Yale University, 1980

This was a study that attempted to eliminate the problem with questionnaires filled out by the subjects themselves. The researchers used observations of actual behavior on a playground rather than responses on probable behavior during confrontations.

Description. Parents of 141 nursery schoolers were given logs to record their children's TV viewing. Trained observers were then sent to the children's schools to watch the children on the playgrounds at recess. The children were rated for aggressiveness based on evidence of their overt behavior towards others. The number of hours of violent action-adventure programming viewed was then compared to the aggressiveness of the children and found to be positively correlated, though with a "weak" correlation coefficient.

Conclusions. The result in this observation study matched the findings of similar questionnaire studies, though with a much weaker correlation coefficient. An explanation of this difference is that the children who watched more violent television might have wanted to respond more aggressively in make-believe situations, but were afraid or otherwise constrained from doing so on the playground.

Criticisms. Critics seized upon the weak correlation coefficient, which seemed to indicate that the relationship between the variables was not all that strong. Singer and Singer, however, argued that:

While the statistical associations found are small and account only for perhaps 10 percent of the possible influences on aggression, such a small effect of television viewing cannot be minimized when we consider the millions of children watching television. Even the small incremental effect of television viewing on the level of aggression in thousands of children must be taken seriously as a public health problem [Singer and Singer, 1989, p. 289].

Other studies have been conducted over extended time periods. That is, children were observed in playground situations from ages 10 to 12 in an attempt to see if aggressive tendencies increased with age, and if that increase could be related to changing television viewing patterns. It was hoped that these studies might resolve the chicken versus egg controversy—does viewing violent television lead to more aggressive behavior, or does more aggressive behavior lead to viewing violent television—but the results were inconclusive.

Further studies have been conducted over different cultures. American television programs have become popular in Europe and some parts of Asia, and children in those countries were observed in playground situations in an attempt to see if aggressive tendencies and television viewing were related to any third factor such as child-rearing methods, social group constraints, or academic school pressures. Again, the results were inconclusive.

What conclusions can be drawn from the full collection of studies? First, researchers have firmly established a positive correlation between the viewing of violent television and the aggressive behavior of children. Nearly everyone agrees on this, and the proof seems virtually irrefutable. However, the correlation is weak, and—even further—correlation does not necessarily mean causation. It is still not clear whether (1) viewing a lot of violent TV causes children to act aggressively, (2) acting aggressively causes children to watch a lot of violent TV, or (3) some third, unknown factor causes children to both watch violent TV and act aggressively.

For most nonacademics who are in-terested in the topic of violence on television it is probably fair to say that the inconclusive results have been disappointing. However, inconclusive and disappointing results may be a natural outcome of all social science research into important national problems. Too many variables may be involved. Many of those variables may be difficult to define and then measure. It is impossible to set up a control group (one that has either been isolated from or exposed to certain variables) because of the potential conflict with human rights. Professor James Wilson of Harvard University has expressed these problems clearly and succinctly:

> When social scientists are asked to measure consequences in terms of a badly conceptualized or hard-to-measure "effect" of one among many highly interrelated "causes," all of which operate (if at all) over long periods of time, they tend to discover that there is no relationship or at best a weak and contingent one. This is one of the reasons, for example, for the controversy over human intelligence: the measures of intelligence are much disputed and the correlates of intelligence (race, class, family status, diet, or whatever) are themselves so intercorrelated as to make it hazardous to guess which one or which few variables, and in what temporal sequence, account for changes in I.Q.
>
> Another example: social science studies of the effects of governmental interventions of a broad and diffuse nature (building "better schools" or running a "community action program" or enrolling students in Project Head Start) on various vague social objectives (improving education or strengthening the sense of community) are usually inconclusive and controversial.

The irony is that social science may be weakest in detecting the broadest and most fundamental changes in social values, precisely because they are broad and fundamental. Intuitively, it seems plausible that the media and other forces have contributed powerfully over the last generation to changes in popular attitudes about sexuality, political action, and perhaps even violence. But for lack of a control group it is unlikely that this will ever be proved scientifically [Wilson, 1974, p. 304].

Given that conclusive evidence supporting a *causal* relationship between violence on television and violence in society may never be established by social science research, it is necessary to turn to the opinions of those on each side of this issue. These include parents, people active in the television industry, educators, clerics, social critics, law enforcement personnel, and the attorneys who represent all of these groups. Their opinions are based upon their personal observations, values and interests, not upon their research findings, but they express clearly the concerns of most of the rest of the population. There are six major areas of contention:

1. Is it "right" to show violence on television, given that violence is an obvious part of American life and a dominant theme in world literature?

People who support the status quo—the unrestricted showing of violence on television—start with the claim that violence is part of American life. Like it or not, they say, murders occur every 24 minutes within the United States, robberies every 55 seconds, and assaults every 33 seconds. It is legitimate to portray that violence on television, they claim, because otherwise the programs would just be sugar-coated fantasies, even further from reality than they currently are alleged to be.

People who support the status quo then go on to explain that violence is also part of world literature. Murder mysteries are among the most popular of all books: Should those novels be banned? Cowboy westerns are widely available: Should they be removed from the shelves? Even classics such as Shakespeare's *Macbeth* and children's stories such as *Little Red Riding Hood* contain violence. Macbeth assassinates both Banquo and Duncan before being slain himself by MacDuff. Little Red Riding Hood's grandmother is eaten by the wolf, who then is hacked to death by the woodsman. Why is violence acceptable in *Macbeth* and *Little Red Riding Hood*, they ask, but not on "Murder She Wrote"?

People who oppose the portrayal of violence on television counter the claim that the programs simply reflect the violence of American life by saying that the violence currently shown on television is excessive in its amount. The number of violent acts per hour, they claim, is well in excess of anything experienced in real life. "Hardball," which aired on NBC in the fall of 1989, averaged 47 violent acts per hour. That same year, "Tour of Duty" on CBS averaged 45 violent acts per hour, and "The Young Riders" on ABC averaged 40 acts per hour. Most people do not experience one tenth of that violence within their entire lifetime, let alone the full amount within one hour. Police shows, some of which have topped over 50 violent acts per hour, are said to be even more unrealistic. The critics of violence on television explain that it is a fact that most police officers never fire their guns, except on the practice range, during their entire careers, and that most arrests are made without a struggle let alone a lengthy fight.

The critics also claim that the violence that is shown on television is excessive in its realism. They admit that violence is part of literature, but explain that there is a vast difference between the verbal and the visual depiction of violence, and that the verbal depiction is often toned down or even eliminated. In *Macbeth*, for example, the killing of Duncan is not even verbally described by Shakespeare; instead, the murder is encouraged by Lady Macbeth, and later her husband reports "T'is done." Television, the critics say, would graphically show the sword play, with Duncan staggering slowly and bloodily towards his death. They make the same point with *Little Red Riding Hood*. It is one thing for a child to read (or have read to him or her) that "the woodsman swung his axe and killed the big, bad wolf"; it is another to portray that death with all the visual imagery of modern-day, full-color, high-resolution television.

2. Is it "right" to restrict violence on television, given that a causal relationship between violence on television and violence in society has never been proven?

Many television executives make the point that their industry should not be condemned on circumstantial evidence. There simply is not proof, they explain, that television violence causes aggressiveness in children, and

that to impose restrictions on television without that proof is acting as if the networks were guilty until proven innocent. There are hundreds of thousands of people, they add, whose livelihoods depend on the broadcasting industry, and it would be unfair to those people to attack television just because *some* of the programs *might be* affecting *some* of the children *some* of the time. Developing theories as to how television violence might affect children is not the same as providing evidence that it does, they say.

> Given the vastness of the audience and the enormity of the programming (something over 5 million hours of broadcasting annually), it is interesting that there is so little traceable impact upon the nation. Even the number of reported untoward incidences—when an impressionable viewer imitates something seen on a show with damaging results—cannot be more than a few dozen a year. The trade-off for our highway system is about 40,000 annually [Fowles, 1984, p. 3].

The critics of violence on television say that network executives are being hypocritical when they claim that there is no proof that hours of violent television viewing have any major, direct or indirect, effect upon children. There is no real proof, the critics go on to say, that the 15-second and 30-second advertisements on television have any major, direct or indirect, effect upon consumers, yet the network executives do not demand clear scientific evidence of causality in this instance. If correlation rather than causality is good enough in the second instance, why is it not good enough in the first?

Television time is sold to sponsors on the conviction that although the Ajax ad will not guarantee that the viewer will buy the product, it raises the probability that he will. Social scientists would simply make the same claim for filmed or televised violence, whether fictitious or real. Viewing the carnage does not guarantee that the viewer will "go forth and do likewise," but it raises the probability that he will [Siegel, 1974, p. 1].

The critics go on to say that it would be nice if there were clear scientific evidence pointing one way or the other, but in reality there simply isn't. Even if the issue is murky on a scientific level, they explain, that doesn't mean it is necessary to suspend all judgment.

Unhappily, all of the major premises on which our society rests derive from the realm of intuition.... Can anyone prove that the family is a desirable institution? That higher education promotes human welfare? That love is better than hate? That democracy is superior to dictatorship? None of these is provable. But this does not stop us from acting on our best judgment, knowing that all human judgment is fallible [Christenson, 1974, p. 311].

Others have explained that policymakers and business managers usually have to make decisions based upon incomplete information, and that common sense often substitutes for scientific evidence:

Methodological squabbles and the call for "more definitive research" have served as an excuse to buy time for producers.... In my opinion, we do not need more research on the latest forms of violence to take action. As concerned citizens all of us need to raise the discourse to a moral level, a level in which

we talk about the commonweal and what we want to teach our children [Friedrich-Cofer, 1985, p. 16].

The moral aspects of the decision to continue showing violence on television has been noted by many authors:

In the case of violence ... it is unlikely that social science can either show harmful effects or prove there are no harmful effects.... These are moral issues and ultimately all judgments about the acceptability of restrictions on various media will have to rest on political and philosophical considerations [Wilson, 1974, p. 370].

3. Is it "right" to restrict violence on television, given that the networks already have regulations in place and review boards to enforce those regulations?

Television executives say that the violence that is shown is part of the plot on the programs that they air, and that excessive or gratuitous violence (i.e., violence that is not related to the dramatic development of the plot) is not permitted on television. All networks have departments that review scripts for content, they add, and excessively violent scenes and unnecessarily violent acts are eliminated prior to screening.

We recognize our responsibility to ensure that when violence is presented in the context of a dramatic program, there exists legitimate and thematic justification for its inclusion. Further, it is our practice to limit the portrayal of violence to that which is reasonably related to plot development and character delineation. The excessive depiction of violence is rarely necessary and gratuitous portrayals are considered inappropriate for the television medium [Research Perspective on Television Violence, 1983, p. 14].

The critics of violence on television reply that industry self-regulation has not worked in the past, and cannot be expected to work in the future.

> I do not understand why network executives cannot adopt the simple rule that the amount of violence shown on television cannot exceed the amount of violence experienced by the typical viewer during his or her lifetime. But, that is not going to happen. As long as television people believe that violence sells, it's going to be shown in excessive amounts with the approval of their internal review boards [Verbal statement of industry critic].

4. Is it "right" to restrict violence on television, given that the parents can, or should, supervise what is watched?

Television executives and many child-rearing experts say that it is the responsibility of the parents much more than the responsibility of the networks to restrict the programs children watch. Parents are using television sets as babysitters, they add, and that is not a function television programs were designed to perform. The parents should consider changing their own behavior, and take a much more active role in supervising their own children:

> It is clear that where mothers establish more rules about television, limiting viewing or allowing particular shows while forbidding others, the children are less likely to show the *negative* effects of television viewing. This study points to the extremely important role of the parent as a guide to the child's con-

structive rather than self-defeating use of the television medium [Singer and Singer, 1984, p. 36].

Critics, of course, respond that given the number of single-parent families, and those in which both parents are working outside the home, and then adding on the other pressures of contemporary family life, it is totally unrealistic to expect that parents will be able to continually supervise their children in front of the TV.

> Throwing the full responsibility on the parents for determining what their children are exposed to is, in this day, naive and almost impossible. Parents need the help of the community with its various protective agencies and resources [Cline, 1974, p. 352].

5. Is it "right" to restrict violence on television, given that the market can, or should, regulate what is shown?

Television executives say that the networks air only what people want to watch. People choose what programs they like; the networks don't choose for them. If the public doesn't like a certain program because it's too violent, all they have to do is stop watching, which will lower the Nielsen ratings, drive away the commercial sponsors, and quickly lead to the program being canceled or changed. This is a market economy, they add, and it should be left to the marketplace to decide what is aired, and what is not:

> If you cannot persuade people (such as the viewing public) to reject that which you consider exploitative or unhealthy, do not ask the government to impose your will on the same people [Lynn, 1985, p. 9].

Critics, however, reply firstly that the marketplace for television programs is not very efficient because alternatives to the predominantly violent shows are not widely available due to cost. It is much cheaper to rerun adult programs during the periods of high children viewing than to produce other programs specifically designed for their interests. In short, they say, money motivates the programming during children's hours, not some sophisticated notion concerning a free and efficient "marketplace" for ideas.

High exposure to violence is more a result of saturation by broadcasters than a strong preference for this type of programming by youngsters. Among first graders, for example, the two most popular programs are sitcom reruns. Preschoolers prefer Sesame Street to the violent cartoons [Liebert, Davidson, and Neale, 1974, p. 117].

Critics also question the entire concept of a "marketplace" for ideas due to the lack of established means of determining "consumer" preferences. Marketplaces for toothpastes and headache remedies obviously exist, they say, and you can easily compute market share by asking how many people put their money down and buy each brand. Marketplaces for ideas are not that simple; you never know how many people "buy" (i.e., accept) a given concept unless there is an election or a survey, and even that acceptance may not be a valid indication of the true worth of the concept:

One should ask whether the best test of the idea of dictatorship, segregation, or genocide is really the marketplace; whether our experience has not taught us that even such ideas can get themselves accepted there, and that a marketplace without rules of civil discourse is no marketplace of ideas, but a bullring [Bickel, 1974, p. 74].

6. Is it legal to restrict violence shown on television, given that the First Amendment of the U.S. Constitution guarantees freedom of speech and freedom of the press to the networks?

Television executives, lawyers representing the networks, public officials, and many others believe that placing restrictions on the content of programs that the networks can and cannot broadcast brings up a whole host of constitutional issues. The First Amendment of the U.S. Constitution focuses on freedom of religion, of speech, of the press, and of assembly. It is very explicit in its wording:

Congress should make no law respecting an establishment of religion, or prohibiting the free exercise thereof; or abridging the freedom of speech, or of the press, or of the right of the people peaceably to assemble, and petition the Government for a redress of grievances [Bill of Rights of the U.S. Constitution].

Freedom of speech is often said to be the hallmark of a free society. It's the bedrock on which the foundations of democracy exist. Freedom of the press is thought to be a necessary condition for a democracy; it is the means of disseminating information beyond the control of the government. Many people value these freedoms highly.

Network executives rely upon these freedoms—and the respect in which they are held—in their argument against restrictions on the total amount or graphic depiction of violence in television programming. If restrictions are placed on the content of network entertainment programs, they ask, what will be next? Network news programs? Local editorial positions? Election day reports? Print as well as electronic media? It is always easy, they say, to find a perfectly valid social reason to restrict one form of speech. But, they explain, that is just the first step in the decay of our freedoms of speech and the press. They go on to cite an Indiana court that struck down an Indianapolis ordinance banning obscenity by observing that you can't have a law against one form of speech without threatening all forms of speech (see Demac, 1985, p. 21).

Restrictions on the content of network programming, television executives believe, would violate both the explicit wording of the First Amendment and the implicit understanding of the U.S. population.

Not so, say critics of the current content of network programming. Restrictions would be constitutional. The intent of the framers of the Bill of Rights was to ensure the free discussion of all matters of public concern, not to limit the authority of the people in determining what was a matter of public concern. And, they go on to explain, nowhere in the Constitution is there any protection for the rights of entertainers, and television is primarily an entertainment media.

The drafters of the Constitution probably and properly intended an absolute ban on efforts by the government to forbid the dissemination of any political, economic, religious, or social ideas ... but the commercial entertainment industry cannot logically claim the same constitu-

tional protection as normal political discourse [Christenson, 1974, p. 311].

There are, the critics say, numerous exceptions to the First Amendment's seemingly inflexible wording already in existence:

False advertising—you can't say anything you want to in business; lying about the performance of your product is against the law.

Public preaching—you can't say anything you want to in education; religious instruction in public schools is against the law.

Improper warning—you can't say anything you want to in public; creating a "clear and present" danger to others is against the law.

Democracy, the critics say, requires a balancing act between self-freedom and self-restraint. Self-restraint and indeed some degree of conformity—imposed on us through laws if necessary—are essential for the functioning of any society. We must have individual freedom, they add, but we must not have exploitive license.

The law is what we want it to be. Society shapes its laws more than the law shapes society. And thus we can permit as much freedom of expression and dramatic license as we wish. There is, however, probably somewhere a cost-benefit ratio. If "speech" becomes too disruptive and society suffers too much, in our self-interest we say "no"; we draw a line; we refuse to tolerate it. However, it takes a sizeable consensus of our citizenry to draw the line. When a minority has attempted to assume the role, historically they have nearly always been rebuffed [Cline, 1974, p. 107].

7. Is it "right" to restrict violence shown on television, given that this is imposing the views of the majority upon the wishes of a minority?

No, say television executives, it is not "right" even if some court should rule that it is legal. Restrictions are wrong because placing restrictions on what people can watch on their television sets is legislating morality. We live, they add, in a pluralistic society. Different groups hold different values, and what is distasteful to one group may be essential to another.

> One person's "gratuitous" exploitation is another's core artistic expression [Lynn, 1985, p. 9].

Simply put, television executives and the attorneys representing the networks claim, the majority of the American public shouldn't be legislating its tastes on the minority. After all, watching violence on TV in your own home is a private act involving no one else and harming no one else. So why should the government, or any other group in favor of restrictions for that matter, be able to invite itself into your living room to regulate your behavior in your home?

The critics of the current unregulated broadcasting of violence on television reply that restrictions would not only be legal, but "right." Society, they say, has to be able to determine what is best for society, and what is best for society will always be resented by some small group:

> Opponents of … censorship sometimes contend that the state should not try to be the moral custodian of the people. Nor should a majority seek to impose its moral standards on a minority, it is said. Yet every criminal law represents a moral judgment. And laws typically constitute a coercion of the minority by the majority. Presumably bigamists resent laws against bigamy, polygamists oppose laws against polygamy, and sexual exhibitionists dislike laws against indecent exposure. Their objections are not decisive once society regards these restrictions as reasonable [Christenson, 1974, p. 313].

Class Assignment

You are the president of one of the major television networks in 1993. The amount of violence in the United States has escalated far beyond that reported in 1988 (in the table on page 95). There are now many more stringent demands from religious groups, political figures, and social welfare workers that the broadcasters severely reduce or even totally eliminate the violent content of their programs. You have to decide what to do. You also have to decide in such a manner that you can convince others—both within your company and within your society—of the "rightness" of your decision. None of the facts reported in the case have changed substantially: that is, the violent programs are still the most popular among all age groups except the very young, and no proof has been found to establish causality in the relationship between violence on television and violence in society.

CHAPTER 4

The Middle Ethical Principles

Moral reasoning, to repeat the earlier definition from Chapter 2, is the method of applying the ethical principles of analysis to a moral problem in which some people are going to be hurt or harmed in some way, while others are going to be benefited or rewarded. How do you arrive at a decision that you believe to be "right" and "just" and "fair" under those circumstances and, even more importantly, how do you convince others of the "rightness," "justness," and "fairness" of your decision? You use the process of moral reasoning, in six steps:

1. Define the moral problem. What appears to be a moral problem to you, with an unjust or unfair impact upon others, may not seem so unjust or unfair to others. Consequently, you should define the problem as clearly as you can so that others will understand and (hopefully) share your concerns.

   Is it right that I (we, you, they) should (the decision that is being considered), given that this may result in (the adverse impact upon the welfare or the rights of others that you foresee)?

2. Develop possible alternatives. Most of the complex moral problems you will encounter are not dichotomous, with just two "Yes, I will" or "No, I won't" types of answers. Think of the alternative solutions that are possible and arrange them in a logical sequence.

   What are the midpoints between the extremes, and what are the major compromises that are possible? Recognize that other people want to be certain that "their" solutions were considered in the decision.

3. Resolve the factual issues. Factual issues are those on which you can get agreement if you can find reliable information. In many instances, you may not be able to get enough data, or some of the data you do get will be conflicting. Show how the different interpretations will affect the eventual outcome.

   Is it a fact that (the issue that is in dispute), and what evidence do we have that this indeed is true? What evidence do those who dispute this fact have, and how can we resolve the two points of view?

4. Consider the personal impacts. Personal impacts are the consequences to the person making the decision or bringing the moral problem to the attention of others. "Whistle-blowers" are not well liked in many organizations because they act contrary to the expected patterns of behavior.

> What will happen to me or to my career if I make this decision or alert others to this problem, and am I prepared to make that sacrifice? Are there informal channels in this organization that could reduce the risk to me?

5. Apply the ethical principles. Ethical principles are the "first" principles or basic conditions for a "good" society in which people voluntarily cooperate for the benefit of all. Apply each of the ethical principles, in sequence, not just the ones that support your intuitive point of view.

> If I think in terms of my long-term self-interests, how will I decide? If I think in terms of the need to be open, honest and truthful, and proud of my actions, how will I decide?

6. Arrive at a decision that you can support, explain, and (if necessary) defend. Express that decision clearly, and the reasons (the ethical principles) that make you think that it is "right" and "just" and "fair." Others may not agree with you, but they should be able to agree that your proposed solution is "thoughtful," "logical," and "reasonable."

The prior chapter looked at the first three ethical principles of self-interests, personal virtues, and religious injunctions. This chapter will examine the next four: government requirements, utilitarian benefits, universal duties, and individual rights.

GOVERNMENT REQUIREMENTS

The principle of government requirements can be expressed very simply in the statement that everyone should always obey the law. The law in a democratic society is said to represent the minimal moral standards of that society. You may or may not agree with those minimal moral standards, but you cannot really fault a person who obeys the law. You may feel that a person or a company that faces a complex moral problem in which some people are going to be harmed and harmed badly should go beyond the law. They, however, may disagree with you. They may say, "If you don't like what we're doing, get together with a majority of your fellow citizens and pass a new law, and we will obey the provisions of that law, but until that happens please do not lecture us on the superiority of your moral standards. We see nothing wrong with what we are doing, and it is legal."

Thomas Hobbes (1588–1679) is the originator of this principle that the sole moral responsibility of men and women is to obey the law, or the supreme governmental authority that sets the law. It is necessary to recognize that Hobbes lived during the Elizabethan Age in England, a period of intellectual excitement—the influence of the Italian Renaissance on the renewal of learning

EXHIBIT 4–1   The Method of Moral Reasoning

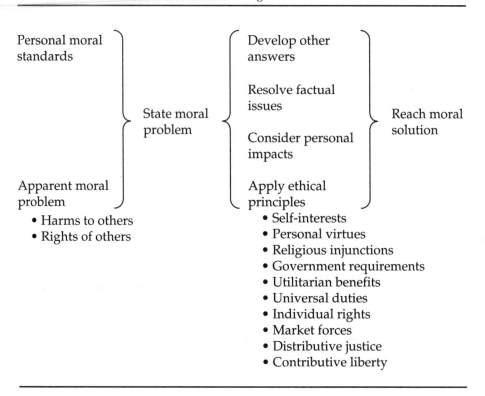

and the impact of the European Reformation on the renewal of the church had just barely begun to be felt—and of civil war, rebellion, and conflict. It was a time when it was natural for a moral philosopher to be interested in the nature of government and the rights of man.

Hobbes wrote *Leviathan*. The name comes from the Bible, and refers to a huge sea monster; it is meant to portray the dominating political force that is needed to impose order on people living in a state of nature which, according to Hobbes, will necessarily be a state of conflict. There are five major points:

1. Men are equal in their strength of both body and mind. Equality of ability leads to equality of hope in the achievement of ends, and therefore to a constant struggle for gain, for safety, and for reputation.

2. The struggle is a war (and here there is a famous quotation): "And such a war as is of every man against every man"). The war is continual, like bad weather, not intermittent like a shower.

3. The conflict "where every man is enemy to every man" results in a lack of

security, and the lack of security leads to a decline in industry and (again, a very famous quotation: "The life of man, solitary, poor, nasty, brutish, and short").

4. To stop this continual struggle, Hobbes says that people living in a "state of nature"—a free association of equal individuals, before the corrupting political and economic institutions have been added—would reach two major conclusions, which he terms "natural laws":

> Men, to gain the benefits of peace, will seek it by all means available to them.

> The only means available to them is for all men to surrender their rights to a central authority.

How do you apply Hobbes, and his "continual war of every man against every man," to ethical problems? At the simplest level, the ethical principle from Hobbes comes out as a requirement that everyone obey the law. What is "just" is what the central authority, which you and all others have agreed to accept, says is "just." You may not like the law, particularly when it has been established by an autocratic dictum rather than through a democratic vote, but to avoid the continual war you have to accept it.

At a more complex level, the ethical principle from Hobbes comes out as a requirement that you determine what people living in a state of nature would accept as the governing rules of society. This is the idea of the "Social Contract," and it is an important concept in moral philosophy.

If you were to take 100 people, somehow separated from all prior cultural influences, and put them on an island, would that society be idyllic or chaotic? Let us assume that it would be idyllic as long as there was enough food, fuel, clothing, and shelter for everyone. But suppose there were a shortage; then what would happen? You might well have the war of "every man against every man" that Hobbes predicted.

A "contractarian"—that is, a person who believes in the ethical worth of the concept of the Social Contract—would argue that whatever agreement those 100 people would make to stop the conflict is the most rigorous definition you can find as to what is "right" and "just" and "fair." The contractarian would say that the people on the island would discuss the distribution of benefits, the imposition of harms, the recognition of rights, and the definition of duties, and that the resulting agreement—which would have to be unanimous to be effective; one person holding out would make the agreement worthless—would be totally without biased self-interest.

Obviously, you cannot put 100 people on an island and record their means of reaching a decision on the benefits, harms, rights, and duties they believe to be "right." But, you can envisage what would happen if the stakeholders in a moral problem in management were put into a room and no one knew what position they would hold when the decision was reached, nor who would turn out to be the hardest working, most intelligent, best educated, or richest. Those

EXHIBIT 4–2
Excerpts from *Leviathan*
Thomas Hobbes

Nature has made men so equal in the faculties of body and mind as that, though there be found one man sometimes manifestly stronger in body or quicker of mind than another, yet when all is reckoned together the difference between man and man is not so considerable as that one man can thereupon claim to himself any benefit to which another may not pretend as well as he.... From this equality of ability ariseth equality of hope in the attaining of our ends. And therefore if any two men desire the same thing, which nevertheless they cannot both enjoy, they become enemies, and in the way to their ends endeavor to destroy or subdue one another.

Hereby it is manifest that during the time men live without a common power to keep them all in awe, they live in that condition which is called war, and such a war as is of every man against every man.

Whatsoever therefore is consequent to a time of war, where every man is enemy to every man, the same is consequent to the time wherein men live without other security than what their own strength and their own invention shall furnish them withal. In such condition there is no place for industry because the fruit thereof is uncertain; and consequently no culture of the earth, no navigation, nor use of the commodities that may be imported by sea; no commodious building; no instruments of moving and removing such things as require much force; no knowledge of the face of the earth; no account of time; no arts; no letters; no society; and which is worst of all, continual fear and danger of violent death; and the life of man, solitary, poor, nasty, brutish, and short.

To this war of every man against every man, this also is consequent; that nothing can be unjust. The notions of right and wrong, justice and injustice have there no place. Where there is no common power there is no law; where no law, no justice or injustice.

The only way to erect such a common power as may be able to defend them from the invasion of foreigners, and the injuries of one another, and thereby to secure them in such sort that, by their own industry and by the fruits of the earth, they may nourish themselves and live contentedly, is to confer all their power and strength upon one man, or upon one assembly of men, that they may reduce all their wills, by plurality of voices, unto one will. This is more than consent, or concord; it is a real unity of them all, in one and the same person, made by the covenant of every man with every man. The multitude so united in one person is called a Commonwealth, or in Latin Civitas. This is the generation of that great Leviathan to which we owe under the immortal God our peace and our defense.

people, ignorant of their interests and advantages in the actual situation, would decide what was "right" and "just" and "fair" without regard to those interests and advantages. This decision would be free of biased self-interest.

John Locke (1632–1704) adds a note of realism to Hobbes' justification of the position of central authority within a productive society, and the need for legal obedience on the part of the members of that society. Locke is worried about the negative aspects of centralized authority, for the person who holds that position can be arbitrary or self-interested and act to repress others. There are four major points:

1. Right to life is no longer the only basic right. Men and women can now "order their actions and dispose of their possessions as they wish." Rights to liberty and property have been added.

2. State of nature is no longer a constant war. With the rights to life, liberty, and property come the duty to preserve those rights for others by punishing all who transgress against them.

3. If men give up their basic rights to a central authority, as recommended by Hobbes, they can become subject to an arbitrary ruler. Consequently, they give up their duty to punish all who transgress against the basic rights.

4. If men keep their rights, they achieve freedom which Locke (in a famous quotation) defined as "to have a standing rule to live by, common to very one of that society ... and not to be subject to inconstant, uncertain, unknown, arbitrary will of another man."

What does all this mean? It is fairly heady stuff for, following over 1,000 years of arbitrary rule on the part of both the secular and religious authorities, here are two writers beginning to think about some very basic issues. The ostensible topic is government, but government is seen only as a means for "living together in peace and unity" in a productive, industrious, and free society. The actual topics are "rights," "duties," "liberty," and "justice." All four of these topics will be considered later in the book, for all four have been expanded further to become the basis of complete ethical systems of belief.

UTILITARIAN BENEFITS

The principle of utilitarian benefits can be summarized in the statement that people should always act in ways that will maximize the net social benefits—the excess of social goods over social harms—of their actions. Obviously it is difficult to measure many of the nonmaterial and nonfinancial goods of a society—the health, education, and security of the citizens, and it is even more difficult to measure the nonmaterial and nonfinancial harms, but the overall rule is that you measure the goods and harms as best you can, and then choose the course of action that results in the greatest net benefits for the society of which you are a part. It is a rule that eliminates self-interests, for they form no part of the calculation.

Jeremy Bentham (1747–1832) was the first advocate of the principle of utilitarian benefits. His intent was to apply rational moral concepts to the government and the law. Common law in England at the time was a confusing set of

---

EXHIBIT 4–3
Excerpts from the *Second Treatise of Government*
John Locke

To understand political power right and derive it from its original, we must consider what state all men are naturally in, and that is a state of perfect freedom to order their actions and dispose of their possessions and persons as they think fit, within the bounds of the law of nature, without asking leave or depending upon the will of any other man.

A state also of equality, wherein all the power and jurisdiction is reciprocal, no one having more than another; there being nothing more evident than that creatures of the same species and rank, born to the same advantages of nature and the same uses of faculties, should also be equal one amongst another without subordination or subjection.

And that all men may be restrained from invading others' rights and from doing hurt to one another, and the law of nature be observed, which wills the peace and preservation of all mankind, the execution of the law of nature is put into every man's hands, whereby everyone has a right to punish the transgressors of that law to such a degree as may hinder its violations, for the law of nature would, as all other laws that concern men in this world, be in vain if there were nobody that in that state of nature had a power to execute that law, and thereby preserve the innocent and restrain offenders.

And here we have the plain difference between the state of nature and the state of war which, however some men have confounded, are as far distant as a state of peace, good-will, mutual assistance, and preservation, and a state of enmity, malice, violence and mutual destruction are one from another. Men living together according to reason, without a common superior on earth with authority to judge between them is properly the state of nature. But force, or the declared design of force, upon the person of another, is the state of war.

To avoid this state of war—wherein there is no appeal but to heaven—is the one great reason of men's putting themselves into society, and quitting the state of nature.

The liberty of man in society is to be under no other legislative power but that established by consent in the commonwealth, nor under the dominion of any will or the restraint of any law but what the legislative shall enact according to the trust put into it. Freedom of men under government is to have a standing rule to live by, common to every one of that society and made by the legislative power erected in it, a liberty to follow his own will in all things where the rule prescribes not, and not to be subject to the inconstant, uncertain, unknown, arbitrary will of another man.

---

precedents from a 500-year history of legal decisions; these decisions were based upon social institutions such as the royal government and an agricultural economy that no longer existed in their original forms. The king had been

---

EXHIBIT 4–4
Excerpts from *An Introduction to the Principles of Morals and Legislation*
Jeremy Bentham

Nature has placed mankind under the governance of two sovereign masters, pain and pleasure. It is for them alone to point out what we ought to do, as well as to determine what we shall do. On the one hand the standard of right and wrong, on the other the chain of causes and effects, are fastened to their throne. They govern us in all we do, in all we say, in all we think; every effort we can make to throw off our subjection, will serve but to demonstrate and confirm it. In words a man may pretend to abjure their empire but in reality he will remain subject to it all the while. The principle of utility recognizes this subjection, and assumes it for the foundation of that system, the object of which is to rear the fabric of felicity by the hands of reason and of law. Systems which attempt to question it deal in sounds instead of senses, in caprice instead of reason, in darkness instead of light.

But enough of metaphor and declamation; it is not by such means the moral science is to be improved.

The principle of utility is the foundation of the present work; it will be proper therefore at the outset to give an explicit and determinate account of what is meant by it. By the principle of utility is meant that principle which approves or disapproves of every action whatsoever, according to the tendency which it appears to have to augment or diminish the happiness of the party whose interest is in question, or, what is the same thing in other words, to promote or to oppose that happiness. I say of any action whatsoever; and therefor not only of every action of a private individual, but of every measure of government.

---

supplanted by an elected parliament, and agriculture was succumbing to industrialization. Bentham sought a simple means of judging the actions of government and the legitimacy of laws within this complex set of changing relationships, and proposed the principle of "utility" as that means. There are five steps in his argument:

1. Mankind is governed by pleasure and pain, the "two sovereign masters." They determine what we do, as well as what we ought to do.

2. Principle of utility, then, is to approve of actions that increase pleasure and decrease pain, and disapprove of actions that have the opposite result.

3. Utility is equal to the "benefit, advantage, pleasure, good, or happiness of the party involved." The "party" can be an individual or a community.

4. Bentham views a community as a fictitious body (not the result of a social contract), composed of the individual persons who constitute its members.

5. Bentham says that acts of government are "good" and laws are legitimate when they augment the benefit, advantage, pleasure, good, or happiness of the persons who constitute the community.

John Stuart Mill (1806–1873) was the primary defender of the concept of utilitarianism. He was a philosopher, economist, administrator (director of the British East India Company), politician (member of Parliament), and reformer. He also wrote exceedingly well, with both precision and clarity. Here are four major points, and their related statements, from the first chapter of *Utilitarianism:*

1. Mill admits that there has been little progress in the search for the criteria that will separate right from wrong in human actions.

   Two thousand years of thought about the Summum Bonum, or the foundations of morality, has resulted only in confusion and uncertainty.

2. Morality is different from science in which the principles are derived from observation. In morality, the principles must come first.

   A test of right and wrong must be the means, one would think, of ascertaining what is right or wrong, and not a consequence of having already ascertained it.

3. Mill rejects the idea of a "natural law" that is inherent and intuitive because it provides no means of deciding what is right and wrong in any particular matter.

   There ought either to be some one fundamental principle or law at the root of all morality, or if there be several, there should be a determined order of precedence among them.

4. The absence of a single principle has not left morality in the complete disarray that might be expected. There has been a tacit acceptance, Mill says, of the principle of utility.

Mill wanted to change the tacit acceptance to an explicit acceptance, and consequently he explained and then defended the theory against objections. One contemporary charge was that the mass of people were not well enough educated to apply the "high aspirations and intellectual effort" needed to understand utilitarianism. Mill responded with a proposal that was certainly unusual for his time: mandatory public education.

   An amount of mental culture sufficient to give an intelligent interest in these objects of contemplation should be the inheritance of everyone born in a civilized country.

Another contemporary charge was that the "positive evils of life"—sickness and death—will prevent the attainment of happiness for most people (remember, this was also the argument of St. Augustine). Mill responded with a second proposal that was unusual for his time: social welfare programs.

   Poverty may be completely extinguished by the wisdom of society. Disease may be indefinitely reduced by good physical and moral education.

The problem with the principle of Utilitarian Benefits is not the lack of public education and social welfare among the population that may prevent those people from attaining the "greater happiness" planned for the community. Instead, the problem is the lack of an accepted means of accurately measuring the benefits and costs that lead towards that community happiness, and the lack of an equitable method of distributing the benefits and harms within the community. Remember, what one group may consider a major benefit, such as a new and uncrowded airport, another group may believe to be a positive curse due to the noise. Utilitarianism provides no means of explaining why those who wish to travel should receive the benefits of the airport, while those who live in the flight path should pay the costs.

Utilitarianism does, however, provide a single principle, not a set of rules or a proposed condition for society, by which to judge the overall benefits of a decision or action for the full community. It is the first of the true single principles. It is also one of the principles that should not be omitted from moral reasoning for it would be hard to say that a given decision or action was "right" and "just" and "proper" if it did not result in greater benefits than harms for the society of which the decision maker was a part.

UNIVERSAL DUTIES

The ethical principle of Universal Duties can be summarized in two statements. Both, as you will soon see, are felt to have exactly the same meaning—you can't apply one to a moral problem without also applying the other—but the two formulations are thought to help in understanding the single principle. The first statement is, "Take no action that you would not be willing that others, faced with the same or an equivalent situation, should also take." The second statement is, "Treat each person as an end in himself or herself, worthy of dignity and respect, never as a means to your own ends."

Immanuel Kant (1724–1804) is one of the dominant figures in moral philosophy. He developed an ethical principle that is totally original, totally outside all earlier work, and—you will find—very useful in moral reasoning.

Kant follows Isaac Newton (1642–1727), and that sequence is essential in understanding the *Groundwork for the Metaphysics of Morals*. Newton had explained all earlier work in physics (which at that time was primarily based on astronomical observations as the building blocks of matter had not yet been discovered) with one elegantly simple formula on gravitational forces:

$$\text{Force} = G \; \frac{Mn \text{ (product of the masses of the objects)}}{R^2 \text{ (square of the distance between them)}}$$

Kant wanted to duplicate, for moral philosophy, the accomplishment of Isaac Newton in natural philosophy. He explains, in the introduction to *Groundwork for the Metaphysics of Morals*, that there are only two sets of laws in the world: natural philosophy or physics, which has determined the laws by which everything in the physical sphere does happen, and moral philosophy or ethics, which needs to determine the law by which everything in the human sphere ought to happen. He goes on to say that he will base his proposed law upon

EXHIBIT 4–5
Excerpts from the First Section of the *Groundwork for the Metaphysics of Morals*
Immanuel Kant

Nothing can possibly be conceived in the world, or even out of it, which can be called good without qualification except a good will. Intelligence, wit, judgment, and the other talents of the mind, however, they may be named, and courage, resolution, perseverance, the qualities of the temperament, are undoubtedly good and desirable in many respects; these gifts of nature may also become extremely bad and mischievous if the will which is to make use of them, and which, therefore constitutes what is called character, is not good.

It is the same with the gifts of fortune. Power, riches, honor, even health, and the general well-being and contentment with one's condition which is called happiness, inspire pride and often presumption if there is not a good will to correct the influence of these on the mind, and with this also to rectify the whole principle of acting and adapt it to its proper end.

There are even some qualities which are of service to this good will itself, and may facilitate its actions, yet which have no intrinsic unconditional value, but always presuppose a good will. This qualifies the esteem that we justly have for them, and does not permit us to regard them as absolutely good by themselves. Moderation in the affections and passions, self control, and calm deliberation are not only good in many respects, but even seem to constitute part of the intrinsic worth of the person; but they are far from deserving to be called good without qualification, although they have been so unconditionally praised by the ancients. For without the principle of a good will, these characteristics may become extremely bad. The coolness, self-control and calm deliberation of a villain not only makes him far more dangerous, but also directly makes him more abominable in our eyes than he would have been without those characteristics.

reason, not observation, and consequently his study will be the metaphysics, not the science, of ethics. Science, he believed, was based upon observations.

Despite that claim, the first section of *Groundwork* is based upon observations. He starts with a famous quotation: "Nothing can possibly be conceived in this world, or even out of it, which can be called good without qualification except a good will." What does he mean by "good will"? He never explains exactly in the first section, but you can translate the term as your personal intent, general wish, sense of duty, or feeling of obligation towards others. He then goes on to make four major claims:

1. All other characteristics—intelligence, judgment, courage, moderation, and self-control—are not good of and by themselves. A villain can be moderate and self-controlled in his villainy.

2. A person's will cannot be influenced or observed by others because it is

private. A person can act from good will, personal advantage, or sudden whim, and no one can tell the difference.

3. If a person's will cannot be observed, then how do we know if it is good? An action draws its moral worth not from the purpose which is unknown, nor from the result which is indefinite, but from the duty that is recognized.

4. Duty is the necessity of acting out of respect for the law; this is not national or natural law, but universal law. Duty, then, is never to act except when you could will that the maxim (rule) you are following could become a universal law.

In the first section, Kant derives the "can you will that the maxim you are following should become a universal law?" test of the moral worth of an action from observations of the ways in which people actually do act (from self-interest, momentary whim, or good will). In the second section, he attempts to determine the same universal law test from pure reason. He starts by observing that it is impossible to know whether people act out of good will or the other motives, and therefore it is possible to doubt the entire concept of morality. This is wrong, he says, for the question is not whether people decide based upon good will and therefore are moral, but whether they should do so. Then come four major steps in deriving the "can you will" test from reason, not experience:

1. Everything in nature works according to laws. (Remember Newton's formula for the actions of the universe.) Rational beings alone have the faculty to act according to an understanding of the principle of those laws.

2. Rational beings have a duty to act rationally; that is, they have a duty to follow a command of reason, or the principle derived from those laws. That command of reason can be termed an "imperative" because it is a duty.

3. Imperatives (commands of reason) can be divided into two different types: Hypothetical (a means to something else) and Categorical (complete in itself, without reference to any other end).

4. There is only one Categorical Imperative (a command of reason, complete in itself), and that is, "Act only on the maxim (rule) that you can at the same time will that it should become a universal law."

Kant has established that there is only one Categorical Imperative (a command of reason, complete in itself, without reference to another end), and that is, "Act only on the maxim that you can at the same time will that it should become a universal law." If you doubt this, try to think of another rule that does not lead to some further end in an ends-means-ends sequence. No one else has been able to do so, and therefore it is necessary to admit that Kant has accomplished part of his objective: he has identified a single universal rule based upon reason that can be used to evaluate individual decisions and actions. The question, however, is whether this rule will be accepted by all human beings. Kant reasons as follows:

EXHIBIT 4–6
Excerpts from the Second Section of the *Groundwork for the Metaphysics of Morals*
Immanuel Kant

Without being an enemy of virtue, a cool observer, one that does not mistake the wish for good, however lively, for its reality, may sometimes doubt whether true virtue is actually found anywhere in the world, and this especially as the years increase and the judgment is partly made wiser by experience, and partly also by more acuteness in observation. This being so, nothing can secure us from falling away altogether from our ideas of duty, or maintain in our souls a well-grounded respect for its law, but the clear conviction that although there may never have been action which really spring from such a pure source yet whether this or that takes place is not at all the question. The question is whether reason of itself, independent of all experience, should ordain what *ought* to take place.

---

1. If duty is to be a practical, unconditional necessity of action, it must hold for all human wills. The will focuses on the end that is desired, and if this end is assigned by reason alone, it must be accepted by all human beings.
2. Men and women exist as ends in themselves. So far this is just a subjective principle (applicable only to a single person), but because everyone has the same end, then it becomes an objective principle (applicable to everyone).
3. The result is the Second Formulation of the Categorical Imperative: "Act so as to treat humanity, whether in thine own person or in that of any other, in every case as an end, worthy of dignity and respect, never as a means only."

What are the problems with the use of Kant's Categorical Imperative in either of the formulations? There are two. Firstly, the Imperative provides no scale between actions. Acts are either morally "right" (yes, I can will that this maxim become a universal law) or morally "wrong" (no, I can't will that this maxim...). Secondly, the Imperative provides no comparison between wills. You can will one universal rule, and I can will another, but there is no way to decide between our two positions without starting to think about the consequences of those rules, which brings in a totally different means of moral reasoning.

What are the advantages of the use of the Categorical Imperative? It totally eliminates self-interest. If it is right for me to take this action (such as breaking an implied contract to provide health insurance to low- and middle-level management retirees), then it is right for everyone to take approximately the same action (break implied contracts). Do I want to live in a world in which implied contracts are worthless? No, I do not, and consequently if I cannot "will" that my action should become a universal law, then I should not take that action.

EXHIBIT 4–7
Excerpts from the Second Section of the *Groundwork for the Metaphysics of Morals*
Immanuel Kant

If then there is a supreme practical principle or, in respect of the human will, a categorical imperative, it must be one which, being drawn from the conception of that which is necessarily an end for everyone because it is an end in itself, constitutes an objective principle of will, and can therefore serve as a universal practical law. The foundation of this principle is: rational nature exists as an end in itself. Each individual necessarily conceives his own existence as being so; so far then this is a subjective principle of human actions (applicable only to a single person). But every other individual regards his existence similarly, just on the same rational principle that holds for me, so that the rational being as an end in itself is at the same time an objective principle (applicable to everyone) from which as a supreme practical law all laws of the will must be capable of being deduced. Accordingly, the practical imperative will be as follows: *So act as to treat humanity, whether in thine own person or in that of any other, in every case as an end withal, never as a means only.*

INDIVIDUAL RIGHTS

The principle of individual rights can be summarized in the statement that people obviously have rights, and that all that is necessary to achieve a decision that is "right" and "just" and "fair" in its impact upon others is to list and agree upon those rights, and then observe them. It is not necessary to search for the greatest good (Summum Bonum). It is not necessary to search for a universal duty (Categorical Imperative). It is only necessary to list the rights of the members of our society, and then ensure that the institutions of society recognize and observe those rights.

Do you have "rights?" You certainly do. Can you list those rights, and then get agreement with others on that listing? Here you probably will run into some difficulty. People have been trying to get agreement on the basic human rights since the time of Hobbes (1588–1679), but with limited success. Look at the wide range of alternative views that have been proposed:

Hobbes   You have a right to life; all of Hobbes is based upon this single very basic right.

Locke   You have a right to life, liberty, and property, provided there is enough property (primarily agricultural land) left over for others to have some too.

EXHIBIT 4–8
Excerpts from the *Declaration of Independence*
Thomas Jefferson

When, in the course of human events, it becomes necessary for one people to dissolve the political bands which have connected them with another, and to assume, among the powers of the earth, the separate and equal station to which the laws of nature and of nature's God entitle them, a decent respect for the opinions of mankind requires that they should declare the causes which impel them to the separation.

We hold these truths to be self-evident, that all men are created equal; that they are endowed by their Creator with certain unalienable rights; that among these are life, liberty, and the pursuit of happiness. That, to secure these rights governments are instituted among men, deriving their just powers from the consent of the governed; that, whenever any form of government becomes destructive of these ends, it is the right of the people to alter or to abolish it, and to institute a new government, laying its foundation on such principles, and organizing its power in such form, as to them shall seem most likely to effect their safety and happiness. Prudence, indeed, will dictate that governments long established should not be changed for light and transient causes and, accordingly, all experience had shown that mankind are more disposed to suffer, while evils are sufferable, than to right themselves by abolishing the forms to which they are accustomed. But, when a long train of abuses and usurpations, pursuing invariably the same object, evinces a design to reduce them under absolute despotism, it is their right, it is their duty, to throw off such government, and to provide new guards for their future security. Such has been the patient sufferance of these colonies, and such is now the necessity, which constrains them to alter their former systems of government. The history of the present King of Great Britain is a history of repeated injuries and usurpations, all having in direct object the establishment of an absolute tyranny over these states.

Declaration of Independence	Life, liberty, and the pursuit of happiness; remember that the author of the Declaration (Thomas Jefferson) was trained in the classics and knew the work of Bentham, so that you can translate "happiness" as either individual worth and the pursuit of excellence (Aristotle) or social benefit, advantage and well-being (Bentham). You should not, however, translate it as pleasure or satisfaction.
Bill of Rights of Constitution	Free exercise of religion, speech, communication, and assembly. Security against the seizure of home, person, papers. Protection against deprivation of life, liberty, or property without due process of law. Guaranteed a prompt and public trial by an impartial jury, together with the assistance of counsel.

EXHIBIT 4–9
The Bill of Rights of the U.S. Constitution

Article One. Congress shall make no law respecting an establishment of religion, or prohibiting the free exercise thereof; or abridging the freedom of speech, or of the press, or the right of the people peaceably to assemble, and to petition the Government for a redress of grievances.

Article Two. A well regulated militia being necessary to the security of a free State, the right of the people to keep and bear arms shall not be infringed.

Article Three. No soldier shall, in time of peace, be quartered in any house, without the consent of the owner, nor in time of war but in a manner to be prescribed by law.

Article Four. The right of the people to be secure in their persons, houses, papers, and effects, against unreasonable searches and seizures, shall not be violated, and no warrants shall issue but upon probable cause, supported by oath or affirmation, and particularly describing the place to be searched, and the person or things to be seized.

Article Five. No person shall be held to answer for a capital, or otherwise infamous crime, unless on a presentment of indictment of a Grand Jury, except in cases arising in the land or naval forces, or in the militia, when in actual service in time of war or public danger, nor shall any person be subject for the same offense to be twice put in jeopardy of life or limb, nor shall be compelled in any criminal trial to be a witness against himself, nor be deprived of life, liberty, or property, without due process of law; nor shall private property be taken for public use without just compensation.

Article Six. In all criminal prosecutions the accused shall enjoy the right to a speedy and public trial, by an impartial jury of the State and district wherein the crime shall have been committed, which district shall have been previously ascertained by law; and to be informed of the nature and cause of the accusation; to be confronted with the witnesses against him; to have compulsory process for obtaining witnesses in his favor; and to have the assistance of counsel for his defense.

Article Seven. In suits at common law, where the value of controversy shall exceed twenty dollars, the right of trial by jury shall be preserved, and no fact tried by a jury shall be otherwise reexamined in any court of the United States, than according to the rules of the common law.

Article Eight. Excessive bail shall not be required, nor excessive fines imposed, nor cruel and unusual punishments inflicted.

Article Nine. The enumeration in the Constitution of certain rights shall not be construed to deny or disparage others retained by the people.

Article Ten. The powers not delegated to the United States by the Constitution, nor prohibited by it to the States are reserved to the States respectively or to the people.

What is left out? These are all negative rights; they can be summarized as the right not to be treated in an arbitrary or capricious way. Even more, they are all negative rights vis-à-vis the government. Business firms, colleges and universities, or the other institutions in society can still treat you in an arbitrary or capricious way as long as they do not contravene an existing law or statute.

Further, you may have some positive rights as well. As a U.S. citizen or resident alien you certainly have the negative right not to be "deprived of life, liberty, or property without due process of law," but many people would be willing to argue that you also have the positive right to a minimal level of the food, clothing, shelter, and medical care necessary to support your life and make your liberty meaningful. An extensive listing of both negative and positive rights is contained in the *Universal Declaration of Human Rights* adopted by the General Assembly of the United Nations in 1948. The problem, of course, is that there has been little agreement upon or support for those rights since that adoption.

Can you use the ethical principle of individual rights in moral reasoning to determine what is "right," what is "just," what is "fair" in managerial decisions and actions? It is difficult. Firstly, there has never been agreement upon exactly what those rights are, except for the few that have been formally expressed and legally enforced in such national documents as the amendments to the U.S. Constitution.

Even more important, however, is the fact that the rights of stakeholders within a moral problem in management often seem to conflict. Owners have a "right" to an adequate return on capital; workers have a "right" to a decent wage; customers have a "right" to reasonable prices. These conflicts over rights can be seen even more clearly in the political area. Campaign contributors have a "right" to express their opinions through financial donations; individual voters have a "right" to elections that are not biased by huge advertising expenditures.

The ethical principle of individual rights is difficult to use in moral reasoning due to the lack of agreement upon the exact listing of those rights and the continual conflict between the holders of those rights. Still, the ethical principle remains meaningful. Examining the positive and negative rights of the individual impacted by a decision or action may not help to determine whether that decision or action is "right" and "just" and "fair," but the examination generally does help to clarify the issues for all of the participants.

This chapter has looked at four ethical principles: government requirements, utilitarian benefits, universal duties, and individual rights. These principles are not necessarily mutually supportive. They do not inevitably lead to the same conclusion. Just because a given decision or action is legal does not mean that it will also (1) result in the greatest net social benefit; nor (2) be of the type that we could will that everyone, faced with the same situation, should be free to take; nor (3) guarantee the negative and positive rights of the individuals and groups affected by the decision or action. Instead,

EXHIBIT 4–10
Excerpts from the Universal Declaration of Human Rights
General Assembly of the United Nations

Article 25. Everyone has the right to a standard of living adequate for the health and well-being of himself and of his family, including food, clothing, housing, medical care and the necessary social services, and everyone has the right to security in the event of unemployment, sickness, disability, widowhood, old age or other lack of livelihood in circumstances beyond his control.

Motherhood and childhood are entitled to special care and assistance. All children, whether born in or out of wedlock, shall enjoy the same social protection.

Article 26. Everyone has the right to education. Education shall be free, at least in the elementary and fundamental stages. Elementary education shall be compulsory. Technical and professional education shall be made generally available and higher education shall be equally accessible to all on the basis of merit.

Education shall be directed to the full development of the human personality and to the strengthening of respect for human rights and fundamental freedoms. It shall promote understanding, tolerance, and friendship among all nations, racial or religious groups, and shall further the activities of the United Nations for the maintenance of peace.

each principle provides a different perspective to judge the "rightness" of that decision or action, and consequently helps to decide what is "right," what is "just," what is "fair" in the decisions and actions of individuals and organizations.

ASSIGNMENT QUESTIONS

1. Read the excerpts from *Leviathan* (Thomas Hobbes) once again. Do you agree that people are generally equal in ability, and that consequently when they compete for gain or reputation, the competition can be destructive? What keeps that competition from being destructive?

2. Read the excerpts from *Second Treatise of Government* (John Locke) once again. Locke defines freedom as having "a standing rule to live by, common to every one of that society and made by the legislative power erected in it...." How would you define freedom?

3. Bentham and Mill are convinced that utilitarianism (a decision or action is "right" if it results in the greatest net social benefits of any alternative under consideration) provides the basic foundation for morality. List the advantages, and the disadvantages, of this ethical principle.

4. Kant believed that the Categorical Imperative (a decision or action is "right" if the decision maker could will that the maxim he or she is

following should become a universal law) provides a better foundation for morality. List the advantages, and the disadvantages, of this ethical principle.

5. As a U.S. citizen or resident alien you have certain rights guaranteed to you by the U.S. Constitution. List those rights which you think are important under current conditions (i.e., protection against the quartering of troops may no longer be crucial). What five additional rights, either positive or negative, do you think that you have?

6. One way to look at a business firm is that it consists of groups of "stakeholders"—customers, employees, suppliers, distributors, creditors, stockholders, local residents, and national citizens—each with certain rights. What "rights" do customers have? Employees? Suppliers? Stockholders? Be specific; what "rights" do you have as the passenger on an airline, or as a student at a university?

Case 4–1

CONFLICT OF DUTIES IN MARKETING

The managers of a business firm obviously have duties to their stockholders who are the owners of the company and benefited by its profits. The managers also have duties to their stakeholders who are the people associated with the company in some way and affected by its actions. These two sets of duties frequently come into conflict. One of the basic moral responsibilities of management is to resolve those conflicts in ways that can be considered to be "right" and "just" and "fair." How would you resolve the following five conflicts in the functional area of marketing; all of these actions were legal at the time they were proposed or considered:

1. Cash payments. Many of the large supermarket chains now demand substantial cash payments from their suppliers before agreeing to stock new products. These payments are called "stocking fees" or "shelving costs." Supermarket managers claim that they do not know whether a new consumer food product will be successful or not before they put it on their shelves, and consequently they want to be reimbursed for the expenses involved before they accept it for retail sale. The payments go to the chains (they are not bribes paid to the purchasing agents), but they are in addition to the price discounts that are standard in the food

distribution industry, and they are not small. Forty percent of the value of the first shipment is not uncommon. Large and well-financed suppliers such as Procter & Gamble or General Mills have no difficulty in making those payments, and they recover the amounts through somewhat higher consumer prices at the start. Small and entrepreneurial food products companies find it very difficult to pay the required amounts and are, in essence, shut out of the markets. Is it "right" for supermarket chains to charge stocking fees to large and small companies alike? What do the executives in those chains "owe" to their suppliers and customers?

2. Distributor changes. Many manufacturers of both consumer and industrial products are streamlining their operations and cutting costs in an attempt to meet foreign and domestic competition. Wholesale distribution is an obvious target for these cost-cutting efforts. Often, either as a result of a recent merger or acquisition that increased sales volume or following a review of the alternative transportation routes and means, a manufacturer will find that it is less costly to establish regional warehouses and then sell direct to retail stores and dealers rather than to rely any longer on wholesale distributors. Distributors usually have contracts with the manufacturers they represent that legally can be broken on 60 days notice "with or without cause." Distributors, however, generally claim that they have a lengthy history of cooperation with the manu-

facturer dating back 20, 30, or even 50 years, and that they had helped in the past to build up the business and expand the sales of the manufacturer, and should not be discarded so quickly now. Is it "right" for manufacturing firms to terminate a wholesaler who has performed well in the past just because it is less costly to sell direct today? What do the executives in those firms "owe" to their distributors?

3. Special discounts. Airlines and hotel chains have recently begun negotiating special rates for large corporations that are, of course, large users of their services. Special rates on the airlines for these customers are said to be 32 percent below the fares for the advance purchase coach tickets available to everyone else, though without the restrictions for advanced purchase or weekend stay overs that are applied to others. Special rates at the hotel chains for large corporate customers are said to be 22 percent less than those assigned to members of the general public. The reason for these special rates is clear; it is to compete for the business of the large corporations that account for 60 percent of all travel expenditures in the United States. Legally it is permissible for suppliers to offer special rates for goods or services to large corporations if it can be shown that those rates reflect economies of scale in providing the goods and services. Small business management associations and travel agency trade groups claim that those economies of scale do not

exist in air travel and hotel accommodations because the reservations are made and the services are provided for individuals or small groups, not for large numbers of people at one time, and that consequently the charges should be equal for all. Is it "right" for airlines and hotel chains to provide special low rates for their large customers that are not made available to small companies or the general public? What do the executives at these firms owe to smaller and less important customers?

4. Incomplete advertisements. Many insurance companies offer "guaranteed" life insurance to elderly persons through advertisements that feature well-known television personalities (Dick Van Dyke, Ed Asner, Art Linkletter, etc.). The advertisements stress the peace of mind that comes from having enough insurance to pay funeral expenses and leave a small inheritance to family members. The policies are said in the ads to be guaranteed because an applicant cannot be rejected because of age or illness and because the rates will not be increased over time. The advertisements do not explain that the rates for these guaranteed policies are 100 percent to 200 percent higher than the rates for people of equivalent age who do submit to medical exams to determine their fitness, and that no payments will be made for death during the first two years of coverage. Is it "right" for insurance companies to promote policies without full disclosure of comparative prices and "small-print" terms? What do the executives at these firms "owe" to older customers who are not as careful in detecting fraud or exploitation?

5. Inaccurate advertisements. Many television advertisements for consumer products are grossly inaccurate if not deliberately untruthful. Cold and flu remedies promise a "24-hour relief." Frozen food ads show colorful pictures of meals that have been prepared in a restaurant rather than taken from the package. Airline appeals portray passenger accommodations with much greater space across seats and between rows than is ever found on the actual commercial flights. Is it "right" for television and magazine ads to misrepresent the appearance or exaggerate the performance of their products? What do the executives at consumer product firms "owe" to their customers?

Case 4–2

APPLYING ALL 10 OF THE ETHICAL PRINCIPLES

An ethical principle is a statement of the most basic requirement for a "good" society. A "good" society, in turn, can be defined as one in which everyone cooperates for the benefit of all. People tend to cooperate for the benefit of others only when they believe that they have been treated in ways that they consider to have been "right" and "just" and "fair." Consequently, an ethical principle is a means of determining what is "right" and "just" and "fair" in the treatment of others, with the objective of leading towards a "good" or "better" or "just" society.

There are 10 ethical principles that are commonly used in management. Each principle provides a different perspective, a different way of looking at decisions and actions when some people associated with a business firm are to be hurt or harmed in some way outside of their own control. The usual managerial perspective is that of economic self-interest: which decision or action will yield the greatest profit for the firm? Somehow that perspective does not seem very satisfactory to those of us who are to be hurt or harmed in some way. We wish that the decision makers would look at the situation in a different light, from a different perspective, and see our self-interests as clearly as they see their own. That is the purpose of the ethical principles. If managers expect us to

enthusiastically cooperate in the future for the benefit of the firm, rather than just grudgingly assent to their actions, they must recognize our self-interests, and combine them into some concept of the common good.

The 10 ethical principles described in this text do not necessarily point to a single conclusion when applied to a moral problem. It is not even claimed in this text that the decision maker should inevitably take the decision or action indicated by a majority of the principles. Instead, the intent is to gain greater insight and understanding into the self-interests of others, and consequently into the decision or action that would balance the self-interests of all of the stakeholders into a coherent whole that can be considered to be "right" and "just" and "fair," and that will contribute to a concept of the common good for all.

Class Assignment

Here are three short moral problems in which some people will be hurt or harmed while others will be benefited or helped. Firstly, relying on your subjective moral standards and intuitive value judgments, decide quickly what you would do in each instance. Then apply all 10 of the objective ethical principles in sequence. That is, start with self-interests; what is in the long-term interests of the organization you represent? Next take up personal virtues. Can you be open and honest about this matter, and will you feel proud and courageous when people know what you plan to do? Continue through religious injunctions, government requirements, utilitarian benefits, etc., until you reach contributive liberty. See if you gain insight and understanding from this effort. Particularly see if you begin to change your mind about halfway through the process.

1. Selling Camel cigarettes. Each year 400,000 Americans die from illnesses (emphysema, throat and lung cancer, and heart disease) the Surgeon General claims are related to smoking cigarettes, and a million others quit, motivated doubtless by a fear of dying. The tobacco companies have attempted to adjust to this decline in their total market by focusing marketing efforts on the general population overseas (where health concerns seem not to be so prevalent) and by concentrating advertising appeals on younger smokers in the United States (whose health concerns seem not to be so dominant).

   R. J. Reynolds, one of the largest tobacco companies, has developed a cartoon character that has been very successful in both efforts. Joe Camel is portrayed in sunglasses, a drooping cigarette, and contemporary costumes as a "cool," "hip," or "smooth" character. Annual expenditures in support of Joe are said to be in excess of $75 million in the United States alone.

   Many critics say that the cartoon camel was designed to appeal to young nonsmokers and induce them to take up the habit. Studies have shown that Camel's share of the illegal under 18 smoker's market has grown to 33 percent, representing sales of $476 million per year, from 0.5 percent before the ad campaign began. Studies have also shown that Joe Camel is now recognized by children under 12 as frequently and as favorably as Mickey Mouse. The company disclaims any responsibility on both counts, and says that its ads were designed to appeal to "smokers 21-years old and older at home and abroad who are dissatisfied with their present brand choices."

   The American Cancer Society recently petitioned the Federal Trade Commission for a ruling that would outlaw the Joe Camel character or any other cartoon that appealed to children in support of harmful products. R. J. Reynolds objected strongly saying, "All we have done is to break through the sameness, the clutter, of cigarette advertising, with an appealing cartoon. You cannot penalize us for that." What would you decide if you were head of the Federal Trade Commission?

2. Protecting reproductive health. Lead and other heavy metals have a known and harmful effect upon the fetus if absorbed into the mother's body even in very minimal amounts prior to or during pregnancy. Companies with industrial processes that require the use of these heavy metals have normally taken the position that they would bar women of childbearing age from employment on the pro-

duction line. The problem, from the point of view of the women involved, was that those jobs tended to be highly skilled and highly paid. Most of the actual assembly work in these semihazardous industries has been automated in recent years, and consequently the employment opportunities now are in quality control, machine maintenance, and laboratory analysis.

Young women who started in nonhazardous work areas at entry-level pay would eventually find their way to promotion blocked because they were barred from those skilled positions. Johnson Controls, a major manufacturer of lead-acid batteries for automobiles, required evidence of surgical sterilization before women under age 55 could be employed in the areas where those batteries were made. Offended by that company rule, and encouraged by other sex discrimination cases, a group of female employees at Johnson Controls sued the company, and won. The Supreme Court in 1991 ruled that employers could not bar women of childbearing age from certain jobs because of the potential risk to a possible fetus. "Women as capable of doing their jobs as their male counterparts may not be forced to choose between having a child and having a job," the high court said in an opinion written by Justice Harry Blackmun [*The Wall Street Journal*, March 21, 1991, p. B1].

Justice Blackmun tried to reassure business firms by saying, "If an employer fully informs the woman of the risk and the employer has not acted negligently, the basis for holding an employer liable seems remote at best" (Ibid., p. B1). Companies, however, were not reassured. The question of legal liability, it was felt, would gradually evolve about the definitions of "acting negligently" and "informing fully."

The Occupational Safety and Health Administration (OSHA) had no standards for permissible exposure of heavy metals to a fetus, and it was expected that the government would take at least three to five years to develop those standards, which could then be applied retroactively. In the meantime, if a child were born with birth defects to a worker exposed as part of her job to heavy metals, even if the worker had insisted upon that job as one of her legal rights, it was thought probable that a jury would view the situation with considerable sympathy and grant a very substantial award.

Further, even if a woman acknowledged that she had been duly warned about the general dangers, she could still claim that she had not been told about any specific defect that might occur. And, the child in later years could sue for damages, claiming that he or she had not been able to participate in the original decision affecting his or her rights and health.

Assume that you are the manager of the lead-acid battery division of Johnson Controls. Assume that this is a very competitive industry, with heavy overseas competition, but that your division has remained profitable until now due to extensive investments in factory automation. Assume that 3,000 people are employed at three plants; currently, only 15 percent are women of childbearing age (who work in secretarial positions and shipping, segregated from the production processes), but that percentage and the subsequent exposure can be expected to increase rapidly with the recent Supreme Court ruling. Assume that you believe your present production processes to be safe; you currently monitor the level of lead in the bloodstream of all workers, male and female, and that this level is well below existing OSHA standards. Assume that you have no data on the probability of harm to a fetus associated with those existing standards, and that you can probably not get that data due to the prior exclusion of women from the relevant work force. Assume lastly that you have only three choices:

- Close all three plants and shift all manufacturing overseas where legal claims for reproductive health would be minimal at best, and probably not recognized by the courts. There would be charges against company earnings for closing the plants, and greatly increased expenses for transportation and communication, but profits over the long-term could be expected to increase about 25 percent due to lower wage rates.

- Continue to operate all three plants at present locations with present safety standards. Attempt to quickly move women

who become pregnant to nonhazardous jobs, and gather data on the incidence of birth defects. Profits would neither increase nor decrease until legal suits were won or lost in court, and even then the chances of birth defects and the costs of settlements might be less than currently feared.

- Continue to operate all three plants at present locations, but with greatly heightened safety standards. Adopt the "clean room" technology of the electronics industry, with zero tolerance for lead in the bloodstream. Clean room technology is expensive, however, and profits could be expected to decrease 60 percent to 75 percent even with substantial wage concessions negotiated with the workers.

3. Cutting old growth timber. The trees in the original forests of the Pacific Northwest were huge, 5' to 12' in diameter, and hundreds of feet high. The wood, because of the tight grain and the limited number of knots, was considered to be very desirable for construction, and lumber from the region was shipped throughout the world starting in about 1870.

By 1990, after 120 years of the utilization and exploitation of this natural resource, 85 percent of the "old growth" forests had been cut. Fifteen percent of the huge old trees remained, primarily in isolated patches in remote locations, generally owned by the U.S. Forest Service. The old growth timber on private lands had largely been cut years earlier.

The ownership of timberland in the Pacific Northwest has traditionally been split approximately evenly between the federal government and private firms. The trees on any specific site in the original forest, regardless of ownership, were generally clear-cut rather than selectively logged because they tended to be from a single species and of a single age. Replanting was seldom practiced until the 1960s; instead cutover land was allowed to gradually "seed in" over time.

The result of these short-sighted forestry practices was that, except for a few very large private firms such as Weyerhaeuser, Georgia Pacific, and Boise-Cascade that had begun reforestation efforts early in their histories, there was an increasing shortage of trees to be cut, milled, and shipped by the mid-1980s.

That shortage was exacerbated in 1990 with the Spotted Owl ruling. The Northern Spotted Owl, a bird that lives only in the old growth forests of the Pacific Northwest, was placed on the endangered species list by the U.S. Fish and Wildlife Service. The U.S. Forest Service is required by law to "retain viable populations of all native and desired vertebrae species," and consequently a number of environmental groups jointly sued the Forest Service, and forced them to set aside most of the remaining blocks of old growth timber as a refuge for the birds.

As explained previously, only 15 percent of the original old growth forest is left, and that may seem to be a fairly small amount, but it was the basic timber supply that had been counted upon to run the sawmills and plywood mills of the West Coast for the next 20 years, until the second growth forest matured and became ready for harvesting. The consequences of the "set aside" were immediate and severe:

1. Local jobs. Immediately, 13,000 jobs were eliminated, and it was estimated that 20,000 jobs would be lost by the end of the decade. These jobs were in the woods, cutting the mature trees and driving the logging trucks, and in the mills, producing lumber and plywood. These jobs were tough, hard, and highly paid; a way of life ended with the employment.

2. Area towns. For every job that was lost in the woods and mills, another 1.3 jobs would be lost in the small rural towns close to the mills. These additional jobs were in the retail stores, service firms, and public agencies such as schools. It was thought that many of the rural towns in Washington and Oregon would simply cease to exist.

3. Government revenues. The U.S. Forest Service sells the timber on public lands by a competitive bidding process; it was estimated that the loss in income from their inability to sell the old growth timber would be $150 million per year immediately, and $250 million per year by the end of the decade. The total loss was estimated at $4 billion.

4. Timber exports. Some of the lumber from the old growth timber had been shipped abroad, primarily to Japan, where the tight grain and absence of knots made it particularly prized and highly valued. Exports of high-grade forest products generate about $200 million per year, and help to correct the adverse balance of trade with Pacific Rim countries.

5. Lumber prices. Construction-grade forest products are a commodity, with prices that are set by supply and demand. The demand side has been lower than normal since 1990, with a severe recession in the housing industry. Any pickup in that industry is expected to result in a 30 percent to 50 percent increase in lumber prices, making housing even less affordable.

6. Environmental and recreational activists. Many people active in environmental and recreational groups acknowledge the adverse economic impacts of the ban on logging in old growth forests, but they are adamant that it is necessary to preserve most if not all of what is left. The old growth forests are awesome, in their opinion, and support a unique ecosystem.

Assume that you are in the position in the U.S. government, perhaps as Secretary of the Interior, that will have to decide upon this "owls versus people" controversy. The law on endangered species does permit economic impacts to be taken into consideration, so that you are not totally bound by the prior court ruling. Assume further that the obvious compromises, such as cutting half the old growth timber and keeping the other half, are opposed strongly by both sides, though that does not mean that these compromises are automatically wrong. What, in your mind, is the "right" thing to do?

Case 4–3

SUSAN SHAPIRO

Susan Shapiro had an undergraduate degree in Chemistry from Smith College, a master's degree in Chemical Engineering from M.I.T., three years' service as a sergeant in the Israeli army, and an MBA from the University of Michigan. The following is a nearly verbatim account of her experiences during the first month of employment with a large chemical company in New York.

We spent about three weeks in New York City, being told about the structure of the company and the uses of the products, and then they took us down to Baton Rouge to look at a chemical plant. You realize that most of the MBAs who go to work for a chemical company have very little knowledge of chemistry. There were 28 of us who started in the training program that year, and the others generally had undergraduate degrees in engineering or economics. I don't know what you learn by looking at a chemical plant, but they flew us down South, put us up at a Holiday Inn, and took us on a tour of their plant the next day.

As part of the tour, we were taken into a drying shed where an intermediate chemical product was being washed with benzine and then dried. The cake was dumped in a rotating screen and sprayed with benzine, which was then partially recovered by a vacuum box under the screen. However, the vacuum box technology is out of date now, and never did work very well. Much of the solvent evaporated within the shed, and the atmosphere was heavy with the fumes despite the "open air" type of construction.

Benzine is a known carcinogen; there is a direct, statistically valid correlation between benzine and leukemia and birth defects. The federal standard is 10 parts per million, and a lab director would get upset if you let the concentration get near 100 parts for more than a few minutes, but in the drying shed it was over 1,000. The air was humid with the vapor, and the eyes of the men who were working in the area were watering. I was glad to get out, and we were only in the drying shed about three minutes.

I told the foreman who was showing us around—he was a big, burly man with probably 30 years' experience—that the conditions in the shed were dangerous to the health of the men working there, but he told me, "Lady, don't worry about it. That is a sign-on-job (a job to which newly hired employees are assigned until they build up their seniority so that they can transfer to more desirable work). We've all done it, and it hasn't hurt any of us."

That night, back at the motel, I went up to the director of personnel who was in charge of the training program and told him about the situation. He was more willing to listen than the foreman, but he said essentially the same thing. "Susan, you can't change the company in the first month. Wait awhile; understand the problems, but don't be a troublemaker right at the start."

The next morning everybody else flew back to New York City. I stayed in Baton Rouge and went to see the plant manager. I got to his office by 8:00, and explained to his secretary why I wanted to see him. He was already there, at work, and he came out to say that he was "up against it that morning" and had no time to meet with me. I said, "Fine, I'll wait."

I did wait, until after lunchtime. Then he came up to me and said he didn't want to keep tripping over me every time he went in and came out of his office, and if I would just go away for awhile, he would promise to see me between 4:30 and 5:00.

It was 5:15 when he invited me to "come in and explain what has you so hot and bothered." I told him. He said that he certainly knew what I was talking about, and that every year he put a capital request into the budget to fix the problem, but that it always came back rejected—"probably by some MBA staff type" were his words—because the project could not show an adequate return on investment, and because the present process was technically "open air" and therefore not contrary to OSHA regulations.

I started to explain that OSHA never seemed to know what it was doing—which is true, in my opinion. But he stopped me. He said that he was leaving to pick up his family because his daughter was playing in a Little League baseball game at 6:30, and then they would have supper at McDonald's. He said I could go along, if I didn't mind sitting next to his five-year-old son "who held the world's record for the number of consecutive times he has spilled his milk in a restaurant." He was a very decent man, working for a very indecent company. I told him I would go back to New York, and see what I could do. He did wish me "good luck," but he also asked me not to get him per-

sonally involved because he thought that "insisting upon funding for a project that won't meet targeted rates of return is a sure-fire way to be shown the door marked exit in large black letters."

Class Assignment

What would you do in this situation? Make a set of specific recommendations for Susan Shapiro.

Case 4–4

COMPARATIVE SALARIES IN THE UNITED STATES

The income distribution within the United States is changing. Over the period 1977 to 1988, families in the first eight deciles (each decile represents 10 percent of the population) suffered a decrease in average family income adjusted for inflation; families in the top two deciles received an increase. Families in the top 5 percent and top 1 percent recorded very substantial increases, as shown in Exhibit 1.

Salaries, bonuses, and commissions for sports stars, entertainment figures, investment bankers, and senior executives, most of whom are members of the top decile if not the top 5 percent or 1 percent, expanded rapidly during the period 1977 to 1988. Total incomes for representatives from each of those groups are shown in Exhibit 2.

The incomes reported for sports stars and entertainment figures are estimates, prepared by persons who are knowledgeable about those two industries. The incomes for investment

bankers also are estimates, as only the amounts paid to the managing partners of publicly held firms must be disclosed. It is said, however, that successful bond traders and merger/acquisition specialists on Wall Street can easily make $5,000,000 to $10,000,000 per year, an amount that seemed to be confirmed when a 25-year-old stock-dividend trader named Alphonse Fletcher sued Kidder Peabody and Company, claiming that he had received less than half of the $6,500,000 he was owed for his work in 1990 (*The Wall Street Journal*, July 30, 1991, p. C1). Even larger amounts are occasionally paid in the brokerage industry; it is acknowledged that Michael Milken received $550,000,000 in 1987 and $200,000,000 in 1988 from Drexel Burnham Lambert for the sale of "junk" bonds.

The incomes reported in Exhibit 2 for senior business executives are reasonably exact. Those payments must

EXHIBIT 1   Income Gains and Losses over the Period 1977 to 1988 in 1987 dollars.

Income Decile	Average Income 1977	Average Income 1988	Dollar Change	Percentage Change
First	$4,113	$3,504	−$609	−14.8%
Second	8,334	7,669	−665	−8.0
Third	13,140	12,327	−813	−6.2
Fourth	18,436	17,212	−1,216	−6.6
Fifth	23,896	22,389	−1,507	−6.3
Sixth	29,824	28,205	−1,619	−5.4
Seventh	36,405	34,828	−1,577	−4.3
Eighth	44,350	43,507	−798	−1.8
Ninth	55,487	56,064	+577	+1.0
Tenth	102,722	119,635	+16,912	+16.5
Top 5%	134,543	166,016	+31,473	+23.4
Top 1%	270,053	404,566	+134,513	+49.8
All families	33,527	34,274	747	+2.2

SOURCE: Phillips, *Politics of Rich and Poor*, 1990, p 17.

be disclosed in the formal reports called "10Ks" filed with the Securities and Exchange Commission by all publicly held firms. Despite this formal reporting requirement, however, the actual amounts received by the executives do vary both above and below the figures that are listed. There are a number of reasons for this variation:

1. Reported incomes are for one year only. In some instances the figures represent a "spike" in the level of income above that which had been received in the past and probably beyond that which will be received in the future. For example, Mr. Frank Wells, president of Walt Disney, Inc., received $50,900,000 in 1989, far beyond the $9,600,000 received by Mr. Michael Eisner, chairman of the same company in the same year. Mr. Wells, however, was not on the list of highest paid executives in either 1988 or 1990, while Mr. Eisner did make that list in both years, with $40,100,000 received in 1988 and $11,200,000 in 1990 [*Business Week,* May 1, 1989, p. 46; May 7, 1990, p 56; and May 6, 1991, p. 90].

Other figures represent the continuation of a trend in payments. Mr. Paul Firman, chairman of Reebok International, received $13,100,000 in 1986, $15,400,000 in 1987, $11,400,000 in 1988, $14,600,000 in 1989, and $14,800,000 in 1990 for a five-year total of $69,300,000 [*Business Week,* 1991, p. 90]. Still other figures are much lower than actually due under the employment contract for a given year because some of the payment was delayed until a subsequent year. Mr. Steven Ross, chairman of Time Warner,

EXHIBIT 2   Reported Incomes for Various Persons and Occupations during 1989

Evander Holyfield, heavyweight boxing champ[a]	$60,500,000
Frank Wells, president of Walt Disney, Inc.[b]	50,900,000
Steven Spielberg, motion picture producer[b]	50,000,000
Oprah Winfrey, talk show host[c]	38,000,000
Steven Ross, chairman of Time Warner, Inc.[b]	34,200,000
Mike Tyson, prior heavyweight boxing champ.[a]	31,500,000
Jack Nicholson, motion picture actor[d]	30,000,000
Madonna Ciccone, rock music singer[e]	23,000,000
Donald Pels, chairman of Lin Broadcasting[b]	22,800,000
Jim Manzi, chairman of Lotus Development[b]	16,363,000
Michael Jordan, basketball player in Chicago[a]	16,000,000
Paul Firman, chairman of Reebok Inter.[b]	14,600,000
George Foreman, prior heavyweight box. champ.[a]	14,500,000
Ayrton Senna, race car driver[a]	13,000,000
Martin Davis, chairman of Paramount Pictures[b]	10,600,000
Robert Goizuela, chairman of Coca-Cola[b]	10,800,000
Michael Eisner, chairman of Walt Disney, Inc.[b]	9,600,000
Arnold Palmer, golf player and course designer[a]	9,300,000
William McGowan, chairman of MCI[b]	8,600,000
Paul McCartney, singer & former Beatle[f]	8,500,000
James Moffet, chairman of Freeport McMoRan[b]	7,400,000
Rand Araskog, chairman of ITT Corp.[g]	7,300,000
Larry Bird, basketball player in Boston[a]	7,200,000
Donald Peterson, chairman of Ford Motor Co.[b]	7,100,000
Roy Vagelos, chairman of Merck, Inc.[b]	6,800,000
Michael Blumenthal, chairman of Unisys[b]	6,500,000
Paula Porizkova, fashion model[f]	6,000,000
David Stern, commissioner of the NBA[b]	5,500,000
Parker Gilbert, chairman of Morgan Stanley[b]	5,400,000
Harry Merlo, chairman of Louisiana-Pacific[b]	5,300,000
Robert Greenhill, vice chairman of Morgan Stanley[b]	5,100,000
Reuben Mark, chairman of Colgate Palmolive[b]	5,000,000
Robert Pfeiffer, chairman of Alexander & Bald.[b]	4,900,000
William Stirtz, chairman of Ralston Purina[b]	4,800,000
Lee Iacocca, chairman of Chrysler Corp.[h]	4,300,000
Patrick Ewing, basketball player in New York[a]	3,600,000
Robin Yount, baseball player in Milwaukee[i]	3,200,000
Isiah Thomas, basketball player in Detroit[i]	2,300,000
Average compensation for 708 senior executives in *Business Week* annual survey for 1989[b]	2,100,000

EXHIBIT 2   Continued

Alan Trammel, baseball player in Detroit[i]	$1,800,000
William Butcher, chairman of Chase Manhattan[b]	1,600,000
Nolan Ryan, baseball player in Texas[i]	1,400,000
Martina Navratilova, tennis player[i]	1,300,000
Douglas Whitwam, chairman of Whirlpool, Inc.[b]	1,100,000
Cathleen Black, publisher of USA Today[j]	600,000
Gary Trudeau, cartoonist of *Doonesbury*[c]	500,000
Walter Mattson, president of *New York Times*[b]	472,000
Orthopedic surgeon, national average[k]	300,000
George Bush, president of the United States[b]	239,000
General surgeon, national average[k]	227,000
Lane Kirkland, president of AFL-CIO[l]	175,000
Attorney in Manhattan, 7 years exper., local average[m]	171,000
James Duderstadt, president of the Univ. of Michigan[n]	163,000
Professor (full) of surgery, Univ. of Michigan[n]	137,000
Mario Cuomo, governor of State of New York[h]	130,000
David Dinkins, mayor of City of New York[h]	130,000
U.S. Senator, salary plus maximum honoraria[b]	125,000
General practitioner M.D., national average[k]	112,000
Justice, U.S. Supreme Court[o]	110,000
Basketball player in NBA, minimum salary[i]	110,000
Richard Cheney, secretary of defense[o]	99,500
Owen Bieber, president of U.A.W.[p]	92,000
Professor (full) of Business, Univ. of Michigan[n]	90,000
Judge of Federal District Court[q]	89,500
Professor (full) of English Literature, Univ. of Mich.[n]	58,000
Public Accountant, 10 years' experience, average[r]	57,200
Harvard MBA, starting salary[s]	57,000
Local TV News Anchor, national average[i]	52,300
Michigan MBA, starting salary[t]	48,300
Police Lieutenant, Ann Arbor, 15 years experience[u]	42,000
Police Officer, Ann Arbor, 1 year experience[u]	28,500
Drug dependency therapist, Ann Arbor, 5 years experience[u]	25,200
Registered nurse, Ann Arbor, starting salary[u]	24,600
Elementary school teacher, Ann Arbor, starting salary[u]	23,000
Refuse collector, Ann Arbor, 10 years experience[u]	22,000
Restaurant cook, Ann Arbor, 5 years experience[v]	20,000
Data entry clerk, Ann Arbor, starting salary[v]	18,500
Restaurant waitstaff, Ann Arbor, including tips[v]	17,800

(continued)

EXHIBIT 2   Concluded

Toxicologist, Ecology Center of Ann Arbor[u]	$16,500
Counselor for homeless teens, Ann Arbor[u]	15,000
Bank teller, Ann Arbor, starting salary[v]	11,000
Restaurant dishwasher, Ann Arbor[v]	11,000
Preschool teacher, Ann Arbor[v]	10,000

SOURCES:
[a] *Ann Arbor News,* August 5, 1991, p. 1.
[b] *Business Week,* May 7, 1990, p. 57f.
[c] *Parade Magazine,* June 23, 1991, p. 4f.
[d] *Detroit Free Press,* May 5, 1990, p. B1.
[e] *Adweek,* May 8, 1989, p 52f.
[g] *The Wall Street Journal,* June 21, 1991, p. B1.
[h] *New York Times,* April 13, 1990, p. 19.
[i] *Adweek,* May 7, 1990, p. 28f.
[j] *Newsweek,* October 15, 1990, p. 62.
[k] Socioeconomic Monitoring System of the AMA, 1990, p. 47.
[l] AFL-CIO Constitution, 1989, p. 23.
[m] *New York Law Journal,* February 26, 1990, p. 1.
[n] Faculty & Staff Salary Record, University of Michigan, 1989.
[o] *Congressional Quarterly,* February 11, 1989, p. 32.
[p] Constitution of the International Union, U.A.W., 1989.
[q] *U.S. News and World Report,* April 3, 1989, p. 32.
[r] *Managerial Accounting,* May 1990, p. 18f.
[s] *Harvard Business School Recruiting Guide,* 1990, p. 2.
[t] *Michigan MBA Placement Report,* 1989, p. 1.
[u] Telephone call to Department of Personnel, Ann Arbor, 1991.
[v] Telephone call to employing organizations, 1991.

for example, would have received a record compensation of $109,000,000 for 1989 had not all but the reported $34,200,000 been paid 10 days into 1990 [Business Week, 1990, p. 56].

2. Reported incomes include salaries and bonuses but not capital gains from stock options and stock grants except in the year that those capital gains are realized. A stock option gives an executive the right to purchase a given number of shares at a given price at a given time in the future; a stock grant gives the executive the immediate ownership of those shares, generally at no cost to the executive. Stock grants, however, are usually restricted; the shares cannot be sold until a given time in the future. Capital gains from the sale of stock options and stock grants are reported to the SEC only in the year when the shares are sold and the capital gains realized. Mr. Donald Pels, Chairman of Lin Broadcasting Company, for example, had a reported income of $22,800,000 in 1989; that amount is shown in Exhibit 2. Two months later he, received $186,200,000 for stock options awarded in the previous year but exercised in 1990 [Business Week, May 7, 1990, p. 56].

3. Reported incomes may deliberately be understated by the companies involved. The salaries, bonuses, and capital gains from stock options and stock grants received by

senior executives have irritated some stockholders and public officials with the result, it is claimed, that many companies attempt to reduce the amount that is formally reported to the SEC. For example, the income of Mr. Rand Araskog, chairman of ITT Corporation, was reported at $7,200,000 for 1989. At the stockholders meeting it was explained after extended questioning that the actual amount paid was $11,400,000. The difference was $4,200,000 of restricted stock that was given to him in that year but could not be sold until 1993, plus $1,400,000 that was due in 1989 but paid in 1990, less $1,200,000 in restricted stock that was given in 1988 and sold in 1989 [*Wall Street Journal,* June 21, 1991, p. B1].

4. Reported incomes do not include expense accounts. Expenses do not have to be included in the amounts reported to the SEC and are usually disclosed only when a company is forced to file for bankruptcy. Mr. James Stewart, chairman of Lone Star Industries, was found to have been reimbursed $2,900,000 for travel and entertainment expenses in 1989 after Lone Star (a cement company) entered Chapter 11 [*Business Week,* December 24, 1990, p. 25]. Mr. David Paul, chairman of CenTrust Savings Bank, was found to have charged $515,000 for insurance premiums and $363,000 for personal bodyguards to the bank, to have had the exclusive use of a $7,000,000 yacht owned by the bank, and to have had the bank pay $29,000,000 for European paintings that he hung in his home. These expenses were disclosed after the

bank was seized by federal regulators [*USA Today,* May 31, 1991, p. 1].

The salaries, bonuses, stock options, stock grants and expense accounts are supported by many people who claim that senior executives have to be well paid because they hold stewardship of billions of dollars worth of assets for their stockholders.

> If Oprah Winfrey is worth $38,000,000 for talking, and Jack Nicholson is worth $30,000,000 for acting, and Madonna is worth $23,000,000 for wearing a torpedo bra and being a "boy toy," surely Dr. Vagelos is worth $6,800,000 for managing $8 billion in assets and 37,000 employees at Merck and Company [Verbal statement of compensation consultant].

Others who support the salaries, bonuses, stock options, and stock grants say that it is necessary to compensate senior executives for exceptional performance. They generally cite four of the persons near the top of the annual listing (Exhibit 2) for reported incomes:

- Mr. Michael Eisner, chairman of Walt Disney, received $60,900,000 between 1987 and 1989, and Mr. Frank Wells, president of the same company, received $50,900,000 in 1989. The earnings at Walt Disney increased from $0.15 per share in 1986 to $6.20 per share in 1990.

- Mr. Robert Goizuela, chairman of Coca-Cola, received $10,800,000 in 1989. The earnings of Coca-Cola increased from $0.88 per share in 1985 to $2.04 per share in 1990.

- Dr. Roy Vagelos, chairman of Merck, received $6,800,000 in 1989. The earnings of Merck increased from $1.20 per share in 1985 to $4.56 per share in 1990.

Lastly, those who support the present system of salaries, bonuses, and capital gains say that it is necessary to pay large amounts to keep skilled executives. "They would leave for other companies if they were not well paid" is a frequent comment.

"Not so," respond those who oppose the present system. "You can't move from an entertainment firm to an automobile company anyway, because the conditions are so different, and even more to the point if the senior executives of a company don't show any loyalty to that company, who will?" The opponents then go on to cite the very substantial increases in senior executive compensation that have occurred over the past few decades relative to other occupations:

- In 1960, at the virtual height of what was to be the American century, the U.S. businessman stood as a leader in the world. He commanded vast respect and sometimes fear from his global competitors. For this premium performance, the big company CEO got premium pay. On average, he drew down a $190,383 paycheck—41 times the average pay of the factory worker, 38 times the $4,995 made by the average school teacher, and 29 times [that of] the engineer.
- That gap has widened dramatically. In 1988, the CEO's record $2,025,484 compensation was 98 times an average factory worker's $21,725, 72

times a teacher's $28,008, and 44 times an engineer's $45,680 [*Business Week*, May 1, 1989, p. 46].

The opponents add that the income of senior executives is often totally unrelated to performance. They cite three very different executives from the "best paid" listing:

- Mr. Michael Blumenthal, chairman of Unisys, received $6,500,000 in 1989 and $12,486,000 for the previous three years [*Business Week*, May 7, 1990, p. 59]. Earnings at Unisys declined from $3.15 in 1987 to a deficit of $3.45 in 1990, and the stock price went, over the same period, from $60.00 per share to $4.50 per share.
- Mr. Rand Araskog, chairman of ITT Corporation, received either $7,300,000 (reported to the SEC) or $11,400,000 (admitted to the stockholders) in 1989. The earnings of ITT went from $7.20 in 1987 to only $8.06 in 1990, and the stock price remained constant over that period at $60.00 per share.
- Mr. Lee Iacocca, chairman of Chrysler, received $4,300,000 in 1989 and $61,900,000 for the previous nine years [*Business Week*, May 7, 1990, p. 60]. Mr. Iacocca had joined Chrysler in 1980 when it was nearly bankrupt and had worked for the first two years at a token salary. Earnings at Chrysler, however, had been going down since 1986, losses had been steady since 1990, and the stock price had declined from $48.00 to $5.50 over that same period.

Large payments to automobile executives, including of course Mr. Iacocca, have long irritated Mr. Owen

Bieber, president of the United Auto Workers, who calls them "annual executive pigouts":

> On the one hand the executives say that intense foreign competition requires sacrifice, restraint, and discipline.... Yet, they then turn around and demonstrate none of those qualities by awarding themselves more personal compensation for a year's effort than could be spent in several lifetimes. [Statement by Mr. Bieber, quoted in *Business Week*, May 1, 1991, p. 49].

Union activists also complain that the performance bonus plans for senior executives are not only far larger but also much more stable than those for the lower-level employees:

> At General Motors, former Chairman Roger B. Smith's annual bonus last year fell 7 percent to $1.4 million in response to a 13 percent profit slide; profit sharing paid to hourly and lower-level salaried workers fell 81 percent to $50 per person. The higher-level bonuses are based on overall corporate results, a spokesperson explained, while lower-level profit sharing is based only on the less profitable North American automotive operations [*The Wall Street Journal*, November 8, 1991, p. B1].

Finally, the opponents of the current compensation system explain that senior executives in American firms receive six to eight times as much as their counterparts in Japan and Europe. In Japan, for example, the chief executive officer of a major corporation would be paid approximately $350,000 per year; in Germany about $250,000.

Class Assignment

Are the amounts listed in Exhibit 2 "fair" and "just" and "proper" in your opinion? Why? What reasons would you use to support your judgment?

1. How has this situation come about? What are the reasons for the larger incomes that are listed on the first page of Exhibit 2? Think in terms of the entertainment figures, sports stars, and business executives.

2. Suppose you were an adviser to the Japanese or German governments. Would you recommend that they adopt the American system of executive compensation? What system would you recommend that they adopt?

Case 4–5

FORD VERSUS GREENPEACE IN THE UNITED KINGDOM

Greenpeace is an organization that historically has been dedicated to the

SOURCE: Based on "Ford Versus Greenpeace in the United Kingdom" prepared by Prof. H. Lewis Gabel of the European Institute for Management.

energetic protection of the global environment. It began in 1971 when a group of Americans and Canadians chartered a boat, which they christened *Greenpeace*, to stage a protest against a planned U.S. nuclear test on the Alaskan island of Amchitka. The protest was successful, the test was canceled, and the members of that early organization went on to stage other protests throughout the world. Targets included the testing of nuclear weapons in the Pacific, the killing of whales and seals in the Arctic, and the dumping of nuclear waste materials at sea. Greenpeace achieved worldwide name recognition in 1985 when one of its ships, the *Rainbow Warrior*, on a mission to oppose French nuclear testing, was bombed and sunk by the French secret service.

By 1988 Greenpeace had 35 offices in 20 countries throughout the world, with 375 paid employees, 2,000,000 enrolled members, and more than 40 ongoing protests. Several characteristics defined the "style" of these protests:

Aggressive. Greenpeace strove to develop a radical, hard-line, in-your-face approach to environmental issues. It was very suspicious of "deals" with governments and businesses and would often refuse to accept verbal declarations of intent without some supporting action. Indeed, Greenpeace thrived on conflict and claimed not to be awed by authority. "In the spectrum of environmental groups, Greenpeace is on the radical edge because of the uncompromising stands it takes," said one of its supporters.

Forthright. Greenpeace also strove to dramatize environmental issues, with limited regard to prevailing standards of courtesy or "good taste." A famous antifur television campaign in 1984 showed a fashion model carrying a fur coat which dripped copious amounts of blood across the floor. Below was the caption, "It takes up to forty dumb animals to make a fur coat but only one to wear it." This ad was one of the few Greenpeace television campaigns ever to be canceled; this was done not in response to protests from fur merchants but after complaints by Inuit Eskimos who depended upon the fur trade for part of their livelihood.

Innovative. Greenpeace continually sought different ways to bring its campaigns to public attention through the use of the media. It quickly learned that spectacular stunts were much more likely to be filmed, and shown on the evening news or the front page, than more mundane rallies and marches. Greenpeace was a nonviolent organization, but its protests sometimes broke the law and often involved physical danger to the protesters. Examples included hanging banners from tall smokestacks, swimming in the path of toxic waste ships, or using small speed boats to harass the hunting of whales at sea. The ads produced by Greenpeace also tended to be memorable, as in the antifur commercial, and generally attempted to hone in on the weakest spot of their opponent's position.

Independent. Greenpeace raised money through public donations, membership fees, and the sale of merchandise such as T-shirts. It remained separate from political parties (including the well-known Green parties of Europe), though it did occasionally join with other environmental groups when, for example, international petitions were being signed. The separation from the political process, the large membership list, and the multiple fund sources meant that Greenpeace could not be influenced by any threat to cut off protest funding.

Group oriented. Although many of the campaign leaders were certainly charismatic persons, they tended to keep a low profile away from the protests and the cameras. Greenpeace preferred the collective strength of dedicated national groups to reliance upon a few world-famous individuals.

The group in the United Kingdom began when four people established an office in London in 1977. This office grew very quickly and by 1988 there were 45 paid employees plus an average of 10 volunteers at any given time who helped out with administrative tasks such as responding to letters. The 1988 budget was about £5 million.

The U.K. office occupied three floors above a small shopping arcade in the fashionably scruffy area of Islington, North London. The atmosphere was informal, relaxed, and personal. Cardboard boxes with leaflets and stationery seemed to be everywhere, and the walls were covered with colorful posters and pictures. The balcony on the first floor was crowded with employees' bikes.

The employees dressed casually with many sporting Greenpeace T-shirts. Most were under 35 years old. What sort of people were they? "It is very hard to generalize," said Alison Reynolds, head of personnel. "A lot of people still think that we all fit the open-toed sandals, bicycle to work, muesli for breakfast stereotype. There is no doubt that the office is unconventional. But people don't realize how professional our approach is. We have a traditional management structure. We also have many experts working for us, both our own employees and outside consultants. People here are very efficient, much more so than in many businesses, and very effective."

Since the issues with which it was involved were often technical as well as controversial, Greenpeace was aware of how important the scientific accuracy of its work was. It had recently formed a Science Division, headed by Dr. Jeremy Leggett, who for 11 years had held the post of Reader in Earth Sciences at Imperial College, London. His role was to provide "quality control" for the campaign documents and protest claims, using both a process of peer review and advice/comments from other scientists. "The issues are getting more complicated, and the level of detail is becoming more sophisticated," he explained.

Greenpeace intended to continue to emphasize the scientific validity of its claims. For example, in one campaign, it bought full-page advertisements in national newspapers to dispute the idea that an expansion of nuclear power would help solve the greenhouse effect in the earth's atmosphere. Headed, "Scientifically speaking, it is just a lot of hot air," the advertisement bore the signatures of 40 well-known scientists including two Nobel prize winners.

Despite its growing size, those in the office were confident that operations would not become too bureaucratic. To the contrary, they prided themselves on how quickly they could move. For example, one Tuesday afternoon the office heard of a toxic shipment of Canadian PCBs being delivered by a Russian vessel to the London docks. A meeting was scheduled for 4:00 that afternoon, Greenpeace's protest volunteers were put on alert, and the Media Department notified the press. At 4:00 the following morning Greenpeace staged its protest in full view of more than 40 journalists; they used small power boats that prevented the Russian ship from edging in to the docks for unloading.

Steven Elsworth was one of the U.K. office employees who both designed and participated in protests. He had earned his degree in English literature and worked as a teacher before writing a number of books, including a dictionary of the environment. That experience was sufficient to convince him to spend all his time on environmental issues. Elsworth did not fit the "open-toed sandals" stereotype. With short blond hair, gold-rimmed glasses, white shirt and bluejeans, he looked like an MBA student and spoke with the same apparent command of technical detail.

Elsworth was in charge of Greenpeace's Global Air Pollution campaign. He had a £30,000 budget, two assistants, and an occasional supplement of unpaid volunteers and outside consultants. His job covered all the issues involved with acid rain and the greenhouse effect. However, he had become particularly interested in automobile emissions following two years of research on that topic. He persuaded the senior U.K. directors that a campaign against automotive pollution should be a Greenpeace priority.

Air pollution was certainly not a new problem to the United Kingdom in the 1980s. Winter smog had polluted London and other large cities in that industrialized country for over a century due to the extensive use of soft coal as a primary source of energy. A combination of the sulphur dioxide and particulates from coal fires together with dank winter weather regularly produced "pea soup fogs" in which visibility was reduced to just a few meters. The infamous London smog of 1952 killed an estimated 4,000 people in just one month.

In response to those deaths the U.K. government passed the 1956 Clear Air Act which raised chimney heights (to improve combustion) and encouraged the use of other fuels. Smoke emissions were reduced nationally by 85 percent over the next 30 years. Due at least in part to this success, air pollution receded for a time as a public policy issue, and the government became complacent. A government official stated in 1987, for example, that "the effects of pollution by motor vehicles can be summarized as follows: there is no evidence that this type of air pollution has any adverse effect on health."

But the U.K. government was behind the times. During the 1980s, environmentalists, scientists, policymakers in other countries, and the general public had all seized upon the issue of air pollution. If any factor may be said to have brought this about, it was the phenomenon now referred to as *Waldsterben* (dying forest), which was caused by acid rain. But other global air pollution problems like the depletion of the ozone layer and global warming had drawn attention as well. In short, air pollution was once more an area of intense public interest, and the automobile was implicated as a major cause.

Public policy attention focused on six air pollutants: sulphur dioxide (SO_2), airborne particulates, carbon monoxide (CO), ozone, nitrogen oxides (NO_x), and carbon dioxide (CO_2). Alone or in combination, these pollutants were primarily responsible for the environmental problems of acid rain and global warming.

Acid rain is formed when a variety of compounds including sulphur dioxide, nitrogen oxides, and hydrocarbons are mixed in the atmosphere to form a "pollution cocktail" of sulfuric acid, sulfates, nitric acid, and ozone which are then washed to earth in the rain water. Acid rain has severely damaged lakes, soil, buildings, wildlife, and vegetation, and the public has been stirred by stories of rainfall with the acidity of lemon juice. More than 17 million acres of forest land in Northern Europe, and more than 50 percent of all trees in West Germany, showed some degree of acid rain damage in 1986.

The United Kingdom was a major net exporter of acid rain, mostly to the Continent. The U.K. Department of the Environment estimated that 77 percent of U.K. emissions went abroad, due to the prevailing northeasterly winds that came off the Atlantic. The United Kingdom was one of the four biggest SO_2 polluters in Europe, and its pollution contributed to a greater NO_2 deposition in Belgium, Denmark, the Netherlands, and Norway than the emissions from those countries themselves—a fact that had earned the United Kingdom the sobriquet of "dirty man of Europe."

Acid rain, ozone depletion, and global warming were not the only consequences of air pollution. Hydrocarbons hindered oxygen transport from blood into human tissues, causing chronic respiratory and cardiac disorders in susceptible individuals. NO_x caused lung problems for people with chronic bronchitis or emphysema. There was some evidence that hydrocarbons caused cancer, and lead (from leaded gasoline) was known to retard the mental development of children.

Most of the public's concern over air pollution focuses on the automobile. Automobiles produce a number of different pollutants, but the most serious are CO, NO_x, hydrocarbons, lead, and CO_2. In 1985 the U.K. Department of the Environment estimated that 5.8 million tons of these pollutants were emitted from cars in the United Kingdom every year. About 40 percent of all NO_x emissions were caused by autos, as are 90 percent of urban CO and 40 percent of urban hydrocarbons. Diesel engines in trucks and buses accounted for 80 percent of urban U.K. particulate pollution.

Each year additional cars circulated on U.K. motorways. If trends were to continue the present 20 million cars in the country would reach 30 million by the end of the century. A graphic forecast by a transport consultant estimated that these extra vehicles would fill a 306-lane motorway from London to Edinburgh!

Of the various ways in which the emissions from automobiles can be reduced, the three-way catalytic converter is the best known. A catalytic converter looks like a muffler and is connected to the exhaust pipe of a car. Exhaust gases are passed through an elaborate honeycomb coated with heavy metal catalysts such as rhodium, platinum, and palladium. Inside the converter, CO and hydrocarbons are converted into CO_2 and water, and NO_x emissions are reduced. Tests on a 1.6 liter Volkswagen equipped with a three-way catalytic converter showed that it reduced emissions of CO by 97 percent, hydrocarbons by 90 percent, and NO_x by 84 percent.

The catalytic converter is the best known, but it is not the only way to reduce air pollution from cars. Other methods include the following:

- Use unleaded gasoline. At the start of the decade, gasoline without lead additives had been nearly unavailable in the United Kingdom. Partially as a result of relative tax reductions for the unleaded brands, and partially as a result of a promotional campaign by an environmental group called "CLEAR" (Campaign for Lead-Free Air), the demand had increased so that by 1986 1 service station in 10 was able to offer this alternative. It was expected, however, that by 1989 nearly half of the U.K. 10,000 stations would have facilities to provide unleaded gasoline. This percentage would be greatly expanded, of course, if catalytic converters were widely used, for the converters require lead-free gas.

- Drive at reduced speeds. Vehicle emissions rise significantly when a car is operating at high speeds. For example, NO_x emissions are six times greater at 130 kph than at 50 kph. In 1988 legislation was proposed in Sweden to reduce the speed limit to 90 kph. Even in West Germany, where the absence of any speed limit on the *autobahns* is a cherished tradition, one could hear occasional voices urging slower driving to reduce air pollution.

- Use lower carbon fuels. The use of lower carbon fuels, such as methanol, would reduce the amount of CO produced. These fuels were still very expensive in 1988 compared with gasoline and were almost totally unavailable in the United Kingdom. There was a definite possibility, however, of combining the lower carbon fuels, if they could be made available, with fuel-efficient "lean-burn" engines to reduce the current cost disadvantage.

- Adopt "lean-burn" technologies. Some car manufacturers such as Ford and Peugeot had invested heavily in the development of "lean-burn" engines, which they believed would provide an attractive alternative to catalytic converters. These engines operate at higher air/fuel ratios than regular engines (20/1 as opposed to 14/1). Combustion occurs at higher temperatures, less fuel is consumed, and harmful emissions are significantly reduced. But, although emission reductions were impressive, they were not adequate to meet U.S. 1983 emission standards which had come to represent a worldwide reference point and a possible new standard for Europe. In particular, the combined hydrocarbon and nitrogen oxide level of a "lean-burn" engine could not be cut below six grams/liter, a level well above the U.S. limit of 4.6 grams/liter.

Catalytic converters and lean-burn engines were viewed as alternative means of achieving approximately the same ends in the late 1980s. It was not possible to fit a true lean-burn engine with a three-way catalytic converter because of the high oxygen content of the lean-burn engine's exhaust, so that the methods were not and could not be made complementary. The choice of which technology was to be the focus of anticipated European Community standards, therefore, was clearly critical for the European car manufacturers. Each of the two alternatives had advantages and disadvantages, and each had proponents and opponents.

Catalytic converter technology was effective and well tested, especially in the United States where it had been required for years as the only technology able to meet automotive environmental standards. Virtually all manufacturers worldwide had experience with the technology, but its adoption in Europe would clearly favor those companies with large exports to the U.S.

Catalytic converters did have a number of disadvantages, however:

- Reduced fuel economy. There was some disagreement on this point, but catalytic converters seemed to raise fuel consumption, perhaps in the range of 4 percent to 10 percent. The uncertainty existed because only large cars had been equipped with converters for testing in Europe.

- Rare metal sources. Catalytic converters required rare metals available only from South Africa, and increased trade with that source was offensive to those people who advocated a strengthening of the existing boycott due to the notorious racial policies of the government.

- Limited life spans. The converters lose efficiency over time and had to be regularly checked to assure that they were working properly, yet obligatory auto inspections were not a common policy in Europe and had never been required in the United Kingdom.

- Warm-up periods. The catalytic converters only function at temperatures above 300°C, but cars release large amounts of pollution before their engines heat to that temperature. This, it was thought, might be a greater problem in Europe than in the United States where commuting distances, and consequently the amount of time available to get up to the proper operating temperatures, tend to be longer.

- Final disposal problems. The catalytic converters do wear out and must be discarded, but the heavy metals provide a continuing health threat in landfills or incinerators. Theoretically, it was possible to recover the heavy metals before the units were discarded, but means of doing that on a commercial scale had not been developed despite the extensive use of the converters in the United States and Japan.

- Car prices. The gasoline in an engine fitted with a catalytic converter must be very precisely metered, so the traditional mechanical carburetors have to be replaced by much more sophisticated electronic fuel injection systems. The cost of the three-way catalytic converter and the fuel injection system was expected to raise the price of large cars (generally defined as those with engines larger than 2 liters) 2 percent to 3 percent, the price of medium-size cars 6 percent to 8 percent, and the price of small cars (below 1.4 liters) 10 percent to 15 percent. The fact that the large cars frequently had electronic fuel injection systems as standard equipment magnified the already disproportionate impact that catalytic converters would have on small car prices. It should be understood that Ford in the United Kingdom, primarily produced small cars.

- Consumer resistance. The increased cost of cars equipped with catalytic converters meant that consumers had no financial incentive to buy them. Either consumers would have to be required to do so by law, or else government subsidies and tax concessions would be needed. Altruism might prompt some to pay the higher price in an effort to preserve the environment, but a study done in the Netherlands in 1988 showed that, without financial incentives or legal requirements from the government, that number would be very low. The prevailing wisdom was, "Nobody ever buys a new car because its got the cleanest tail pipe."

Even supporters of the catalytic converter technology admitted that due to the problems described briefly above it was not a suitable long-term solution to the problem of automobile air pollution. In their opinion it was simply better than any other alternative available in 1989.

Supporters of lean-burn technology felt, in contrast, that they had the long-term solution close at hand. That solution, in simple terms, was to build lower pollution into the engine with improved combustion, ignition, and fuel economy rather than clear up the pollution once it was created. Forced adoption of catalytic converters would kill lean-burn technology just when the investment was due to pay dividends, in the opinion of these car engineers and scientists. They cited the following advantages:

- Improved fuel economy. One potentially significant advantage of lean-burn engines was the 8 percent to 10 percent improvement in fuel economy. By the end of the century, fuel economy standards could well be obligatory in Western Europe just as they were in the United States. Even if they were not, improved fuel economy provided an inducement for consumers to adopt lean-burn engines without the necessity of governmental compulsion.

- Reduced CO_2 emissions. Not only was improved fuel economy directly beneficial, but it also implied reduced CO_2 emissions. This might be significant should the European Commission add CO_2 (one of the major greenhouse gases) to the CO, NO_x, and hydrocarbons that were already the object of its proposed regulations.

- Longer life span. Another potentially significant advantage of lean-burn engines was the fact that they were more robust and more reliable than catalytic converters. It was possible, and a study by the U.S. Environmental Protection Agency apparently supported this view, that they might cause lower pollution over the full life span of an engine even under the current stage of development.

Yet to opponents, lean-burn engines that could match the environmental performance of catalytic converters were just a promise, a "phantom technology" in the words of Dr. Laurens-Jan Brinkhorst, European Commission Director General for the Environment. Current lean-burn engines could only reduce harmful emissions by about 50 percent, and they were especially ineffective for NO_x pollutants. Most of the engines that were actually in use ran on just slightly leaner air/fuel mixtures of 16/1 or 18/1 rather than the 20/1 that was desirable, and consequently were hard pressed even to meet the 50 percent reduction standard.

Despite the uncertainties that were present on both sides, Greenpeace gave catalytic converters its *de facto* support in 1988. Steven Elsworth argued that Greenpeace should not formally campaign for catalytic converters per se, but should accept them as the best means to reduce harmful auto air emissions available at that time. "If the 1983 U.S. emission standards could have been met by lean burn, we would have accepted that technology just as well. Unfortunately the manufacturers of lean burn could never deliver in practice what they believed to be possible in theory."

At that time, the European Community had no clear-cut policy on motor vehicle exhausts, unlike the United States which had set "technology forcing" standards for a 90 percent reduction in the three major exhaust pollutants in 1970, had required catalytic converters on all cars built after 1975, and had then solidified these requirements with even tougher legislation in 1983. Contributing to the relative lack of accomplishment in Europe was a continual disagreement among member states over the extent and timing of the proper standards. West Germany, Denmark, and the Netherlands were pushing for quick implementation of legislation similar to that in the United States, while France, the United Kingdom, Italy, and Spain wanted more gradual adoption of less strict controls.

Arguments over these matters meant that in 1988 there was general agreement among the European states only that large cars should use catalytic converters while the medium-sized vehicles might choose between the converters and lean-burn engines, and the smaller vehicles might or might not be exempted from either requirement. The positions of the various nations generally varied with the types of cars produced in the area (large, medium, or small), and the percentage of cars exported to the United States where catalytic converters were required on all models, regardless of size.

The situation in the United Kingdom at this time was even less clear cut—if that were possible—than in the European Community (E.C.). The U.K. government still opposed E. C. adoption of the 1983 U.S. standards, and seemed to suggest that lean-burn engine technology would suffice for all sized cars.

Ford U.K. primarily made small and medium-sized cars for the home market and the European Community and so avoided any need under current requirements for catalytic converters on those models. Despite its obvious association with the parent U.S. firm, Ford U.K. also tended to ship very few vehicles to the United States, where converters would have been required regardless of size. The company had spent over £90 million on research and development of the lean-burn technology, and had invested £175 million in a production line to build a lean-burn 1.6 liter engine that was installed on all Escort, Orion, and Fiesta models sold in the United Kingdom since 1986.

In short, Ford U.K. was committed to the lean-burn technology and was working, albeit slowly, to improve that technology. The company held a 28 percent market share position in its home market, and had been financially successful since a series of losses in the early 1980s. Executives were worried, however, by the obvious trade liberalization that could be expected following the 1992 economic integration of the European Community, and by signs that the existing system of bilateral export agreements between individual European countries and Japan was coming apart. Car markets in Europe were expected to become much more competitive in the very near future, and Ford U.K. executives wished to have European auto emission standards set firmly in their favor for their small, low-priced cars before that competition intensified.

Ford lobbied its case for lean-burn engines with the U.K. government and with the European Community via the U.K. Department of Trade and Industry. The Society of Motor Manufacturers and Traders, an umbrella organization of U.K. auto firms, similarly advocated the lean-burn technology.

The U.K. government sided with lean-burn engines when it and the other nations comprising the majority of the European Council of Ministers decided on small car standards in June 1988. Criticizing the minority group of countries which were in favor of tighter standards, the U.K. minister for the environment said that such standards would effectively terminate development of the lean-burn engine in return for only modest improvements to the environment and that at great additional cost.

In the summer of 1988 Toyota launched the Celica GT-Four, which was the first car to be sold in the United Kingdom with a catalytic converter as standard equipment. Three months later Volkswagen announced that three of its models (the Golf, Passat, and Jetta) would be offered with converters. Volkswagen said its decision was motivated by respect for the environment rather than by any expected U.K. legislation.

These announcements were enthusiastically received at Greenpeace's offices in London. "With the Germans and the Japanese now offering converters in the United Kingdom, we felt that we really had something on which to build our campaign," explained Steve Elsworth, the prospective head of that campaign.

Elsworth persuaded his senior colleagues that a campaign for catalytic converters now had a realistic chance for success. He described the process. "A campaign is very much like a product launch. We always look for three things. First, there must be clear scientific evidence of major environmental harm. Second, there must be a visible polluter so that we can target somebody easily and focus public attention on that specific person or company. Third, we must have a strong moral argument in order to win the support of the public in the face of potentially strong opposition."

Elsworth was already convinced of the harm caused by auto emissions from the work he had done on acid rain. But what especially attracted his attention in this instance was the difference in the international policies of the auto manufacturers themselves. "I found it very interesting, to say the least, that a global manufacturer was supplying cars with different standards to different parts of the world. If we can find an area where we can see differences of opinion between governments or businesses, we can leverage this disunity. It makes our job an awful lot easier."

For the next two weeks, Elsworth and one of his assistants laid out the guidelines for the campaign. They wanted to start on a "level playing field" by giving the manufacturers a chance to reply to Greenpeace's demand. Assuming some would rebuff them, they next decided to target just one of that group. This, they reasoned, would increase the chance that the targeted manufacturer would eventually change its policy, and it would reduce the likelihood of an industrywide defense.

"Whereas the objective of the campaign was to change the entire accepted norm for vehicle pollution around the world, we considered that Ford was a good target because it was the biggest manufacturer in the United Kingdom, which formed the biggest obstacle to that process. If the outcome of the campaign had been a change in the legal standards requiring catalytic converters we would, of course, have been satisfied too." explained Elsworth. "A further objective of the campaign was to destabilize the friendly image of the family car which had been the result of years of careful advertising by the manufacturers."

Greenpeace sent letters to the public relations directors of the 18 car manufacturers that had more than 1 percent of the U.K. market. Eleven of the companies quickly replied that catalysts either were supplied or would be in the near future. Greenpeace categorized these replies as favorable. Greenpeace regarded another four of the replies as unsatisfactory but not entirely negative. Three manufacturers' replies—those of Ford, Mercedes-Benz, and Peugeot-Citroen—were thought to be "extremely negative."

Ford's "extremely negative" reply came in an eight-page letter from the public relations director. The letter gave no indication of when Ford would make catalyst-equipped cars available in the United Kingdom, but it did attempt a detailed defense of Ford's support for lean-burn engines. The author argued that Ford shared Greenpeace's concern for the environment but that the company believed that lean burn was the best long-term technical solution.

Pressure in favor of catalytic converters increased over the fall of 1988 when Volkswagen announced that it would supply catalysts on all its models by September 1989. The following month the Greenpeace team concluded that Ford would be the target.

"We had several reasons for choosing Ford," explained Elsworth. "First, Ford was the market leader in the United Kingdom. If you can judo throw the leader, there will always be a follow-on effect from the others. If you target the number-two firm, it can then reply, 'Why me? Why not number one?' Tackling the leader fits with our style, anyway. We don't mind confrontation. Second, Ford was a prime example of double standards. In the United States, Ford boasts about its achievements in reducing emissions 90 percent through converters. Ford supplies cars in the rest of Europe equipped with converters. We had received a reply from Ford Austria saying it was 'proud its cars passed the strict Austrian emission tests.' Third, we did not accept Ford's arguments about lean burn. In our view, lean burn was just 'jam tomorrow.' We have evidence that shows it was promised back in 1984, but today, even under the best possible conditions, lean burn can only reduce emissions by a maximum of 60 percent. We know that converters are not the ultimate solution, but we support the principle of the best available technology, and lean-burn engines simply are not good enough. We decided to start our campaign immediately."

Class Assignment

1. Is the Greenpeace position entirely ethical? Who can be hurt by the proposed campaign? If Steven Elsworth asked for your advice on whether or not to launch it, what would you tell him?

2. Put yourself in the position of Steven Elsworth and develop a protest campaign against the Ford decision to continue with its lean-burn technology on all cars sold in the United Kingdom. Remember that you are working for an organization (Greenpeace) that prides itself on being "aggressive, forthright, and uncompromising," that searches for "innovative weak spots" in its opponents position, that doesn't mind being considered "confrontational," and that likes to leverage its advertising expenditures with free publicity. What will you do? Specifically, what will you do to get "40 journalists viewing your protest" as in the instance where a Canadian PCB shipment was turned away—at least temporarily—from the London docks?

3. Is the Ford position entirely ethical? Who can be hurt by its continued opposition to catalytic converters? If the managing director of Ford U.K. asked for your advice about a possible switch in positions, what would you tell him or her?

4. Now put yourself in the position of the managing director of Ford U.K. Are you prepared to withstand the pressures that an "aggressive, forthright, and uncompromising" opponent may bring to bear? What, if anything, can you do to strengthen your position, to get some of the free publicity on your side?

CHAPTER 5

The Modern Ethical Principles

Why be moral? Why should a person worry about what is "right" and "just" and "fair" in the distribution of benefits and harms, or in the recognition of duties and obligations, that are owed to other people? Why should all of us not simply resolve never to lie, cheat, or steal, and then begin to look after our own long-term self-interests? As seen in Chapter 3, ethical egoism (you look after your long-term self-interests, and I will look after mine) is a valid ethical principle. The argument of this book is that ethical egoism, by itself, is not enough. The argument of this book is that we have to add concepts from the personal virtues (be open and truthful in what you do and be proud of what you have done), the religious injunctions (be compassionate and attempt to build a sense of community), government requirements (obey righteous laws and understand the social contract as the logical basis for those laws), and so on. The argument of this book is that we have to look at the decisions and actions that impact others from a number of different perspectives to determine what is "right" and "just" and fair."

But, why should we do this? Why should we use those different perspectives? Why should we worry about "rightness," and "justice," and "fairness"? A totally amoral person—one who did not worry about "rightness" and "justice" and "fairness" for others and instead concentrated upon his or her own self-interests—might be expected to be more successful in purely financial terms over a given period of time. Why should we not do this?

The answer on one level is that if we want others to worry about whether their treatment of us is "right," and "just," and "fair," then we have to worry about our treatment of them. Reciprocity is the most logical reason for morality. But, the world is filled with people who are not logical in the sense of recognizing reciprocity and the need to be consistent. The world is filled with people who might well say, "We'll take our chances on your treatment of us later on, after we get what we want now, and if we do get what we want now, we won't have to worry about your treatment of us later on." What do we do about them? Do we simply cede to them the first place in material benefits and managerial positions, and hope that eventually they will learn that "what goes around comes around"? That is not a very satisfactory solution for most of the rest of us.

Beyond reciprocity, however, as the reason for moral action is—or should be—our concern for the quality of our lives. If we are concerned about the sort

EXHIBIT 5–1

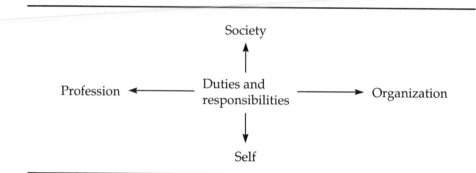

of profession we have entered, the sort of organization we have joined, the sort of society we have made, and the sort of people we have become, then we have to start thinking about our duties and responsibilities to our professions, our organizations, our fellow citizens, and our selves.

The ethical principles are a means of sorting out your duties and responsibilities to each of these entities *on your terms.* What do you owe to your profession? What do you owe to your organization? What do you owe to your society? What do you owe to your self? Socrates, in 399 B.C., made the statement that "the unexamined life is not worth living." You can certainly interpret that statement following your own understanding, but perhaps he is saying that you should examine your duties and obligations to your profession, your organization, your society, and your self.

The most basic question in ethics is, "Do you have an obligation to leave the world a little better than you found it, or can you simply take what you need now and let the next generation worry about remedies and improvements later on?" Most people do recognize that obligation, but have never thought strongly about its nature and terms, and have never sorted that obligation into their duties and responsibilities to their professions, their organizations, their communities, and their selves. Still, it has to be realized that there are others who choose to ignore this obligation to "leave the world a little better than they found it," and the question once again is do we cede to those people the first place in material rewards and managerial positions, and only hope that eventually they too will become concerned with the quality of their lives and the nature and terms of their duties and responsibilities to others?

Beyond reciprocity of treatment and quality of life, the third argument in favor of moral action is that of expansion of effort. Organizations are composed of stakeholders. The stakeholders in a business firm include the workers, managers, engineers, suppliers, distributors, customers, creditors, owners, and so on. All have an interest, a "stake," in the future of that firm. All must contribute their best efforts if that future is to be successful and secure.

But, why should the various stakeholders contribute their best efforts to an organization they do not manage and may not be able to influence? This is one

EXHIBIT 5–2

Corporate mgt. in extended organizations	Recognition of moral responsibility • What is "duty"?	Trust Commitment Effort
	Application of moral reasoning • What is "right"?	
	Possession of moral character • What is "integrity"?	

of the most basic questions in management, and the answer may require more than compensation payments and incentive rewards. Perhaps effort requires commitment, and commitment requires trust. The argument of this book is that trust is based upon the recognition of moral responsibility, the understanding of moral reasoning, and the possession of moral character by the management of the firm.

Why be moral? Logically you should be moral because of your eventual need for reciprocal action from others. Emotionally you should be moral because of your subjective desire for improved quality of life. Pragmatically you should be moral because of your managerial responsibility to build trust, commitment, and effort among all of the stakeholders within the firm.

How do you know that your actions are moral, that they are "right" and "just" and "proper," and that they will help to build the needed trust, commitment, and effort? You use the ethical principles of analysis. Chapter 3 looked at the early ethical principles: (1) self-interests, (2) personal virtues, and (3) religious injunctions. Chapter 4 reported on the middle ethical principles: (4) government requirements, (5) utilitarian benefits, (6) universal duties, and (7) individual rights. Chapter 5 will explain the modern ethical principles: (8) market forces, (9) distributive justice, and (10) contributive liberty.

MARKET FORCES

The ethical principle of market forces can be summarized very briefly as the statement that it is possible to rely on the input factor markets to set the cost and provide the supply for material, labor, and capital, and on the output product markets to set the price and establish the demand for the various goods and services, and that the only responsibility of management is to convert those scarce resources into the wanted goods and services as efficiently as possible.

Efficiently means substituting capital for labor through equipment

modernization, or material for capital through overseas purchase of components, to find the lowest unit cost of production. Efficiently also means making
full use of the economies of scale, the economies of scope, and the economies of
experience (the learning-curve effect) to maintain that lowest unit cost position.
Efficiently in economic terms does *not* mean cutting corners on product quality,
worker safety, or environmental protection.

When a company is operating as efficiently as possible, of course, it is also
operating as profitably as possible. Consequently it is possible to say that the
only responsibility of management is to maximize the profits of the firm. This
view has been stated very succinctly and very clearly by both James McKie of
the Brookings Institution and Milton Friedman of the University of Chicago:

> The primary goal and motivating force for business organizations is profit.
> The firm attempts to make as large a profit as it can, thereby maintaining its
> efficiency and taking advantage of available opportunities to innovate and
> contribute to growth. Profits are kept to reasonable or appropriate levels by
> market competition, which leads the firm pursuing its own self-interest to
> an end that is not part of its conscious intention: enhancement of the public
> welfare. [James McKie, *Changing Views, Social Responsibility and the Business
> Predicament,* 1974, p. 19].

> The view has been gaining widespread acceptance that corporate offi-
> cials . . . have a "social responsibility" that goes beyond serving the inter-
> ests of their stockholders or their members. This view shows a fundamental
> misconception of the character and nature of a free economy. In such an
> economy, there is one and only one social responsibility of business—to use
> its resources and engage in activities designed to increase its profits, so long
> as it stays within the rules of the game, which is to say, engages in open and
> free competition, without deception or fraud. . . . Few trends could so thor-
> oughly undermine the very foundations of our free society as the accep-
> tance by corporate officials of a social responsibility other than to make as
> much money for their stockholders as possible [Milton Friedman, *Capital-
> ism and Freedom,* 1962, p. 13].

The ethical principle of market forces is dependent upon the economic
concept of the "invisible hand" which, of course, comes from Adam Smith.
People pursue their own self-interests, but as long as they pursue those self-
interests through the mechanism of price competition within a market, then the
public welfare is improved because the scarce resources of society—capital,
material, and labor—are used as efficiently as possible to generate more goods
and services for society.

Suppose I were to start a new company to provide simple health care and
"assisted living" services for older people who wish to remain in their own
homes. There is, I understand, a growing need for this service as our society
ages. Suppose I were to staff this new company by hiring, training, and then
providing transportation for inner city residents. There is, again I understand, a
growing need for this opportunity as many of those people are unemployed.
The argument of Adam Smith, James McKie, Milton Friedman, and all others

---

EXHIBIT 5–3
Excerpts from *The Wealth of Nations*
Adam Smith

In almost every other race of animal each individual, when it is grown up to maturity, is entirely independent, and in its natural state has occasion for the assistance of no other living creature. But man has almost constant occasion for the help of his brethren, and it is in vain for him to expect it from their benevolence only. He will be more likely to prevail if he can interest their self-love in his favour, and show them that it is for their own advantage to do for him what he requires of them. Whoever offers to another a bargain of any kind, proposes to do this. Give me what I want, and you shall have this which you want, is the meaning of every such offer; and it is in this manner that we obtain from one another the far greater part of those good offices which we stand in need of. It is not from the benevolence of the butcher, the brewer, or the baker that we expect our dinner, but from their regard to their own interest. We address ourselves not to their humanity but to their self-love, and never talk to them of our necessities, but of their advantages.

. . . . . .

Every individual is continually exerting himself to find out the most advantageous employment of whatever capital he can command. It is his own advantage, indeed, and not that of the society which he has in view. But the study of his own advantage naturally, or rather necessarily, leads him to prefer that employment which is most advantageous to the society. . . . Every individual necessarily labours to render the annual revenue of the society as great as he can. He generally indeed, neither intends to promote the public interest, nor knows how much he is promoting it. By preferring the support of domestic to that of foreign industry, he intends only his own security; and by directing that industry in such a manner as its produce may be of the greatest value, he intends only his own gain, and he is in this, as in many other cases, led by an *invisible hand* to promote an end which was not part of his intention. . . . By pursuing his own interest he frequently promotes that of the society more effectually than when he really intends to promote it. I have never known much good done by those who affected to trade for the public good. It is an affectation, indeed, not very common among merchants, and very few words need be employed in dissuading them from it.

---

who believe in the ethical principle of market forces is that I may make large profits from my new company, but that society is better off because older people have a residential service they want and city residents have an employment opportunity they need. I am prevented from charging too high a price to the older people because of competition in the product market, and I am also blocked from paying too low a wage to the city residents because of competition in the labor market. Market forces ensure that I may follow my self-interests very energetically, and attempt to make as much money for myself as humanly possible, yet society as a whole will benefit from my efforts.

What do you think of this ethical principle? It is certainly simple and easy—almost pleasant—to follow: Make as much money for yourself as is humanly possible, staying within market and legal constraints of course, and then the "invisible hand" of the factor and product markets will allocate the benefits and distribute the harms equitably among the stakeholders. Simple and easy to follow, certainly, but there are three basic difficulties:

1. Noncompetitive markets. It has to be admitted that not all markets are fully competitive. Many product markets—particularly for the standardized and easily comparable commodities—are competitive, with an open bidding process. But in others the number of competitors participating in the market may be low, the amount of information available to the buyer may be limited, or the ease of comparison between goods and (particularly) services may be insufficient. I have started my company to provide "assisted living" services to seniors; you have an elderly parent in dire need of those services. Can you easily judge the quality and reliability of my offering versus those of my competitors? Probably not, and one of the reasons for my success may be the lack of competition, given the newness of the service.

2. Noninclusive costs. There is an assumption in economic theory that all of the costs, including those that are external to the production process, have been covered in the price for the product. External costs are those that do not show up in the usual accounting records; they are the environmental damages, workplace dangers, product hazards. They have to be estimated, but it is difficult to estimate them accurately. I want to drill for oil off the coast of Southern California; you are a surfer who enjoys the beaches in that area. Are we going to agree on the costs of a potential oil spill? Probably not, and remember that we have to settle not only on the total cost for the potential spill but also on the statistical probability of its occurrence in order to include this external "cost" in the unit price for the product.

3. Nonparticipative persons. There is a further assumption in economic theory that all of the members of a society are able to participate in the output product markets for the goods and services produced by that society, and in the input factor markets for the capital, material, and—particularly—labor needed by that society. There may, however, be some people who are so poorly trained that they have very few skills to sell in the labor market, and who consequently are so poorly paid that they have very few dollars to buy in the product market. It is the argument of most market economists that the government has to set minimum wages, provide skill training, and arrange transfer payments to enable members of these poorly trained and low-paid groups to participate in the product and factor markets, but these government programs are often not widely available or effectively run.

The ethical principle of market forces differs from the ethical principle of self-interests in that the former adds the provision of staying within market constraints. This is a crucial provision. The important question, when you apply this principle, is *not* whether you can make substantial profits. That would be pure self-interest. The important question is whether within your industry there are competitive factor markets with full information so that suppliers can make informed rational choices to sell the resources—labor, capital, and material—that you need; and whether there are competitive product markets, again with full information, so that customers can make informed rational choices to buy the products—both goods and services—that you produce. If those competitive markets with full information do exist, it is hard to fault a person or a company for making use of them.

What do you think of the ethical principle that the existence of competitive markets with full information tends to make acts "right" and "proper" and "fair"? It is certainly simple and easy to apply, and it is outwardly attractive because it removes the responsibility from the manager and places it upon the market—it is perfectly all right to fire this kindly old person who has worked for our company for years because there is a labor market out there, and he or she will soon gain employment at a wage which reflects his or her true value to the employer—but there are the problems that all of the markets may not be competitive, that all of the costs may not be included, and that all of the members of our society may not be able to participate. Once again we are left with a principle that gives another perspective on a moral problem, but that cannot be conclusive by itself.

DISTRIBUTIVE JUSTICE

The ethical principle of distributive justice can be summarized very simply: take no action which might harm those who could be considered to be the least among us, those with the least education, the least skills, the least material goods, and the least lifetime opportunities. This is another principle that seems to come back close to that of self-interest, but with the critical provision that we must look out for those who are least able to look out for themselves.

Distributive justice is an ethical principle developed by John Rawls (b. 1921), currently a faculty member emeritus at Harvard. It is based upon the concept of the social contract. What agreement would people in an original position of absolute equality make for the distribution of the benefits of social cooperation? Human society, wrote Rawls, is marked by a conflict in interests as well as an identity of interests. The identity of interests comes from the social cooperation that is needed to produce the benefits—the goods and services—of society; the conflict comes from the individual striving that is generated in the distribution of those benefits. Rawls says that "to further their own aims each [person] prefers a larger to a lesser share."

How should the benefits that are produced within a society be distributed? Traditionally there are six methods for this distribution, and all six are used within our society:

EXHIBIT 5–4
Excerpts from *Distributive Justice*
John Rawls

We may think of a human society as a more or less self-sufficient association regulated by a common conception of justice and aimed at advancing the good of its members. As a co-operative venture for mutual advantage, it is characterized by a conflict as well as an identity of interests. There is an identity of interests since social co-operation makes possible a better life for all than any would have if everyone were to try to live by his own efforts; yet at the same time men are not indifferent as to how the greater benefits produced by their joint labours are distributed, for in order to further their own aims each prefers a larger to a lesser share. A conception of justice is a set of principles for choosing between the social arrangements which determine this division and for underwriting a consensus as to the proper distributive shares.

---

1. To each person equally. Public schooling and public transportation are both available on a relatively equal basis.
2. To each person according to his or her need. Welfare payments and (to some extent) health care are distributed by need.
3. To each person according to his or her effort. Commissions are often paid based upon effort.
4. To each person according to his or her contribution. Bonuses are intended to reward contributions.
5. To each person according to his or her competence. Salaries are ideally set through market comparisons of competence.
6. To each person according to his or her ancestry. Inheritances are the obvious example here, but education and health care also traditionally seem to be more available to some groups than to others.

Rawls claims that each of these six methods is somewhat unjust. If benefits are made available equally or based upon need, then those who put forth greater effort and/or have greater competence will suffer. If benefits are distributed according to contributions, then we have the dual problem of measuring those contributions and establishing the rewards, while those who cannot contribute due to a lack of innate skills will be shortchanged.

Rawls suggests a totally different method of distributing benefits, and that is to establish the rule that inequalities in distribution are arbitrary and unjust unless it is reasonable to expect that those inequalities will work out to the benefit of all. That is, it is perfectly all right to pay scientists more than day laborers for the additional pay will attract more scientists who will invent new products and processes that will make all of us better off, including the day laborers.

EXHIBIT 5–5
Excerpts from *Distributive Justice*
John Rawls

If, then, we believe that as a matter of principle each member of society has an inviolability founded on justice which even the welfare of everyone else cannot override, and that a loss of freedom for some is not made right by a greater sum of satisfactions enjoyed by many, we shall have to look elsewhere (beyond utilitarianism) to account for the principles of justice . . . Now, the most natural alternative to the principle of utility is its traditional rival, the theory of the social contract. The aim of the contract doctrine is precisely to account for the strictness of justice by supposing that its principles arise from an agreement among free and independent persons in an original position of equality and hence reflect the integrity and equal sovereignty of the rational persons who are the contractees. Instead of supposing that a conception of right, and so a conception of justice, is simply an extension of the principle of choice for one man to society as a whole, the contract doctrine assumes that the rational individuals who belong to society must choose together, in one joint act, what is to count among them as just and unjust. They are to decide among themselves once and for all what is to be their conception of justice. This decision is thought of as being made in a suitably defined initial situation one of the significant features of which is that no one knows his position in society, nor even his place in the distribution of natural talents and abilities. The principles of justice to which all are forever bound are chosen in the absence of this sort of specific information. A veil of ignorance prevents anyone from being advantaged or disadvantaged by the contingencies of social class and fortune; and hence the bargaining problems, which arise in everyday life from the possession of this knowledge do not affect the choice of principles. On the contract doctrine, then, the theory of justice, and indeed ethics itself, is part of the general theory of rational choice, a fact perfectly clear in its Kantian formulation.

Rawls says that it is difficult to compute the impact of most inequalities in benefit distribution upon the life prospects of everyone within society—unlike the scientists who, it is hoped, will benefit everyone by their discoveries—and consequently the rule is that you should compute the impact upon the "least among us," those with the least education, the least income, and the least skills, and consequently the ones most likely to be left out of the usual distribution methods.

What do you think of this ethical principle? One of the advantages is that it states clearly, "Yes, you do have an obligation to a specific group within society, and this is the precise nature of that obligation." Another advantage is that it is based upon the social contract; if you were able to put together a group of people who were ignorant of their skills and abilities and their prospective levels of education, income, and energy, and then asked them to set up rules for the distribution of income you might well find a rule such as the one Rawls has proposed to be the result. Members of society would want to protect their own interests, and—since they would be uncertain who would be on the bottom of society—they would specifically include those people on the bottom in the distribution system.

You will find, however, that the ethical principle that inequalities in income distribution are "wrong" unless they work out to the advantage of those on the bottom of society is not as useful in application as it might appear. It is hard to define "advantage." For example, is it all right to hold a lavish birthday party for a popular entertainer or sports figure during a severe economic recession if you distribute the leftover lobster salad to a charity? Perhaps not. Also, it is not at all clear that people in a state of ignorance about their personal skills and abilities would focus on the distribution of the benefits generated by those skills and abilities through social cooperation. People in that state of ignorance might be more interested in guaranteeing their freedom to develop whatever skills and abilities they would have to the best of their own ability. In short, they might be more interested in liberty than justice. This brings us to the last ethical principle: that of contributive liberty.

CONTRIBUTIVE LIBERTY

The ethical principle of contributive liberty—the name is my own, devised to contrast with distributive justice; it does not come from the chief proponent of this principle, Professor Robert Nozick—can be summarized very briefly. Never take any action that might interfere with another person's right to self-development and self-fulfillment. If you think about it, you will realize that this is the exact opposite of distributive justice.

Contributive liberty is an ethical principle developed by Robert Nozick (b. 1938), currently a faculty member at Harvard. Nozick agrees that society is an association of individuals, and that cooperation between those individuals is necessary to generate social benefits, both goods and services, but he would argue that the cooperation comes about as the result of the exchange of goods and services to satisfy individual desires, and that any exchange that is voluntary is just. He uses the example of Wilt Chamberlain, a well-known basketball player of the 1960s and 1970s, to establish his point. He says that you could set up whatever distribution of the benefits of social cooperation you might like—everyone could have an equal share, or the shares could be based upon some mixture of social contribution and personal need—but that if people were willing to pay to see Wilt Chamberlain play basketball, that ideal distribution would be different after the season ended. Would the new distribution be unjust? It would be hard to make that claim because the benefit exchanges between Wilt and the fans were all voluntary.

If all voluntary exchanges of benefits are just, then the rule from distributive justice that all inequalities in benefit holdings have to be shown to work for the benefit of everyone in society—and particularly for the benefit of those least able to look after their own benefits due to a lack of education, income, position,

EXHIBIT 5–6
Excerpts from *Justice as Entitlement*
Robert Nozick

The term "distributive justice" is not a neutral one. Hearing the term "distribution," most people presume that some thing or mechanism uses some principle or criterion to give out a supply of things. Into this process of distributing shares some error may have crept. So it is an open question, at least, whether redistribution should take place; whether we should do again what has already been done once, though poorly. However, we are not in the position of children who have been given portions of pie by someone who now makes last minute adjustments to rectify careless cutting. There is no central distribution, no person or group entitled to control all the resources, jointly deciding how they are to be doled out. What each person gets, he gets from others who give to him in exchange for something, or as a gift. In a free society, diverse persons control different resources, and new holdings arise out of the voluntary exchanges and actions of persons.

. . . . .

If the world were wholly just, the following inductive definitions would exhaustively cover the subject of justice in holdings:

1. A person who acquires a holding in accordance with the principle of justice in acquisition is entitled to that holding.

2. A person who acquires a holding in accordance with the principle of justice in transfer, from someone else entitled to the holding, is entitled to the holding.

3. No one is entitled to a holding except by repeated applications of rules 1 and 2.

. . . . .

It is not clear how those holding alternative conceptions of distributive justice can reject the entitlement conception of justice in holding. For suppose a distribution favored by one of these non-entitlement concepts is realized. Let us suppose it is your favorite one, and let us call this distribution D_1. Perhaps everyone has an equal share; perhaps shares vary in accordance with some dimension you treasure. Now suppose that Wilt Chamberlain is greatly in demand by basketball teams, being a great gate attraction. He signs the following sort of contract with a team: In each home game, 25 cents from the price of each ticket of admission goes to him. The season starts, and people cheerfully attend his team's games; they buy their tickets, each time dropping a separate 25 cents of their admission price into a special box with Chamberlain's name on it. Let us suppose that in one season one million persons attend his home games, and Wilt Chamberlain winds up with $250,000. Is he entitled to this income? Is this new distribution, D_2, unjust? If so, why?

or power—is obviously wrong. Nozick proposes the rule that we not interfere with those voluntary exchanges, and particularly that we not interfere with people's self-development so that everyone can arrange those voluntary exchanges in their own interests. Liberty, the right to self-development and self-fulfillment, is more important than justice according to Nozick, because self-development leads to greater personal skills and abilities and consequently to greater social benefits. Nozick believes that people in a state of ignorance would recognize the importance of self-development, and consequently would place liberty before justice in their version of the social contract.

What is the problem with this ethical principle that we should never interfere with the rights of others to develop to their full potential, given that this development will obviously contribute to the total sum of benefits within the society as a result of social cooperation? Again, you will find that it is hard to apply in practice. What exactly is interference? Is it enough just not to take any action that impedes a person's right to self-development and eventual self-fulfillment, or should we take some actions that assist that person's right? This is the vexing difference between negative and positive rights that we have encountered previously, and once again there are no easy answers. You will find, however, that the principle of contributive liberty does provide one more perspective—one more way of looking at moral problems—and does offer one more bit of help in your attempt to decide what is "right" and "just" and "fair" in your managerial decisions and actions.

SUMMARY OF ETHICAL PRINCIPLES

The intent of the last three chapters of this book describing the various ethical principles is *not* to tell readers *what* to think about moral problems, but to explain *how* to think about those problems. A moral problem, once again, is one in which some individuals or groups within our society are going to be hurt or harmed in some way, or in which their rights are going to be abridged or ignored in some other way.

Given that people will subjectively differ in their moral standards of behavior and in their value judgments of priority, we need an objective means of comparing the alternative decisions and actions that are possible in a managerial situation in which some people are going to be harmed, or in which their rights are going to be abridged. The objective means of comparison are the ethical principles. These ethical principles do not change as we move from one country to another, or from one culture to another. They remain exactly the same, and the methods of applying them remain exactly the same. Applying these ethical principles to a moral problem does not result in a single solution of absolute certainty. There are no "absolutes" in moral reasoning; that is, there are no answers that are totally and completely "right" and "just" and "fair." But, there are answers to moral problems that are "more right," "more just," and "more fair" than others, and the application of the full range of ethical principles helps you to find those answers.

Ethical principles provide different perspectives, or different ways of looking at moral problems. Each, of course, represents the first principle of what constitutes a good society in which people willingly cooperate for the benefit of all. They are summarized here for easy comparison:

1. Ethical egoism. If everyone would look after their own self-interests, without forcefully interfering with others, then society as a collection of free individuals will benefit.

2. Personal virtues. The lack of forceful interference is not enough. As we each pursue our own self-interests, we have to be honest, truthful, and temperate with each other.

3. Religious injunctions. Honesty, truthfulness, and temperance aren't enough; we have to have some degree of compassion and kindness towards others to form a true community.

4. Government requirements. Compassion and kindness would be ideal if everyone would be so, but everyone won't. Therefore, we have to agree to obey basic rules from a central authority.

5. Utilitarian benefits. Common obedience to basic rules would work if the central authority did not have self-interests. It does. We have to evaluate rules based upon social benefit.

6. Universal rules. Greatest social benefit is elegant in theory, but the theory says nothing about distribution based upon self-interest. We need a rule to eliminate self-interest.

7. Individual rights. Eliminating self-interest isn't possible within society, given what people are really like. We need a list of basic rights that must be upheld by all for all.

8. Economic efficiency. Basic rights are meaningless without the essentials of food, clothing, and shelter. Maximize the production and distribute the output by following market forces.

9. Distributive justice. Market forces exclude the "least among us": the poor; the uneducated, the unaccepted. We need a rule to ensure that they are not left out.

10. Contributive liberty. The rule that ensures that no one will be left out interferes with the self-development of others. We need a process that ensures liberty more than justice.

These 10 ethical principles provide a means for an individual to decide in his or her own mind what is "right" and "just" and "fair" when faced with a moral problem. The ability to decide what is "right" and "just" and "fair" is certainly helpful, but it is not enough in most business organizations. Someone has to lead everyone within the organization towards moral actions, and imbue the organization with moral standards. That is the responsibility of the leader of the organization, and the subject of the next chapter.

ASSIGNMENT QUESTIONS

1. The graphic in Exhibit 5–2 on page 157 of this chapter asks three questions: (1) What is "duty"? (2) What is "right"? and (3) What is "integrity"? Answer those three questions in your own terms, paying particular attention to the last. How would you define "integrity"?

2. Professor Milton Friedman, in the brief quotation that was given in this chapter, wrote, "Few trends could so thoroughly undermine the very foundations of our free society as the acceptance by corporate officials of a social responsibility other than to make as much money for their stockholders as possible." Do you agree? If you agree, explain why. If you don't agree, explain why.

3. Read the excerpts from *The Wealth of Nations* once again. Adam Smith states that, "In almost every other race of animal each individual, when it is grown up to maturity, is entirely independent, and in its natural state has occasion for the assistance of no other living creature. But man has almost constant occasion for the help of his brethren ..." Do you agree? If you agree, why is this so? Why do people need the help of other people?

4. Read the first excerpt from *Distributive Justice* on page 162 once again. Do Adam Smith and John Rawls have the same view of human society? If so, what are the similarities? If not, how do their views differ?

5. Read the second excerpt from *Distributive Justice* on page 163 once again. Rawls again brings up the ideas of the social contract (which we first encountered in Hobbes *Leviathan*). Define this idea of a social contract in your own terms. What does it mean to you, and why is it important to Hobbes, Locke, Rawls, and Nozick?

6. As you study the various ethical principles you keep encountering concepts of justice, liberty, and equality. Define each of these concepts in your own terms.

   If you want to look back, and see how others defined these terms before attempting your own definitions, here are some references:

   a. You will find "justice" described in Plato, Aristotle, the Bible (not included in any of the excerpts, but you must know the "eye for an eye, tooth for a tooth" quotation), St. Thomas Aquinas, Hobbes, Locke, Jefferson, Rawls, and Nozick.

   b. You will find "liberty" defined in Hobbes, Locke, Jefferson, Rawls, and Nozick. Read carefully the definition by John Locke.

   c. You will find "equality" explicitly mentioned in Hobbes, Jefferson, Rawls, and Nozick, and it is implicitly assumed (though in different forms) by most of the other authors.

   Are there any conflicts between your definitions of "justice," "liberty," and "equality"? That is, can you envisage a society that is absolutely "just," totally "free," and completely "equal"?

Case 5–1

CONFLICT OF DUTIES IN ACCOUNTING AND FINANCE

The managers of a business firm obviously have duties to their stockholders who are the owners of the company and benefited by its profits. The managers also have duties to their stakeholders who are the people associated with the company in some way and affected by its actions. These two sets of duties frequently come into conflict. One of the basic moral responsibilities of management is to resolve those conflicts in ways that can be considered to be "right" and "just" and "fair." How would you resolve the following three conflicts in the functional areas of accounting and finance? All of these actions were legal at the time they were proposed or considered:

1. Reorganizing a company to reduce unemployment costs. In the southeastern United States during the late 1980s many of the companies in the petroleum and construction industries had to substantially reduce employment. The discharged workers collected unemployment benefits from the states within the area, of course, but the reserves for those benefits were soon exhausted. The state of Texas passed a law to raise the unemployment compensation tax to replenish those reserves. The amount of the additional tax to be paid by each company was to be proportional to the number of workers that had been laid off by that company over

the past five years. Large firms that had laid off large numbers of workers found that it would be far less expensive to reorganize operations, combine divisions, and charter a new company. The new company, which could be chartered for less than $100,000 in legal and accounting fees, would of course have no prior history of laying off workers and would therefore be exempt from the additional tax. For some large firms, which had laid off hundreds or even thousands of workers in the past, the savings from a new charter would be in the range of $250,000 to $2,500,000 per year. Is it "right" for these large firms to reorganize operations, combine divisions, and charter a new company to lower their unemployment compensation costs? What do the senior executives in a company "owe" to other citizens in the state in which it is located?

2. Using nonverbal language to convey inside information. During the period of unfriendly takeovers and forced acquisitions in the late 1980s many brokerage firms formed risk arbitrage departments to invest in the stocks of companies that were considered "in play." The profits were immense if a brokerage firm could buy stock in a company during the "run up" before the final price was set and announced. The risks, however, were equally great

because many of the acquisitions that were widely talked about and largely expected never took place. Access to reliable information was the key, but the investment bankers, lawyers, and accountants who were involved in the takeover and acquisition process were forbidden by law to discuss any details of their activities with persons outside that process. Robert Freeman, at that time the head of risk arbitrage at Goldman, Sachs & Company and a well-known, wealthy figure on Wall Street, took the approach of calling the principal investment banker involved in a proposed takeover to discuss recently publicized information as the process neared completion; he said that he could tell by the "anxious tone of voice" (*New York Times*, August 28, 1989, p. 22) whenever there was likely to be a problem. The U.S. Government attempted to arrest Mr. Freeman for the use of inside information; government officials pointed out that few other arbitrageurs and no small investors would have been able to reach these investment bankers by telephone, let alone know them well enough to judge their outlook by their tone of voice or, as the government alleged, by the very brief and enigmatic tips that were exchanged. One attorney for Mr. Freeman admitted that Mr. Freeman's wide range of friendships did give him an advantage, but said that was immaterial. "The market is not and never has been a level playing field," he explained (Ibid.). Another attorney for Mr. Freeman said that the government would

have to define insider trading much more clearly before indicting his client. "A legitimate businessman is entitled to know what the rules of the game are before he gets carted off to jail," he claimed (Ibid.). Is it "right" for Mr. Freeman to obtain market information through professional friendships and personal telephone calls? What, if anything, does a brokerage firm executive "owe" to other investors in the financial markets?

3. Changing transfer prices and overhead costs to reduce taxes. It is well known that many foreign companies that operate in the United States pay substantially less in corporate income taxes than American firms in exactly the same industry with approximately the same cost structure. The reason is that the foreign countries in which these companies are based usually have corporate income tax rates that are much lower than those in the United States, and consequently it is in the self-interests of the foreign companies to recognize their profits at home. This can be done by changing the transfer prices at which their products are moved from one country to another, and by allocating the shared costs of their overhead budgets more to one country than another. It is not so well known that globalized American companies often do exactly the same thing, but in reverse. An American company with manufacturing and marketing operations throughout the world can arrange to recognize its profits abroad. Is it "right" for globalized American companies to reduce their tax lia-

bilities by recognizing their profits in foreign countries? What do the managers of large American com- panies owe to the other citizens of their country?

Case 5–2

WHAT DOES "BEING RESPONSIBLE" REALLY MEAN?

"Responsible" is a term that has numerous meanings. The primary definition in *Webster's New World Dictionary* is "expected or obliged to account for something to someone, as he/she is responsible for the car." The secondary definition is "involving accountability, obligation, or duties, as he/she has a responsible position." The tertiary definition is "answerable or accountable as being the cause, agent or source of some outcome, as he/she is responsible for this state of affairs."

None of us would quarrel with those definitions taken from a respected source, but perhaps they do not fully encapsulate the concept of liability, of being subject to a penalty of some sort if the "thing" is not maintained in good order, if the "duties" are not performed in good faith, if the "outcome" is not generally beneficial to all. Harry S. Truman, president of the United States from 1945 to 1952, is said to have kept a sign on his desk that read "The Buck Stops Here"; perhaps that is a more accurately stated though more crudely worded definition of responsibility than all of the others.

Many corporate executives, however, have refused to accept responsibility in this ultimate "the buck stops here" sense for the actions of their organizations. Their arguments are that they cannot be held liable for decisions they made that happened —through unforeseeable circumstances—to turn out badly, or for actions taken by their subordinates who unknown to the chief executive cut moral corners to achieve corporate goals. Here are four examples of moral problems in which some individuals or groups were hurt or harmed in some way outside of their own control. Who should be held liable for these actions, and what should be the extent of that liability?

1. False auto repairs. The California Department of Consumer Affairs in 1992 accused Sears, Roebuck & Company of systematically overcharging auto repair customers. An inspector from the Consumer Affairs Department would drive an older car with worn brakes but no other mechanical defects into the auto repair center at a Sears store, and ask for "a brake job" at a locally advertised price. Eighty nine percent of the time the inspector— who of course was not in uniform but disguised as a normal working man or woman—would be told that additional parts were needed,

and those additional parts cost an average of $224.00 for all of the statewide tests. The worst case was in Concord, California where the inspector was overcharged $585.00 to replace the front and rear springs, the front and rear shock absorbers, and the front and rear master cylinders, all of which were in good working order. Officials at the Consumer Affairs Department believe that pressure from corporate headquarters led to the overcharges. They explained that Sears had established a quota of parts and services for every eight-hour shift, and repair supervisors who failed to meet those quotas would be transferred back to regular shop work at a substantial decrease in pay. Repair supervisors who did meet the quotas received a substantial weekly bonus. Mr. Brennan, chairman of Sears, Roebuck & Company, said that he did not know of the practice, and could not be held responsible. "We deny allegations of fraud or systematic problems at our auto centers. Isolated errors by our employees? Yes. A pattern of misconduct by our management? Absolutely not" [*New York Times,* June 23, 1992, p. C1].

2. Worthless employee pensions. Mr. Charles Hurowitz purchased the Pacific Lumber Company, a large producer of redwood lumber located on the northern coast of California, in 1988. As the new owner he was responsible for pensions averaging $1,000 per month that had been promised to slightly over 500 retirees who had lengthy records of service with the firm. The company had funded a reserve of $93 million from which to make those pension payments. Mr. Hurowitz asked for bids from life insurance companies to replace the pensions with annuities (guarantees to make exactly the same payments over the lifetime of the recipients), and received a low bid of $36 billion from First Executive Insurance Company of Los Angeles. Mr. Hurowitz paid the $36 million to the insurance company, and pocketed the balance of $57 million. Four years later First Executive defaulted on the payments of the annuities. The problem was that the insurance company had counted on the income from the $36 million invested in "junk" bonds (high-income but high-risk securities) to make the guaranteed payments. The recession of the early 1990s destroyed the value of those bonds, First Executive declared bankruptcy, and the pension payments came to an abrupt halt. Mr. Hurowitz claimed that he was not responsible; he had accepted a bid from a reputable insurance company. The owner of First Executive said that he was not responsible; he had purchased the bonds from a reputable brokerage firm. The partners in the brokerage firm said that they were not responsible, that no one could have foreseen the decline in the bond market. Mr. Hurowitz, the owner of First Executive, and the partners in the brokerage firm are all wealthy individuals, enjoying very high standards of living in Southern California. The 500 retirees who have had their pensions discontinued are not wealthy individuals; they are "just

getting by" on Social Security and their rapidly dwindling personal savings, and in many instances have lost their homes through their inability to pay the insurance and taxes.

3. Cheating small banks. E. F. Hutton in 1986 was a national brokerage firm with over 1,800 individual offices. A brokerage firm, of course, has a very substantial and predictable cash flow as investors are required by law to pay for their investments within three calendar days. Managers at the 1,800 branch offices would hand carry the cash receipts each day to a local bank for deposit, but then make out a check larger than the amount deposited to be wired to their central office in New York. By the time that check returned from the central office to the local bank, the overdraft would be covered by deposits from subsequent days. This form of overdraft, which relies upon differences in the time of transmission of deposits versus payments, is known as "check kiting." It is highly illegal if practiced by a single individual. It was highly profitable, as practiced by E. F. Hutton: the company earned interest of $32 million per year on fictitious bank balances of over $400 million. The scheme was discovered only when a branch manager in Oregon refused to participate, and the overdrafts became visible at other branches. Mr. Robert Fomon, the head of E. F. Hutton at the time, refused to accept any responsibility, saying, "No chief executive can be held responsible for every single thing that happens in a large, corporate organization" [*The Wall Street Journal*, July 30, 1990, p. B1]. He explained that the check kiting was not a company policy, but had been undertaken independently by the managers of the branch offices as a means of increasing their profits and consequently their bonuses. Mr. Fomon bristled at the suggestion of one reporter that he repay personally a portion of the debt: "I didn't do it; why should I pay for it?"

4. Damaging customers' property. The *Ann Arbor News*, a local newspaper in southeastern Michigan, on September 28 ran a series of letters from readers who were angered by the tree-trimming practices of a contractor for the public utility in the area. Two of the letters are reproduced here, slightly edited to remove extraneous material.

Letter 1

I would like to add my own "horror" story to the list. About a month ago, while entertaining out-of-town visitors, we were startled by a very loud noise. Our friend's children came running in to report a sparking wire. Indeed, a high power wire had broken, narrowly missing our friends' car, and was actively jumping, sparking, and burning on our lawn.

Trying to quickly call the Detroit Edison became the first in a series of exasperating and educational experiences. A new 800 number slowly works you through a labyrinth of choices and recorded announcements until you are finally able to speak with a human being who states, "We'll report it."

My next call was to the Ann Arbor Fire Department. They arrived within five minutes, cordoned off the area, and stood watch for the next two hours while the utility decided who would respond. This was on a weekend with good weather and presumably no overload of emergency calls. A crew finally did arrive and cut the line and the fire department left.

I could see that a limb from a large willow tree was the probable cause and within a week had received a call from the Edison tree-trimming crew. I spoke to the supervisor and because of a past experience with them (resulting in the death of a prized maple) I made it very clear that I expected them to trim with care and caution. My fears were realized. Their corporate policy is clear: brutal trimming is much more efficient and much less costly than careful work.

My numerous attempts to get through to a single individual at Edison who would hear and respond to my complaints were met by a maze of obfuscation. What do you do when the only company from whom you can buy electricity due to their monopoly of the service area obviously has no respect for you or your property?

Letter 2

Like many people, I received a brochure in the mail describing the likelihood of a visit by line clearance crews. I have trees hanging over the lines in my front yard. Expert clearing seemed like a good idea. Then, in early June, I had a visit from a line clearance contractor. One of my trees, a huge old mulberry, was in bad shape, he said, and posed considerable danger to the lines. The Edison representative and I agreed that the tree should go.

Later in June we had a fierce storm. The wind blew hard out of the east and tumbled a major part of the tree onto the guy-wire secured between two Edison poles. The cable was stretched tight against all three electric wires attached to a large transformer on one of the poles. Also the poles were pulled together by the weight of the tree, making the electric wires excessively taut up and down the street on both sides of the poles.

I immediately called Edison. That same day two people came out and looked at the mess. "We'll take care of it," they said. Well, they never did. After complaints from a neighbor about the stretched wires in mid-July I called the Edison contractor again. By August I had still had no action. I called Edison a third time.

A few days latter a crew arrived as I was going to work. When I returned that evening I found that the only trimming done was to an old apple tree which had branches no nearer than six feet to the wires. The mulberry tree hanging on the cable abrading the electric wires had not been touched.

Next day I called Edison for the fourth time. When I got home from work, I found that the crew had indeed came back. The branch that had actually rested on the cables had been cut. The Edison arborists simply sawed through the offending limb, along with a few other branches, dropping everything on the ground. The debris was left strewn there, for me to clean up.

Telephone Response from Detroit Edison Executive

These people are contractors, not employees. We are not responsible for their actions.

Class Assignment

Where does "the buck stop" in each of these four organizations? Who, if anyone, should be subject to a penalty of some sort in each instance, and what should be the nature of that penalty? In short, do you believe that senior executives should be held responsible for the actions and decisions taken by other members of their organizations that happen, due to unforeseen circumstances, to harm at least one of the stakeholder groups?

Case 5–3

GEORGE KACMAREK

George Kacmarek was a graduate of the B.B.A. program at the University of Michigan. He went to work for one of the large auto supply firms in Detroit that produced stamped metal parts for the car companies. The following is an almost verbatim account of a moral problem he encountered during his first week on the job.

On the second or third day at work I was sent from the office out to the plant to pick up some requisition slips from the foreman in one of the tool rooms. I don't know if you have ever been in a big stamping plant, but they are noisy and confusing. They have these big presses going up and coming down, and you can't hear yourself think. In our plant they have more than 100 presses, all under one roof, but with paint booths, tool cribs, loading docks, and storage bins scattered all around. I got lost.

I didn't want to admit that I was lost, so I couldn't ask any of the workers for directions. They probably couldn't hear me anyway. I went into what I thought would be an office where I could ask for directions, but it was a record storage area, with row after row of steel shelving reaching close to the ceiling, loaded with thousands of cardboard files, each marked by a number. There was a door at one end, and I was heading in that direction when I heard the voice of the plant manager talking to another person. The plant manager was from New York City, and had an accent that you could remember very easily. I had only met him once, but I recognized his voice right away.

The plant manager said, "I want $5,000 this time. That's a nice round figure, and it will help me to remember (name of a large steel supply firm) for the rest of the year."

The other person said, "George you're getting greedy. You've given us good business, and we appreciate it, but it's not worth five bills."

The plant manager got upset and told the man, "Look, you'll be out on your fat rear end if I say the word. We'll start running quality checks on your stuff until we find some that won't meet specs, and then we'll reject everything you've sent us for a month."

This didn't faze the other guy at all; he said, "George, we know the score. You don't have to tell us. But we can't go $5,000. We'll go $3,000 now, and $3,000 at the end of the year if everything stays smooth and if your volume holds up, but that's the best that we can do."

The plant manager grumbled about that but eventually he agreed to it, and both men went out the door at the end without seeing me. I went out the other door as fast as I could, and wandered around on the shop floor for awhile. I didn't know what to do.

Class Assignment

What would you do in this situation? Make a set of specific recommendations for George Kacmarek.

Case 5–4

U.S. TRADE NEGOTIATORS AND JAPANESE FIRMS

It is expected that the trade relationships between Japan and the United States will be extensively redefined during the early 1990s. For years it has been felt by some American companies and some American officials that those trade relationships were imbalanced, in favor of the Japanese. Japanese semiconductor firms, for example, came to dominate the American market during the 1980s, while American firms felt that they were excluded from the Japanese market. Japanese construction companies received over $2 billion in revenues from American building projects in 1989, to give an even more specific example, while American construction companies were limited to less than $50 million in revenues from equivalent Japanese projects. The Japanese response, of course, has always been that American companies have made very little effort to sell in Japan.

The trade relationships between Japan and the United States will be redefined through a series of negotiating sessions between the two countries that are to be held in both Washington and Tokyo. Mrs. Carla Hills, an active and articulate woman who has held numerous high-level positions within the government, will be in charge of the American delegation as U.S. Trade Representative. She will be joined by Mrs. Sidney Williams, Assistant Secretary at the Department of Commerce, and Mr. Julius Katz, Assistant Secretary at the Department of State, both of whom have been formally designated as Deputy Trade Representatives. All three are attorneys and/or economists who in between periods of government service have worked for large law firms and/or consulting firms in the Washington, D.C. area. All three have been employed in the past in their capacities as attorneys and/or consultants by Japanese manufacturing and exporting firms. All three may legally expect to be employed in the future, after this period of government service has been completed, by Japanese manufacturing and exporting firms.

If history is any guide, these and other top officials with the Office of the U.S. Trade Representative will have the chance to return to the payroll of Japanese interests. Indeed, since the early 1970s, fully one-half of the roughly 60 former top officials at the USTR have gone on to represent foreign clients or register as foreign agents, most for Japanese interests [*The Wall Street Journal*, February 23, 1990, p. A1].

Some American officials have objected to this "revolving door" practice because of the very apparent possibility for conflicts of interest. It is traditional in Washington for the higher-level governmental officials, both those who have been elected and those who have been appointed, to work as highly paid consultants and lobbyists after they leave government service. In most instances, however, those consultants and lobbyists have worked for American firms. Somehow, it is felt, the Japanese connection adds a new element.

"It's a national tragedy," says Senator John Heinz, the Pennsylvania Republican. "So many people who once worked to further the national interests now go to work for Japan. In Japan anyone doing that would be ostracized for life." [*Wall Street Journal*, February 23, 1990, p. A1]

On the other side of the issue, of course, is the fact that anyone who has worked for Japanese firms has a much better understanding of their policies and methods, if not of their language, and can subsequently become a much better negotiator for the United States. It is also said that it is almost impossible for an experienced trade negotiator in the Washington area to avoid working for the Japanese; they have both the money to hire representatives and the need to settle disputes. There have been so many "dumping" cases (allegedly selling products in the United States at unfairly low prices, or at prices below those at which the same products can be purchased in Japan) filed against Japanese companies that the Japanese have had to search for legal representation. The

United States has a tradition that everyone, whether an individual or a corporation, and whether native or foreign, is entitled to legal representation.

> A foreign corporation ought to be able to come into our market, and buy our services such as legal counsel [Mrs. Carla Hills, quoted in *The Wall Street Journal*, February 23, 1990, p. A5].

Still, the possibility of a conflict of interest exists in the minds of many observers.

> "Government officials are put in situations where they could pull their punches, and it would be very lucrative to do so," says Clyde Prestowitz, a former Commerce Department official in the Reagan Administration, and now a loud critic of the Japan lobby. "If you are a government trade negotiator, you know sooner or later you'll leave government service. Clearly it's not advantageous to make enemies" [*The Wall Street Journal*, February 23, 1990, p. A5].

Mrs. Hills strongly objects to the inferences that have been expressed about her past and (supposedly) future relationships with Japanese firms, saying that she looks upon her previous Japanese clients as "personal friends."

Mrs. Hills has little patience with questions about her links to Japan, dismissing them as something akin to McCarthyism. "I do have Japanese friends," she says, "I have French friends. I have black friends." She glares to a reporter. "And I don't want to have to be defensive about my friends who don't look exactly like you" [*The Wall Street Journal*, February 23, 1990, p. A1].

Class Assignment

Assume that you have been asked to be on a panel that is to consider the question, "Should American trade negotiators be prevented from being employed by foreign firms for a period of five years after they leave office?" Mrs. Carla Hills is to be a member of that panel, which will be held in a college auditorium in Washington, D.C. What will be your position? How will you support it in debate? Assume that you have been told that each participant will have 10 minutes to explain his or her position, before the moderator opens the panel discussion to general debate and questions from the audience.

Case 5–5

AFFIRMATIVE ACTION IN BIRMINGHAM, ALABAMA

Birmingham, Alabama was founded in 1872 during the reconstruction of the South following the Civil War.

Northern investors were attracted to the area by the abundant deposits of iron, limestone, and coal that were found in the region. Iron, limestone, and coal are the raw materials for steel, and the city was formed around the first steel mill in the southern states. It was named for Birmingham, England, the largest steel center in Europe.

The city grew rapidly. Jobs were plentiful in the mills and on the railroads and at the mines that served the mills, though most of the jobs were hard and dangerous, and they tended to attract a work force that could also be described as hard and dangerous. The jobs were segregated from the start. Skilled positions were reserved for whites; only the menial tasks were open to blacks. There were, however, many menial tasks in the steel industry before it was mechanized: shoveling ore and coal, lifting ingots, riveting girders, loading rails, laying tracks, and cleaning cars. Many black laborers migrated to the city from the rural sections of the South, and Birmingham became one of the first metropolitan areas in the United States to have a substantial black population. Members of that population, however, were strictly segregated in housing, education, employment, and government. Until 1958, for example, all job applications for governmental positions in the city of Birmingham were marked "whites only."

With a population of 350,000, Birmingham was in 1960 Alabama's largest city. A steel town, it was one of the region's major business centers. Blacks accounted for 40 percent of the city's population, but were three times less likely than white residents to hold a high-school diploma. Only one of every six black employees was a skilled or trained worker, as opposed to three quarters of the whites. The median income for blacks was $3,000, less than half that for white people [Williams, *Eyes on the Prize*, p. 185].

Continued income and educational inequality and a growing resistance to change marked the early days of the civil rights movement in Birmingham. In 1962, for example, the city closed 68 parks, 38 playgrounds, 6 swimming pools, and 4 golf courses rather than comply with a federal court order desegregating all public facilities. In 1963, after a handful of downtown merchants had removed the "whites" and "colored" signs on separate restrooms and drinking fountains, the head of the Public Safety Commission—a person soon to become known nationwide as "Bull" Connor—sent city inspectors to fine those stores for building-code violations. Eighteen bombings occurred in black neighborhoods during the same year; these were not investigated by the Public Safety Commissioner due to an alleged lack of staff.

Black civil rights leaders in Birmingham were frustrated and angry in the spring of 1963. They had received no assistance from the city officials, and they expected no help from the state governor, George Wallace, who had ended his inauguration speech in January of that year with the words: "Segregation now! Segregation tomorrow! Segregation forever!" The local leaders turned to the Southern Christian Leadership Conference (SCLC) whose director, another person soon to become known nationwide as Dr. Martin Luther King, offered to organize civil disobedience demonstrations aimed at getting blacks hired as clerks in the downtown stores, and at desegregating public facilities in the downtown area.

The black community started a boycott of the downtown stores on April 2, 1962, and conducted marches through the downtown area, but the Public Safety Commissioner acted with restraint, avoided violence, and little public sympathy was generated for the cause of greater equality. Reverend King was arrested as he led one demonstration, but instead of offering support, members of the white clergy within the city took out a full-page ad in *The Birmingham News* the following day to criticize him as an "outside agitator" and to denounce his ideas as "unwise and untimely." Dr. King responded with his famous "Letter from the Birmingham Jail".

The "Letter from the Birmingham Jail" provoked an immediate response. Volunteers, black and white, came to demonstrate in front of the Birmingham City Hall. Black high school students from the surrounding counties joined the demonstrations en masse. Bull Connor reacted. The students were arrested and forced into police cars and then school buses, and finally national guard trucks. The city and county jails were filled, and then a stockade was erected to hold the overflow at the state fairgrounds.

Students and volunteers kept coming, television cameras kept recording, and Bull Connor kept reacting. He ordered the Birmingham Fire Department to turn its hoses on the demonstrators. These hoses had 100 pounds of pressure per square inch; they were powerful enough to knock demonstrators off their feet and wash them down the street. He ordered the Birmingham Police Department to use its dogs on the demonstrators. These were large German shepherd animals; they were also strong enough to knock demonstrators off their feet. The hoses and dogs turned back the demonstrators, but only so far.

In 1963 I remember being washed down Fourth Avenue by Bull Connor's fire hoses. They [Dr. King and his organizers] told us to just fall down and protect ourselves, but my parents were scared that if you got caught they'd bomb your house, so I'd run. You couldn't fight the hose, but it could wash you down the street just so far. I was fortunate I never got bitten by the dogs. I was fast then. I got up and flew [Statement of a black fire fighter, quoted in the *Los Angeles Times*, February 7, 1990, p. A-1].

My Dear Fellow Clergymen:

While confined here in the Birmingham city jail, I came across your recent statement calling my present activities "unwise and untimely." Seldom do I pause to answer criticism of my work and ideas. If I sought to answer all the criticisms that cross my desk, my secretaries would have little time for anything other than such correspondence in the course of the day, and I would have no time for constructive work. But since I feel that you are men of genuine good will and that your criticisms are sincerely set forth, I want to try to answer your statement in what I hope will be patient and reasonable terms.

I think I should indicate why I am here in Birmingham, since you have been influenced by the view which argues against "outsiders coming in." I have the honor of serving as president of the Southern Christian Leadership Conference, an organization operating in every southern state, with headquarters in Atlanta, Georgia. . . . Several months ago the affiliate here in Birmingham asked us to be on call to engage in a nonviolent direct-action program if such were deemed necessary. We readily consented, and when the hour came we lived up to our promise. So I, along with several members of my staff, am here because I was invited here. I am here because I have organizational ties here.

But, more basically, I am in Birmingham because injustice is here. Just as the prophets of the eighth century B.C. left their villages and carried their "thus saith the Lord" message far beyond the boundaries of their towns, and just as the Apostle Paul left his village of Tarsus and carried the gospel of Jesus Christ to the far corners of the Greco-Roman world, so am I compelled to carry the gospel of freedom beyond my own home city.

Moreover, I am cognizant of the interrelatedness of all communities and states. I cannot sit idly by in Atlanta and not be concerned about what happens in Birmingham. Injustice anywhere is a threat to justice everywhere. Whatever affects one person directly, affects all persons indirectly. Never again can we afford to live with the narrow, provincial "outsider agitator" idea. Anyone who lives inside the United States can never be considered an outsider anywhere within its bounds.

You deplore the demonstrations taking place in Birmingham. But your statement, I am sorry to say, fails to express a similar concern for the conditions that brought about those demonstrations. I am sure that none of you would want to rest content with the superficial kind of social analysis that deals merely with effects and does not grapple with underlying causes. It is unfortunate that demonstrations are taking place in Birmingham, but it is even more unfortunate that the city's white power structure left the Negro community with no alternative.

. . . . .

If I have said anything in this letter that overstates the truth and indicates an unreasonable impatience, I beg you to forgive me. If I have said anything that understates the truth and indicates my having a patience that allows me to settle for anything less than brotherhood, I beg God to forgive me.

I hope this letter finds you strong in the faith. I also hope that circumstances will soon make it possible for me to meet each of you, not as an integrationist or a civil rights leader but as a fellow clergyman and a Christian brother. Let us all hope that the dark clouds of racial prejudice will soon pass away and the deep fog of misunderstanding will be lifted from our fear-drenched communities, and in some not too distant tomorrow the radiant stars of love and brotherhood will shine over our great nation with all their scintillating beauty.

Yours for the cause of Peace and Brotherhood,

Martin Luther King, Jr.

President John Kennedy dispatched the Assistant Attorney General for Civil Rights, Burke Marshall, to Birmingham. With Burke Marshall watching and the television cameras recording, with the downtown merchants fearing major riots, looting, and damage, with the members of the Birmingham Police and Fire Departments growing increasingly exhausted by the long hours and constant turmoil, and with the ranks of the demonstrators undiminished by the continual arrests, the city agreed on May 10 to desegregate the department stores, lunch counters, drinking fountains, and public washrooms in the downtown area.

The next night the Ku Klux Klan rallied in anger just outside Birmingham. Bombs exploded in homes and churches within the black community and at the hotel where Dr. King was staying. Riots broke out, seven stores were burned and looted, and 40 persons were injured. President Kennedy sent troops from the U.S. Army to restore order. Demonstrators were released from jail. Bull Connor was removed from office. Robert Kennedy, the brother of the President and the Attorney General of the United States, drafted the Civil Rights Act of 1964.

The Civil Rights Act of 1964 was a landmark in equal rights legislation. With numerous parts—called "titles"—the document was over 100 pages long, and dealt with everything from discrimination in voting to segregation in housing. Title VII focused on discrimination in employment, and in Section 703a it stated:

It shall be an unlawful employment practice for an employer:
(1) to fail or refuse to hire or to dis-

charge or attempt to discharge any individual, or otherwise to discriminate against any individual with respect to his compensation, terms, conditions, or privileges of employment, because of such individual's race, color, religion, sex, or national origin; or
(2) to limit, segregate, or classify an employee in any way which would deprive or tend to deprive any individual of employment opportunities or otherwise adversely affect his status as employee, because of such individual's race, color, religion, sex, or national origin [Civil Rights Act of 1964, p. 255].

Just 10 paragraphs later Section 703j specifically rejected any intent to create preferential treatment based upon race, color, or previous denial of opportunity:

Nothing contained in this title shall be interpreted to require any employer to grant preferential treatment to any individual or to any group because of the race, color, religion, sex, or national origin of such individual or group, or on the account of an imbalance which may exist with respect to the total number or percentage of persons of any race, color, religion, sex, or national origin employed by any employer in comparison with the total number or percentage of persons of such race, color, religion, sex, or national origin in any community, state, section, or other area [Civil Rights Act of 1964, p. 257].

It was not until 1968, four years after the passage of the Civil Rights Act of 1964, that the first black was hired by the Birmingham Fire Department. He joined 400 white firemen within that department. No further blacks were hired until 1974 when the local chapter of the National Association for the Advancement of Colored People (NAACP) filed suit in federal court against the City of Birmingham, the Birmingham Fire Department, Jefferson County (the county surrounding the city of Birmingham), and the Jefferson County Personnel Board. Three days later, a second class action suit was filed against the same defendants on behalf of three black individuals who had been denied jobs at the Birmingham Fire Department.

Jefferson County and the Personnel Board of Jefferson County were included in the suits because of the hiring and promotion procedures followed by the City of Birmingham. All applicants interested in working for the city went to the Personnel Board and filled out an application that listed the specific departments where they wished to work. Then periodically throughout the year the Personnel Board administered certification tests for the different positions within each of the departments to screen out unlikely candidates. The Personnel Board would then draw up a certification list of the passing applicants, ranked by the test scores from top to bottom, and would pass along the names of the first three persons on the list for hiring interviews by the city.

The board and the city followed a similar process for promotions. Those interested in moving up would take a promotional exam offered by the board once each year. The score on that exam, plus a point added for each year a person had served within a particular department, would determine the three people who would be recommended to the city for promotional interviews.

Everyone, then, seeking employment or promotion within any of the city's departments, had to take and pass the appropriate test. The board argued that the tests were very objective, and that they were the best way to determine who should or should not be employed or promoted by the city.

Pressured by the lawsuits, the board and the city began to certify and employ more black workers. Eight more blacks were hired by the Birmingham Fire Department between 1974 and 1976, bringing the total number to 9 out of a total staff of more than 400. The NAACP, however, continued to argue that the tests and the interviews were biased, and that the percentage of applicants of each race who passed both the test and the interview supported their view:

	Black	White
Total taking test	285	1,530
Total passing test	69 (25%)	1,263 (82%)
Total offered employment	9 (3%)	215 (14%)

In January 1977 the suits of the NAACP and the three black individuals who had been denied employment at the Birmingham Fire Department came to trial. The judge, Samuel Pointer of the U.S. District Court of the Northern District of Alabama, ruled that the tests were not job related, had a "severe adverse impact on black applicants," and were therefore in violation of Title VII of the Civil Rights Act of 1964. He commented that while there seemed to be no design or intent on the part of the board to discriminate, the effect had been to discriminate.

Judge Pointer ordered the board to take whatever steps were necessary to make certain that in the future the tests did not have an adverse impact upon black applicants. He stated that the tests should certify a percentage of blacks equivalent to the percentage of blacks taking the exam. Since 18.6 percent (285/1,530) of the recent examinees were black, then 18.6 percent of the examinees certified for hiring by the city needed to be black or there would be de facto evidence of racial discrimination. The city and the board quickly appealed Judge Pointer's ruling to Fifth Circuit Court of Appeals in New Orleans.

Three and one-half years later, in May 1980, the United States Court of Appeals for the Fifth Circuit upheld Judge Pointer's original ruling. The city and the county began negotiations with the NAACP and the black litigants to reach an out-of-court settlement that would resolve future problems but not cause either the city or the county to be liable financially for past actions. This out-of-court settlement eventually took the form of two consent decrees that were accepted by all parties in the spring of 1981.

The text of both consent decrees was over 100 pages long, but the five key points affecting the hiring and promoting of black fire fighters at the Birmingham Fire Department could be summarized briefly as follows:

1. Long-term goal. The city would hire and promote fire fighters in percentages which would approximate their respective racial divisions in the civilian labor force of Jefferson County. Since the civilian labor force of Jefferson County was 28 percent black in 1980, this became the long-term target for the Birmingham Fire Department.

2. Short-term goal. In order to reach the long-term goal in a reasonable amount of time, it was agreed that over half the fire fighters hired by the city or promoted to lieutenant in any given year would be black.

3. Certification goal. The board would certify enough blacks in any one year to meet the city's hiring needs.

4. Expiration date. The consent decrees would be dissolved after six years when, it was felt, the long-term goal would have been met.

5. Qualifying clause. The consent decrees would not require the board to certify or the city to promote a less-qualified person in preference to a person who was "demonstrably better qualified."

Judge Pointer, whose court had to either arrange for a consent decree or enforce his earlier order that the board should certify and the city should hire a percentage of blacks equivalent to the percentage taking the exam (18.6 percent in the period 1974–1976, but much higher at this time), approved of the terms:

> The settlement represents a fair, adequate, and reasonable compromise of the issues between the parties to which it is addressed and is not inequitable, unconstitutional, or otherwise against public policy [Judge Pointer, quoted in *Federal Reporter, United States Courts of Appeal*, 1984, p. 1492].

The decrees were signed by the contending parties in June 1981, and a community fairness hearing was held in August of that year. Some white fire fighters objected to the provisions on promotion, but Judge Pointer again emphasized that the settlement was not "inequitable, unconstitutional, or otherwise against public policy" and the two decrees became binding on August 18, 1981.

The board and the city stated that they intended to observe both the letter and the spirit of the two consent decrees, and by March 1988 the Birmingham Fire Department had come close to meeting the 28 percent long-term goal in total employees, and by February 1989 did meet that goal in officer positions:

Fire Department	Total Employees	Number Black	Percent Black	Percent Goal
August 1981	453	42	10.2%	28.0%
March 1988	492	124	25.2%	28.0%

Fire Department	Officer Positions	Number Black	Percent Black	Percent Goal
August 1981	140	0	0.0%	28.0%
February 1989	136	38	27.9%	28.0%

Some of the white fire fighters, however, objected strongly to being passed over for promotion. They claimed that they had scored well on the tests, but then had not been promoted due to the short-term goal of ensuring that at least 50 percent of all fire fighters promoted each year were black. Fourteen white members of the Birmingham Fire Department sued, claiming that this reverse discrimination was detrimental to their careers, and that it was clearly illegal under Title VII of the Civil Rights Act of 1964. The attorneys for these men made four major points:

1. The white fire fighters were being denied promotion on the basis of their race, not on the basis of their competence or performance. The Fire Department admitted that it was promoting equal numbers of the highest-ranking whites and the highest-ranking blacks, regardless of where the whites and blacks fell on the list relative to each other. The city did not release either the actual scores or the relative rankings of the people taking the tests; it did, however, notify each individual where he or she stood on the list and the relative rankings could then be reconstructed by the individuals "comparing notes." The 14 white fire fighters involved in the legal action had all either determined or been told that they were high enough on the list in a given year to have been promoted were it not for the short-term 50 percent goal of the consent agreement.

Chief Gallant told me I was number three on the list, but due to the fact that he had to promote more blacks, I was to be number six. Five men were promoted. [Statement of white fire fighter, quoted in *The Birmingham News*, December 17, 1985, p. A-4].

Chief Gallant told me he didn't have anything against promoting me, but that I probably wouldn't be promoted because of the consent decree. He said my position would probably change from seventh to about sixteenth [Statement of white fire fighter, quoted in *The Birmingham Post-Herald*, December 18, 1985, p. C-1].

Chief Gallant congratulated me but said he wasn't going to promote me because of the consent decree. I was very discouraged [Statement of white fire fighter, quoted in *The Birmingham News*, December 19, 1985, p. A-4].

One of the white fire fighters reported that he had been eighth on the promotion list in 1982 when 12 men were promoted, but he was not one of them. He was third on the list in 1983 when five were promoted, but was again passed over. He was ninth on the list in 1984 when 11 were promoted, but was not among them that year either. He did not bother to take the test a fourth time.

2. The white fire fighters had no control over the format or content of the test, and had to assume that it was not biased in their favor. They admitted that adding one point to the test score for each year of service did give them an advantage because they had been employed longer than the blacks, but they argued firstly that seniority was not a hollow issue—a fire lieutenant needed years of experience to safely lead other fire fighters into a dangerous situation—and secondly that they were willing to give

up those points because they did not greatly affect the relative rankings.

We are not wedded to the current paper test. It's up to the City to choose [and redesign the test if necessary]. But then apply the results evenly [Statement of white fire fighter, quoted in the *Los Angeles Times*, February 7, 1990, p. A-14].

3. The white fire fighters were being punished for a situation that they did not create. The 14 whites involved in the lawsuit were all too young to have actively participated in the overt discrimination that existed against blacks in the city of Birmingham up until 1965, or to have been responsible for the covert discrimination that existed against blacks in the fire department of Birmingham up until 1981. They claimed that consequently it was not "fair" to deny them the promotions they deserved on the basis of the test scores:

Hell, it's not fair, it's not right to give jobs or promotions on the basis of skin color. We didn't discriminate against anyone. Don't hang it on us. We weren't the ones who put up those "no blacks need apply" signs. I want to shake those people now and say to them, "So you're going to do it to me now, discriminate against me on the basis of race, but now it's all right?" It wasn't all right then, and it isn't all right now [Statement of a white fire fighter, quoted in the *Los Angeles Times*, February 7, 1990, p. A-15].

Your honor, there is a human factor here. There are people behind these goals and quotas. The plaintiffs are human beings who have been pushed aside. We feel that the City has been far too aggressive in pushing aside some employees in favor of others [Statement of an attorney representing the white fire fighters, quoted in the *Birmingham Post-Herald,* December 29, 1985, p. A-2].

4. The white fire fighters did not participate in the discussions that led to the consent decrees. The officers of the white union, the Birmingham Fire Fighters Association, were never invited to attend any of the meetings, and none of their members were permitted to be present. Officers from the black union, the Black Fire Fighters Association, were invited to attend, and many times they took members of their union with them.

Legally, this was an important issue because it seemed to indicate that the white fire fighters had not been a party to the decrees, and consequently that they had a right to now legally challenge those decrees in court. This issue was also important from the standpoint of democratic processes; the white fire fighters felt that the terms of the decrees had been dictated to them without their participation, and were resentful of that method of reaching a decision. They claimed that they were being asked to make sacrifices they weren't prepared to make, and had never agreed to make.

Attorneys for the black fire fighters, along with representatives of the City of Birmingham and the Employment Board of Jefferson County, defended the existing consent decrees. They made three major points:

1. The black fire fighters should not be forced to wait for normal changes in age patterns to create promotion opportunities, or for gradual improvements in regional

school systems to raise test scores. The last was a critical point. Lower test scores were not, it was claimed, an indication of lower competence; they were just a proof of poorer education. Schools in the predominantly black sections of the South, it was said, even 40 years after the end of formally segregated education in that region, tended to place less emphasis upon the basic skills of reading and writing than did schools in the predominantly white areas. Consequently, the black fire fighters read and responded to the questions on the tests somewhat more slowly than did the whites, and had much less experience in the psychological pressures of doing well on written exams.

Are we qualified for promotion to fire lieutenant? All I can tell you is that there has been no increase in the loss of property or the loss of life caused by fires within the city of Birmingham since the consent decrees went into effect, and black firemen were promoted to command positions [Statement of black fire lieutenant, quoted in *The New York Times,* June 14, 1989, p. A-10].

2. The black fire fighters needed active antidiscrimination steps to redress past wrongs. No black officers existed prior to the consent decrees, even though there had been a few black fire fighters since the early 1970s. It had to be expected that the future pace of promotions for black fire fighters would have continued to be slow without the short-term goals of the consent decrees.

They're not totally fair, but was it fair that I couldn't be a fireman back in the '60s? If there had been black firemen in the 1960s, there wouldn't have been consent decrees in the 1980s [Statement of black fire fighter, quoted in the *Los Angeles Times*, February 7, 1990, p. A-15].

Could we have been less intrusive? What you're really asking is, could we have done it over 30 years instead of six? Well, sure, yes we could have. But then we wouldn't have dealt with the problem for two whole generations [Statement of attorney for the black fire fighters, quoted in the *Los Angeles Times*, February 7, 1990, p. A-14].

For years now I have heard the word "Wait!" It rings in the ear of every Negro with piercing familiarity. This "Wait!" has almost always meant "Never!" We must come to see, with one of our distinguished jurists, that "justice too long delayed is justice denied." We have waited for more than 340 years for our constitutional and God-given rights [Dr. King, *Letter from the Birmingham Jail*, p. 8].

The 14 white firemen filed the suit charging racial discrimination in both the hiring and the promotion policies of the city and the board. Judge Pointer ruled in December 1985 once again that the consent decrees were not "inequitable, unconstitutional, or otherwise against public policy" and he noted that the decrees were limited in duration and consequently in effect, and could not be that damaging to anyone's career for very long, if at all.

Judge Pointer's decision was appealed to the U.S. Court of Appeals. That court ruled in December 1987 that the relief intended by the consent decrees was expected to come from the city and the county, not from the individual fire fighters. It ruled that Birmingham might actively recruit black persons to apply for positions, and might offer classes or tutorials to ensure that black candidates would be able to qualify for open positions, but that the city could not, as part of an affirmative action program, ignore higher test results from equally qualified white candidates.

The city and board appealed the circuit court's decision to the U.S. Supreme Court. In June 1989, the Supreme Court upheld the decision of the circuit court and found against the city, the board, and the black fire fighters. The white fire fighters were now able to file suit against the city and the county for monetary damages. They did so in 1990.

At the same time, the racial composition of both the City of Birmingham and Jefferson County had changed since the 28 percent black hiring and promotion goal had been set in 1980. Birmingham was now over 50 percent black, Jefferson County over 40 percent. Black civil rights groups, consequently, sued to continue the consent decrees beyond the six-year limit, and to raise the hiring and promotion goals to 42 percent. It was expected that both lawsuits would continue for at least five years, eventually reaching the Supreme Court once again:

> The city has been put into a situation where they'll be defending their position no matter what they do. I anticipate seeing both reverse discrimination and traditional discrimination suits tried at the same time, maybe in the same court. We are on the horns of a dilemma. All we know is that whatever we do, the losing side is going to sue us. This might never end [Statement of attorney for the City of Birmingham, quoted in the *Los Angeles Times*, February 7, 1990, p. A-15].

As I sat in the Supreme Court today, I wondered how long would this type of thing go on, and how many different stumbling blocks will be put in our path before they correct the wrong doings. Back in 1963 when I was demonstrating, I had hopes that within some short term—two or three years—some of these things would be resolved. But here we are in 1989, and we're still talking about some of the things I was demonstrating against back in 1963. When does it stop? [Statement of black fire fighter, quoted in *The Birmingham News*, January 19, 1989, p. B-1]

Where's affirmative action going to end? I say end it now. My kids shouldn't have to pay for the past. There's got to be an end. Sooner or later you pay off the car [Statement of white fire fighter, quoted in the *Los Angeles Times*, February 1990, p. A-15].

Class Assignment

You have recently been appointed the chief of the Birmingham Fire Department. The effectiveness of the department has declined markedly over the past four years as a result of the constant turmoil and legal squabbling. What do you do to end the turmoil and increase the effectiveness?

CHAPTER 6
Moral Responsibility in Management

In Chapter 5, it was suggested that a basic reason for a business manager to be moral, a basic reason to be concerned about what is "right" and "just" and "fair" in the treatment of others, is the need to build trust, commitment, and effort among all of the stakeholders of the firm. This is the managerial responsibility view of the importance of ethics.

Certainly it is possible to say that you owe moral decisions and actions to yourself, to your concept of your own dignity and self-worth. The argument here is that you have a *personal* responsibility to act in ways that are "right" and "just" and "fair." Certainly it is also possible to say that you owe moral decisions and actions to your fellow human beings, to your acceptance of their dignity and self-worth. The argument in this instance is that you have a *social* responsibility to treat others in ways that are "right" and "just" and "fair." Certainly it is further possible to say that you owe moral decisions and actions to those people who are dependent upon your special knowledge of the law, or medicine, or marketing. The argument in this instance is that you have a *professional* responsibility to treat citizens in the society—the people who in the past have educated you and then employed you to practice your expertise—in ways that are "right" and "just" and "fair." Lastly, and perhaps most important of all, however, is the claim that you owe moral decisions and actions to those people who are dependent upon your direction of the activities of the firm. The argument in this instance is that you have a *managerial* responsibility to treat stakeholders in the organization—people who in the past have worked with you for the successful performance of the firm—in ways that can be considered to be "right" and "just" and "fair." That treatment may be due to their past performance, but it should help to ensure their future trust, commitment, and effort.

The first major thesis of this chapter is that (1) treating people in ways that can be considered to be "right" and "just" and "fair" creates trust, (2) trust builds commitment, (3) commitment ensures effort, and (4) effort is essential for success. Certainly there will be disagreements among the stakeholder groups on exactly what distribution of benefits and allocation of harms, on exactly what

EXHIBIT 6–1

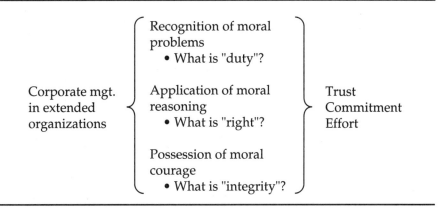

recognition of rights and performance of duties, can be considered to be "right" and "just" and "fair" in any given situation. Certainly some stakeholder groups will prefer one decision outcome, while other stakeholder groups will prefer another. But, the thesis of this chapter is that as long as all of the groups together can agree that the decision process itself has been "right" and "just" and "fair"—that is, that the decision process has considered the interests of each of the groups according to known and consistent principles—then there should be an increase in trust and commitment among all of the stakeholder groups, and that increase in trust and commitment should in turn lead to an increase in effort.

The second major thesis of this chapter is that the effort that results from stakeholder trust and commitment goes far beyond that which is based only upon financial incentives or commercial contracts. Stakeholder trust and commitment result in a willingness to contribute "something extra," a readiness to act with both energy and enthusiasm for the benefit of the firm.

A story by Edward Carlson, then president of United Airlines, illustrates very succinctly this willingness to contribute something extra. Mr. Carlson is quoted as saying, "The president of a company has a constituency much like that of a politician. The employees may not actually go to the polls, but each one does elect to do his or her job in a better or worse fashion every day" [Thomas Peters and Robert Waterman, *In Search of Excellence: Lessons from America's Best-Run Companies* (New York: Harper & Row, 1982), p. 289]. Electing to do his or her job in a better rather than a worse fashion is what is meant in this text by contributing something extra. That committed attitude among all of the stakeholders—not just the workers—is essential for the success of most organizations.

The third major thesis of this chapter is that this committed attitude, this willingness to contribute something extra, this readiness to act with energy and enthusiasm for the benefit of the organization on the part of all of the stakeholder groups, is much more important now than in the past given the changed conditions of global management. Competitors have become more aggressive. Technologies have become more advanced. Products have become more complex. Markets have become more diverse. Processes have become more oriented towards quality and cost. Customers in both the industrial and consumer segments have become more insistent upon value and choice. Changes in competitors, technologies, products, markets, methods, and customers have become more frequent. And the thoughtfulness, speed, and cost of the firm's reactions to those changes—or even better in their anticipations of them—have become more critical.

It is no longer possible to manage organizations that must respond intelligently, quickly, and efficiently to technological, product, market, process, or customer changes on a "command and control" basis. Innovation is required, but a corporate manager cannot command innovation. Cooperation is essential, but a corporate manager cannot control cooperation. The problem is that many of the groups who must first innovate and then cooperate are outside the formal command and control hierarchy of the firm.

Material and component suppliers, for example, are clearly outside the formal hierarchy of the firm, yet they can easily influence the quality and cost of the company's goods and services. Many suppliers now participate in the design of those goods and services, almost on a partnership basis, and most are now relied upon for "just-in-time" inventory systems where failure to deliver could shut down the production lines of their customers.

Wholesale and retail distributors, as another example, are also outside the formal hierarchy of the firm, yet here again they can influence the price of the product, the level of service, and the degree of satisfaction received by the customer. Many distributors are now relied upon not only for the prompt transmission of information about current sales trends, but also for the accurate anticipation of future customer needs. Both are obviously essential for the long-term success of the firm.

Commercial banks, investment companies, research labs, and educational institutions are further examples of organizations that are outside the formal command and control hierarchy of the firm yet can influence the long-term success of that firm. They provide personnel, technology, equity, and debt. Their cooperation is essential, given the changed conditions of management. Companies with untrained employees, obsolete methods, or inadequate funds cannot compete in a global economy.

Lastly, industry trade associations, public interest groups, and domestic political agencies are further examples of organizations that are outside the formal command and control hierarchy of the firm. These associations, groups, and agencies help in determining (1) the national financial policies that set tax rules and interest rates, (2) the national regulatory policies that influence product/process designs and environmental requirements, (3) the national social policies that establish educational achievement levels and health care costs, and (4) the national infrastructure systems which include the communication networks and the transportation methods.

EXHIBIT 6–2   An Extended View of Business Organizations

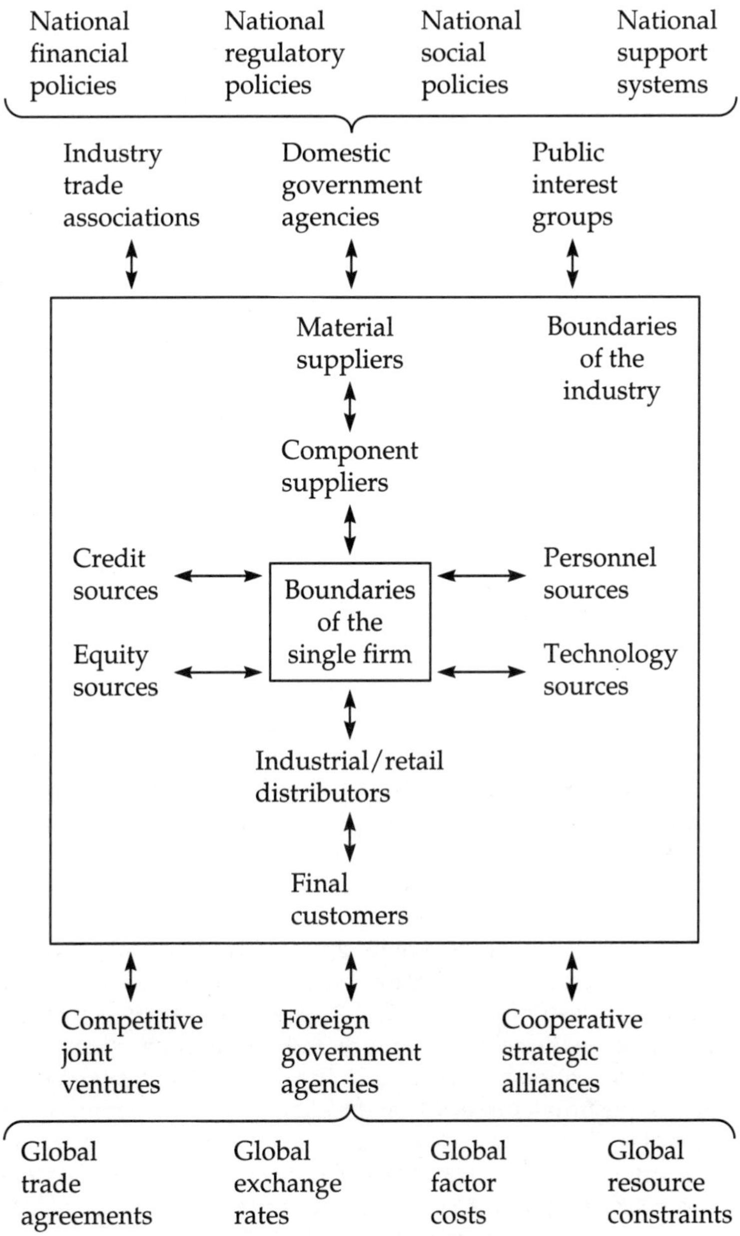

National financial policies

National regulatory policies

National social policies

National support systems

Industry trade associations

Domestic government agencies

Public interest groups

Material suppliers

Boundaries of the industry

Component suppliers

Credit sources

Boundaries of the single firm

Personnel sources

Equity sources

Technology sources

Industrial/retail distributors

Final customers

Competitive joint ventures

Foreign government agencies

Cooperative strategic alliances

Global trade agreements

Global exchange rates

Global factor costs

Global resource constraints

If you doubt that companies are now dependent upon the governmental policies and national systems listed above, think for a minute about the domestic automobile manufacturers who must meet mileage, safety, and emission standards in their cars, and provide educational training and health care benefits for their workers. In 1992 it was said that health care benefits added $1,100 to the cost of each American car, a charge not included in the cost of automobiles produced in Europe or Japan where the health care system is financed by public, not private revenues. Companies are starting to compete based upon their country's education and health care systems, in addition to their own product designs, manufacturing costs, and advertising messages.

Let us assume that you accept for now the proposal that the old "command and control" form of management is no longer viable. Let us further assume that you also agree that the stakeholder groups that can affect the success or failure of the organization are now too diverse, and that they now extend too far beyond the hierarchical bounds of its structure, for the older method to survive. Innovation is too important, given the rapid changes occurring in technologies, products, markets, and methods, yet innovation cannot be commanded. Cooperation is too essential, given the need to react quickly and efficiently to those changes, but cooperation cannot be controlled. The question is, then, what takes the place of the outmoded "command and control" model? What generates a sense of trust, commitment, and *directed* effort?

Directed effort is obviously important. Undirected effort results only in chaos and confusion. But, the effort has to be the result of trust and commitment as well as direction and planning. This leads us to the fourth major argument of this chapter: Moral reasoning—the process that leads to a determination of what is "right" and "just" and "fair" in the treatment of others—is not peripheral to corporate management. It is not something to be considered—if at all—only after the important operating, functional, technical, and strategic decisions have been made. It is not something to be published as a code of conduct that will be handed to each new employee on the first day at work, and then promptly forgotten. Moral reasoning has to become an integral part of the managerial process. It has to be combined with the other managerial decisions at all levels of the organization to ensure trust, commitment, and directed effort.

The need for trust, commitment, and directed effort leads to a form of management that might be called "unify and guide" rather than "command and control." Unification is the key. Unification means bringing all of the stakeholders of the firm—those within the company, those within the industry, and those within the society—together into an innovative and cooperative whole. Unification requires recognizing the impacts of company actions—both benefits and harms—upon the stakeholders of the firm, and then distributing those impacts through a process that is thought to be "right" and "just" and "fair," in order to ensure the willingness to innovate and to cooperate. Unification, based upon trust, commitment, and effort, is *the* moral responsibility of management.

EXHIBIT 6–3   Levels of Managerial Activity

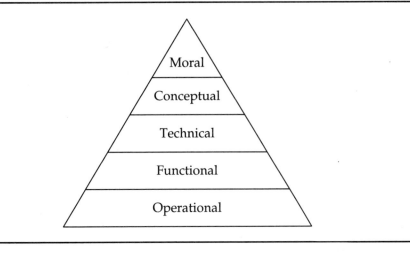

Unification through the process of moral reasoning is the moral responsibility of management, but there are other responsibilities as well, at the conceptual, technical, functional, and operational levels. What are these other responsibilities? They are necessarily associated with the activities within the firm that lead towards the long-term success of the company. The long-term success of an organization is, of course, the ultimate responsibility of management.

It is not possible to describe all of the activities that take place at each level of management within the firm. It is possible, however, to summarize the activities at each level that are critical for long-term success, and then to identify specific measures for the performance of those activities. Those measures of performance form the operational, functional, technical, and conceptual responsibilities of management for the activities at each level that have to be done, and done well, for the organization to succeed:

1. *Operational level.* At the bottom of the administrative hierarchy is the operational level where products are manufactured, customers are served, revenues are generated, and bills are paid. For many smaller firms, particularly in the retail and service industries, this is the primary level of activity. In these small organizations there is little need for quantitative analysis in the functional areas of marketing, production, or finance; close contacts with customers, workers, and creditors seem to be more effective. There is little need for advanced systems in the technical areas of human staffing, data processing, and product or process design; intuitive assessments, desktop computers, and gradual improvements seem to be quite suitable. There is even limited concern for the strategic concepts of the economies of scale or scope, barriers to entry, and learning curves; a good shop or store location with plenty of free parking seems to be more desirable.

EXHIBIT 6–4   Changes between Responsibility Levels

| Operational level | Functional level | Technical level | Conceptual level | Moral level |

Good operating level companies don't plan, they do. They seem to adapt naturally to local conditions, and they usually remain successful as long as the local economies upon which they are dependent continue to prosper. Personal time and effort are all required, of course, but the owners and managers—often combined in one person or one family or one group—appear to look upon their primary tasks as satisfying customers, improving methods, and conserving assets. These are also the basic performance outcomes we should be able to expect from managers at the operational level in larger companies. They often seem to be forgotten in this larger context, unfortunately, but some of the most famous managerial texts of the 1980s, such as *In Search of Excellence* and *The Art of Japanese Management,* have done little more than remind corporate managers and others of these basic operational responsibilities.

2. *Functional level.* The next level of activity at most corporations is that of functional management, where planning begins to supplant doing. Marketing policies are established through analytical approaches to pricing levels, distribution channels, and promotional means. Production policies are arranged by mathematical programs for machine scheduling, line balancing, and job sequencing. Financial policies are developed through economic comparisons of investment projects, asset prices, and debt-equity structures. Here we have the province of the quantitative techniques that are taught so extensively in most schools of business administration. The expected outcomes of the application of these techniques are the maximization of revenues, the minimization of costs, and the optimization of returns. These can be considered to be the performance criteria of managers at the functional level at medium-sized and larger firms.

3. *Technical level.* The third level of activity is that of technical management where the human and machine capabilities for improved performance are developed and where plans become at least as important as actions. Human resource departments are set up to select, train, and moti-

vate people. Data processing departments are established to reco.
nize, and transmit information. R&D departments are formed to co.
design, and establish new products and processes. The expected outc.
of corporate activities at this level include the development of people, ι
utilization of information, and the improvement of products and processes.
These can also serve as the performance criteria for managers at the technical level.

4. *Conceptual level.* The fourth level of activity is that of conceptual
management where plans almost totally replace actions. This is the level
that was originally termed strategic planning or strategic management. In
the early 1970s, strategic planning primarily focused on the objectives of
the firm. Strategy was defined as the "pattern of goals and objectives for an
organization and the major policies and procedures to achieve those goals
and objectives stated in such a way as to define the nature of the business
and the character of the company" [Kenneth Andrews, *The Concept of
Corporate Strategy* (Homewood, Ill.: Richard D. Irwin, Inc., 1971), p. 3]. It
was felt that any strategy could be successful if it matched the opportunities and risks in the environment (what should we do?) with the strengths
and weaknesses of the firm (what can we do?) with the values and attitudes
of the management (what do we want to do?).

The optimistic belief that any thoughtful strategic plan that matched opportunities, skills, and values could be successful came to an end in the early
1980s with the advent of global rather than domestic competition. Strategic
planning became not so much the direction of the firm to achieve corporate
objectives as the positioning of the firm to gain competitive advantages. The
five forces that determined industry profitability were described as supplier
power, customer power, new entrants, substitute products, and producer ri-
valry. It was now necessary to establish a defensible posture for the company
within each industry through the consideration of entry barriers, value chains,
scale and scope economies, experience curves, distributor constraints, and competitor intentions [Michael Porter, *Competitive Strategy: Techniques for Analyzing
Industries and Competitors* (New York: Free Press, 1980)]. Companies were also
told to build an overall framework of industry strategies based upon a foundation of core competences [C. K. Prahalad and Gary Hamel, "The Core Competences of the Corporation," Harvard Business Review, May–June 1991, p. 71–
91]. The expected outcomes of managerial activities at the conceptual level
could then be defined as setting achievable objectives, gaining competitive
advantages, and building core competences.

5. *Moral level.* The activities of management at the moral level are the
distribution of the benefits and the allocation of the harms generated by the
firm. Distributing benefits, of course, is easy and pleasant work. It is always
easy to raise salaries, pay bonuses, announce expansions. It is always
pleasant to offer contracts, build plants, raise dividends.

EXHIBIT 6–5   Levels of Managerial Responsibility

Moral responsibilities	Gaining trust Generating commitment Producing effort	⎫
Conceptual responsibilities	Setting objectives Forging advantages Building competence	
Technical responsibilities	Developing people Utilizing information Creating products	⎬ Economic efficiency Comp. effectiveness Social beneficiency
Functional responsibilities	Maximizing revenues Minimizing costs Optimizing returns	
Operational responsibilities	Satisfying customers Improving methods Conserving assets	⎭

Allocating harms, however, is not easy and pleasant work. It is not easy to cut salaries, eliminate bonuses, announce restructurings. It is not pleasant to cancel contracts, close plants, reduce dividends. Yet, this often has to be done given the severity of global competition. And, just as with the other activities in the hierarchy of managerial responsibilities, it has to be done well.

Distributing benefits and allocating harms "well" does not mean just performing those activities harshly or sternly or with a lack of care or compassion. Performing those activities "well" means that the distribution of benefits and the allocation of harms is accomplished in such a way that the stakeholders within the firm, within the industry, and within the society can agree that the process—if not the decision—has been "right" and "just" and "fair." This is the recognition of moral problems, the process of moral reasoning, and the possession of moral courage applied to the basic mission or purpose of the firm. This leads to the trust, commitment, and effort by all of the stakeholders of the firm that are the performance criteria for managers at the moral level.

The fifth, and last, major argument of this chapter is that if the activities at all of these levels of management are performed "well"—that is, if the moral, conceptual, technical, functional, and operational responsibilities of management are met and met fully—then the result will be an extended organization that is economically efficient, competitively effective, and socially beneficial.

Economic efficiency means that the company is able to convert the scarce resources of society—the financial capital, the raw material, and the trained people—into needed goods and services as inexpensively as possible. Economic efficiency is one indication of the long-term success of the firm; it can be measured by the profits of the company.

Competitive effectiveness means that the company is able to improve its position relative to other firms by building upon its competitive advantages and core competences as thoughtfully as possible. Competitive effectiveness is a second indication of the long-term success of the firm; it can be measured by the growth of the company.

Social beneficiency means that the company is able to distribute the benefits and allocate the harms generated by the firm as equitably as possible. Social beneficiency or betterment is the third indication of the long-term success of the firm; it can be measured by the trust of the company.

The moral responsibility of management is key to this high-profit, high-growth, and high-trust outcome. It provides the unification of the stakeholders within the company, within the industry, and within the society, that is essential for total long-term success.

ASSIGNMENT QUESTIONS

1. Look once again at the graphic An Extended View of Business Organizations in Exhibit 6–2. It has been said that this graphic is just a recognition of the simple fact that "we're all in this together." Do you agree? If so, why? If not, why not?

2. Look once again at the graphic Levels of Managerial Activity in Exhibit 6–3. It has been said that placing the moral level at the top of that hierarchy is just an understanding of the obvious reality that adversarial relationships among stakeholders are no longer very productive. Do you agree? If so, why? If not, why not?

3. Think once again about the changes that have occurred to the old "command and control" form of management. The text suggests that it is being replaced by a new form that might be called "unify and guide." Explain what the term "unify and guide" means to you. Do you agree that this new form will replace the older method? If so, why? If not, why not?

4. Look once again at the graphic Levels of Managerial Responsibility in Exhibit 6–5. Explain what the term "responsibilities of management" means to you. Is this list complete? What, if anything, would you add to it? Why, for example, is a responsibility to preserve the environment not on that list?

5. This chapter has expressed five major theses or arguments that are stated below, in sequence. Do you agree, or disagree, with each?

   • The first major thesis of this chapter is that (1) treating people in ways that can be considered to be "right" and "just" and "fair" creates trust,

(2) trust builds commitment, (3) commitment ensures effort, and (4) effort is essential for success.

- The second major thesis of this chapter is that the effort that results from stakeholder trust and commitment goes far beyond that which is based only upon financial incentives or commercial contracts, and becomes a willingness to contribute "something extra" for the benefit of the organization.

- The third major thesis of this chapter is that this committed attitude, this willingness to contribute "something extra" for the benefit of the organization, is much more important now than in the past due to the changed conditions of global competition.

- The fourth major thesis of this chapter is that moral reasoning—the process that leads to a determination of what is "right" and "just" and "fair" in the treatment of others—is not peripheral to corporate management. It is, or should be, a dominant part of the managerial process.

- The fifth major thesis of this chapter is that when moral reasoning *does* become an integral part of the managerial process, and when the managerial responsibilities at the operational, functional, technical, conceptual *and moral* levels are fulfilled, the long-term success of the firm is greatly enhanced.

Case 6–1

EXPLAINING YOUR MORAL DECISIONS TO OTHERS

When you make a moral decision as a private individual within our society you have only to explain that decision to yourself. You may or may not wish to justify your decision to others, but you are not forced to do so. When you make a moral decision as a senior executive within a company you have to explain that decision to others who may or may not share your standards of behavior and your judgments of priority. How do you do this, and particularly how do you do this in a logical, convincing way to people who oppose your point of view: It is difficult, but it is essential if you are going to change other people's actions and priorities.

Here are three examples of actions that you may or may not believe to be "wrong." In each instance the action was completely legal, and the people involved felt strongly that there was "absolutely nothing improper in any sense" even though considerable opposition was aroused and considerable disagreement was expressed. How would you convince these people that their actions were "wrong," if that is your judgment? How would you convince members of the opposition that the actions were "right," if that is your choice?

1. Stock sales by company officials just prior to an adverse earning report. In September 1992 it was disclosed that two officials of Browning Ferris, Inc.—an industrial and municipal waste disposal firm— had both sold half their stock holdings two weeks before an announcement by the company that third- and fourth-quarter earnings would be substantially below analysts' expectations. The chief financial officer sold 60,000 shares at $27.34 each, while the general counsel sold 15,000 shares for $27.00 each. Immediately after the formal announcement the stock price declined to $17.67 per share. Both men claimed afterwards that there was absolutely nothing wrong with what they had done, saying that it was perfectly legal as long as it could not be proven that they had acted solely to prevent financial losses prior to the earning decline becoming public knowledge. The chief financial officer added that he sold the shares only because "it wasn't very prudent to have that many eggs in one basket." The general counsel said that implications he had acted improperly were "an insult to his personal integrity." How would you respond to each?

2. Foreign trips arranged at no personal cost by U.S. Supreme Court justices. In September 1992 it was reported that Justice Sandra Day O'Connor had expressed an interest in visiting Rwanda (a small country in central Africa) to see the rare mountain gorillas that reside there. The U.S. Information Agency arranged the trip at no cost to Justice O'Connor on the condition that she give a talk to college students in the capital city of Kigali (population 25,000). At the same time it was reported that Chief Justice William Rehnquist had expressed an interest in visiting Ireland. The U.S. Information Agency paid for that trip also at no cost to Justice Rehnquist, again on the condition that he address a gathering of luncheon guests at the U.S. embassy. It was estimated that the two trips, both just one week long, cost somewhat over $10,000 each for first-class air fare, a car and driver, and housing at the embassy. Each beneficiary expressed the opinion that "there was absolutely nothing wrong." How would you respond to each?

3. Vacation housing constructed for a U.S. senator at 53.8 percent of the actual cost. Mr. Philip Gramm, U.S. senator from Texas and a member of the Senate Banking Committee, disclosed that a Texas constituent who specialized in building large office buildings near Houston had constructed Senator Gramm's vacation home on the Maryland shore for $63,400 and had charged off the balance of the $117,000 expense to a "cost overrun." The constituent had a number of issues pending before the Senate Banking Committee, and Senator Gramm admitted that he had helped the contractor with advice on banking issues and letters to banking regulators, etc. Senator Gramm, however, claimed

that there was "absolutely nothing wrong with his actions," and said that he had picked the Texas contractor, rather than a local builder, to "stimulate the Texas economy," and that the cost overrun had been a natural mistake in bidding. The chairman of the Senate Ethics Committee agreed that the $53,600 not charged was a "contractual cost overrun" and not a gift. How would you respond to each?

Class Assignment

In each instance put yourself in a position where you are superior to the participants, perhaps as chair of the U.S. Ethics Commission (there is no such commission, but perhaps there should be). In short, put yourself in an authoritative position where people have to listen to you; you do not have to listen to them. How will you convince senior company officials, justices of the U.S. Supreme Court, or members of the U.S. Senate, that you are "right"?

Case 6–2

TUNA FISH, DOLPHINS, AND H. J. HEINZ

Assume that you have just started work at the H. J. Heinz Company. Heinz, if you are not familiar with the firm, is a large food products company, headquartered in Pittsburgh, that was one of the first to become active in international manufacturing and marketing. Over half of its sales revenues now come from outside the United States.

Assume that you were very pleased to receive a job offer from Heinz. It is a rapidly growing company, with numerous opportunities for younger managers. Further, it tends to recruit very few business students, and then only for positions in international marketing and finance. Domestic positions have traditionally been filled by promotion from within the company.

Assume lastly that at the end of your first week on the job you, and

approximately 25 other recent graduates of business schools and law schools in both the United States and Europe who were part of the training program, were invited to a reception to meet Mr. A. J. H. O'Reilly, the chairman of Heinz.

You were particularly pleased to have an opportunity to meet Mr. O'Reilly. He has an unusual reputation in business circles. He is a native of Ireland, and still maintains his home in that country, flying to Pittsburgh (headquarters for the global corporation and the U.S. division), London (headquarters of the European division), and Sydney, Australia (headquarters for the Pacific division). He is an urbane, sophisticated man who attempts to keep a low profile in the business press. A number of years ago he was quoted as saying that the function of a chairman is to set a clear direction and explicit goals for the company, select good people to achieve those goals, and then keep well out of their way. The phrase "keep well out of their way" seemed to appeal to the media. Numerous magazines published pictures of Mr. O'Reilly salmon fishing on his estate in Ireland, or riding in a fox hunt across the picturesque Irish landscape, under that title. Mr. O'Reilly simply ignored those jibes implying that he works very little. He could afford to do so. H. J. Heinz has increased its earnings substantially each year for the 19 years that he has been chairman.

In addition to the unusual reputation in business circles, Mr. O'Reilly has an unusual background, which includes an undergraduate degree in moral philosophy from Dublin College, a Ph.D. in economics from Bradford University, and a law degree from the University of Paris. He was appointed president of Heinz at age 37, after 10 years as firstly a marketing executive and then general manager of the very successful European division.

At the reception, Mr. O'Reilly talked to your group about his view of a truly global economy, bound together by rapid advances in telecommunication technologies and responding to equally rapid changes in market segments. He finished by describing his vision of the future of H. J. Heinz as part of that economy, those technologies, and those markets. It was not a mundane address. It obviously reflected his deeply held beliefs. He then circulated around the room, guided by the vice president of human resources who introduced each recent hiree with a brief comment about that person's interests or background. For example, the person standing next to you happened to be from the University of Paris, and Mr. O'Reilly said a few words about the days when he was a student at that university and asked about changes in the curriculum.

When it was your turn, the vice president introduced you by name, and then explained that you had taken a course in ethics at your university. You wondered why she had picked upon such a minor portion of your background, but Mr. O'Reilly was immediately interested. He asked about the content in the course. You described very briefly the moral reasoning process designed to deal with situations in which some people may be hurt or harmed in ways outside of their own control, and then mentioned a few of the early ethical principles such as self-interests, personal virtues, and religious injunctions that help to decide what is "right" and "just" and "fair" in those situations. Then you stopped, for you wondered just how much detail he really wanted. He nodded his head and said, "Yes, yes, do go on," so you completed the listing with Hobbes, Mill, Kant, Jefferson, Smith, Rawls, and Nozick. He asked you to comment on Kant's Second Formulation of the Categorical Imperative (treat each person as an end, valuable in himself or herself, not as a means to an end) which you were very happy to realize you remembered in some detail. He asked which side of the debate of Rawls (who believes that justice is the primary "good" or goal for society) or Nozick (who takes the opposite side, that freedom is more important than justice) you were on. You responded.

It seemed as if he were testing your knowledge of the basic concepts, and your understanding of the first principles. He appeared satisfied, however, for he nodded his head and said "exactly" or "of course" a number of times as you spoke. He chatted for a few more minutes about his own thoughts upon the latter subject (Rawls versus Nozick), and upon his belief that modern managers should have a better understanding of what he termed "the moral and political economy of business."

Then, he turned to the vice president of human resources and said, "Susan, I should like to borrow this young person for a few days next week, if you can spare him (her) from the training program for that period of time." There was, of course, rapid agreement from the vice president. Mr. O'Reilly then turned back to you, and explained that he would like you to write a short report addressed to him explaining what H. J. Heinz should do relative to the killing and maiming of dolphins that seemed to be an unavoidable consequence of fishing for tuna. Starkist tuna fish, you already knew from one of the introductory lectures about the company, was one of the major brands produced by the firm, and accounted for 9 percent of sales and 11 percent of profits. "Don't tell me what you think I want to hear" was his parting comment as he went on to talk with others in the room; "tell me what you think the company ought to do." He emphasized the word "ought." Then he finished by saying, "Give the report to my secretary next Wednesday. If you

tell people in the company you are working for me, I feel fairly certain that you will be able to get the background information you will need. Susan [the personnel vice president] can help you get started."

You spent the weekend learning as much as you could about commercial tuna fishing, from reports accumulated by the staff of the personnel vice president. You found that the basic facts were depressingly familiar to everyone who wrote on the subject. The best tuna is termed "albacore," and it comes from the eastern tropics of the Pacific, a 6 million square mile section of that ocean that extends between 200 to 600 miles off the coast from northern Chile to southern California.

There is also an Atlantic species of the fish which is termed "horse mackerel" (due to its larger size than the standard Atlantic mackerel). Horse mackerel is of much lower quality (an oilier and coarser consistency) than albacore tuna. There is a second Pacific species termed "white" tuna which is found only in the western tropics of the Pacific but that is heavily fished by the Pacific nations, including Japan, Taiwan, and Indonesia. Finally, there used to be a Mediterranean species called "yellow" tuna, but that has been largely depleted by overfishing.

Albacore tuna are large fish, ranging in size from 15 to 35 pounds. They swim in schools, feeding on the small shrimp and brine minnows that thrive in the warm waters of the eastern tropical Pacific. The Humboldt Current, which is a cold water current from the Antarctic, flows directly along the coasts of South and Central America, and brings nutrients that mix with the warmer waters of the Pacific. The result is a very prolific spawning ground for a wide variety of commercial fish and marine mammals.

Commercial fishing is very active in the area, which is outside the territorial waters of any of the countries along the coast. Fishing fleets come from Italy and Spain in Europe, Japan and Korea in Asia, and most of the American nations.

The problem that arises in commercial fishing for albacore tuna is that, for reasons that are not at all understood despite extensive research by oceanographic scientists, the schools of this species of tuna tend to congregate directly under herds of dolphins. It may be that the tuna and the dolphins are attracted by the same food sources, or by the same water temperatures. It may be that a symbiotic (helping) relationship exists between the two species. It remains a fact that schools of albacore tuna are seldom found, in the entire 6 million square miles of the eastern tropics of the Pacific, if they are not associated in some way with herds of dolphins.

Dolphins, of course, are mammals, not fish. They have a reputation of being highly intelligent, able to communicate with one another through a series of squeaks, grunts, and whistles. They also have a reputation of being highly playful, often riding the bow waves of boats or leaping over ocean waves in an apparent game of "follow the leader." They have even been known to play tag with swimmers along the coast, which can be unnerving for the swimmer but apparently is "fun" for the dolphin.

Fishing boat captains locate schools of tuna by finding herds of dolphins playing or feeding on the surface. In the earlier methods of fishing, called "hand lining," the presence of the dolphins caused no problem. Lines, with baited hooks, were dropped to the level of the tuna and the fish were reeled in, by hand. Modern methods of fishing make use of floating nets, called *purse seines*, that are up to 3 miles long and perhaps 100 feet deep. The nets are laid to encircle the visible dolphins and the invisible tuna (though the presence of schools of tuna can now be confirmed by underwater sonar) and pulled tight. The dolphins could easily leap over the floating buoys and cables that support the net, but they seem to become confused, swim in circles, and finally are either suffocated (dolphins are air-breathing mammals) when trapped in the nets, or crushed as the nets are hauled by mechanical winches aboard the boats.

In 1972, during the early days of the environmental movement, Congress passed the Marine Mammal Protection Act which regulated the killing of dolphins in purse seine nets (so named because they look like an old-fashioned string purse, with a single opening at the bottom). The Act set a maximum number of dolphins which could be killed by U.S. boats fishing for tuna, and that number was to decline over time from 320,000 in 1972 to 20,000 in 1987.

The Marine Mammal Protection Act of 1972 passed by the U.S. Congress, of course, applied only to U.S.–registered fishing boats. Most U.S.–registered boats, though not those owned or under contract to H. J. Heinz, simply changed their registry to Mexico,

Panama, or Peru. H. J. Heinz attempted to find a means of complying with the law. It used speedboats within the circle of the net, immediately after it was first laid, to chase dolphins and attempt to force them to jump over the supporting buoys and cables. The dolphins ignored the speedboats, or seemed to consider them part of an enjoyable game designed for their amusement, while the tuna were irritated by the propeller sounds and dived under the net. Small explosive charges were tried, with equally discouraging results.

The United States had negotiated treaties with the other countries active in tuna fishing, attempting to place foreign boats under the same restrictions as the remaining ships in the U.S. fleet. Unfortunately, no observers were permitted on foreign boats and consequently the negotiated restrictions were said to be largely ignored. The result was that the dolphin population within the eastern tropics of the Pacific Ocean began to decline rapidly.

You found that in 1989 H. J. Heinz operated within the law because it was the only company to contract with the U.S.–registered boats and thus was "entitled" to the full U.S.–approved kill (20,000 per year) for those boats. Foreign boats have their own "approved" kill levels, allocated per nation agreeing to the treaty. H. J. Heinz, however, bore the major brunt of the public opposition, partially because it reports the estimated kill each year (as required by U.S. law), but also because two years ago a representative of an environmental group (Greenpeace) signed onto one of the company's boats as a crew member, and took surreptitious videotapes of the killing and maiming of dolphins. These videotapes were considered too "distressing" to be shown publicly on U.S. television, but they have been shown privately within this country and abroad by various conservation and church groups, and have resulted in a boycott of the company's canned tuna products. The boycott has not been economically effective—sales of Starkist canned tuna continue to increase each year both in the United States and in Europe—but there was general agreement that it did not help to build the overall image and reputation of H. J. Heinz as a concerned global citizen.

In short, you found that H. J. Heinz was the only food products company selling tuna in the United States that was actively obeying the U.S. law against killing dolphins, yet it was also the prime target by environmental groups for that killing. And, despite the apparently misdirected anger of the environmental groups, it was necessary to admit that the company did cause the deaths of approximately 20,000 dolphins each year.

There were five basic alternatives beyond the obvious effort to discover a new means of either luring or chasing the dolphins playing on the surface away from the tuna feeding at greater depths. H. J. Heinz had spent $2.5 million dollars supporting oceanographic research, but up to 1989 without a positive result. Some of the more ingenious methods involved broadcasting under water. Sound travels well in water (much further than in the air), and the call of a killer whale, the appeal of an amorous dolphin, and the music of a rock group had all been tried. The first frightened the tuna as well as the dolphins, the second attracted only a very few of the dolphins, while the last apparently was enjoyed by both species. The more serious alternatives open to the company are as follows:

1. Continue commercial fishing for albacore tuna in the eastern Pacific, using U.S. boats with the purse seine technology. The U.S. boats are large, expensive, and efficient; they are able to land tuna in the United States for canning at a cost equal to that of any of the foreign boats. The advantage of this alternative is that the company would remain cost competitive and have access to the highest grade of tuna. The disadvantage is that the dolphin deaths would continue, though at a rate that would be within the legal limits imposed by U.S. law. A public relations campaign could be started to convince the environmentalists that Heinz was the only firm observing those limits and obeying that law, though of course the success of that public relations campaign could not be guaranteed.

2. Continue commercial fishing for albacore tuna in the eastern Pacific, using U.S. boats with the purse seine technology, but sell the tuna in Japan and the other nations of the Far East where albacore tuna is regarded as a specialty product and may be sold at a premium price, and where the killing of dolphins is not regarded as an environmental crime. In 1989, albacore tuna was one of the few packaged food products that could be imported into Japan without encountering re-strictive trade practices. Indeed, the dolphins that were killed as a result of this fishing could also be exported to Japan and the other nations of the Far East as pet food. The advantage of this alternative was that it would generate by far the highest profit for the company and would probably end the boycott. The disadvantage was that it would not end the killing of dolphins.

3. Continue commercial fishing for albacore tuna in the eastern Pacific, using U.S. boats with a "hand-line" technology. Hand-line fishing with baited hooks in a school of tuna can be a semiefficient method; the fish are caught quickly but at a considerably higher labor cost. There are numerous advantages to this alternative. The U.S. boats could be converted to this older technology for the crane used to position and lift the nets could be used to launch and recover the dories, which are small, seaworthy power boats needed for hand-line fishing. The disadvantage was that hand-line fishing would cost about 35 percent more per pound of tuna. Customers could be asked to pay this premium (estimated to add $0.25 to the price of a typical 6 oz. tin) for "dolphin-free" tuna, or workers from the poverty-stricken cities of South America could be hired to man the dories at much lower wages. A problem with the second alternative was that those workers would not be experienced at sea. Fishing from small boats, even when supported by a large "mother" ship, is considered to be dangerous for inexperienced per

sons. The new workers could be trained, of course, but it was not certain that trained but inexperienced seamen would react properly in emergencies, such as a sudden storm that caught them in their dories.

4. Change to fishing for yellow tuna in the western Pacific, using foreign boats and the purse seine technology. Herds of dolphins are seldom associated with schools of tuna in the western Pacific, again for reasons that are not fully understood. It would therefore be possible to catch "dolphin-free" tuna. There seemed to be few advantages to this alternative, however, beyond that ability. The disadvantages were numerous. The U.S. boats which had fished exclusively for Heinz over the past 20 years could not continue; they did not have large enough fuel tanks to reach the western Pacific, nor large enough refrigerated holds to carry the catch back to the United States. The U.S. canneries, which employed over 2,000 people in southern California, would have to be closed. Foreign canneries, which tended to be less conscientious in quality control, would have to be opened. And, it was thought that foreign fishing fleets which did not observe the U.S. law would simply replace the U.S. boats in the eastern Pacific, and kill many more dolphins.

5. Discontinue the production and marketing of canned tuna. Canned tuna, to repeat the facts stated earlier, accounted in 1989 for 9 percent of sales and 11 percent of profits of H. J. Heinz.

Class Assignment

Prepare a recommendation on the future of the Starkist canned tuna product line for the chairman of the H. J. Heinz company. Obviously, you can select any alternative that you believe to be "right," ranging from ignoring the dolphin problem to discontinuing the tuna product, but you should state as clearly as possible why you believe that course of action to be correct. Accept the recommendation of Mr. O'Reilly that you not tell him what you think he wants to hear; instead, tell him what you think is the "right" thing for the company to do.

Case 6–3

RESISTOL SALES IN CENTRAL AMERICA

This is a shortened version of an earlier case written by Professors Norman Bowie and Stefanie Lenway, both of the Carlson School of Management at the University of Minnesota, and is used with their permission.

Resistol is a fast-drying, solvent-based liquid adhesive used to glue paper, cardboard, wood, leather, plastic, rubber, and textile products. In essence it is an industrial-strength form of the familiar airplane glue or rubber cement, with the properties of rapid set, strong adhesion, and water resistance.

Resistol is widely used in Central and South America by the small shoe and clothing manufacturers, leather workers, wood workers, carpenters, and repair shops that are typical of the region. It is also widely used by individual customers for the quick repair of shoes, clothing, and household goods. It is easily available from industrial suppliers in large containers and from retail shops in small tubes. The easy availability is part of the problem.

Fumes from the solvent in Resistol are a hallucinogenic, and street children in four of the poorest countries of Central America—Guatemala, Honduras, Nicaragua, and El Salvador— have started using those fumes as a mood-altering drug.

> They lie senseless on doorsteps and pavements, grimy and loose limbed, like discarded rag dolls.
>
> Some are just five or six years old. Others are already young adults, and all are addicted to sniffing a commonly sold glue that is doing them irreversible brain damage.
>
> Roger, 21, has been sniffing Resistol for eight years. Today, even when he is not high, Roger walks with a stagger, his motor control wrecked. His scarred face puckers with concentration, his right foot taps nervously, incessantly, as he talks.
>
> Since he was 11, when he ran away from the aunt who raised him, Roger's home has been the streets of [Tegucigalpa] the capital of Honduras, the second poorest nation in the western hemisphere after Haiti.

> Roger spends his time begging, shining shoes, washing car windows, scratching together a few pesos a day, and sleeping in doorways at night.
>
> Sniffing glue, he says, "makes me feel happy, makes me feel big. I know that it's doing me damage, but it's a habit I've got, and a habit's a habit. I cannot give it up even though I wish to."
>
> No one knows how many of Tegucigalpa's street urchins seek escape from the squalor and misery of their daily existence through the hallucinogenic fumes of Resistol. No one has spent the time and money needed to study the question.
>
> But, one thing is clear, according to Dr. Rosalio Zavala, head of the Health Ministry's Department of Mental Health, "These children come from the poorest slums of the big cities. They have grown up as illegal squatters in very disturbed states of mental health, tense, depressed, aggressive."
>
> "Some turn that aggression on society, and start stealing. Others turn it on themselves, and adopt self-destructive behavior."
>
> But, he understands the attraction of the glue whose solvent, toluene, produces feelings of elation. "It gives you delusions of grandeur, you feel powerful, and that compensates these kids for reality, where they feel completely worthless, like nobodies" [InterPress News Service, July 16, 1985, p. 1].

Resistol is manufactured by H.B. Fuller Company of St. Paul, Minnesota, a specialty chemical company frequently confused with the better known but much smaller Fuller Brush Company. The adhesive is marketed in Central America by

Kativo Chemical Industries, S.A., a wholly owned subsidiary of H.B. Fuller.

Traditionally the H.B. Fuller Company has given regional executives in foreign subsidiaries a great deal of autonomy to respond quickly to currency fluctuations, political changes, and market needs. When the story quoted above appeared in the Honduran newspapers under the title "Los Resistoleros" (the users of Resistol), Humberto "Beto" Larach, the manager of Kativo's Adhesive Division, quickly informed the editors that Resistol was not the only substance abused by Honduran street children and that the image of the manufacturer was being damaged by taking a prestigious trademark as a synonym for drug abusers. He threatened to sue the newspaper for defamation of character.

Señor Larach felt strongly that the glue-sniffing problem was not caused by the solvent in the product, but by the poverty of the region for which he and H.B. Fuller were not responsible. He recommended to the St. Paul office that no action be taken to change the formulation or the distribution of the product. It was possible, for example, to use a much less volatile solvent that would decrease the hallucinogenic effect of the fumes but would also lengthen the drying time of the adhesive. Señor Larach said that in third world countries most industrial supply firms and retail stores would stock only one brand of a product and that if the product specifications were changed in an unsatisfactory way the users would demand that their suppliers switch brands to a readily available competitor with the desired qualities. Resistol at the date of the case was by far the dominant quick-setting adhesive sold in the region, with a market share over 80 percent, but competitive products were readily available from companies in both France and West Germany.

Señor Larach also explained that reducing the volatility of only the solvent of the adhesive sold through the retail stores (that is, keeping the adhesive sold through industrial suppliers at full "industrial" strength) would not solve the problem either. The street children currently obtained the glue in small tubes from the retail stores and in small jars from adults who either bought it from the industrial suppliers or stole it from the industrial users.

In 1986 a Peace Corps volunteer in Honduras, disturbed by the situation and angered by what he perceived as a lack of response on the part of Kativo, formed a committee of local religious and social leaders to attempt to reduce the use of the drug by the street children. The first act of this committee was to petition the government to pass a law dictating that allyl isothiocyanate (also known as "oil of mustard") be added to all quick-setting adhesives sold in the country to prevent their abuse. Allyl isothiocyanate is a chemical that irritates the mucous membranes of the upper respiratory tract; it can also cause burns to the eyes and skin. When used in full strength it is the "mustard gas" that caused horrendous casualties in World War I. Members of the committee had no intention that the chemical be used in full strength in Resistol; they conceded, however, that its presence even in diluted form would make the adhesive unpleasant to apply in normal industrial and consumer use but felt that situation was better than its continued misuse by children. During the 1970s allyl isothiocyanate had been added to airplane glue in the United States to prevent a similar form of abuse.

The Peace Corps volunteer in Honduras also started a letter-writing campaign directed both to the senior executives at H.B. Fuller and to the trust officers and pension managers who held much of that company's common stock. The letters were accompanied by photographs of the street children, translations from news accounts, statements by the local clergy, and invitations to visit the region and observe the situation.

The senior executives at H.B. Fuller commissioned a study by a large international consulting firm which reached seven major conclusions:

1. Oil of mustard is not only a skin and lung irritant; prolonged exposure even in diluted form can cause nausea, dizziness, headaches, and asthma.

2. No less hallucinogenic solvent is readily available that will not severely detract from the present quick-setting, high-adhesion, and water-resistant qualities of the product.

3. No less harmful additive is readily available that will both decrease the use of the adhesive as a street drug and maintain the present desirable product qualities.

4. It would be possible to search for a less hallucinogenic solvent or a less harmful additive, but the search would be expensive and no guarantee of success could be offered.

5. Sales of Resistol in Central America amounted to over $12,000,000 per year; profits were not listed in the report released to the public but they were assumed to be high.

6. Sales of Resistol in Central America were thought to be important to the industrial development of the region. Water-based adhesives are used in Europe, the United States, and Japan, but these require microwave dryers and presses for curing. Those dryers and presses are not available in Central America due to their capital cost.

7. Sales of Resistol in Central America were thought to be related to the sales of paint (the major product of both H.B. Fuller and Kativo); that is, if the suppliers and retailers purchased industrial adhesives from other sources they were likely to purchase industrial finishes from those sources as well. Paint sales by Kativo were over $50,000,000 per year.

In 1987, two events occurred that forced the senior executives at H.B. Fuller to address directly the problem of Resistol sales in Central America. Firstly, the National Assembly of Honduras passed a law mandating the use of allyl isothiocyanate in all solvent-based adhesives sold in that country. Señor Larach, however, reported that the National Assembly had included no mechanism for enforcement of the law, that he had been assured by members of the Assembly that the law had been passed to placate the committee of religious and social leaders, and that there was no intent to enforce it. Señor Larach also said that the National Assembly was likely to be dissolved in the near future (which would overturn all laws passed during its recent session) as part of the political instability that troubled the region.

Secondly, the president of H.B. Fuller Company received a telephone call from the editor of one of the major statewide newspapers in Minnesota. The editor explained that his daughter was a member of the Peace Corps in Central America, had complained that "a company in St. Paul is selling a product that is literally burning out the brains of children down here," that the paper had sent a reporter to Honduras and planned to run a story on the allegation if true, and that the call from the editor was a courtesy to alert the executives at H.B. Fuller and enable them to "tell their side of the story if they wished to."

Class Assignment

You are president of H.B. Fuller Company. What would you do?

Case 6–4

CRYSTAL RIVER GOLF COURSE

The proposal to construct a "world-class" golf course on protected wetlands located just to the east of Glen Arbor on the Leelanau Peninsula in northwestern Michigan is, in 1992, probably the most controversial environmental issue in the state. Proponents of the golf course say that its construction is vital to the economic development of a region that is totally dependent upon tourism for survival. Opponents say that its construction will destroy the last absolutely clear, clean river in the Midwest, and eliminate a major wildlife breeding and refuge area.

The Crystal River runs from Glen Lake to Lake Michigan, a geographic distance of only one mile. The river meanders back and forth over that distance, however, and is six miles long. Much of its length is contained within the boundaries of the Sleeping Bear Dunes National Park, an area of large sand dunes which have been protected against development since the mid-1960s. Prior to that time the sand was strip mined and shipped by lake freighters to Chicago and Milwaukee for use in concrete bridge, building, and highway construction, but that practice was totally stopped with the advent of the National Lakeshore Park.

The water in the Crystal River is crystal clear. The reason is that much of the bed of the river is sand or gravel, and that most of the soil in the wetlands surrounding the river has never been disturbed, so that there has been limited erosion to "muddy" the water. Further, the Leelanau Peninsula is an area of heavy "lake-effect" snowfall during the winter. The pre-

EXHIBIT 1

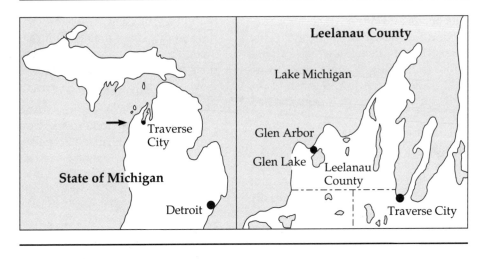

vailing winds from the west blow across Lake Michigan and pick up water vapor which is then deposited in the form of snow on the coastal counties of the state. When the snow melts in the springtime, Glen Lake, which is the source of Crystal River, and the other lakes within these counties are replenished with clear water.

The wetlands surrounding the Crystal River form a unique ecosystem. As with all wetlands, they serve as spawning grounds for fish, hatcheries for waterfowl and marsh birds, and natural habitats for fur-bearing animals and whitetailed deer. In addition, these are among the few surviving wetlands on the western shore of the state, and consequently act as an important resting place and refuge for migrating ducks, geese, herons, wrens, sandpipers, and hawks. Two thirds of all the fish, birds, and animals on Michigan's endangered species list can be found at one time or another during the year within the 468

acres that comprise the Crystal River wetlands.

The wetlands surrounding the Crystal River also have a unique geological structure. They are composed of high sand ridges running parallel with low rock depressions or swales. Both the ridges and the swales were formed by glaciers thousands of years in the past. The swales have filled in since that time with a very rich soil built up from decaying aquatic plants. It has been years since the area was logged, and the borders between the ridges and the swales are now covered with tall pine, birch, cedar, and aspen trees. The swales are thick with cattails, bulrushes, and the other vegetation normally found in marshlands. The ridges, due to the sandy soil, are dominated by low plants such as bracken fern, blueberry, wintergreen, and rice grass.

The Crystal River itself is an ideal spawning ground for fish due to the clear, cold water which encourages activity, the sandy bottom which provides breeding sites, and the numerous bends and turns which offer protection for the young. It is one of the few rivers in Michigan which still has runs of steelhead trout and coho salmon in the spring. Sunfish, bass, and chub fill the river during the balance of the year.

Unfortunately from an environmentalist's point of view, the Crystal River wetlands have the potential for a nearly perfect "world-class" golf course. The sand ridges could easily be sculpted into long, narrow fairways. The deep swales, bordered by trees, would isolate the tees and greens. The river, wandering back and forth, would create interest and challenge. And, the northwestern border of the proposed golf course would have an elegant view; it looks out over a long bend in the river, the attractive village of Glen Arbor, and the waters of Lake Michigan, only one-fourth mile away.

Unfortunately also from the environmentalists' point of view, the Crystal River wetlands are owned by a person who wants to convert them to a "world-class" golf course. Mr. Robert Kuras, who has built a large vacation area called The Homestead Resort just to the north of Glen Arbor, purchased all of the wetlands surrounding the Crystal River except for the sections included in the Sleeping Bear Dunes National Park a number of years ago.

Mr. Kuras, who has the reputation of an active, aggressive, and occasionally abrasive personality, has expressed a number of points in favor of the proposed golf course:

1. He owns the land and, subject to any zoning restrictions imposed by the village of Glen Arbor, has the right to do what he likes with that land. There are no zoning restrictions in Glen Arbor that pertain to golf course construction.

2. The golf course is needed to expand business at The Homestead. Currently that resort is filled to capacity during July and August, and is moderately busy during the winter ski season. The golf course, if built to a truly "world-class" design worthy of its site, would attract large numbers of vacationers during the May–June and September–October periods. The late spring and early fall periods offer almost ideal weather on the Leelanau Peninsula, but currently there are few outdoor sporting activities to bring those people to the region. Mr. Kuras believes that a "world-class" course —by that, he means one that is outstandingly attractive in appearance and challenging to play—would bring affluent foreign visitors and Professional Golf Association tournaments in addition to the expected business meetings and family vacationers from Chicago, Grand Rapids, and Detroit.

3. The expanded business at The Homestead Resort would increase employment opportunities there. Presently 400 people (200 local residents and 200 college students) work at the resort during the summer months. These numbers are cut back immediately after Labor Day to a permanent staff of only 35 until the start of the ski season brings the

EXHIBIT 2

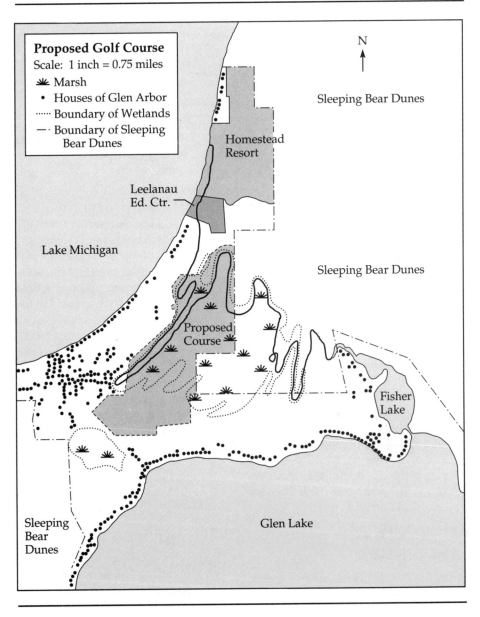

Proposed Golf Course
Scale: 1 inch = 0.75 miles
※ Marsh
• Houses of Glen Arbor
····· Boundary of Wetlands
—· Boundary of Sleeping
    Bear Dunes

N

Sleeping Bear Dunes

Homestead
Resort

Leelanau
Ed. Ctr.

Lake Michigan

Sleeping Bear Dunes

Proposed
Course

Fisher
Lake

Glen Lake

Sleeping
Bear
Dunes

need for additional workers. It is expected that the permanent staff will be stabilized at 210 with the construction of the golf course.

4. The expanded business at the Homestead Resort would also expand employment opportunities throughout Leelanau County. Each visitor to the resort is estimated to spend $30 per day outside of the resort for restaurant meals and travel assistance. This is expected to translate into an additional 100 jobs providing those services. Each member of the permanent staff at the resort is believed to require one third of a person employed outside of the resort for retail sales and home services. This translates into a further 60 jobs (175 additional permanent staff times 33 percent).

5. The expanded employment is badly needed in Leelanau County. Unemployment in the area has averaged 15 percent since auto part factories and food-processing plants (the area grows both cherries and apples) shut down in nearby Traverse City. In addition to employment opportunities, the new golf course and the new homes/ condominiums to be built alongside the golf course would increase taxes paid to the local community by nearly $1 million per year.

6. The golf course is badly needed by The Homestead Resort to remain competitive. Other resort complexes have been built in northwestern Michigan since 1970 when Mr. Kuras began the construction of The Homestead. These resort complexes, at Shanty Creek, Schuss Mountain, Boyne Highlands, Boyne Mountain, Hidden Valley, Crystal Mountain, and Sugar Loaf, all have conference meeting facilities, downhill ski areas, and private golf courses. They are located 25 to 50 miles further to the north, and don't directly compete with The Homestead in Leelanau County, but Mr. Kuras has stated, "All major northern Michigan resorts now have golf courses; we're dead in the water without one."

7. Lastly, Mr. Kuras continually stressed that there was no other site available for the construction of a golf course close enough to be associated with his resort. Sleeping Bear Dunes National Park extends to the northeast *and* to the southwest of The Homestead Resort and the village of Glen Arbor, while Glen Lake is to the south and Lake Michigan to the west. Further, he claimed, there was no other site available anywhere in northern Michigan that would make such an attractive and challenging course, with the river, the swales, the ridges, and the views of Lake Michigan. "What God had in mind when he made Crystal River was a golf course" was a statement that Mr. Kuras often used to summarize his views regarding the desirability of converting the area adjacent to his Homestead Resort into a recreational facility.

The opponents of the plan to convert the Crystal River wetlands into recreational facilities are many and vocal. They are, as might be expected, particularly incensed by Mr. Kuras's

"God had in mind" statement, and reply with some heat that "God made Crystal River and the wetlands for all of His living creatures and does not need Mr. Kuras to blacktop the paths, bulldoze the ridges, and dredge the swales just for golfers."

These people, who have banded together in a group called Friends of Crystal River, make the following points to substantiate their opposition:

1. The proposed changes to convert the wetlands into a golf course will be much larger than at first admitted by Mr. Kuras. Originally, the opponents claim, he spoke of "sculpting" the sand ridges to create fairways. Now, plans call for 85,000 cubic yards of fill to be brought in to build up the tees, expand the greens, and provide bends and "dog legs" in the course for more challenge and greater interest. Some of the fill will come from the swales, which now will be dredged in places to create lakes and water hazards. Most of the fill will come from a dune area outside the national park that will be leveled. In addition, six stone bridges will be constructed across the river, and extensive pathways of gravel will be laid down, to facilitate the movement of the golfers and their carts. A 3 acre parking lot and all of the access roads will be covered with asphalt. It is feared that the earth-moving equipment and heavy trucks needed to accomplish these changes will compact the soil, kill the vegetation, and cause extensive erosion. Soil washed into the river will remain there for years, and the present water clarity probably will be destroyed.

2. The chemical treatments to maintain the fairways and greens are much more extensive than at first admitted by Mr. Kuras. Golf course grasses are genetically bred firstly for their green color and fine texture, secondly for their ability to grow compactly and withstand frequent mowing, and only thirdly for their resistance to disease and drought. The conditions on the ridges are not ideal for these "laboratory grasses," and consequently extensive watering and chemical treatments will be needed. Fertilizers will be spread to enrich the soil which is too sandy to naturally support the turf. Fungicides will be used to kill the moss and mildews that will follow the extensive watering. Herbicides will be applied to eliminate the weeds that will seed in from the surviving swales. And, pesticides will have to be sprayed to kill the flies and mosquitoes that are numerous and annoying in wetland areas. The fear is that all of these chemicals, which are applied to other golf courses in less environmentally sensitive areas at the rate of 17 tons per year, will leach into the wetlands and the river, and kill the fish, birds, and small animals. There is even fear that the fertilizers will pass rapidly through the sandy soil and concentrate in the river where they can result in "algae bloom," a rapid growth of unicell creatures that occurs in nutrient-rich water, and which could clog the river and deplete the oxygen in the water, suffocating the fish.

The Friends of Crystal River believe that the local residents oppose the construction of the golf course, but that claim is open to interpretation. A referendum was held in 1990 in an attempt to extend residential zoning to all of the proposed area which would exclude commercial ventures, such as the golf course; that effort was defeated by a vote of 238 to 209. However, only full-time residents of the area were registered to vote and consequently were able to participate in the referendum. The part-time residents who own 80 percent of the homes in the village of Glen Arbor were not registered to vote, and thus were excluded from the referendum. Many of these part-time residents have been coming to this vacation area for years from their permanent homes in Chicago, Grand Rapids, or Detroit and hold a deep affection for the natural beauty of the setting. Surveys among this group indicate an opposition rate of over 90 percent.

Class Assignment

You are the director of the Michigan Department of Natural Resources, a state agency. Because of the dredging of the swales and the filling for the tees and greens, you have to approve the construction of the golf course. Yours is the only vote that is needed before the construction can begin. You have listened to all sides in the dispute:

All major northern Michigan resorts have golf courses. We're dead in the water without one [Mr. Robert Kuras, developer of the proposed golf course, quoted in *The Detroit News*, September 2, 1990, p. C5].

It [the golf course] will be on the same level of quality and sensitivity you can see at The Homestead now [which is, all parties to the dispute agree, remarkably attractive and well maintained]. The current plan will leave over 80 acres forever green as environmental reserves, along with major stretches of open space. The golf course will not ruin the river. That's in my own best interest. Aesthetics are what sell this place [Mr. Robert Kuras, developer of the proposed golf course, quoted in *The Detroit News*, September 27, 1987, p. K2].

Crystal River is a major development, and is important to our economy and tourism [Mr. John Engler, governor of the state of Michigan, quoted in *The Detroit News*, March 15, 1992, p. B2].

The vacation industry is a key element of the Michigan economy as it supports approximately 7 percent of statewide employment and provides approximately 11 percent of our revenues. It has outpaced the growth of the state's economy as a whole, and, consequently, has been targeted as a key element of the strategic plan for long-term growth and diversification away from the declining automobile industry. We need more and better vacation destinations [Statement of supporter for the proposed golf course].

Golf is more than a game. It's getting outdoors. It's blue sky and green grass, rippling creeks and ponds (oops; there goes another ball) and forests of pine, cedar, and oak. It's springtime green, lush summers and glorious autumns with a color display to remember through the too-long winters. Crystal River can provide all that, and more: hundreds of jobs for the local community, and thousands of dollars for the state government [Statement of supporter of the proposed golf course].

Nobody is against a golf course. We aren't. I love golf myself. But why does he [Mr. Kuras] have to build it on the wetlands? That has to be some of the most environmentally sensitive land in northwestern Michigan. What he's talking about is a desecration of a very rare natural resource [Statement of opponent of the proposed golf course].

If you look at all of the alternative sites within a reasonable distance from The Homestead, you have to conclude that there simply is no other place to build the golf course than the one Mr. Kuras has selected, and now owns. Sixty-eight percent of the land in the area is the property of the National Park Service, and 17 percent is covered by Glen Lake and Fisher Lakes, so that leaves only 15 percent and most of that is under the town of Glen Arbor [Statement of supporter of the proposed golf course].

Crystal River is a landmark case in environmental ethics. It's known coast-to-coast. We have a chance to preserve one of the most beautiful rivers in the Midwest, one of the last wetland areas on the Lake Michigan shoreline, and provide a nesting/hatching/ breeding area for many of our disappearing birds, fish, and mammals. We're not going to give up. This is too important. We've got to win [Statement of opponent of the proposed golf course].

This is one of the worst fights I can remember. Friends have been set against friends, and local residents against summer vacationists. Some people are so worked up over this "employment versus environment" issue that they peek into the windows of our post office to see who's there before going in. They just want to avoid any more arguments, and any more confrontations [Statement of resident of the town of Glen Arbor].

Once again, you are the director of the Michigan Department of Natural Resources. You have listened to all sides in the dispute, and have reviewed all of the facts as stated in the case. The relevant law is clear: wetlands can be altered with the approval of the director of the Department of Natural Resources. You hold a political appointment as that director, but you can be removed only by a vote of the state legislature which may or may not agree with the governor. What do you decide?

Case 6–5

"SIXTY MINUTES" AND THE CONSUMERS POWER COMPANY

In November 1990 the Consumers Power Company of Jackson, Michigan received a request from the producers of "Sixty Minutes," the popular Sunday evening news program, for a company spokesperson to appear on a future program segment. The future program segment was to be titled "Stray Voltage," and the company spokesperson was to respond to allegations that Consumers Power had ignored repeated requests for help from a dairy farmer in western Michigan in alleviating a problem with stray voltage from the company's lines.

Stray voltage is an electrical

phenomenon that is associated with electrical lines that are old, worn, heavily overloaded, or poorly installed. Stray voltage is *not* the result of a short circuit in which the insulation on an electrical conductor becomes so brittle or broken that the full voltage can jump to a nearby conductor. A short circuit is a direct transfer of current on a metal-to-metal basis; it will cause such an increase in current flow (amperage) that fuses will blow or disconnects will trip, and the problem can easily be identified and repaired.

Stray voltage, instead, is the result of a small "leakage" of current, with no metal-to-metal contact. Generally the current passes through insulation that may be worn but is not broken or along conductors that are not metallic and consequently have a relatively high resistance. Dust and cobwebs in a control box, if slightly damp, would be an example of a nonmetallic conductor that would have relatively high resistance. The resistance decreases the current flow, and consequently fuse boxes and circuit breakers are unaffected and the identification and repair of the problem is much more difficult.

The analogy is not really accurate, but stray voltage is somewhat similar to a water main made out of slightly porous materials. If you had a large leak in that main, water would spray all over the place and you could find the problem and fix it. With a water main made out of slightly porous materials, the leaks are too small to find. You won't lose enough water to notice any drop in the pressure or volume and, while you may see some water dripping off the pipe, you will find that the water has been running on the outside of that pipe for some distance and is dripping off at the low point, not where the leaks are located. You probably will give up trying to find the source, and say it doesn't really matter, but over time the ground near the main will get very wet [Statement of electrical engineer asked for assistance in defining the concept of stray voltage].

Stray voltage is technically defined as "neutral-to-earth" voltage. That is, stray voltage is considered to be a positive electric potential (measured in volts) between the earth and the neutral or "return" wire in an electrical power system. The following explanation may seem somewhat technical, but bear with it; some understanding of the technology is necessary for readers to fully accept that the sources of stray voltage cannot easily be traced and fixed.

Electrical power in rural areas is distributed along roadside lines that are single phase and charged at a nominal 4,400 volts. Single phase means that there are just two wires: one is powered or "hot" and the other is neutral.

At each farm or other customer location, transformers are installed on a nearby pole to reduce the voltage from 4,400 volts to 220 and 110 volts, the common farm and household currents. Three wires lead from the pole transformer to an entrance box on the house or barn. Two of these entrance wires are powered or hot, and the other is known as a "grounded neutral." The potential between the two powered lines is 220 volts, while the potential between either of the powered lines and the grounded neutral is 110 volts.

EXHIBIT 1   Electric Utility to Farm Customer Connections

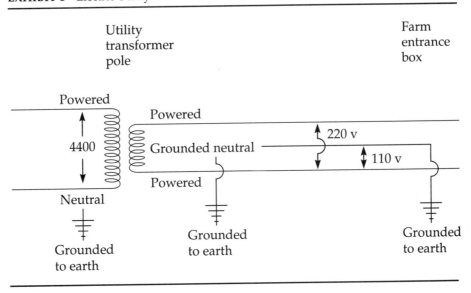

The neutral is grounded to the earth at three locations in the typical farm service installation: on both sides of the pole transformer (remember, in a transformer there is no direct connection of the input and output wires; instead currents at reduced voltages are "induced" on the output wires through coils that interface rather than interconnect) and at the entrance box.

Motors, controls, lights, and switches throughout the farm are grounded back to the entrance box by the use of metallic conduit or by the use of a ground wire. That is, if a short circuit should develop anywhere on the farm, in a motor or light, the current from that short circuit would flow back rapidly to the entrance box, passed through to the earth, and the flow would be high enough to melt fuses or trip circuit breakers. If a short circuit should develop in the entrance box, it would be drawn back rapidly to the output side of the transformer,

passed through to the earth, and again melt fuses or trip circuit breakers. If a short circuit should develop in the transformer, it would be drawn back rapidly to the input side, passed through to the earth, and shut off service. In short, the farm is completely protected against short circuits, and the harms that can come to either people, animals, or property through encountering full voltage.

The farm is not, however, protected against stray voltage, which has a greatly reduced flow due to the resistance on the nonmetallic contacts, and does not melt any fuses or trip any disconnects. These nonmetallic contacts are, once again, dirt and dust in motors and controls and worn insulation in light fixtures and switches. Even old ballast starters in fluorescent lamps have been found to be a source of stray voltage.

Other sources of stray voltage are loose connections in the conduit or ground wire that do not permit short circuits to return to the entrance box for grounding to the earth. Instead, the current is likely to jump through nonmetallic high resistance contacts to metal buildings, water pipes, and steel supports. Or, a powered line with inadequate insulation passing close to those metal objects can induce a secondary current that becomes stray voltage. Lastly, the 110-volt loads throughout the farm must be "balanced" between the two 220-volt power lines and the grounded neutral wire, and that grounded neutral wire must be adequately sized to carry those loads or stray voltage will be formed at the load sites.

The electrical potential (measured in volts) is very low in most stray voltage situations because of the nonmetallic contacts and/or the induced currents. Three to 7 volts is common, 7 to 10 volts is uncommon but possible, while anything over 10 volts very seldom occurs. A person touching an iron water pipe that was conducting a 7-volt stray voltage current would not feel any shock because his or her natural resistance is greater than that which could be overcome by 7 volts. Remember, to use the somewhat misleading analogy of a water system once again, that the voltage is the pressure and the amperage is the flow of the electrical current; when the pressure is low the impact upon human beings is minimal.

People who touch an electrical conductor carrying low voltage stray currents will feel no shock. Dairy cattle, however, will. Dairy cattle are said to be 10 times more sensitive than human beings to electricity and, of course, dairy cattle tend to stand in wet barnyards and/or on wet barn floors which provide ideal contacts for the charges to pass through their bodies.

This is as far as agreement on the nature, cause, and effect of stray voltage extends. Everyone agrees that stray voltage is either transmitted by nonmetallic contacts or electromagnetically induced, an indirect leakage from wires that are old, worn, overloaded, and/or poorly installed. Everyone agrees that because stray voltage is an indirect leakage it is very difficult to pinpoint the exact source, particularly on farms that tend to have electrical systems that are old, worn, overloaded, and/or poorly installed. Everyone agrees that because stray voltage is characterized by both low voltage and low amperage it has no noticeable effects upon people. Everyone agrees that because dairy cattle are so much more sensitive to electricity than human beings it does have a noticeable effect upon them. There is no agreement, however, on whether this noticeable effect is harmful to the dairy cattle, or on how to cure the problem in the event that a rural customer of a public utility comes to believe it to be harmful to his or her cattle.

One argument on the harm of stray voltage, put forth by many farmers and some agricultural extension service workers, is that it is obvious that cattle do feel the shocks, and that repeated shocks from steel barn stanchions, metal drinking troughs, and stainless steel milking machines change the behavior of cows, and lead inexorably to low milk production, to various illnesses and breeding problems, and eventually even to death.

If you were a cow producing milk by the gallon you would need to drink water by the gallon, but if every time you went to the drinking trough out in the barnyard you got a bad shock, you would stop drinking water. If every time you rubbed up against the metal stanchions in your barn stall you got an equally bad shock you would stop moving around and stand rock still. If every time you went into the milking room you got an even worse shock on a particularly sensitive part of your anatomy, you would have to be driven into the milking room.

You can go onto any farm that is troubled with stray voltage and you can see cattle that don't drink enough water, that don't move about in their stalls, and that have to be driven into the milking room. Milk production falls way off. Cattle illnesses, particularly mastitis (a chronic disease of the udder), go way up. Calves are born deformed, or die soon after birth. Cows die in their stalls. It is a horrible situation [Statement of agricultural extension worker, asked for assistance in defining the problems caused by stray voltage].

Another view is that stray voltage is only one of the many possible causes of decreased milk production, increased herd diseases, deformed calves, and premature deaths. This is the view advanced by most public utility companies that serve rural areas and by many researchers at agricultural colleges and universities. The argument here is that modern breeding and feeding techniques have produced dairy cattle that are very productive in gallons of milk per day, but also very susceptible to various illnesses and birth defects. These diseases and defects can be caused by poor feed, poor care, poor management.

Problems initially attributed to stray voltage often are due to factors not related to the farm's electric service. These factors include overall farm management techniques being used, such as the health of the herd or the dietary practices.

Experts in Michigan State University's School of Agriculture are considered among the most competent on this issue in the United States. Elsewhere, Dr. Ronald Gorewit, of Cornell University's Animal Science Department, is the nation's leading expert on stray voltage research and has conducted more animal research on this topic than any other scientist. *These experts have determined that stray voltage is usually not a contributing factor to decreased milk production on dairy farms* [Statement from an internal memo of Consumers Power Company dated April 18, 1991, and quoted with its permission. The italics for emphasis are in the original document].

There is little agreement on the actual effects of stray voltage upon dairy cattle. There is even less agreement upon the real sources of stray voltage on dairy farms:

Correctly diagnosing the source of stray voltage is often a painstaking, time-consuming process for both the farmer and the utility. This is due to the multiplicity of potential sources, including:

Improper grounding of electric lines.

Defective electrical equipment on the farm.

Inadequate connections on the neutral or ground wires.

Undersized neutral wire, inadequate for the current it carries.

Unbalanced electric loads.

Dirty, dusty, corroded, cobwebbed or damaged electric boxes and devices.

Of the approximately 100 requests from farmers for investigation of stray voltage we receive each year, a defect with the farmer's wiring system is usually the cause in 99 cases. These defects can include any or all of the conditions listed above. In perhaps one case per year we resolve the problem by making changes on our system. Occasionally stray voltage originates from a neighbor's electric system and is carried by a connecting water or sewer pipe. In the vast majority of cases we are able to cooperatively resolve the problem [Statement from an internal memo of Consumers Power Company dated April 18, 1991, and again quoted with its permission].

Officials at Consumers Power Company explained verbally to the case writer that one of the causes of stray voltage in Michigan in their opinion was the exemption in state law that enables farmers to do their own wiring on their own farms. All other commercial enterprises within the state were required to meet the National Electrical Code, and that code mandated the use of a qualified and licensed electrician whenever industrial equipment using 220-volt or 440-volt current was installed or changed. Many farmers wished to save the expense of hiring an electrician, did the wiring themselves, and as a result often had improper groundings, inadequate connections, undersized wires, or unbalanced loads, all mentioned in the company memo as possible causes of stray voltage. Company officials went on to explain that they distributed folders (see Exhibits 3 and 4) to their farm customers warning about stray voltage, and offering free inspections to help in finding and eliminating these causes.

Many farmers and farm extension workers associated with state agencies or agricultural colleges, however, still believe that the public utilities have done far too little in helping to resolve the problems caused by stray voltage. They claim that the utilities are too eager to blame the farmers for conditions which may be secondary or even tertiary causes of stray voltage, but are not the primary or basic causes. They also say that the problems of stray voltage are much more severe and widespread than has been admitted by the public utilities and their hired consultants and experts:

Veterinarian John Ryder, who studies stray voltage for the Wisconsin Agricultural Department, said he once saw eight cows leap simultaneously as they were being milked. "They were obviously getting hit with some very heavy jolts," he explained.

"About 30 percent of the farms [in Wisconsin] are affected by it or could potentially have stray voltage problems," said Dan Dasho, head of a three-year-old state-sponsored stray voltage task force.... "It can hurt your milk production and over a long period of time it can really hurt your financial status so you can't farm any more."

With livelihoods on the line, emotions can sometimes run high. In Wisconsin, a small but vocal group of stray voltage activists has sprung up in response to what they claim is foot-dragging on resolving the issue by state and utility officials. Several farmers have slapped utilities with lawsuits and won judgements ranging to more than $1 million....

"The problem is that the utility distribution systems are 30 to 50 years old and they have not been upgraded even though electrical use has gone up dramatically," argued Brad Kolpin, a dairy farmer who was awarded $738,000 after he took his utility to court over stray voltage–related losses ... [*The Los Angeles Times*, March 17, 1991, p. 21].

The argument that the utility distribution systems are old and have not been upgraded is particularly telling to many electrical engineers. They explain that the original electrification method used in rural areas was a very simple single phase (*phase* refers to the cycle of the current; *single phase* means that there is only one cycle at a time to provide the potential for electric power) two-wire system. Usage on farms and at homes has increased substantially, however, and the single-phase system is now thought to be operating at or very close to capacity. In addition, parts of the system have deteriorated over time. Insulation has weathered, connections have loosened, switch boxes have become dirty, and some equipment has failed. In brief, many of the conditions which are said to cause stray voltage on the farm are now found at the utility's own transformer pole and entrance meter.

In all of the diagrams that you see printed by utilities and consultants, the sources of stray voltage are shown at a location on the farm with little black arrows leading back to the grounded neutral at the entrance meter or transformer pole of the utility. And probably in the majority of cases those diagrams are right. But, in a substantial number of cases those diagrams are absolutely wrong. The source is the utility's own power distribution system, and those little black arrows should be shown pointing the other way, from the grounded neutral back to the farm [Statement of electric engineer asked for

assistance in defining the sources and problems of stray voltage].

Any leakage of current at the transformer pole or the entrance box is conveyed, through the grounded neutral, to the earth and through the earth, particularly if wet, to the farm. Those leaked currents on the farm charge the iron water pipes, the metal building supports, and the steel reinforcing rods in the concrete pads under the milking machines. When a cow touches any of those metal parts or comes in contact with any equipment connected to those metal parts she completes the circuit, and receives a shock.

How can you cure all of this? You can spend hours trying to trace down the source, but remember that stray voltage is "leaked" through worn insulation, poor connections, dirty or damaged switches, temporary overloads, faulty equipment, etc. The leaks aren't consistent and they aren't major so that it is hard to find them. The direction of the flow can't be noted. The result is that you spend hours arguing about the source of the leaks. The problem, of course, is that when it gets right down to an argument between a farm customer and a public utility about who is responsible for a given condition, the customer is going to lose 98 percent of the time.

The utility could fix the entire problem. They could separate the neutral wire and ground wire, instead of using the present combined "grounded neutral." And, as part of that change, they could replace the old transformers and meter boxes, tighten the old connections, and generally upgrade the entire rural distribution system. I don't know how much that would cost; maybe you could do it for $3,000 to $5,000 per customer. You can't do this for just one customer, however; you have to rewire an entire section leading back towards

EXHIBIT 2 Typical Diagram Showing Source of Stray Voltage

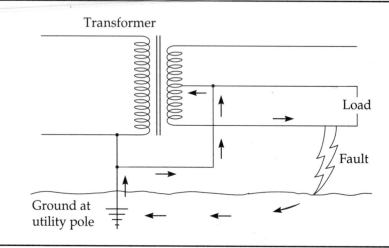

SOURCE: Truman Surbrook and Norman Reese, "Stray Voltage on Farms" (Cooperative Extension Service of Michigan State University, not dated).

a distribution substation, at least 100 to 200 rural customers at a time.

But if you are going to upgrade the entire rural distribution system you might as well do it right, and install a three-phase system (three powered wires and a single neutral) to replace the existing single-phase system. That would solve the capacity problem. Three-phase power is available in cities and towns, but rural customers have always been excluded. That would cost big bucks: at least $10,000 per customer, and here again you would have to do entire sections at a time.

The problem is that at the present time most utilities serving rural areas can't even afford to keep the brush and tree limbs trimmed back, away from their lines; that is why you get so many power outages after a storm. Those utilities certainly can't afford to make the investment required to either update the existing system or convert to a four-wire three-phase system without a substantial rate increase that would affect all of their customers. Is it right to charge residential users and industrial plants for system improvements that benefit only dairy farmers? I don't know.

The dairy farmers alone could never afford to pay for the needed system improvements. But, of course, if the system improvements are not made then in essence some of the dairy farmers are left by themselves, to pay the costs of the stray voltage on their farms in terms of decreased milk production and increased cattle illness. I don't know what to recommend [Statement of electrical engineer asked for assistance in defining the sources and problems of stray voltage].

The "Sixty Minutes" program, to which Consumers Power Company had been asked to respond, portrayed the plight of Paul and Judy VanDen-Berg, dairy farmers in western Michigan, who had long felt that they had been left by themselves to pay the costs of stray voltage on their farm in terms of decreased milk production and increased cattle illness. They sued the Consumers Power Company in 1985, claiming that the source of stray voltage in their instance was a "wrongly placed and improperly grounded utility pole," and in 1988 received a $750,000 negotiated settlement. A local paper reported the events that led up to that settlement:

For the VanDenBergs, problems began in 1978.

In that year, Paul VanDenBerg, 42, and his father, Donald, 69 and now semiretired, had a dairy operation with production far above the state average. So they began building a new 365-cow facility.

But in the past decade, milk production fell steadily. They also lost about 500 head of cattle, replaced their milking system three times, and hired a steady stream of experts to help them pinpoint the cause of their problems.

They suspected an electrical problem off the farm, but frequent checks by Jackson-based Consumers always ended with the same finding: the problem is on the farm, probably poor management. That charge stung Paul VanDenBerg.

The family had its feed analyzed, the cows' rations balanced, and metal pipe replaced with plastic. Four different electricians checked every wire and ground connection on the farm, and they found nothing wrong. But the couple's expenses mounted and cows kept dying.

An ice storm on New Year's Eve 1984 turned things around.

"This whole area was out of power, and we used a generator for seven days," VanDenBerg said. "Our milk production went up a thousand pounds that week, and that's when we knew it wasn't us."

According to Judy VanDenBerg, her husband sat her down with their four sons and told them they could leave the farm or stay and fight the utility.

In simple terms, the VanDenBergs alleged that their dairy barn, and the cows in it, became part of the power-return loop to Consumers Power's substation because of a poorly placed and inadequately grounded transformer pole on their farm. And when cows came into the barn to eat, drink, and be milked, they got jolted with shocks of varying intensity.

The jolts caused them to avoid eating and drinking properly. And since good milk producers must drink as much as 30 gallons of water a day, refusal to drink resulted in an immediate milk production drop and eventual sickness.

Even the light jolts made the cows so nervous they suffered from high blood pressure, stomach ulcers, and other diseases, said Kenneth Main, an Allegan veterinarian who has worked with the VanDenBergs for eight years [*Grand Rapids Press*, December 11, 1988, p. 1E].

The case never went to trial. Instead, it was settled out of court for considerably less than the $3 million originally claimed by the plaintiffs for damages. Consumers Power Company did not discuss with the case writer the arguments it would have offered in court to offset those claims, but it can be assumed that the company would have explained that it could not be proven that the source of stray voltage was its pole, and that it could not be proven that the stray voltage, whatever the source, caused the decreased milk production or the increased disease rate.

At the time of the settlement, both Paul and Judy VanDenBerg signed a confidentiality agreement that they

EXHIBIT 3 Stray Voltage on the Farm

Secondary neutral
from transformer

In most utility systems the
earth is used as a conductor for
returning power to its source.
When poor grounding occurs
either on a farm complex or
along the path to a substation,
farm animals can become links
in an alternate power return
loop. Because common points
of contact with dairy cows are
water dishes, affected animals
can unknowingly be trained to
avoid water, causing losses in
milk production, dehydration,
and eventually death.

Transformer and
utility pole grounds

Electrically grounded
stanchion and
water pipe

Wet floor and soil

Ground rod

SOURCE: Minnesota Extension Service, University of Minnesota.

would not discuss "the terms and amount of the settlement with others." Such an agreement is common in negotiated settlements: the defendant in a civil suit obviously does not want to have the conditions that led to a large financial settlement widely publicized by the plaintiff for fear that such publicity will attract still further litigants. Immediately after the settlement, which involved both the payment of $750,000 and the "isolation" of the farm by providing 3-wire ungrounded service, it was clear that Paul VanDenBerg had discussed the terms and the amount of the settlement with others; he was quoted in the article partially reprinted above as having said, "The farm game's been rough this year. We can survive the farm game, but we can't survive electrocution."

He went on to explain to the reporter that the reason he was speaking out was that he wanted to warn other dairy farmers about the dangers of stray voltage, and their need to know that, in the case of his family at least, he felt that the public utility had deliberately misled him and other family members about both the effects and causes of stray voltage. "We trusted those people with our lives. I don't trust them at all now" was his final statement to the reporter.

Class Assignment

It is now two years after the settlement with the VanDenBergs. You are the senior officer at Consumers Power Company in charge of public and governmental relations. You are obviously concerned that Mr. and Mrs. VanDenBerg are still talking about the problems and causes of stray voltage

from their point of view, and that their story has now come to the attention of "Sixty Minutes." You know that "Sixty Minutes" is one of the most watched shows on television, primarily because it produces very dramatic and often touching vignettes of life in the United States. Many of those vignettes, each 16 minutes long so that three fit into an hour-length program with 12 minutes left for sponsor advertisements and network promotions, are built around the theme of "the little man or woman fighting against the big corporation, government agency, or professional group." Lastly, you know that "Sixty Minutes" has the reputation of "hard-hitting journalism"; that is, the programs are likely to make charges with limited substantiation and then let the opponents attempt to defend themselves against those charges. It is a journalistic practice that can hardly be described as "fair," but it does make for lively, entertaining, and commercially successful television.

1. Will you accept the offer of "Sixty Minutes" for a spokesman from Consumers Power Company to appear on the "Stray Voltage" program segment? The corporate attorney for Consumers Power is strongly against anyone from the company appearing on the program; he feels that the company would have no legal standing in attempting to enforce the confidentiality agreement with the VanDenBergs if a company spokesperson appeared on national television and discussed the same issues. Regardless of the legal aspects, recognize that both of the VanDenBergs

EXHIBIT 4

If you suspect stray voltage, we can help.
Stray voltage is low-level electrical alternating current found on metal objects, such as
stanchions, feeders and pipes. It may be caused by deteriorated wiring, wiring that
adoesn't conform with the National Electrical Code, or sources located off the farm.

Call us for a free inspection.
Stray voltage may cause livestock to be nervous, reluctant to eat or drink and unwilling
to enter barns, stanchions and other areas. (Note: This type of behavior may be caused
by nonelectrical problems.) Usually, humans cannot feel stray voltage.

If you feel a shock, you may have defective wiring. This could cause a fire or serious
personal injury.

If you suspect stray voltage on your farm, or if anyone receives an electrical shock for an
unknown reason, please call us right away at the telephone number shown on the front
of your bill. We'll inspect your farm free of charge to find the source of the problem.

---

are articulate, photogenic people; they will be, in show business terms, a "hard act to follow."

2. If you do accept the offer for a spokesperson to appear, and assume that the chairman of Consumers Power has said that he will rely upon your judgment, what will you say, or suggest that the spokesperson say? Recognize that you or that spokesperson will probably have approximately two to three minutes to make whatever points you wish to get across to the audience, and that you or the spokesperson will doubtless be interrupted during the response. Recognize further that the interviewer for "Sixty Minutes," Mr. Ed Bradley for this particular segment, will probably start by asking an accusatory question such as, "Why didn't you just fix the problem back in 1978? Five hundred cows were killed over the next 10 years. You must have known something was wrong; 500 cows don't just fall over and die by accident. Why didn't you save the cows, and avoid all the grief you caused the VanDen-

Berg family, and just fix the problem?"

3. Remember that you are the official at Consumers Power Company responsible for both public and governmental relations. Recognize that probably all of the members of the Public Service Commission (the regulatory agency for public utilities in Michigan) and that most of the members of the state House of Representatives and Senate will be watching the program. You will be limited to two to three minutes in your response on television (if you accept the offer to appear); you will not be limited in your follow-up calls and letters to the public officials. What will you say to them?

4. What do you think that the company should do now? There are 6,700 dairy farms in your service area; one estimate is that 30 percent of them—over 2,000 farms—have potentially severe problems with stray voltage. Recognize all of the unknowns. The sources of stray voltage on any particular farm cannot be identified with absolute accuracy. The effects of stray voltage on any particular farm animal cannot be projected with absolute certainty. Recognize also the magnitude of the investment that will be required to totally fix any problem that does exist. The question here is, then, given the uncertainty and the expense, what do you—as Consumers Power Company—owe your customers?

5. Lastly, turn the last question around. What do the producers and interviewers from "Sixty Minutes"—as television journalists who have a unique opportunity to reach a substantial number of American citizens each week, an opportunity denied to most other persons because of the restrictive nature of network licensing—owe to their customers?

CHAPTER 7

Moral Leadership in Business

In Chapter 6, it was proposed that the moral responsibility of management is to build trust, commitment, and effort among all of the stakeholder groups. It was further proposed that this could be accomplished by integrating moral reasoning—the process of determining what is "right" and "just" and "fair" in the treatment of others—into all of the levels of managerial activity. It was lastly proposed that an extended organization that could successfully achieve this integration while also meeting managerial responsibilities at the conceptual, technical, functional, and operational levels would be economically efficient, competitively effective, and socially beneficial:

The belief that a company might—at one and the same time—be economically efficient, competitively effective, and socially beneficial is not widely accepted. Generally it is felt that economic efficiency and social beneficiency or betterment are contradictory. Usually it is thought that the management of a company has to choose between its responsibility to the stockholders to increase profits and its responsibility to the stakeholders to recognize rights. In an attempt to show that these outcomes are not contradictory, it is worth repeating the five major arguments of Chapter 6 that build up to this disputed conclusion:

1. Treating stakeholders in ways that can be considered to be "right," "just," and "fair" through the recognition of moral problems and the application of moral reasoning creates trust; trust builds commitment; commitment ensures effort; and effort is essential for organizational success.

2. The effort that results from trust and commitment goes far beyond that which is based only upon financial incentives and commercial contracts. The effort based on trust results in a willingness to contribute "something extra," to act with energy and enthusiasm for the benefit of the organization.

3. The willingness to contribute "something extra," to act with energy and enthusiasm, is much more important now than in the past due to the changed conditions of global competition. Companies are now dependent upon stakeholder groups that are far outside the "command and control" hierarchy of the firm.

4. Given that the old "command and control" form of management is no longer effective, it must be replaced with a new "unify and guide" form.

EXHIBIT 7–1   Levels of Managerial Responsibility

Moral responsibilities	Gaining trust Generating commitment Producing effort	
Conceptual responsibilities	Setting objectives Forging advantages Building competence	
Technical responsibilities	Developing people Utilizing information Creating products	Economic efficiency Comp. effectiveness Social beneficiency
Functional responsibilities	Maximizing revenues Minimizing costs Optimizing returns	
Operational responsibilities	Satisfying customers Improving methods Conserving assets	

Unification is dependent upon moral reasoning, which must dominate the managerial activities at the conceptual, technical, functional, and operational levels of the firm.

5. If the managerial activities at all five levels of the firm are done, and done well, as measured by the performance criteria that have been established for each level, then the company will operate with economic efficiency, with competitive effectiveness, and with social beneficiency.

In short, a successful company as measured by economic efficiency and competitive effectiveness will also be successful as measured by social betterment. The managers will be "good global citizens"—paying attention to the welfare of their constituent groups—because otherwise they will be unable to gain the trust, commitment, and enthusiastic effort of those constituent groups. This is the major argument of this text. Without the trust, commitment, and enthusiastic effort on the part of all of the constituent groups—those within the company, those within the industry, and those within the society—modern business firms will be unable to be successful over time in a highly competitive global economy.

Obviously, you are free to accept or reject this argument. If you reject it,

EXHIBIT 7–2
Process of Moral Reasoning

Define the moral problem clearly: Is it "right" to take this action which may bring hurt or harm upon one or more groups within the constituencies of the firm?

Examine the alternative actions: What else could be done that would either avoid the harm brought upon this group, or that would spread the harms—and the benefits—more equitably?

Resolve the factual issues: What further information do we need so that all of the constituent groups can agree on the basic choices, and is that information available and reliable?

Consider the personal impacts: What, if any, will be the impact upon the careers of the people who first define and then resolve the moral problem, and are they willing to bear that cost?

Apply the ethical principles: What interim decisions seem to be reached when the problem is examined from the point of view of each of the 10 ethical principles, in sequence?

Reach a firm conclusion: What is the final decision, given the differing points of view of each of the ethical principles, and can that decision be explained clearly and convincingly?

then you have to explain why stakeholder groups outside the company and outside the industry will innovate and cooperate for the benefit of the firm. You cannot "command" innovation. You cannot "control" cooperation. What do the stakeholders owe to you, as the manager of the firm, beyond what you owe to them? Why should they continually elect to do their jobs in a better rather than a worse fashion if you continually decide to treat them in an adversarial fashion? How, in short, can you create trust, commitment, and *enthusiastic* effort without moral reasoning?

If you do accept this argument that the moral responsibility of management is to extend moral sensitivity and moral reasoning through all of the levels of the firm in order to create trust, commitment, and enthusiastic effort among all of the stakeholders of the company, then you have to worry about the means by which you will accomplish this goal. You know how to arrive at a decision that you feel to be "right" and "just" and "fair" in the treatment of others. You know how to explain that decision, with reference to the ethical principles of analysis, so that others, even if they do not agree with the outcome, at least can agree that the process which led to your decision was "right" and "just" and "fair."

That is the process of moral reasoning. It is the final argument of this text that the senior executives within a firm can achieve the unity based upon trust, commitment, and effort by ensuring that the process of moral reasoning pervades the organizational values, the strategic plans, the resource programs, the

EXHIBIT 7–3 Moral Leadership in Business

$$
\text{Process of moral reasoning}
\left\{
\begin{array}{l}
\text{Statement of organizational values} \\[4pt]
\text{Statement of planning objectives} \\[4pt]
\text{Review of strategic plans} \\[4pt]
\text{Review of resource programs} \\[4pt]
\text{Review of revenue/expense budgets} \\[4pt]
\text{Review of performance measures} \\[4pt]
\text{Review of incentive payments} \\[4pt]
\text{Statement of behavioral standards}
\end{array}
\right.
$$

annual budgets, the performance measures, and the incentive payments of the firm. This, in the terms of the title of this chapter, is moral leadership in business.

But, how can this be done? How can the senior executives of a company assume this leadership role? How can they ensure that managerial decisions throughout the firm will be made on the basis of what is most "right" and "just" and "fair" for all of the stakeholders of the firm rather than on the basis of what is most profitable for the company or most remunerative for the managers?

This chapter has eight recommendations that should enable senior executives to assume the leadership role. These recommendations require that the senior executives—the leaders of the firm—take a positive approach towards preparing a statement of organizational values and towards reviewing the impacts of the strategic plans, the resource programs, the revenue and expense budgets, the performance measures, and the incentive payments upon the various constituency groups of the firm:

1. *Prepare a statement of organizational values.* Values, as were described earlier (see Chapter 2) are priorities among the goals, norms, and beliefs of people. They are the gauges we all use to judge the relative importance of what we want to achieve, how we want to act, and why we want to believe those goals and those acts to be truly worthwhile. Most people do not consider that all of their goals, norms, and beliefs are of equal importance; generally there are some that seem more important, more "valued," than others.

Organizations also have goals, norms, and beliefs that are valued. Or, more properly, individuals within organizations have goals, norms, and beliefs that are valued, and often those values are shared by so many other individuals within the same organization that they appear to belong to the organization. Shared values tend to unite the holders. They tend to provide a consistent view of "why we exist," "how we act," and "what we believe."

It is the first recommendation of this chapter, in order to unite the members of the organization and to provide this consistent view of the goals, norms, and beliefs of the organization, that the senior executives deliberately select and then clearly state the values that they wish to have known and would like to have shared throughout the extended organization.

It is not easy to prepare this statement of values that are to be known and—if possible—shared throughout the organization. Firstly, organizational values cannot be imposed upon people. They have to appeal to people. They have to contain the goals, norms, and beliefs that most people can agree to be "right" and "just" and "fair." They have to be prepared, in short, from a basis in moral reasoning.

Secondly, organizational values cannot be stated in absolute terms. "Absolute," of course, means complete, precise, exact, and undeviating. No one could describe the preferred ways of acting towards employees, for one example, or the preferred ways of thinking about products for another, in terms that were "complete, precise, exact, and undeviating." Too much can change. Too much can't be measured. Too much is relative. It is impossible for the senior executives at a firm to say exactly how employees should be treated, under any and all circumstances, or to explain precisely how products should be designed, given the multitude of designs that are possible.

It is possible, however, for the senior executives to list the constituencies of the firm in an order of priority, and then to explain—again, in general terms—the considerations that the senior executives would like the managers at the operational, functional, technical, and conceptual levels to bear in mind as they make their decisions and take their actions that impact those constituencies.

The Credo prepared by Johnson & Johnson is an example of this type of value statement. It obviously has been prepared in a known sequence or order of priority. It obviously has been written in very general terms. "We are responsible to our employees, the men and women who work with us throughout the world. Everyone must be considered as an individual. We must respect their dignity and recognize their merit. They must have a sense of security in their jobs" Those statements that everyone must be considered as an individual, respected for their dignity, recognized for their merit, and given a sense of security in their jobs are not "complete, precise, exact and undeviating." It is not clear exactly what is meant by a "sense of security," nor precisely how people will be "recognized for their merit."

The values expressed in the Credo of Johnson & Johnson are clearly

EXHIBIT 7–4
Credo of Johnson & Johnson

We believe our first responsibility is to the doctors, nurses, and patients, to mothers and all others who use our products and services.

In meeting their needs everything we do must be of high quality.

We must constantly strive to reduce our costs in order to maintain reasonable prices.

Customer orders must be serviced promptly and accurately.

Our suppliers and distributors must have an opportunity to make a fair profit.

We are responsible to our employees, the men and women who work with us throughout the world.

Everyone must be considered as an individual. We must respect their dignity and recognize their merit.

They must have a sense of security in their jobs. Compensation must be fair and adequate, and working conditions clean, orderly, and safe.

Employees must feel free to make suggestions and complaints.

There must be equal opportunity for employment, development and advancement for those qualified.

We must provide competent management and their actions must be just and ethical.

We are responsible to the communities in which we live and work and to the world community as well.

We must be good citizens—support good works and charities and bear our fair share of taxes.

We must encourage civic improvements and better health and education.

We must maintain in good order the property we are privileged to use, protecting the environment and natural resources.

Our final responsibility is to our stockholders. Business must make a sound profit.

We must experiment with new ideas. Research must be carried on, innovative programs developed, and mistakes paid for.

New equipment must be purchased, new facilities provided and new products launched.

Reserves must be created to provide for adverse times.

When we operate according to these principles, the stockholders should realize a fair return.

not absolute. They are clearly not required in each and every instance. But, those values are clearly important in the minds of the senior executives, and company managers throughout the firm are obviously expected to keep them in mind as they make their decisions and take their actions.

EXHIBIT 7–5   Graphic Display of the Annual Planning Cycle Integrating Strategies, Programs, and Budgets

	March	April	May	June	July	August	September
Corporate executives		Statement of planning objectives	Approval of divisional strategies		Approval of divisional programs		Approval of divisional ⟶ budgets
Corporate staff		Forecast economic conditions	Review consistency and format		Review calculations and format		Review calculations and format
Divisional managers		Prepare divisional strategies			Support divisional programs		Support divisional budgets
Divisional staff		Assist strategic planning			Prepare divisional plans		Coordinate budgetary planning
Functional and technical units		Supply, market, cost, and technology data			Supply time and capital estimates		Prepare divisional budgets

2. *Prepare a statement of planning objectives.* The statement of organizational values is normally prepared only once. It usually is updated on a regular basis, but the essential message remains the same over time: "Here is what we think is important, stated very generally and very idealistically, but in a definite order of priority among the constituent groups of our firm."

Statements of organizational values, because they are written in very general and idealistic terms, and because they are prepared only once and then occasionally updated, tend to be neglected unless the message is continually reinforced. An excellent time for reinforcement is at the start of the annual planning cycle.

Most large and medium-sized business firms are divided into product divisions, and those product divisions are expected—usually on an annual basis—to prepare strategic plans for the next 5 to 10 years that are then submitted to the senior corporate executives for approval. This is termed the annual planning cycle, for the strategic plans on the proposed method of competition are usually followed in sequence by program plans for the allocation of resources and then by budgetary plans for the estimation of revenues and expenses and the setting of standards.

At the start of this planning cycle it is the recommendation of this chapter that the senior executives submit to each of the divisional managers a short restatement of the organizational values. "We expect from your division a "x" increase in sales, a "y" increase in profits, and a "z" return on investment over the next five years of your plan, but it does matter how you achieve these goals. You are to explain the impact of your strategic plan upon each of the constituent groups of our company."

3. *Review of strategic plans.* Strategic plans refer to the long-term method of competition chosen for a business firm—how will the company compete within a given industry or industries—and to the position selected for that firm within an industry or across industries for long-term sustainable advantage. The two definitions are nearly identical. "How will it compete?" means what products, markets, prices, promotions, and methods will the company adopt. "What position will it take?" means what economies of scale, scope, and experience does the company have, and what entry barriers and core competences can it build upon.

The strategic plans for a company are normally developed after a consideration of (1) the competitive structure of the industry; (2) the economic, technological, social, and political trends of the environment; and (3) the financial and physical resources and the functional and technical skills of the company. For any given firm at any given point in time there are a number of alternative methods of competition that could be adopted. The intent of strategic planning is to select the "best" method of competition, the one that most closely matches the industry conditions, the environmental trends, and the company competences.

The selection of this "best" method of competition normally takes place on an annual basis. Each year the recent changes in industry conditions, environmental trends, and company competences are evaluated, the alternative strategies open to the firm are considered, and one long-term method of competition is selected. Changes in this long-term method of competition during the annual planning cycle are usually more minor adjustments than major redirections.

Regardless of whether those alterations are minor adjustments or major redirections, it is the recommendation of this chapter that the impact of each change upon the constituencies of the company be clearly stated and then examined. Who will be hurt, and how badly? Who will be benefited, and how much? What is the *potential* for harm or benefit? If either

EXHIBIT 7–6   Strategic Planning Process

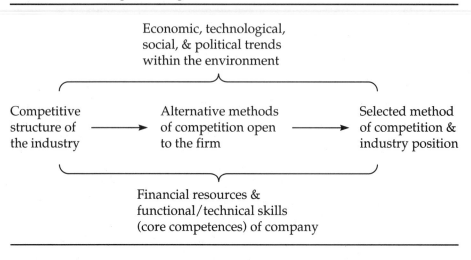

Economic, technological,
social, & political trends
within the environment

Competitive
structure of
the industry → Alternative methods
of competition open
to the firm → Selected method
of competition &
industry position

Financial resources &
functional/technical skills
(core competences) of company

actual hurt or potential harm can be shown, then the moral question has to be asked: "Is it right to take this action, given the actual or potential hurt or harm to others?" This is the integration of moral reasoning—ethics—with managerial decisions in the strategic planning process.

4. *Review of resource programs.* Resource programs allocate the resources—money, people, and property—to achieve the competitive posture envisaged in the strategic plan. A program can be thought of as a set of activities extending across multiple functional and technical departments. The development of a product, the expansion of a market, and the modernization of a factory are all examples of programs.

The resources in a program—once again, money, people, and property—are normally converted to financial equivalents, and then the allocation of those resources is usually approved by the senior executives of the firm as the second stage in the annual planning cycle. Sometimes that approval is delayed, when the alternative uses are found to be more pressing. Sometimes that approval is denied, when the financial returns are found to be too low.

When the resources for a specific program are either denied or delayed, it is the recommendation of this chapter that the impact of that denial or delay upon each of the constituencies of the firm be examined. Once again, if there is an actual hurt or a potential harm, then the moral question has to be asked, and resolved. This is the integration of moral reasoning—ethics—with managerial decisions in the resource allocation process.

5. *Review of revenue/expense budgets.* Budgets are estimates of the revenues and expenses associated with each of the programs developed to

EXHIBIT 7–7   Differences between Strategic Plans, Resource Programs and
Revenue/Expense Budgets

Planning Stage	Organization Level	Time Horizon	Major Component
Strategic	Corporate	5–10 years	Selection of the competitive position of the firm, lead-towards long-term advantage
Program	Divisional	3–5 years	Allocation of the resources needed to achieve the competitive position/advantage
Budgetary	Functional & technical	1 year	Estimation of revenues & expenses associated with each unit working on the program

achieve the competitive position envisaged in the selected strategy for the firm. Budgets also assign responsibility for the activities contained in the programs. This assignment of responsibility is probably the most important element in the definition of the concept: a budget is not so much a forecast of results as it is a commitment by members of a unit within the organization to achieve those results.

Strategies, programs, and budgets are obviously related. Exhibit 7–7 shows the differences between these three forms of planning in terms of organizational levels, time horizons, and managerial intentions. Exhibit 7–8 shows the similarities: the programs and budgets together form a structure for the strategy of the firm.

Budgetary plans forecast the revenues and expenses associated with the different programs of the firm, and they set the goals and objectives for the functional and technical departments assigned to those programs. The goals and objectives are the results that are expected in engineering, marketing, production, etc.; they are statements of where the functional and technical departments are expected to be at specific times in the future.

The goals of the annual budgets give members of the various departments the sense of direction and purpose that is necessary to coordinate their efforts, and they permit evaluation of the performance of those units. These goals serve, in short, as targets for achievement and as standards for control.

The "targets for achievement and standards for control" are primarily financial (expressed in dollars), but they can also be quantitative (expressed in units, ratios, or comparative scales). The financial measures are based upon anticipated revenues or expenses over a 12-month period, and give the appearance of precision and detail, but in reality revenues, costs, and profits are summary figures for many diverse activities and are subject, of course, to the accounting conventions. The financial measures need to be

EXHIBIT 7–8 Integration of Strategic Plans, Program Plans, and Budgetary Plans

	Engineering budget	Marketing budget	Production budget
Program for existing business			
Program for product development			
Program for market expansion		**Overall Strategy of the Firm**	
Program for cost improvement			
Program for capacity increase			

supplemented by quantitative measures, which can be expressed in units (total output), ratios (output per worker), or scales (customer satisfaction).

The revenue and expense budgets, supplemented by quantitative measures of performance, are usually approved by senior executives after the strategy has been selected and the resources have been allocated. Changes often occur at this stage in the planning process, generally to reduce costs or increase profits. It is the recommendation of this chapter that the impacts of those changes upon each of the constituencies of the firm be examined. Once again, if there is an actual hurt or a potential harm, then the moral question has to be asked, and resolved. This is the integration of moral reasoning—ethics—with managerial decisions in the annual budgeting process.

6. *Review of performance measures.* Most managers within a firm are measured by their performance levels against their strategic plans, programs plans, and budgetary plans. These measures involve a comparison of planned outcomes versus actual results through an analysis of the variances, and the intent is—or should be—to provide those managers with information for the improvement of their performance. What has gone wrong, and why? What has gone right, and why? What can we do now, to build upon what has gone right and correct what has gone wrong? Those are the three basic questions in managerial evaluation, often termed "managerial control."

Managerial control is usually exercised at three levels corresponding to the three stages in the planning process: strategic plans, resource programs, and revenue/expense budgets.

Strategic control. The strategic plans define the long-term method of competition selected for a firm and the industry position chosen for a sustainable advantage. It is difficult to measure progress in achieving that competitive method and in building that sustainable advantage, but the effort certainly has to be made. Improvements in customer loyalty, over time. Increases in technological capability, over time. Expansion in the economies of scale, scope, or experience, over time. All can be measured roughly, and actual results can be compared to planned outcomes.

Program control. The resource programs allocate the money, people, and property needed to achieve the competitive positions and build the sustainable advantages envisaged in the strategic plans for the firm. Produce developments, market expansions, process improvements, and cost reductions were said to be examples of programs. Again, it is difficult to measure progress in developing products, expanding markets, improving methods, and reducing costs over the three- to five-year time span of a program, but the attempt has to be made, and the actual results compared to the planned outcomes.

Budgetary controls. The annual budgets forecast the revenues and expenses associated with the different programs of the firm, and they set the goals and objectives for the functional and technical departments assigned to those programs in both financial and quantitative terms. Here it is much easier to compare the actual results to the planned outcomes because the financial results are recorded as a product of the accounting system, and the quantitative outputs can be computed as a by-product of that system.

It is important to recognize in the application of managerial controls at the strategic, program, or budgetary levels that some of the factors in the measures of performance of an organizational unit are subject to the direction of the manager of that unit, and some are not. Factors that are not subject to the direction of the manager are usually external to the unit, and include such problems as reductions in the level of economic activity or increases in the degree of competitive intensity.

It is also important to remember in the application of managerial controls that the intent is the improvement of future performance, not the condemnation of past performance. It is all too easy to set excessive standards that cannot be met. It is all too easy to neglect external problems that cannot be solved. It is all too easy to say, "If you can't meet your goals, we'll find someone who can."

The problem is that any control system can be manipulated to meet unrealistic standards or to avoid unsolvable problems over a short period of time. Revenues can be taken in advance of the actual sales; costs can be delayed into the subsequent periods; programs can be portrayed as nearer to completion than they really are; suppliers, distributors, and customers can be described as more loyal than they actually are. It is the recommendation of this chapter that the impacts of those possible manipulations upon each of the constituencies of the firm be examined. Once again, if there is an actual hurt or a potential harm, then the moral question has to be asked, and resolved. This is the integration of moral reasoning—ethics—with managerial decisions in the design of the control system.

7. *Review of incentive payments.* Most managers within a firm are rewarded when their performance levels measured against their strategic plans, program plans, or budgetary plans meet or exceed expectations. These rewards are for the purpose of motivation. The intent is to encourage effort in the fulfillment of the plans.

Most incentive payments in the motivation system are tied to the performance measures of the control system. This means, unfortunately, that they are subject to exactly the same possible abuses as the performance measures, and they seem to encourage those abuses over short time periods. This is particularly true when the amounts to be paid are "counted upon" to maintain a given standard of living. If an annual bonus is needed to maintain a manager's life-style, or the life-style of his or her family, and if that bonus will be paid only if the manager meets a given performance standard in the control system, then the temptation to overstate revenues, postpone costs, or exploit employees, suppliers, distributors, customers, creditors, and owners becomes very high.

It is the recommendation of this chapter that the impacts of these possible abuses upon each of the constituencies of the firm be examined. Once again, if there is an actual hurt or a potential harm, then the moral question has to be asked, and resolved. This is the integration of moral reasoning—ethics—with managerial decisions in the design of the motivation system.

8. *Statement of behavioral standards.* Given the impact of the control system upon the promotions, pay rates, and jobs of managers, and given the effect of the motivation system upon their financial rewards, it is not surprising that there is often a temptation to cut costs and corners and perhaps harm employees, suppliers, distributors, customers, creditors, or owners.

It is the final recommendation of this chapter that the senior executives at a firm recognize these temptations, and prepare a statement of the behavioral standards that are expected to be followed by all of the members of the firm. This statement on behavioral standards differs in two important ways from the earlier statement on organizational values. The earlier statement was very idealistic; this is very realistic. The earlier statement was very general; this is very specific.

EXHIBIT 7–9
Summary Code of Conduct of Exxon Company, U.S.A.

Our company policy is one of strict observance of all laws applicable to its business.

A reputation for scrupulous dealing is itself a priceless company asset.

We do care how we get results.

We expect candor at all levels and compliance with accounting rules and controls.

It is the established policy of the company to conduct its business in compliance with all state and federal antitrust laws.

Individual employees are responsible for seeing that they comply with the law.

Employees must avoid even the appearance of violation.

Competing or conducting business with the company is not permitted, except with the knowledge and consent of management.

Accepting and providing gifts, entertainment, and services must comply with specific requirements.

An employee may not use company personnel, information, or other assets for personal benefit.

Participating in certain outside activities requires the prior approval of management.

The statement of behavioral standards lists a number of possible actions by members of the organization that are forbidden. One problem is that those members are usually at the lower end of the organization; executives at the top of the hierarchy often seem to be excluded. Another problem is that those actions seem to stress conflicts of interest, where the organization itself will be hurt, and not conflicts of conscience where employees, suppliers, distributors, customers, etc., may be harmed. Still, a statement of the minimal standards of acceptable behavior, such as that prepared by the Exxon Company, does help in providing moral guidance for the members of an organization.

Moral leadership in business provides moral guidance through the statements of organizational values (why we exist), of planning objectives (what we want), and of behavioral standards (how we act). Moral leadership in business also reviews the strategic plans, program plans, budgetary plans, performance measures, and incentive payments for harmful impacts upon the constituency groups within the firm, within the industry, and within the society. Moral leadership in business, in brief, is the integration of moral reasoning—the determination of what is "right" and "just" and "fair"—throughout an extended organization in order to build trust, commitment, and effort.

ASSIGNMENT QUESTIONS

1. Look again at the list of recommended activities in Exhibit 7–3, Moral Leadership in Business. Are there any other ways in which the leaders of a firm can set the moral tone of that organization? Is that "moral tone" important, in your opinion?

2. Read once again the Credo of Johnson & Johnson in Exhibit 7–4. Now, think of yourself as chairperson of that company in 1982 when some bottles of Tylenol (a pain relief remedy) were found to be poisoned. What would you do? How would you explain what you decided to do to the directors?

3. Look once again at the graphic of the annual planning cycle in Exhibit 7–5. Now, think of yourself as chairperson of a large company, such as Johnson & Johnson. How do you influence the direction of that company? Are there any other ways to let people know what you want them to do?

4. Look once again at the Summary Code of Conduct of the Exxon Company, U.S.A. in Exhibit 7–9. This sets the behavioral standards of that company. Express in your own words those standards. As an employee, what actions are you forbidden to take? As the chairperson, what actions would you add to the list?

Case 7–1

WHAT DO YOU DO NOW?

Frequently as a manager you will find that your views as to what is "right" and "just" and "proper" are not as widely shared as you might have thought. Then you are either forced to take some action, or to ignore the situation. What would you do in each of these instances?

1. You are the senior vice president of a machinery manufacturing firm that builds and sells equipment for complete chemical processes on a worldwide basis. The design of this equipment is highly technical, and almost all of your younger employees have an engineering back-ground. Perhaps 15 percent of those engineers are women, who started joining the company about five years previously. It is accepted that the career path for younger employees has to include overseas assignment in developing countries, and you plan to appoint a woman to the next available opportunity. The vice president of the South American sales division calls you—evidently anticipating your intention—and asks you not to do so. He says that the firm's clients in those Latin countries will not accept women in a technical capacity. "The older men will be polite to

her, and treat her like a daughter. The younger ones will engage in some harmless flirting which I assume she can handle with ease, and some not so harmless which she will have to learn to live with. But, neither the older nor the younger customers will accept technical recommendations from a woman, so that she will be useless in a sales capacity. If she wants to work in design at our central office and have no contact with clients, that's fine, but otherwise I think you should send her to Europe." Company sales in Europe were minimal, due to strong competition from technically advanced German, French, and Italian firms.

2. You are the chief financial officer of a chain of retail stores. One of your most valued employees came to your department when your company acquired a much smaller chain for which he worked. Most of the staff employees of that chain were discharged as part of a cost reduction program at the time of the acquisition, but you kept this person because his background was very good—his resume showed that he was the graduate of a well-known Eastern business school—and because he was obviously very bright and competent. He has been promoted a number of times since then, and now works regularly as your assistant. You have been asked to give a talk to the students at the well-known Eastern business school. After that talk, at lunch, you mention to the director of placement how pleased you are with the work of your assistant, and you give his name (which hap-

pens to be unusual and memorable) and say that he graduated six years ago. There is an awkward silence. Then the director of placement asks, "Are you certain?" He repeats the name and says, "He used to work for me, as my assistant, but if we are talking about the same person, I don't believe he is a graduate of this school."

3. You are the executive vice president of the automotive division at Sears, Roebuck & Co. The automotive division sells tires, batteries, repair parts, and auto accessories, and provides repair/maintenance services, at Sears stores nationwide. You have just learned that the California Department of Consumer Affairs (CDCA) is going to sue Sears, Roebuck for customer fraud. The CDCA says that it brought special "test" cars to 48 Sears Auto Centers within the state of California a total of 285 times. The cars were older, but all of the wheel suspension and brake parts—with the exception of the brake pads themselves—had either been recently replaced or had been certified to be in good working order. The driver of the test car, often a woman, asked to have the brake pads—which were worn—replaced under a Sears' printed advertisement offering a "complete brake job for just $48.00." In 247 of those 285 test cases the customer was told that the brake calipers, shock absorbers, coil springs, idler arms, or master cylinders also needed to be replaced at a much higher price. In some instances the undercover investigators were charged as much as $500 for need-

needless repairs. The CDCA claimed that the "customer service representatives" in the auto service areas of Sears stores were paid an escalating commission for the higher value parts, and also were evaluated by a control system that specified the number of these higher value parts that should be solldduringeveryeight-hourshift.Cus-tomer sales reps who did not meet those sales targets were demoted to the position of regular salesclerks. You had designed both the incentive system and the control system about three years previously, and have since received substantial bonuses based upon the expanded sales and profits that came from the introduction of those systems.

Case 7–2

THREE COMPANIES IN NEED OF MORAL DIRECTION

Three short cases that depicted moral problems encountered by recent graduates of a program in business administration were included earlier in the book. These cases—"Sarah Goodwin," "Susan Shapiro," and "George Kacmarek"—depicted very fundamental moral problems for in each instance they placed the career of the individual in jeopardy if he or she refused to accept the situation. The recent graduates had to decide what they would or would not accept; that is, they had to decide where they would "draw the line."

Now, you have been promoted. Put yourself in the place of the president of one of those companies. Just to help your memory, the moral problems involved (1) a retail store that was shipping defective food products to the ghetto for sale to the poor, (2) a chemical company that maintained a production process even though it was harmful to the health and well-being of the employees, and (3) a plant manager for a metal stamping company who was accepting kickbacks from a steel supplier.

You are the president or a senior vice president, clearly at a managerial level where you can make whatever decision you believe would serve the best interests of your company and your society. You also have a reputation as a "doer," a man or woman who has managed the company very successfully in the past, with continually rising sales and profits, and consequently a person who tends to get his or her own way in dealing with stockholders, board members, and immediate subordinates. In short, no one will openly oppose you. That does not mean, however, that people further down in the organization, at the functional or operating levels, will automatically accept your directions just because they are your directions. You probably will have to convince people that it is in their best interests to follow your directions.

Lastly, you have just found that the situation described in the case actually exists in your firm and, even worse, you have hard evidence that it is endemic throughout the firm. That is, if you decided to be president of the metal stamping company, you have irrefutable evidence that numerous people throughout the company are accepting small kickbacks. If, instead, you put yourself in the place of the president of the chemical company, you now understand that almost all of your chemical plants have at least one production process that is technically legal but medically and environmentally harmful. You are shocked. You say to your spouse that night, "I had no idea this was going on, but it obviously is and I've got to do something about it."

Class Assignment

What exactly will you do? You can fire the people involved, but will that really cure the problem? What actions can you take that will "cure the problem"?

Case 7–3

CODE OF ETHICS FOR A SCHOOL OF BUSINESS ADMINISTRATION

Your school may or may not have a formal Code of Ethics or a written Code of Conduct. The two are basically the same; only the terms in the title seem to differ, as well as some degree of emphasis upon what is "wrong" (ethics) or what is "prohibited" (conduct).

If your school does have such a code, get a copy and look at it closely. What actions are prohibited? Are there any actions that you feel probably should be added to the code? Any that should be removed? Does the code apply only to students, or does it extend to cover actions by faculty, administrators, recruiters, etc.? Is the code known and followed by those to whom it was designed to apply?

If your school does not have such a code, start to think about how you would form one. It is suggested that you begin by looking at the two codes that are included in Chapter 70. The code of the Exxon Corporation tends to be negative; it lists a series of the actions that are prohibited. The code of Johnson & Johnson tends to be positive; it lists a series of duties towards each of the constituent groups. Decide which type you prefer, or whether you would like some mixture of the two. Then, outline the areas that you think should be included in the final version.

1. The code of ethics (Credo) of Johnson & Johnson puts the customers in the first place. If you selected a positive type of code, similar to the Credo, which group do you place first?

2. The code of ethics of the Exxon Corporation specifically prohibits a series of actions by employees. If you selected a negative type of code, what actions do you prohibit?

3. If a person (student, faculty, administrator, or recruiter), broke one of the provisions of your code, what penalty, if any, would be invoked? What process should be followed?

Case 7–4

THE BOSTON COMPANY

The Boston Safe Deposit and Trust Company, generally called the Boston Company for short, was founded shortly after the Civil War to provide trust management and investment custody services for wealthy New England families. The latter half of the 19th century and the early part of the 20th century were periods of rapid industrial growth within the region. Textile mills, machine tool factories, railroad equipment companies, and specialty chemical plants all expanded. Many of these were family owned, and the Boston Company established a reputation as the premier financial institution to manage the wealth of its well-born clients.

By 1960, however, the industrial prosperity of New England had come to an end. The textile mills had moved to the South, in search of less expensive labor. The machine tool factories had moved to the Midwest, to be close to their major customers: the automobile, farm machinery, and home appliance industries. The specialty chemical plants, which primarily produced paint, varnish, and the early plastics, had moved to Texas and Louisiana to make use of the petrochemical feed stocks discovered in those states. The railroad equipment companies had simply closed, when cars, trucks, and airplanes replaced the railroads as the major modes of transportation.

The Boston Company opened offices in Chicago, Houston, and Los Angeles in an attempt to move closer to the new centers of wealth, but it found that its reputation had less meaning in those new areas and, it was said, many of its new customers found it somewhat stodgy and old fashioned. Its investment performance had been excellent. Investment officers at the Boston Company had recognized very early the growth potential of microelectronics, data processing, pharmaceutical drugs, and packaged foods, and had moved their clients' money into the common stock of companies in those industries, but somehow this record of growth in the pension funds and trust funds under their control exceeding that of the common stock indexes was not enough. The Boston Company remained profitable, polite, and stagnant.

In an interesting sidelight, the Houston office formed a consulting group to advise on investments in oil and natural gas exploration and production; this became known as the

Boston Consulting Group, but it was sold by the Boston Company shortly after it was moved back to Boston. After the sale it went on to become one of the premier corporate-level consulting firms in the country.

In 1981 the Boston Company was purchased by Shearson Loeb Rhoades (later to be known as Shearson Lehman Brothers), a division of American Express. Shearson Loeb Rhoades was a large investment bank and brokerage firm with offices throughout the country. The intent of the merger was to market the mutual funds and investment services offered by the Boston Company through the branch offices of Shearson Loeb Rhoades. It was a strategy that was almost immediately successful, and the Boston Company became the fastest growing bank and trust company in the United States during the period 1982 to 1988.

James von Germeten, a financial services executive from Chicago, was appointed president in 1982 to oversee, as was phrased in the *Institutional Investor*, "Boston Company's transformation from a banking and trust culture to a Wall Street performance culture" [July 1987, p 129].

Mr. von Germeten brought in a new director of marketing, a new director of finance, and a new treasurer. Together they set out to remake the company. Young people were recruited, often with backgrounds in quantitative finance. Older people were let go, unable to keep pace with the changes. The Boston Company continued its focus on the wealthy, limiting its clients to those with over $1 million in net worth, but the sources of this wealth changed from basic manufac-

turing to the real estate, retail sales, and entertainment industries. In short, the bank began to appeal to celebrities:

> When Donald Trump bought his yacht *The Princess* in 1988, he didn't have to throw a lavish celebration party. His lender threw it for him. Boston Company, the American Express subsidiary that loaned Trump the $29 million purchase price, spared no expense. Champagne and caviar flowed as top executives from the area toured the 282-foot yacht in Boston Harbor. For Boston Company Chairman James N. von Germeten, the Trump loan represented the transformation of his firm from a stodgy trust-fund manager for New England's old-line elite to a big-time backer of the nouveaux riches, especially celebrities and real estate developers [*Business Week,* July 22, 1991, p. 58].

The Boston Company financed expensive homes as well as yachts; it built up a $4.2 billion portfolio of "jumbo" mortgages in amounts ranging from $350,000 to $3,500,000. These large mortgages were generally unavailable from other financial institutions, and consequently carried higher-than-normal interest rates. Large personal loans were also issued to the bank's wealthy clientele, often with special collateral or repayment provisions that again permitted higher-than-normal rates. The record of successful management of client funds also continued, which allowed higher-than-normal fees to be charged for that management.

The emphasis throughout the period 1982 to 1988 was on growth. Deposits increased 18-fold; mortgages and loans 10-fold; private trust funds

8-fold; public pension funds 6-fold; after-tax earnings 12-fold. Clear targets for growth in assets, loans, revenues, and profits were set for each of the divisions within the company, and large cash incentives were arranged to reward the managers who met or exceeded those goals:

A large part of the firm's success, particularly in active investment management, stems from companywide incentive compensation schemes von Germeten introduced. It began with portfolio managers and analysts but has since expanded. Now, he points out, all managers have pools to "incentivize" their staffs, and bonuses have been as high as 100 percent of salary [*Institutional Investor*, July 1987, p. 131].

Growth in assets, revenues, profits, salaries, and bonuses was accompanied by a growth in "perks" which were felt to be necessary to attract the wealthy clients and reward the successful managers:

Mr. von Germeten brought a go-go style to the Boston Company's State Street headquarters. The company soon was throwing lavish parties complete with caviar and ice sculptures. Mr. von Germeten, unlike his predecessor, rode around Boston in stretch limousines; when in London, he opted for a Rolls Royce.

· · · · ·

In November, he flew out to Los Angeles, where Boston Company opened a new office with a party so lavish it featured a 66-piece orchestra. A guest at the party says he was flabbergasted to find that Boston Company had hired dozens of parking valets to whisk away celebrities' Mercedes and Jaguars.

· · · · ·

As the Boston Ballet finished a Saturday matinee of *The Nutcracker* last month, a mock balloon descended from the stage rafters, carrying, of all people, James N. von Germeten, Boston Company's flamboyant president. The thousand-odd Boston Company employees who had bought out the hall looked on, dumbfounded and slightly embarrassed. Mr. von Germeten, in full business suit regalia, didn't miss a beat, however. He happily mingled with the dancers and took a bow with the ballerinas [*The Wall Street Journal*, January 30, 1989, p. 1f].

Such a dramatic entrance deserved an equally dramatic exit, and that exit occurred just two months later: Mr. von Germeten was asked to resign on January 20, 1989 when the Boston Company was forced to recognize $45 million of "accounting irregularities" that had falsely inflated profits for the prior year.

In explanation of this request, it was revealed that the comptroller of the Boston Company had refused to "sign off" on the internally prepared financial statements for the third quarter of 1988. She maintained that revenues were being recognized before they occurred and that expenses were being recorded after they became due which, of course, had the effect of substantially increasing profits for the period. The comptroller claimed that this had been happening on a much smaller scale for years, but that it had now reached the stage where she could no longer agree, as an accounting professional, that the statements represented fairly the financial position of the firm.

Mr. von Germeten claimed, in response, that he had immediately informed executives at Shearson Loeb Rhoades about the allegations, but surprisingly there was no accounting follow up, no audit of the books by a public accounting firm. Ms. Aronin, the comptroller, was persuaded to stay and not make her statement public as she had originally threatened to do. In November, however, Mr. Patrick Thewlis, the manager of the Boston Company's internal investment portfolio which had been exceedingly profitable for the prior five years, committed suicide at his home. A public audit of the $1.1 billion fund was required by law, given the circumstances of the manager's death, and that audit quickly revealed an unrecorded loss of $10 million on a $100 million investment in esoteric securities known as collateralized mortgage obligation residuals. These are securities whose value fluctuates sharply with changes in interest rates; they were, in essence, a bet that interest rates would go down. Instead, they went up.

This stark evidence of an unrecorded loss in an unsuitable investment for a trust company obviously supported the earlier allegations of the comptroller, and a public audit of the entire company was quickly arranged:

By mid-December, the company's outside auditors, Coopers & Lybrand, and accountants from Shearson were crawling all over Boston Company, and they didn't like what they found. On December 23, Shearson announced that Mr. von Germeten, Boston Company Chief Financial Officer Joseph Murphy, and Boston Company Treasurer Michael Walsh had been put on paid leave.

Shearson also said it had uncovered $10 million to $15 million of accounting irregularities—a figure that later tripled when the investigation was completed in January [*The Wall Street Journal*, January 30, 1989, p. 1f].

Outside directors of the firm—those not associated with either Shearson Loeb Rhoades or the Boston Company—were dismayed by the size of the loss caused by accounting deceptions, and by the size of the investment in unsuitable securities. Both were felt to have been caused by the pressures from senior executives to meet quarterly goals for revenue and profit increases:

A Boston Company director says the deceptive accounting began soon after the stockmarket crash of October 1987, when Boston Company was in danger of falling short of its performance goals. Missing the goals would mean sharply lower management bonuses, which sometimes approached $1 million for top executives, company sources say [*The Wall Street Journal*, January 30, 1989, p. 1f].

The outside directors of the firm met on January 20 and accepted the resignations of Mr. Murphy and Mr. Walsh (chief financial officer and treasurer, respectively). Mr. von Germeten refused to resign, and in a series of interviews sought to minimize the severity of the accounting problems and his involvement in them:

"At no time during this year did I believe there was improper accounting going on," he is reported to have said. "I'm not an accountant. I'm required to follow the judgments and advice of other people. This was a series of judgmental errors by professional accountants" [*The Wall Street Journal*, January 20, 1989, p. C14].

In a series of interviews this month, Mr. von Germeten insisted he hasn't done anything wrong. He has accused Shearson of conducting a "witch hunt" in its investigations, and he has said that any earnings problems merely reflect "judgmental errors by accountants." Asked whether subordinates might have thought he wanted rapid growth no matter what it took, Mr. von Germeten says: "That's what the pressures of business are all about" [*The Wall Street Journal*, January 30, 1989, p. A1].

Mr. von Germeten was not without support in the financial community. Many fellow executives and some people in the media thought that he had been instructed to achieve growth in sales and profits, that he had done so "in spades," and that now he was being condemned for lower-level activities over which he had no control:

> Another troubling issue is executive responsibility—and motivation. Some clients and Shearson insiders believe Boston Company felt compelled by Shearson to produce extraordinary results at a time when most other units of Shearson, an American Express Company subsidiary, were struggling. During the probe, says one Shearson source, Murphy and Walsh "claimed that they were under tremendous pressure from von Germeten. Von Germeten claimed he was under tremendous pressure from Phillips," who is Shearson's vice chairman [*Business Week*, February 6, 1989, p. 87].
>
> I'm one of those who think that James von Germeten is getting a raw deal from Shearson. He did exactly what they told him to do. He raised profits from $10 million in 1982 to $150 million in 1988. Certainly there were losses from the accounting errors. Certainly there were

losses from the investment mistakes. Certainly they've now had to repossess Trump's yacht, and write off about $90 million in their jumbo mortgage portfolio [as of January 1991]. But you've got to compare that to the overall return to Shearson, which was immense.

You cannot hold the chief executive officer of a business firm responsible for everything that happens within that firm. You have to hold him [or her] responsible for profitable operations, and as long as he [or she] produces the targeted rate of return, maintains the expected competitive position, and follows the letter and spirit of the law, then you have to support that executive. Boston Company broke no laws. No institutional or private investors were hurt. No government funds were lost. Instead, von Germeten transformed an old-line trust company into a modern money machine. He is being condemned for mistakes made by subordinates far down in the corporate structure, in the process of that transformation. He should be retained as president [Statement of industry observer].

Class Assignment

1. You are a senior executive at Shearson, and a member of the committee that oversees the Boston Company. What action would you take regarding James von Germeten who refuses to resign? Assume that you are the oldest member of that committee, and doubtless will be the one assigned to meet with him and announce the committee's decision. What will you say at that meeting?

2. Assume now that you are Mr. von Germeten (if the committee decides to retain him as president), or the replacement for Mr. von Germeten

(if the committee decides to fire him). What actions would you take? Specifically, it is a common rule of management that you can accomplish only three things in any one year: What three things would you want to accomplish in your first year as president?

Case 7–5

THE WRECK OF THE *EXXON VALDEZ*

The wreck was an accident. What have accidents got to do with ethics? [Verbal statement of an Exxon public relations official on May 24, 1989]

At 9:30 P.M. on Thursday, the 22nd of March, the oil tanker *Exxon Valdez* left the oil terminal at Valdez, Alaska loaded with 1.26 million barrels of oil. The *Valdez* is the largest tanker owned by Exxon. It is nearly 1,000 feet long and weighs, fully loaded, 280,000 tons.

When the ship left port, it was under the command of Captain William Murphy, the harbor pilot. Harbor pilots are responsible for steering both incoming and outgoing tankers through the Valdez Narrows, a ½ mile wide approach to the port of Valdez. After exiting the Narrows and achieving the sea lanes in Prince William Sound, Captain Murphy turned over command to Captain Joseph Hazelwood and left the ship. Captain Murphy testified later that he had smelled alcohol on the breath of Captain Hazelwood, but that he made no comment and took no action. He knew that it was common practice for both the officers and crew of oil tankers to drink while in port.

Captain Hazelwood, immediately after assuming command, radioed the Coast Guard and requested permission to alter course to avoid large chunks of ice that had broken loose from the Columbia Glacier and were floating in the outbound shipping lane. The permission was granted. Captain Hazelwood then turned over command of the vessel to Third Mate Mr. Gregory Cousins and went below to his cabin. Mr. Cousins was not licensed to pilot a ship in the sea channels approaching Valdez. Mr. Cousins and others later testified that it was common practice to turn over command of oil tankers to nonlicensed officers.

Captain Hazelwood had set the automatic pilot to steer the ship southward into the inbound shipping lane, and he had instructed Mr. Cousins to maintain the course until after the ice chunks from the glaciers were passed, and then to return northward to the outbound lane. No inbound traffic was expected, and permission for this course change had been granted by the Coast Guard, so no danger was anticipated. At 11:55 Mr. Cousins ordered a course change of 10 degrees right rudder to bring the tanker back to the proper lane within the channel. There was no response. At 12:04 the lookout, who was on the bridge rather than at the normal station on the bow of the tanker, sighted the lighted buoy marking Bligh Reef, a rock outcropping only 30 to 40 feet beneath the surface. Mr. Cousins ordered emergency hard right rudder. Again there was no response. In the hearings which followed the accident, it was determined that either Captain Hazelwood had not informed Mr. Cousins that he had placed the ship on automatic pilot, or that Mr. Cousins and the helmsman had not remembered to disconnect the automatic pilot, which prevented manual steering of the vessel.

At 12:05 A.M. the *Exxon Valdez* ran aground on Bligh Reef. The hull was punctured in numerous places; 260,000 barrels, approximately 11,000,000 gallons of crude oil, spilled from the badly ruptured tanks. It was the largest oil spill in the history of the North American petroleum industry.

At 12:28 A.M. one of the officers on the ship radioed to the Coast Guard that it was aground on Bligh Reef. "Are you leaking oil?" a Coast Guard operator asked. "I think so" was the reply.

At 3:23 A.M. members of the Coast Guard boarded the *Exxon Valdez*, and reported that oil was gushing from the tanker. "We've got a serious problem" radioed the Coast Guard officer on board the tanker. "There's nobody here.... Where's Alyeska?"

"Alyeska" was the Alyeska Pipeline Service Company which both managed the oil pipeline, which brought crude oil 800 miles from the oil fields at Prudhoe Bay to Valdez,

and ran the oil terminal at Valdez. It was responsible through a formal agreement with the state of Alaska for the containment and recovery of all oil spills within the harbor and sea lanes. That agreement was expressed in a detailed written plan, 250 pages long, that listed the equipment and personnel that were to be kept available by Alyeska, and the actions that were to be taken by Alyeska, to react promptly to oil spills. The stated goal of the plan was to encircle any serious oil spill with floating containment booms within five hours of the first report of the occurrence, and to recover 50 percent of the spill within 48 hours. The stated goal was well known within the area, and accounted for the perplexity of the Coast Guard officer. When he reported, "There's nobody here," he was referring not to the captain and crew of the tanker, but to the oil spill recovery team and equipment from Alyeska.

The Coast Guard officer also noted the smell of alcohol on the breath of Captain Hazelwood, and reported to his base in very blunt terms that he suspected that the captain was drunk. He was unable to establish the degree of intoxication, due to the lack of a testing kit, but he did request the assistance of the Alaska State Police to conduct the tests as soon as possible. Those tests were conducted the following morning, and did establish that the level of alcohol in Captain Hazelwood's bloodstream at that time (approximately nine hours after the accident) was twice the legal limit.

At 6:00 A.M. on Friday, March 23 (six hours after the accident), officials from Exxon flew over the grounded tanker for the first time, and reported a massive oil slick streaming away from the tanker. They contacted the Alyeska oil terminal, and ordered a quicker response and greater effort from the personnel at the terminal. The problem, the manager at the terminal reported, was that the single barge capable of handling the long containment booms had been out of service for two weeks, and had been unloaded for repairs. Workers were preparing to reload the barge at that time, but the employee who was capable of operating the crane needed for reloading had not yet reported for work. Later that morning, the loading was completed and the barge was taken in tow by a harbor tug. At 2:30 P.M. the barge arrived at the wreck site, carrying all of the containment booms that were available at the terminal, and a number of centrifugal pumps to help in removing the remaining oil from the Valdez.

At 7:36 A.M. on Saturday, March 24 (31½ hours after the accident), Exxon began pumping oil from the *Valdez* to a second tanker moored alongside, the *Baton Rouge*. At about the same time, seven Alyeska "skimmers," or barges with vacuum equipment designed to siphon oil off the surface of the water, arrived at the site. The skimmers, however, were designed to recover oil that had been bunched in a compact mass by the containment booms. Those booms were still not in place, due to a shortage of tugs and some degree of confusion in the means of unloading the booms and placing them in the sea. By nightfall, only 1,200 barrels of oil had been recovered.

At 11:00 A.M. on Sunday, March 25 (59 hours after the accident), the *Exxon Valdez* was finally encircled by containment booms. It had taken 2½ days to get the booms in place, despite the original plan which called for full containment of any spill within five hours. Most of the oil was now outside the booms in a slick that covered 12 square miles, and the wave action had begun to convert the crude oil to an emulsified "mousse" mixture of oil and water that quadrupled the volume. This emulsified mixture now lay 5 to 9 inches thick upon the surface of the sea. The specific gravity of the emulsified mixture was very different from the specific gravity of either water or oil, and the skimmers were no longer effective except when working on fresh seepages close to the grounded tanker, within the booms.

At 6:00 A.M. on Monday, March 26 (78 hours after the accident), the Coast Guard admitted that the situation was out of control. The first two days had been calm, but Sunday night winds as high as 73 miles per hour had arisen, and driven the emulsified oil and water mixture 37 miles from the wreck site. It was swathing the islands and beaches throughout Prince William Sound with solid bands of black petroleum "gunk," the accepted term for the residue that is left after the more volatile elements in crude oil have evaporated. The skimmer barges and boom-tending boats had been forced to retreat to sheltered water. Flights into the Valdez airport, bringing additional supplies and people, had been halted. Most of the oil that had remained in the unruptured tanks of the *Exxon Valdez* had been pumped out, but it was now thought to be impossible to recover any further substantial amount of the spill. Eventually the marks of this spill stretched 700 miles along the coast, spoiling fishery resources, wildlife refuges, and national parks in one of the most scenic regions of the country, and killing sea birds, fish, and mammals in one of the prime marine habitats of the world.

Nearly two months after the biggest oil spill in American history, Alaskan officials say not a single mile of beach has been completely cleaned and that the death tolls of birds, fish and mammals continues to mount.

Large patches of oil, untended in rough and remote seas, are still washing up on pristine Alaskan beaches more than 500 miles from the reef in Prince William Sound where the *Exxon Valdez* went aground March 24.

The oil from the spill of 11 million gallons hit 730 miles of coastline, Alaskan state officials said today. Of that, only four miles have been declared cleaned. Less than one mile is totally free of oil, the officials said.

. . . . .

The ecological toll of the spill thus far includes more than 11,000 birds of 300 different species, 700 Pacific sea otters, and 20 bald eagles, according to a tally by the State Department of Environmental Conservation.

Biologists say [that] the actual numbers of dead wildlife could be three to five times higher than those found because many of the animals have been washed out to sea or taken by predators.

. . . . .

On some beaches in Prince William Sound the oil is more than three feet thick, lodged in the rocks and providing a reservoir of fresh contamination at every high tide [*The New York Times*, May 19, 1989, p. 1].

The causes of the accident, while obviously related to the intoxication of the captain and the subsequent command of the ship by an unlicensed third mate, were thought to be more complex than that simple explanation. Three additional factors were mentioned in the hearings of the Federal Transportation Safety Board that followed the oil spill.

The crew members on the tanker were tired from working long watches, and were said not to have been alert. The *Exxon Valdez* normally carried a crew of 20 persons. This crew size was considered to be typical for large oil tankers, but it was substantially smaller than that required by Coast Guard regulations and union requirements on merchant cargo ships. The oil companies had argued that the new technology automated the operation of the crude oil carriers, and eliminated the need for a larger crew. The modern equipment, however, had to be manned and maintained, and consequently the automation did not keep the officers and crew from frequently going long stretches with little or no sleep, and working extensive overtime. Crew members on the *Exxon Valdez* testified that they had worked an average of 140 hours of overtime a month per person for the six months prior to the accident. One hundred forty hours of overtime per month and 20 days at sea per month plus the regular 8-hour watches works out to be 15 hours per day.

Many of the crew members were exhausted, a routine feeling on Exxon ships, they testified [*The New York Times*, May 22, 1989, p. 10].

There were definite violations of sailing rules. Captain Hazelwood advised the Coast Guard that he was taking the ship on a southwesterly course, into the inbound shipping channel, to avoid floating ice chunks. That was considered to be perfectly proper, and normal under the circumstances, though permission was never granted for this maneuver except when the inbound lanes were completely free. He did not advise the Coast Guard that he then altered course almost due south, rather than southwesterly, nor that he had engaged the autopilot. Coast Guard rules are very definite that the autopilot should be used only in the open sea. The due south course on the autopilot brought the ship obviously out of the channel, which at that point was five miles wide, and permission would almost certainly have been refused had the Coast Guard been informed.

> Your children could drive a tanker up through that channel [Statement of Paul Yost, commandant of the Coast Guard, quoted in *The Wall Street Journal*, March 31, 1989, p. 1].

There was a definite lack of attention by members of the Coast Guard. The radar at the Coast Guard station, which was capable of tracking the *Exxon Valdez* past Bligh Reef, lost contact with the tanker when it made its course adjustment due south. Instead of maintaining radio contact with the ship's officers, as was required when visual contact on the radar screen was lost, the personnel at the tracking station assumed that there was a malfunction in the radar set and that the *Exxon Valdez* was continuing on its acknowledged course.

> "We started downgrading in 1984," said Commander Steven A. McCall of the Coast Guard, captain of the *Valdez Port*, referring to the vessel tracking center at the terminus of the 800-mile Trans-Alaska pipeline. Since then, he said, there developed "a gradual, obviously false sense of security" [*The New York Times*, May 22, 1989, p. 10].

Within Alaska, public reactions to the accident and to the lackadaisical practices that apparently led to the accident centered on the potential damage to the fishing resources, and consequently on the harm to the livelihood of a substantial portion of the state's population. The Alaskan coast from Prince William Sound northward is known as the richest salmon and crab fishing ground in the world. Exxon assured the fishing boat operators that they would be compensated for any losses they suffered as a result of the oil spill and explained that the company had insurance that would protect it against claims for negligence up to $500 million.

Outside of Alaska, public reactions to the accident and to the lackadaisical practices revealed in the hearings focused on the fouling of the environment and the destruction of the wildlife.

> Already thousands of birds have died, and biologists fear that a significant portion of the Sound's 12,000 sea otters—which lose buoyancy when just 10 percent of their body is covered in oil—may be in jeopardy.
>
> Those who know these bejeweled waters—rich in fish, fowl and fauna like few other places on earth—believe the

damage will be monumental and long-lasting [*The Wall Street Journal*, March 31, 1989, p. 1].

Right now I'm still finding dead sea otters on the beach (61 days after the accident). Bald eagles feed on them, so I'm finding dead eagles.... Here I am a scientist with a Ph.D. and as I watch these oiled birds trying to take off I start to cry [Statement of biologist at the Kenai Fjords National Park, quoted in *The New York Times*, May 19, 1989, p. 1f].

Public reactions to the accident were not mollified when a contractor employed by Exxon wrote a letter to *The New York Times* that was published under the heading "Valdez: Do-Gooders' Feeding Frenzy."

Hired by Exxon, I took a television camera to Valdez, Alaska, in late April. My mission, almost a month after the messy oil tanker accident, was to impartially document the scene, the activity and the cleanup....

Today, I have two three-person camera crews there. We are making a video report for Exxon's annual meeting. We have made considerable parts of our footage available to television stations.

Because the Sound can't be photographed in its entirety for a TV set, Valdez fishermen and tourism boosters are rightfully concerned, for economic and other good reasons, that most of us in the lower 48 states have gotten a distorted view of their situation. The key word, they say, is "perspective." From what I saw, they make an unassailable point.

To be sure, the *Exxon Valdez* spill was horrible, a costly international embarrassment for the company, a calamity. None of my recent acquaintances in Alaska minimizes it in the slightest. But, if you think the whole Sound is a despoiled pool of goo, let me convey some Valdez perspectives.

The Sound is about three times larger than Rhode Island. It contains an estimated 262 trillion gallons of water, in which more than 10 million gallons of crude oil were plunked. That's the equivalent, they say in Valdez, of a teaspoon of fluid in an Olympic-sized swimming pool. The toxicity level rose only momentarily—and microscopically [Letter from Mr. Jack Hilton, published in *The New York Times*, May 23, 1989].

Public reactions to the accident also were not mollified when the chairman of Exxon, Mr. Lawrence Rawl, decided not to go to Alaska and supervise the cleanup operations directly. Instead, he remained in New York City, and made no direct comment upon the oil spill or cleanup operations for seven days. Other officials within Exxon also refused to comment. The first statement by the president of Exxon U.S.A., the holding company for Exxon Shipping which owned the grounded tanker, was made on May 9:

We do not know what caused this accident.... Exxon's response was prompt and consistent with the previously approved contingency plan [Mr.Bill Stevens, quoted in the *Detroit Free Press*, May 9, 1989, p. 7A].

In fairness to Exxon, it should be explained that company officials felt that public reactions to the oil spill were extreme, and did not take into account several mitigating factors. Firstly, they thought that the public did not really understand that the company could not be held responsible for the intoxication of Captain Hazelwood. Secondly, they thought that the public did not fully realize that the company had been prevented from using chemical dispersants on the oil.

Chemical dispersants, it should be understood, do not destroy the oil. Instead, the effect of the dispersant is to lower the surface tension of the oil to the point where it will break up and disperse in the water in the form of tiny droplets. The standard text on environmental chemistry states that the "break-up" action requires special wind and wave conditions, and that the resulting "droplets" can pose hazards to marine life:

Dispersants are usually applied by spraying. Agitation is necessary to make them effective. This makes them very useful on oil slicks in rough open sea where nature does the agitating. Evaluation of the results of their use in the past indicates that dispersants should be used with caution. The high degree of dispersion they create leads to greater solubility and higher concentrations of oil in the water than would be possible if natural dispersion were allowed to take place. Also, the oil droplets formed are in a size range that is easily ingested and assimilated by marine organisms on the low end of the marine food chain. In the case of the *Torrey Canyon* incident [wreck of an oil tanker off the southern coast of Britain in 1974; the floating oil went ashore in Normandy, and allegedly destroyed 85 percent of the marine life along that coast] the dispersants were found to be as toxic to aquatic life as the oil itself [Stephen Stoker and Spencer Seager, *Environmental Chemistry: Air and Water Pollution* (Glenview, Ill.: Scott Foresman, 1978), p. 185].

Company officials, however, thought that chemical dispersants should have been used as soon as it was apparent that the containment and recovery efforts had failed, and

before the beaches were fouled and the wildlife killed. Mr. Rawl, the chairman of the Exxon Corporation, in an interview with *Fortune* magazine, said environmentalists acting with the State of Alaska had prevented the company from applying the dispersants promptly.

One of the things I feel strongly about—this catching hell for two days' delay—is that I don't think that we got a fair shake. The basic problem we ran into was that we had environmentalists advising the Alaskan Department of Environmental Conservation that the dispersants could be toxic [Lawrence Rawl, quoted in *The New York Times*, May 22, 1989, p. 10].

Mr. Lee Kelso, director of the Alaskan Department of Environmental Conservation, disagreed strongly that his department was responsible for the delay in the use of dispersants.

Exxon was free to use dispersants on the vast majority of the oil slick, and did not do so [Statement by Lee Kelso, quoted in *The Wall Street Journal*, April 3, 1989, p. 1].

Mr. Lee Raymond, president of the Exxon Corporation, said that he blamed "ultimately the Coast Guard" [*The Wall Street Journal*, April 3, 1989, p. 1] for the delay in the use of dispersants, explaining that it had required a test before granting permission.

Coast Guard officials denied that they had required testing, saying that it was only common sense procedure to gauge the effectiveness of the treatment under the wind, wave, and water temperature conditions that existed at the time.

Governmental reactions to the oil

spill centered not on the causes of the accident, not on the consequences of the oil spill, nor on the dispute about testing, but on the slowness and ineffectual nature of the cleanup. The government attitude seemed to be that accidents do occur, that seamen have been known to consume excessive amounts of alcohol in the past, and that under conditions of stress people may forget about test conditions and requirements, but that there was no excuse for the inability firstly of Alyeska and then of Exxon to deal promptly and effectively with the spill itself.

The contingency plan that had been developed by Alyeska and approved by the state of Alaska envisaged containment within five hours and recovery of a minimum of 50 percent of the oil by skimmers within 48 hours. Containment, as stated previously, took 59 hours and estimates of the amount of oil actually recovered ranged from 0.4 percent to 2.5 percent. A number of reasons for the ineffectiveness of the response by Alyeska and Exxon were given in the hearings held by the National Transportation Safety Board.

It should be explained, before discussing the results of the hearings before the National Transportation Safety Board, that the Alyeska Pipeline Service Company is not a subsidiary of the Exxon Corporation. It is a consortium owned by the seven oil companies who have drilling rights on the North Slope of Alaska and ship crude oil from Prudhoe Bay to Valdez. Representatives of all seven companies serve on the board of directors. Exxon is the second largest owner, and is said to participate actively in the management of the company.

The first reason given for the slowness of response was a shortage of equipment. The oil spill contingency plan required Alyeska to maintain two barges, loaded with containment booms ready for use. At the time of the spill, only one barge was available. The other had been scrapped as old and obsolete, but its replacement was still in Seattle. There was a requirement in the contingency plan that Alyeska notify the state Department of Environmental Conservation if any equipment was out of service for any period of time. Alyeska now concedes that it failed to provide this notification.

The barge that was available had been damaged by a storm in January. It was still considered to be seaworthy, but the containment booms had been unloaded to facilitate repair. Repairs had been delayed, according to testimony by Alyeska officials, because the company had been unable to locate a licensed marine welder. Environmentalists at the hearing displayed the Valdez telephone book that listed four companies that claimed to provide licensed marine welding services.

Seven thousand one hundred feet of containment booms were stored at the oil terminal. The contingency plan did not specify an exact lineal footage that was to be kept in stock, but it can be understood that 7,100 feet would be enough to contain a spill around a 1,000 foot tanker only if the booms could be placed quickly, before the oil spread out upon the surface of the water. Three thousand feet would be required just to encircle the hull.

Ten skimmers, which are large suction units that can be mounted on barges and used, in essence, to vacuum oil from the surface of the sea, were available as promised in the contingency plan. However, replacement parts were not kept in stock, and equipment breakdowns were common as the machines were not designed to work on the emulsified mixture of oil and water that was formed rapidly through wave actions in the noncontained spill.

Other equipment that was needed either was missing, or could not be found quickly. Heavy ship fenders, essential for the second tanker to come alongside the *Exxon Valdez* and pump out its remaining oil, couldn't be located for hours because they were buried under 14 feet of snow. Half of the required six-inch hose, needed for the pumping, never was found and replacements had to be flown in from Seattle. The emergency lighting system, to illuminate the boom-laying and oil transfer work at night, was finally discovered off base, being readied for use in the Valdez winter carnival.

As a final example of the shortage of equipment, it was determined after the accident that there never had been enough chemical dispersant stored in Valdez to treat the oil spill, even had there been no disagreement or misunderstanding about permission to use the material.

Records made available this week show there was prior approval to use dispersants in the area of the spill and that only 69 barrels of dispersants were on hand in Valdez for a job that called for nearly 10,000 barrels.

Six days after the spill, Exxon still had only a fraction of the amount needed to fight the disaster, according to records

and the company's testimony this week [*The New York Times*, May 22, 1989, p. 10].

In addition to the shortage of equipment, there was also a shortage of personnel. The oil spill contingency plan required Alyeska to have a crew of 15 persons on duty at all times. These were not oil spill experts. These were the hourly paid workers responsible for the normal operations of the terminal, but according to the plan they should have included all of the skills and trades necessary to respond to emergencies, whether oil spills at sea, oil leaks on land, or oil fires which are always a concern to petroleum shipping and refining facilities.

At the time of the spill, only 11 workers were on duty. Unfortunately, none of those people knew how to operate the crane, which was needed to reload the barge with the long and heavy containment booms. A crane operator was finally located, but he was also the only one who knew how to drive the fork lift, and he spent the morning of March 23, when speed in response was essential, running back and forth between the fork lift and the loading crane.

Lastly, there was a lack of training. Alyeska had dismissed its oil spill response team in 1981. This was a group of 12 persons originally set up to contain and then clean up spills throughout Valdez Harbor and Prince William Sound. The duties of the spill response team were assigned to the regular employees at the plant. At the time of dismissal, Alyeska had claimed that this arrangement would be superior as they would have "120 people trained in oil spill response rather than 12."

Some of the cited 120 scoff at this. One senior employee says he has had "zero oil spill training, none." He recalls being summoned to two spills over the years. "I didn't know what the hell I was supposed to do, and when I found the guy I was supposed to report to, he did not know what the hell we were supposed to do either. We just stood there watching" [*The Wall Street Journal*, July 6, 1989, p. 1].

Some of the operating managers within the oil industry have been greatly concerned by this tendency to replace specialized teams with personnel from the general work force.

You either have a team of people who are dedicated to a specific task, and trained to perform that task under any and all conditions, or you have nothing. The Valdez terminal didn't have that trained team, and it showed.

We run into this same problem continually with fire drills. Previously, every refinery had a fire department, with fire engines, a fire chief and a fire crew. Now, they just have the engines and, if they are lucky, they still have a fire chief who knows what he is doing and can teach the others. We are not lucky, and we don't still have a fire chief. It is company policy to run a drill once every six months. The bell rings, and all of the 9:00 to 5:00 desk jockeys jump on the truck, and away they go. When they get there, they don't know how to turn on the hydrants, they don't know how to work the pumps, and they don't know how to lay the hoses, and they don't know what is safe and what isn't. We have not had a fire since the department was disbanded, but when we do it is going to get very bad very fast.

I can understand exactly what happened at Valdez. They had not had a major spill in 18 years, but when they

did it got very bad very fast [Statement of oil industry executive made in confidence to the case writer].

The concern over the dismissal of the trained response teams that is said to be widespread among operating executives within the oil industry apparently was illustrated by training practices at the Valdez terminal prior to the March 24 accident. *The Wall Street Journal* reported a number of mishaps:

Drills for honing responses to oil spills, fires and other troubles sometimes were near-disasters themselves."Drills were a farce, a comic opera," says Mr. Nebel, the former oil-spill coordinator (who claims that he was fired in 1981 for protesting the dismissal of his 12-member response team). In an early 1980s drill, a boat carrying the top Alyeska manager in Valdez and other oil-industry executives ran aground. In 1984, state inspector Tom McCarty witnessed a chaotic drill that had to be canceled when a containment boom sank; in a memo to superiors, he said that Alyeska's spill response capability had "regressed to a dangerous level."

A year later, an Alyeska official told another state inspector at a sloppily run drill that Alyeska wouldn't practice deploying a hose because "it would be too much trouble to roll it up again," state documents show [*The Wall Street Journal*, July 6, 1989, p. 1].

As a final indication of the lack of training, it was said that neither Alyeska nor Exxon knew how to test the effectiveness of chemical dispersants under the varying conditions of wind speed and wave action.

The oil companies weren't ready to test for dispersants for 18 hours, and they then did so by ineffectually tossing buckets of chemicals out of the door of a helicopter.

The test was a flop. The helicopter's rotor wash dispersed the dispersant, and it missed its target. The state says helicopter applications aren't recommended—for exactly this reason [*The Wall Street Journal*, April 3, 1989, p.1].

The shortage of equipment, the shortage of personnel, and the lack of training were caused, it now appears, by deliberate policy decisions reached by the senior management of Exxon Corporation who pushed strongly for cost reductions at Alyeska during the mid-1980s. These policy decisions were not taken arbitrarily. They were in response to a change in the basic economic conditions of the oil industry.

Oil prices fell from $32/barrel in 1981, at the height of the power of OPEC (Organization of Petroleum Exporting Countries) to $12/barrel in 1986, and then rose slightly to stabilize in the range of $15 to $20/barrel. The large oil companies are vertically integrated, with divisions for the exploration, production, and refining of crude oil, and for the distribution and marketing of oil products. The lower price for crude oil, however, brought exploration nearly to a halt, and severely reduced the profits that came from production. States in the American Southwest, particularly Texas and Oklahoma, entered an economic depression that has continued unabated until the present day.

The large vertically integrated oil companies reacted slowly to the changed economic conditions, but the reaction—when it came—was dramatic and harsh. Costs were reduced. Employees were discharged. The changes at Exxon were particularly dramatic and harsh because the company for years had prided itself on a generous, almost paternal attitude towards its employees. In January 1986 Mr. Clifton Garvin, chairman of Exxon Corporation since 1975, commented to *Fortune* magazine about personnel policies upon his company's selection as one of the 10 "most admired" firms within the United States:

Exxon hasn't existed 104 years without having developed a lot of strengths. No. 1 is the people who are in this company. We have more than our fair share of good people. And particularly over the past five years, those people have done well. We also have the financial strength to weather difficult times. In the unsettled recent past of the oil industry, we have been able to adjust to the ups and downs of OPEC and crude-oil pricing [Statement by Mr. Clifton Garvin, quoted in *Fortune,* January 6, 1986, p. 20].

Six months later, Exxon Corporation was in the midst of an extensive restructuring effort:

Exxon is giving workers until May 30 to decide whether to resign. If it doesn't get enough volunteers, it will resort to involuntary terminations. Based on Exxon's earlier announcement of a 26 percent budget cut, guesses on the final body count range from 15 percent to more than a third of all its employees. Analysts figure that the restructuring will provide Exxon with gains in efficiency and profitability, and that by conserving cash the company will be better able to buy oil properties if prices stay low [*Business Week,* May 5, 1986, p. 32].

The generous, almost paternal attitude of the company towards Exxon employees had disappeared:

> With oil companies cutting production in the face of falling crude prices and a hard-nosed head chopper named Lawrence Rawl in the president's chair, at least part of Exxon's worldwide work force of 145,000 seemed destined for the block. In late April, the world's largest oil company offered 40,500 employees the option to retire early or quit with compensation [*Fortune,* May 26, 1986, p.11].

The new chairman of Exxon, Mr. Lawrence Rawl, apparently believed that he had been elected by the board of directors to reduce costs and increase earnings, despite the probable impact upon employee morale:

> Rawl isn't saying, but the prospect of shaking people up does not rattle him. His operating style, he brags, is treading on toes: "That's my M.O." Like most top Exxon executives, he has been essentially invisible to the outside world during his 34-year climb up the corporate ladder. Inside the company, however, Rawl has earned a reputation as a waste cutter and head chopper.
>
> "The current structure of the Exxon Corp. has been in place for about 20 years," he complains. With the restructuring of international operations under way, he will turn next to Exxon's corporate headquarters in New York City, where, he says, "We still have things to do."....Says Rawl: "I'm bottom-line oriented. I look at the revenues, and I look at everything that comes in between. When I find something that looks a little bit soft, I take a *hard* look. When the good times are rolling, you can ignore some of that stuff. But when times get difficult, you've got to do something." In fact, he concedes, "you should do it

anyway. That's management. That's what shareholders pay us for" [*Fortune,* April 14, 1986].

Operating personnel with oil spill experience were among those managers within Exxon who either elected to retire early or were forced to resign:

> At least nine experts on oil spills, including Exxon Corporation's senior environmental officer, left the company in 1985 and 1986 when the work force was being reduced, a specialist in oil pollution said today.
>
> It was not clear if the departures affected the company's response when one of its tankers struck a reef near Valdez, Alaska and spilled 10.1 million gallons of crude oil, said Richard S. Golob, publisher of *Golob's Oil Pollution Bulletin.*
>
> "It might be a contributing factor,"Mr. Golob said, "because they do not have the same experienced cadre of oil spill professional that they had prior to the 1986 early retirement offer" [*The New York Times,* March 30, 1989, p. A20].

Executives at Exxon claimed, following the accident, that the cutbacks in personnel had not affected the company's ability to deal with oil spills, primarily because those who had left could be hired again, as consultants:

> Les Rogers, a spokesman for Exxon Company, U.S.A., the parent company of Exxon Shipping Company, owner of the tanker responsible for Friday's spill in Prince William Sound, said the company was confident it had the expertise needed to deal with the situation. In addition to its own staff, he said, those who have retired were readily available and the company had already engaged two former employees as consultants [*The New York Times,* March 30, 1989, p. A20].

Some operating personnel within the oil industry did not accept the claim that company employees who had been forced to accept early retirement would be "readily available":

I did not know any of the oil spill and environmental people who were let go, but I did know quite a few of the refinery and marketing men who were forced out and let me tell you that they do not harbor kind thoughts towards Exxon.

These were men, 40 to 50 years of age with children in college or just approaching college, and Exxon told them "Here is your pension, which isn't fully funded, and here is a couple of thousand bucks. Goodbye." When you are 50 years old, and have spent 25 of those years working for one company, you don't find another job easily. I know one Exxon refinery engineer who is now a shoe clerk out at the mall in my hometown.

The men I know wouldn't step outside their front door for Exxon on a sunny morning in April. They would, however, buy tickets for a public hanging of Lawrence Rawl [Statement of oil industry executive made in confidence to the case writer].

The cutbacks in staff extended throughout Exxon to the Exxon Shipping Company—the 20-person crew on that company's oil tankers reportedly was to have been reduced to 15 persons, had the accident not intervened—and to the Alyeska Pipeline Service Company.

When oil prices began falling in 1981, the owners of Alyeska ordered it to save even more on costs. In late 1982, Alyeska managers prepared what they thought was a lean budget and

presented it to a meeting of the owner's committee in San Francisco. According to former Alyeska officials who were briefed on the meeting at the time, committee members cited a figure, roughly $220 million, and asked if the budget was under that; told that it wasn't, they rejected it out of hand.

"There was an overall attitude of petty cheapness that severely affected our ability to operate safely," recalls Mr. Woodle who came over from the Coast Guard to run the terminal's marine operations just in time to see their budget slashed by about a third. "I was shocked at the shabbiness of the operations"[*The Wall Street Journal,* July 6, 1989, p.1].

Class Assignment

Concerned environmentalists and some public officials called for the resignation of Mr. Lawrence Rawl, chairman of the Exxon Corporation. They alleged that the disastrous wreck of the *Exxon Valdez*, and the subsequent slow cleanup, had occurred on "his watch," and that he ought to accept personal responsibility and resign.

1. In your opinion, should Mr. Rawl resign as chairman of the Exxon Corporation? List the reasons that support your judgment.

2. What, again in your opinion, were the causes of the wreck of the *Exxon Valdez?* List 10 factors that contributed to that wreck.

3. If you were chairman of Exxon for the three years prior to the wreck and cleanup, what would you have done differently? List five mistakes made by Mr. Rawl.

CHAPTER 8

Moral Leadership in Society

Why should a manager be moral? The argument of this text is that success in business management is dependent upon the cooperation and innovation of all of the stakeholders of the firm. The intensity of global competition and the complexity of technological development mean that everyone must contribute to the operational performance and the strategic position of the company. Workers, managers, functional and technical staff members, material and component suppliers, wholesale and retail distributors, creditors, owners, and customers are all affected by the operations and strategy of the firm, and in turn are able to affect the outcome of those operations and the achievement of that strategy, for better or for worse.

Cooperation between stakeholders is needed, but it is not enough to ensure that the overall performance will be better, not worse. Innovation by the stakeholders is also required. Cooperation between stakeholders outside the formal boundaries of the company cannot be commanded, however, and innovation among stakeholders whether inside or outside those formal boundaries cannot be controlled. The managerial task, therefore, becomes unify and guide rather than command and control.

Unification requires trust. Trust is an essential element in management, and building trust is dependent upon (1) a recognition of the mixture of benefits and harms that are the natural outcome of economic operations, (2) a distribution of those benefits and an allocation of those harms that may be considered to be "right" and "just" and "fair", and (3) a determination to adhere to that allocation and that distribution despite any apparent short-term disadvantages to the organization or to the management. The use of moral reasoning guarantees that the interests of the organization and the senior executives do not necessarily take precedence over the interests of all of the other stakeholders, and confidence in the equity of the decision process builds trust, commitment, and effort (see Exhibit 8–1, page 269).

But what about the rest of us? Lots of us have no formal stakeholder relationship with the large companies in this country and abroad. We don't use their products in such volume that our cooperation is needed, or our innovation is required. We don't work for them or know anyone who does well enough to be able to influence their actions. We don't own their shares, provide their loans,

EXHIBIT 8–1

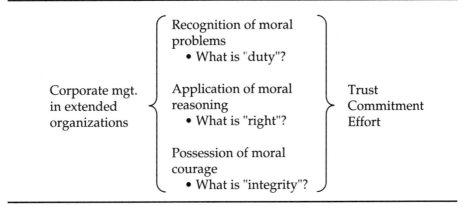

Corporate mgt. in extended organizations	Recognition of moral problems • What is "duty"? Application of moral reasoning • What is "right"? Possession of moral courage • What is "integrity"?	Trust Commitment Effort

EXHIBIT 8–2   Levels of Managerial Responsibility

Moral responsibilities	Gaining trust Generating commitment Producing effort	
Conceptual responsibilities	Setting objectives Forging advantages Building competence	
Technical responsibilities	Developing people Utilizing information Creating products	Economic efficiency Comp. effectiveness Social beneficiency
Functional responsibilities	Maximizing revenues Minimizing costs Optimizing returns	
Operational responsibilities	Satisfying customers Improving methods Conserving assets	

EXHIBIT 8–3   Growth in Global Population

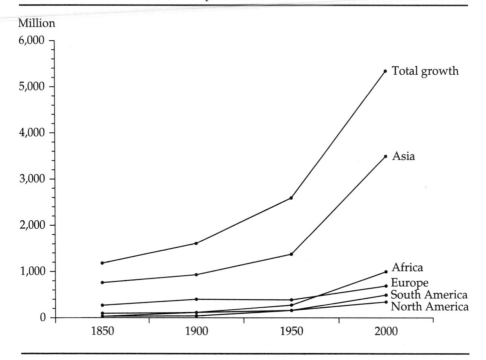

SOURCE: N. Keyfitz, *World Population Growth and Aging* (Chicago: University of Chicago Press, 1990), p. 5; *World Almanac and Book of Facts* (1992), p. 822.

supply their factories, distribute their goods, or develop their technologies. Consequently we are not included, except peripherally, on the list of responsibilities of senior executives in major corporations (see Exhibit 8–2, page 269).

Do the executives in those companies owe the rest of us anything? Do they have any duties towards those of us who are not stakeholders in the formal sense of being affected by and in turn able to affect the operational and strategic performance of the firm? Do those executives, in short, have any responsibility to the society of which both they and we are a part?

The argument of this text is, "Yes, they do." And once again the rationale is the long-term self-interest of the firm. Corporations and the executives who direct them are dependent upon the society of which they are a part for economic growth, political stability, environmental health, resource availability, government help, and social support.

Increasingly the society of which these managers are a part and upon which they are dependent for economic growth and political stability, etc., is global, not national, in scope. Increasingly that society of which they are a part and upon which they are dependent is also complex, crowded, and confused. Let me give a few examples of the complex, crowded, and confused nature of

EXHIBIT 8–4   Growth in Gross National Income per Capita of Selected Countries

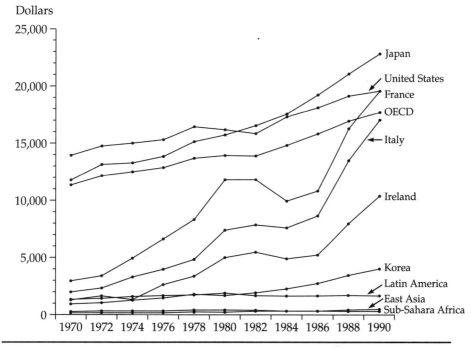

SOURCE: World Bank, *World Tables* (New York: Johns Hopkins University Press, 1992), pp. 6–9.

EXHIBIT 8–5   Growth in Global Energy Use Measured by SO_2 and CO_2, 1850–2000

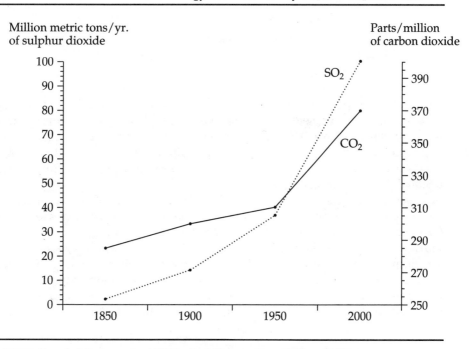

SOURCE: *Atmospheric Environment*, vol. 18 (New York: Pergamon Press, 1989), pp. 19–27.

EXHIBIT 8–6   Growth in Global Surface Air Temperature, 1900–1990

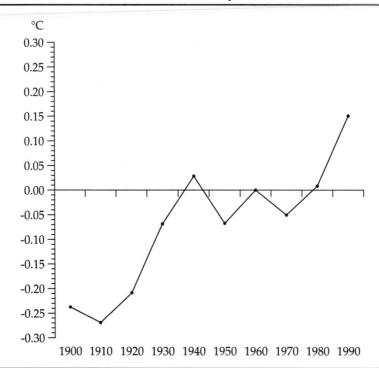

SOURCE: *The State of the Environment* (Paris: Organization of Economic Cooperation and Development, 1991), p. 26.

this global society. Most are well known. Some, not so well known, are very indicative of trends that will require trust, commitment, and effort by all of us to overcome.

Firstly, the population of the earth (as seen in Exhibit 8–3) is increasing rapidly. Better public health and improved medical care have reduced infant mortality rates and extended adult life spans in all of the countries of the world.

Secondly, gross national income per capita (as seen in Exhibit 8–4, page 271) is also increasing rapidly, though the effects of this increase are distributed unequally among the countries of the world.

Increases in gross national income have been the result of industrialization, which is dependent upon the use of large amounts of energy. Increases in the use of energy can be measured by concentrations of sulphur dioxide and carbon dioxide in the atmosphere (as seen in Exhibit 8–5, page 271).

Sulphur dioxide and carbon dioxide are the "greenhouse" gases; they may or may not have resulted in a warming of the surface air temperature. This is a phenomena that is not felt to be proven due to the unexplained trend reversals that occurred between 1930 and 1970 (as seen in Exhibit 8–6).

EXHIBIT 8–7 Growth in Fuelwood Consumption and Decline in New Tree Growth in the Sudan

Million cubic meters

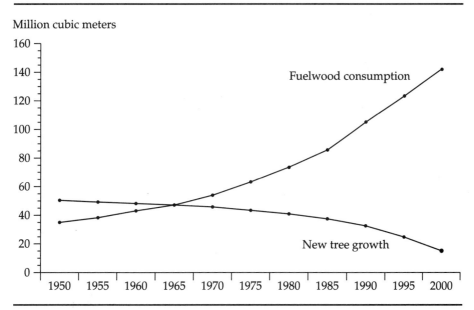

SOURCE: L. Brown, *Reversing Africa's Decline*, Paper 65 (Washington, D.C.: Worldwatch Institute, 1985), p. 15.

EXHIBIT 8–8 Decline in Stock of Trees in the Sudan

Million cubic meters

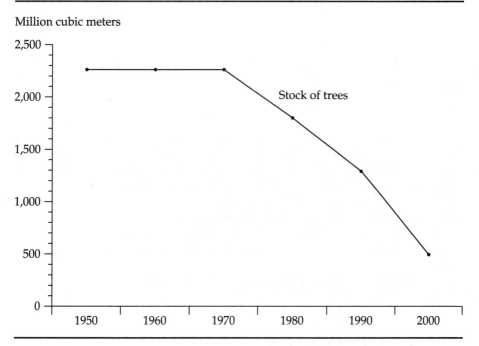

SOURCE: L. Brown, *Reversing Africa's Decline*, Paper 65 (Washington, D.C.: Worldwatch Institute, 1985), p. 15.

EXHIBIT 8–9   Decline in Stock of Ducks in North America

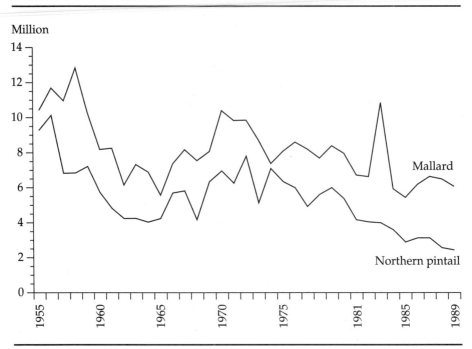

Million

SOURCE: U.S. Council on Environmental Quality, *Environmental Quality, 21st Annual Report,* vol. 20 (Washington, D.C., 1990), p. 489.

Increases in the global surface air temperature cannot be proven, despite the apparent consistencies in the overall trend line. Other environmental changes such as decreases in the stock of trees in the Sudan or in the stock of ducks in North America (as seen in Exhibits 8–7, 8–8, and 8–9 on pages 273–274), are much more obvious.

The decrease in the stock of trees in North Africa and the decrease in the stock of ducks in North America are doubtless due to the population pressures and industrialization impacts that have cut forests for fuel and converted wetlands for farming. Population pressures and industrial impacts, however, result in changes that extend beyond the physical environment. These changes can be seen most easily in the United States where reliable statistics have been kept for years on population increases (as seen in Exhibit 8–10, page 275), economic changes, energy uses, income groups, health expenditures, crime rates, waste amounts, and political costs.

One of the critical assumptions of most population forecasting models has always been that the annual growth of industrial countries would stabilize and eventually decline as the age groups and economic institutions both matured. This has not occurred within the United States, as seen in Exhibits 8–10 and 8–11 (see page 275).

EXHIBIT 8–10   Growth in U.S. Population

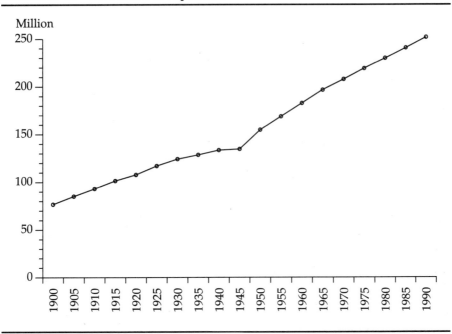

SOURCE: *Historical Statistics of the U.S., Colonial Times to 1970* (Washington, D.C..: U.S. Bureau of the Census, 1975), p. 8; *Statistical Abstract of the U.S.* (Washington, D.C.: U.S. Bureau of the Census, 1992), p. 8.

EXHIBIT 8–11   Growth in U.S. Gross NationalProduct

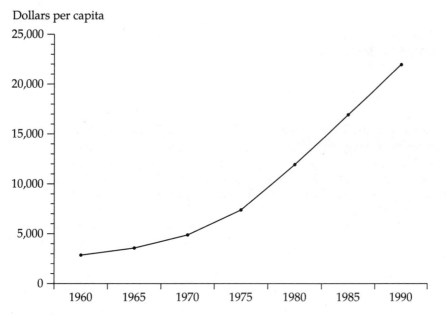

SOURCE: *Statistical Abstract of the U.S.* (Washington, D.C.: U.S. Bureau of the Census, 1992), p. 431.

EXHIBIT 8–12   Growth in U.S. Energy Consumption

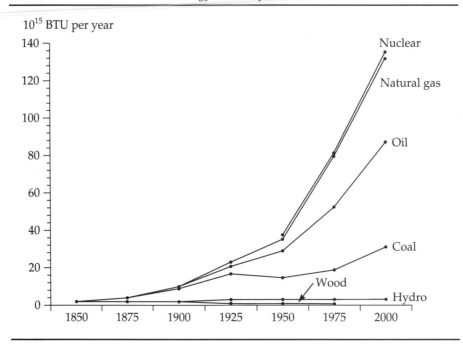

SOURCE: Energy: *Readings from Scientific American* (San Francisco: W. H. Freeman, 1979), p. 11.

Both population numbers and economic outputs have continued to expand within the United States. This has resulted in a sharp growth in the use of all forms of energy, as shown in Exhibit 8–12.

Industrialization and energy usage have led to a high standard of living in the United States and other developed countries. Income disparity between groups, however, has expanded rather than contracted, as shown in Exhibit 8–13 (see page 277).

It is probably a mistake to ascribe all of the growth in income disparity during the period 1980 to 1987 to political influences. This also was a time of increasing social reliance upon technical, medical, legal, and managerial skills. People with those specialized skills tended to earn increasingly higher incomes. One result was a continual increase in the expenditures for health care (see Exhibit 8–14, page 277), which combined a need for all four areas of expertise.

Another outcome of the increasing national population and prosperity was a growth in the amount of solid waste from industrial, municipal, and residential sources as shown in Exhibit 8–15.

A trend that may or may not be explainable through reference to increasing population pressures, industrialization impacts, and income disparities is the very definite growth in the amount of violent crime (see Exhibit 8–16, page 279).

EXHIBIT 8–13   Growth in Income Disparity (Percentage of Gross National Income
Received by Richest 5% and Poorest 40%)

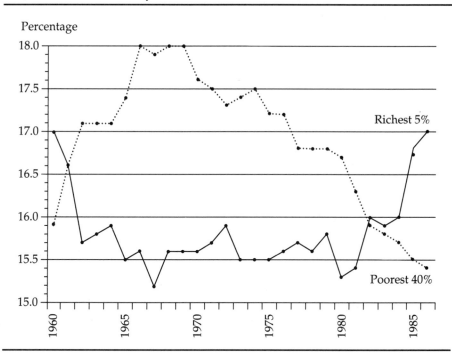

SOURCE: J. Reiman, *The Rich Get Richer and the Poor Get Prison: Ideology, Class and Criminal Justice* (New York: Macmillan, 1990).

EXHIBIT 8–14   Growth in Total U.S. Health Care Costs

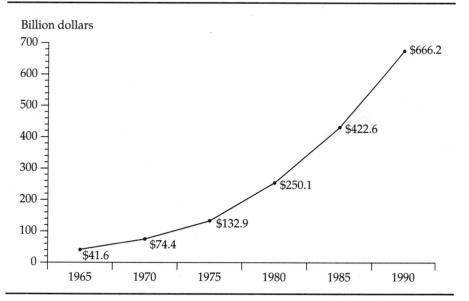

SOURCE: *Statistical Abstract of the U.S.* (Washington, D.C.: U.S. Bureau of the Census, 1992), p. 97.

EXHIBIT 8–15   Growth in U.S. Solid Waste

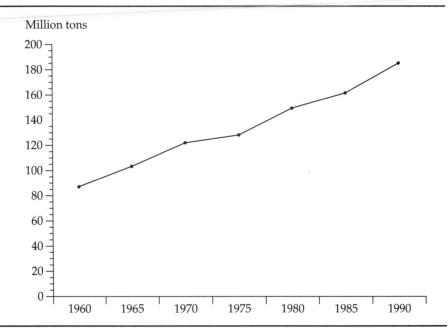

Million tons

SOURCE: *Statistical Abstract of the U.S.* (Washington, D.C.: U.S. Bureau of the Census, 1991), p. 212.

A last trend that may or may not be explainable through reference to increasing population pressures, industrialization impacts, and income disparities is the very definite growth in the level of political expenditures (see Exhibit 8–17, page 279), particularly for the incumbent.

The intent of publishing these 15 charts that show major and often disturbing trends firstly on a global and then a national scale was not to depict the world or the country as approaching an irreducible crisis. After all, the world and the country have grown in population numbers, economic outputs, and energy uses for centuries, and we have not yet reached a limit to growth.

Instead, the intent was to supply some visual dimensions to the economic, social, political, and environmental problems that we do face. Most of these problems have a distinct moral content in that some of the stakeholders in each will be hurt or harmed in some way by any attempt at resolution. Think about health care, for example. Any attempt to reduce expenditures will doubtless lower incomes. Any effort to expand coverage will doubtless raise costs. Any proposal to limit availability will doubtless shorten lives.

Many people who have taken leadership roles in our society have spoken of the need for "hard choices" in health care as in the other economic, social, political, and environmental areas. These hard choices inevitably mean somewhat less for one individual or group, and somewhat more for another. They are moral, and they require the application of moral reasoning to resolve in a

EXHIBIT 8–16   Growth in U.S. Crime

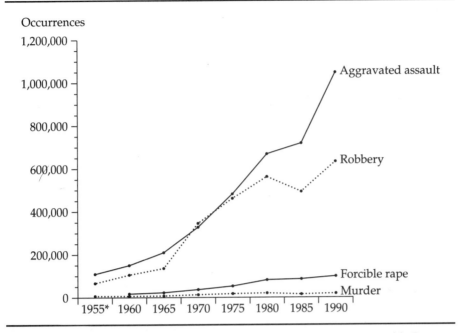

SOURCE: *Historical Statistics of the U.S., Colonial Times to 1970* (Washington, D.C..: U.S. Bureau of the Census, 1975), p. 413; *Statistical Abstract of the U.S.* (Washington, D.C.: U.S. Bureau of the Census, 1991), p. 108.

EXHIBIT 8–17   Growth in U.S. Political Costs (Expenditures for House of Representatives Candidates)

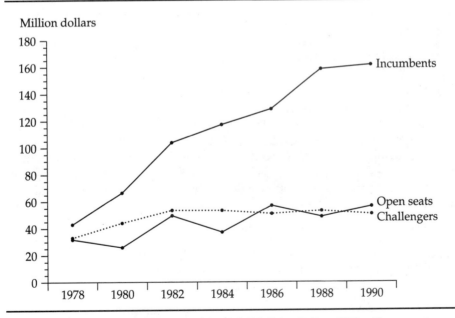

SOURCE: Frank Sorauf, *Inside Campaign Finance* (New York: Yale University Press, 1992), p. 17.

EXHIBIT 8–18   The Method of Moral Reasoning

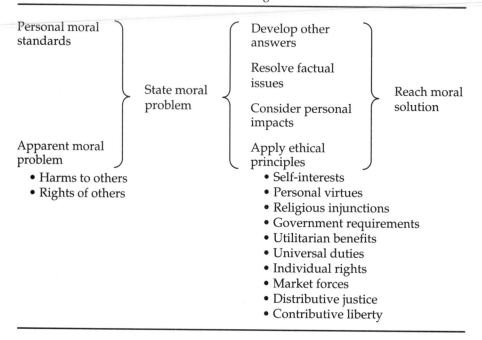

Personal moral
standards

Apparent moral
problem
- Harms to others
- Rights of others

State moral
problem

Develop other
answers

Resolve factual
issues

Consider personal
impacts

Apply ethical
principles
- Self-interests
- Personal virtues
- Religious injunctions
- Government requirements
- Utilitarian benefits
- Universal duties
- Individual rights
- Market forces
- Distributive justice
- Contributive liberty

Reach moral
solution

way that results in cooperation rather than conflict, in innovation rather than injury (see Exhibit 8–18).

All of us within society have a choice. We can either ignore the economic, social, political, and environmental problems that we face, or we can contribute to the solutions of those problems in ways that we believe to be "right" and "just" and "fair." Those people with managerial and professional responsibilities within our society have a somewhat greater burden. If they contribute to the solutions in ways that they can truthfully say they believe to be "right" and "just" and "fair," it will doubtless be at some cost to their organizations and, perhaps, to their careers. Why should they do this? Even more to the point, why should you—the reader—do this when you reach the appropriate level of managerial or professional responsibility? The concluding argument of this text is that it is necessary for you—and others—to decide upon:

The sort of person you want to be.

The sort of profession to which you want to belong.

The sort of organization for which you want to work.

The sort of society in which you want to live.

The sort of world you want to leave to your children.

ASSIGNMENT QUESTIONS

1. Are there, in your opinion, limits to the growth of the global economy? Are there limits to the growth of the national (U.S.) economy?

2. If you believe there are no limits to either the global or national economies, what assumptions are you making about about future increases in productivity and changes in technology?

3. If you believe there are firm limits, where will those limits first become apparent: living standards, food shortages, environmental conditions, or social disruptions?

4. Regardless of your decision on limits to growth, how would you define the responsibilities of a senior executive in a global corporation?

Case 8–1

THE SHORTEST CASE IN ANY UNDERGRADUATE OR MBA PROGRAM

Clarence Walton, formerly dean of the College of General Studies at Columbia and now president of the Catholic College of America, provides a very different concept of leadership in the first chapter of his recent book *The Moral Manager* (Ballinger Publishing Company, 1988, p. 4):

Leadership, an ill-defined word, comes from understanding and respecting four crucial ideas: equality, justice, truth and freedom.

Class Assignment

1. Do you agree with Professor Walton, and why or why not?

2. If you do agree with Professor Walton, why do almost all programs in business administration spend so much time on accounting, statistics, computers, marketing, production and finance, and so little on "equality, justice, truth and freedom"?

3. If you don't agree with Professor Walton, what "four crucial ideas" would you substitute? List them below:

1st crucial idea _____

2nd crucial idea _____

3rd crucial idea _____

4th crucial idea _____

Case 8–2

FINANCIAL COMPENSATION FOR THE VICTIMS OF BHOPAL

On December 3, 1984, some 2,000 people were killed and 200,000 were injured when a cloud of poisonous methyl isocyanate gas was accidentally released from the Union Carbide Company plant in Bhopal, India. The methyl isocyanate was used to manufacture Sevin, a plant pesticide that was distributed widely throughout India for use on that country's corn, rice, soybean, cotton, and alfalfa crops. It was said that the use of Sevin increased the harvest of the food crops by over 10 percent, enough to feed 70 million people.

The accident apparently occurred when between 120 and 240 gallons of water were introduced into a tank containing 90,000 pounds of methyl isocyanate.* The tank also contained approximately 3,000 pounds of chloroform, used as a solvent in the manufacture of methyl isocyanate; the two

_____

*Seven engineers and scientists from the Union Carbide Corporation were sent to Bhopal to assist in the safe disposal of the remaining methyl isocyanate at that site and to investigate the reasons for the accident. They were not permitted to interview operators of the Sevin process or to inspect the methyl isocyanate storage tank and related piping. They were permitted to obtain samples of the residues from the nearly ruptured tank; through experimentation they were able to replicate reactions that led to residues with the same chemical properties in the same proportions. The account, therefore, is a hypothesis for the tragedy, not a proven series of events.

chemicals should have been separated before storage, but that had not been done for some time in the operating process at Bhopal.

The water reacted exothermically (producing heat) with the chloroform, generating chlorine ions, which led to corrosion of the tank walls, and the iron oxide from the corrosion in turn reacted exothermically with the methyl isocyanate. The increase in heat and pressure was rapid but unnoticed because the pressure gauge on the tank had been inoperable for four months, and the operators in the control room monitoring a remote temperature gauge were accustomed to higher-than-specified heat levels (25° C. rather than the 0°. in the operating instructions) due to the continual presence of the chloroform and some water vapor in the tank. The refrigeration unit built to cool the storage tank had been disconnected six months previously. The "scrubber," a safety device to neutralize the methyl isocyanate with caustic soda, had been under repair since June. An operator, alarmed by the suddenly increasing temperature, attempted to cool the tank by spraying it with water, but by then the reaction was unstoppable, at a probable 200°C. The rupture disc (a steel plate in the line to prevent accidental operation of the safety valve) broke, the safety valve opened (just before, it is assumed, the tank would have burst), and over half the 45 tons of methyl isocyanate in storage were discharged into the air.

Following the accident, Union Carbide officials in the United States denied strongly that their firm was responsible for the tragedy. They made the following three statements in support of that position:

1. The Bhopal plant was 50.9 percent owned by the American firm, but the parent corporation had been able to exercise very little control. All managerial and technical personnel were citizens of India at the insistence of the Indian government. No Americans were permanently employed at the plant. Safety warnings from visiting American inspectors about the Sevin manufacturing process had been ignored.

2. Five automatic safety devices that had originally been installed as part of the Sevin manufacturing process had, by the time of the accident, been either replaced by manual safety methods to increase employment, shut down for repairs, or disconnected as part of a cost reduction program. The automatic temperature and pressure warning signals had been removed soon after construction. The repairs on the automatic scrubber unit had extended over six months. The refrigeration unit had never been used to cool the tank and had been inoperable for over a year.

3. The Bhopal plant had been built in partnership with the Indian government to increase employment in that country. Union Carbide would have preferred to make Sevin in the United States and ship it to India for distribution and sale because the insecticide could be made less expensively in the United States due to substantial economies of scale in the manufacturing process.

Warren Anderson, chairman of Union Carbide, stated that while he believed that the American company was not legally liable for the tragedy due to the three points above, it was still "morally" responsible, and he suggested that the firm should pay prompt financial compensation to those killed and injured in the accident.

Class Assignment

Assume that the question of legal liability for the accident at Bhopal never will be settled, due to differences in the law between the two countries and the difficulties of establishing jurisdiction. Assume, however, that the American company is morally responsible for the tragedy, as admitted by the chairman, because it was the majority owner and yet did not insist that the unsafe process be shut down. What factors would you consider in setting "just" financial compensation for each of the victims?

Case 8–3

IMPORTATION OF TROPICAL PLYWOODS

The tropical forests of the world are being destroyed at a rate that is far greater than the annual losses that had previously been reported by government officials. Recent surveys taken by satellite reveal that each year 40 million acres of rain forest simply disappear, with the valuable trees cut for timber while the remaining species are either so severely damaged by the logging operations that they cannot recover, or are totally demolished by the "slash-and-burn" agricultural practices of the inhabitants of the area who follow the roads and trails of the logging companies into the woods. The report based upon the satellite survey was prepared by the World Resources Institute in cooperation with the United Nations. It shows that in the nine largest tropical countries (which account for 73 percent of the total reported destruction) the actual annual losses of tropical forest acreage are four times greater than those estimated by officials in the countries involved as recently as 1985.

The satellite surveys revealed that in some countries, areas of tropical forest that were still officially classified as state or national preserves and parks were treeless. In a particularly telling comment, the report explained that the figures on actual losses might have been undercounted because smoke from burning brush and logging debris obscured some of the satellite photos; only areas that could be clearly seen to be deforested were included in the official results. Officials at the World Resource Institute, members of the United States Congress, and international economists were dismayed at the totals:

> Tropical deforestation is an unparalleled tragedy. If we don't reverse the trend now, it will soon be too late [James Speth, chairman of World Resource Institute, reported in *The New York Times*, June 8, 1990, p. A10].
>
> This is the first reliable data we've had on tropical deforestation in 10 years. A situation we knew was bleak is now shown to be truly horrendous [Patrick Leahy, chairman of the Agriculture Committee of the U.S. Senate, reported in *The New York Times*, June 8, 1990, p. A10].
>
> The destruction of tropical forests is one of the worst ecological disasters of the 20th century. It is the key to the most serious environmental problems: mass extinctions, global warming, shortages of natural resources, and the displacement and suffering of the tribal people who live in the forest [Sara Oldfield, "The Tropical Chainsaw Massacre," *New Scientist*, September 23, 1989, p. 55].

There are three reasons the destruction of the tropical forests is termed "bleak," "horrendous," "an unparalleled tragedy," and "one of the worst ecological disasters of the 20th century." The first, of course, is the possibility of global warming and the greenhouse effect. Green plants absorb carbon dioxide, and through photosynthesis (the action of sunlight upon chlorophyll) convert the carbon dioxide

EXHIBIT 1   Estimated versus Actual Annual Losses in Tropical Forest Acreage

	Annual Losses Estimated during 1981–1985 (in acres)	Annual Losses Revealed by 1988 Satellite Survey
Brazil	3,647,000	19,768,000
Cameroon	198,000	247,000
Costa Rica	160,000	306,000
India	363,000	3,707,000
Indonesia	1,482,000	2,224,000
Myanmar (Burma)	254,000	1,673,000
Philippines	227,000	353,000
Thailand	437,000	981,000
Vietnam	161,000	427,000
	6,939,000	29,686,000

SOURCE: World Resource Institute, reported in *The New York Times*, June 8, 1990, p. A10.

and water into carbohydrates which are basic to the growth of all living organisms, both plants and animals. Trees are the largest green plants, and consequently absorb the greatest amounts of carbon dioxide. Trees in the tropical rain forests receive the largest amounts of water and of sunlight, and consequently are the most effective at absorbing carbon dioxide.

Carbon dioxide is formed in the atmosphere as the result of burning fossil fuels (coal and oil) or natural fuels (wood). The amount of carbon dioxide in the atmosphere has, of course, expanded tremendously as a result of the industrial revolution and the greater use of energy to power the manufacturing and transportation associated with that revolution. The concern of the scientific community is that the greater amounts of carbon dioxide in the upper atmosphere act as a porous haze that reflects infrared energy back onto the earth, increasing surface temperatures and changing weather patterns.

There is a scientific uncertainty about the relationship of the greenhouse gases and the greenhouse effect, primarily due to the difficulties of measuring increases in surface temperatures. Surface temperatures vary by season, by region, and by hour, and are affected by wind streams, cloud patterns, rainfall amounts, and solar radiation, in a complex interdependent system. Increases in surface temperatures can be definitely established for some regions at some seasons, but they seem to be at least partially offset by decreases in other regions and other seasons. Further, global temperatures have varied in the past, as evidenced by the successive ice ages of the late Neolithic period, and those changes could not have been caused by excessive amounts of carbon dioxide in the atmosphere as this period predated the burning of fossil fuels.

The greenhouse effect has not been proven. The concern of many atmosphere scientists and meteorologists is that when it can be proven (about 2010 when adequate data will have been accumulated to prove—or disprove

—the relationship of atmosphere carbon dioxide and global weather patterns), it will be far too late to take meaningful action. The amount of carbon dioxide in the air will be irreversible if the tropical forests no longer exist. The nonexistence of the tropical forests is a true possibility. If the current rate of cutting and burning continues, only scattered remnants in the higher and more inaccessible locations will be left.

The possibility of irreversible global warming is only one of the adverse impacts of the destruction of the rain forests. The second is the extinction of plant and animal species. The tropical rain forests originally accounted for less than 7 percent of the earth's surface, yet they were reputed to hold more than half of all of the earth's living species. Many were never identified. Most were never studied. It is felt that some, particularly among the plants, had medicinal effects that now will never be known.

The third adverse impact of the destruction of the rain forests is the increased poverty of the tropical nations that will come with the final depletion of this resource. The nine nations listed in Exhibit 1 are (with the exception of Brazil) third world countries: poor, underdeveloped, and overpopulated. The export value of tropical hardwood timber was reported to be $7 billion per year in the early 1980s [*Futures*, October 1985, p. 451]; it was expected to decline to $2 billion by the year 2000 and to become negative in 2010. "Become negative" means that the tropical nations will have to import timber for building and other local uses by that year.

The last and perhaps the most serious proven (remember, global warming has not yet been proven) impact of the destruction of the rain forests is the unfortunate result the cutting had upon the lives of the indigenous peoples living within the forests. Rain forests were not unpopulated. They provided a rich environment for human beings as well as tropical plants and animals. It is easily possible for communal villages to live on fish, game, wild fruit, and small plantations of root crops such as sweet potatoes (the Amazon) or manioc (southeast Asia) on land cleared from the jungle. That life is not possible following deforestation.

Native residents were either forcefully removed from the land prior to cutting, or were economically forced to move after the logging operations were completed. A particularly poignant aspect of this forced movement was the belief by the indigenous peoples in the tropical forests as communal property, owned by all for the benefit of all. This communal belief was reflected in the national law of most tropical countries; the forests were legally owned by the individual nations for the benefit of their citizens. The land could not be sold to the timber companies. Instead, "concessions" or rights to cut the timber growing upon the land for a limited number of years were sold to those companies. Consequently, these "concessionaires" (the formal title for all timber companies operating in southeast Asia) had no long-term interest in preserving the timber land. Their most profitable action was to cut everything that grew, drag the logs by tractor to the nearest road, and leave.

When they left, the land rapidly deteriorated even if it was not burned for agricultural use. Tropical forests are not similar to those in the more temperate Northern Hemisphere in at least one very important aspect. The nutrients that support the plants, vines, and trees are not contained in the forest soil; instead they are contained in the "biomass" or the decaying debris of plants, vines, and trees that lies upon the forest floor. This debris decays rapidly, helped by the heat, the water, and the insects and spores common in the tropics. After cutting it is easily washed away by the heavy rainfalls that are also typical of the region, leaving a raw clay that will support little except coarse grass.

Environmentalists in the Northern Hemisphere have strongly encouraged the concept of "selective logging," taking only a few of the mature trees per acre, and leaving the rest to regenerate. Selective logging is also known as "sustained yield" forestry. If a timber concessionaire were to take out only selected trees during the first cutting, it would then be able to recut the land on a 25-year or 40-year cycle, harvesting the cumulative growth each time.

Selective cutting and sustained yield forestry are widely practiced in northern Europe and southeastern United States, but the concepts are not easily transferred to the tropics. Firstly, the timber in northern Europe and southeastern United States is predominantly softwood—pine, spruce, and fir—that grows to a merchantable size in 30 to 50 years. The valuable timber in the tropical rain forests is exclusively hardwood—mahogany, rosewood, and teak—that grows much more slowly. Secondly, the timberlands in northern Europe and southeastern United States are dominated by a limited number of species that easily reproduce themselves through seeding. Timberlands in the tropics contain a much wider variety of species. It is estimated that Indonesia is the home of 700 different trees that grow large enough to be harvested, yet only 20 of those trees produce lumber with the grain, color, and "workability" needed for export. A few of the remaining trees have some value for local construction, but many are valueless except for pulp, and few pulp and paper mills have been built in the developing countries. When the desired trees are selectively logged, there often are not enough specimens left for natural seeding.

Lastly, in a tropical forest, the desired, mature trees tend to be huge. They also tend to be connected to other trees by vines and creepers. When cut, they generally flatten a considerable section of the forest. The logs, of course, are also large and heavy. In mountainous regions, and much of the tropical landmass is mountainous, exceptionally powerful tractors are required to drag the logs to the nearest road that is suitable for a truck. Dragging a large and heavy log down mountainous terrain destroys much of the remaining vegetation. Photographs of tropical forests that allegedly have been selectively logged show a wasted landscape, with broken tree stubs, crushed undergrowth, and churned-up soil.

There is one further reason that selective logging and sustained growth forestry have not been successful in the tropical rain forests, and that is a reason that is seldom discussed at international conferences but that is nonetheless recognized by most if not all of the participants: economic exploitation and political corruption. Profits in logging the concessions offered by the national governments can be immense. The *Far Eastern Economic Review* [November 24, 1988, p. 50] estimated that a concessionaire in the Philippines, after meeting all reasonable costs and paying all expected taxes, would make a net profit of P100,000 (US$4,673) per hectare (a metric surface measure equal to 2.471 acres). The *Review* also reported that one concessionaire in Palawan (an island in the Philippines, southwest of Luzon) had been awarded cutting rights on 168,000 hectares. Simple mathematics converts this award to a potential profit, over the five years of the grant, of $785,000,000. Profits of that magnitude have been alleged to buy political influence in third world countries such as the Philippines:

Palawan is being plundered. Its destruction, spurred by a lack of the political will to stop it and administrative neglect, has set the stage for a last-ditch struggle by conservationists. The fight over Palawan's resources contains in miniature the structure and workings of Philippine politics: the interlocking interests of politicians, government officials, military officers and the businessmen who control the province's economy [Ibid., p. 49].

Local residents were unable to stop the private destruction of the public forests. The *Review* reported that the concessionaire on Palawan "maintains a considerable number of private security guards and has an intemperate reputation" [Ibid., p. 50].

The same combination of profits,

politics, government, and the military was said in 1989 to have defeated an attempt to convert to sustained-yield forestry in Thailand. Villages in the southern portion of that country had been carried away by flash floods in November 1988, or had been buried in mud and logs washed down from hillsides denuded by recent logging. Three thousand five hundred people had been killed. A government report on the causes blamed a "complete failure in the entire system of forestry protection" [*Far Eastern Economic Review*, January 12, 1989, p. 40].

There were 301 logging concessions throughout the country, most of which were granted in 1972. All carried a 30-year lease.

Adverse environmental impact would have been minimal if the logging procedures had been strictly observed. Each of the concessions was divided into 30 plots; the concessionaires were to fell systematically only the large trees on a one-year-per-plot basis whereby at the end of the lease, smaller trees in the initially logged plots would have grown enough for relogging.

But because of rampant corruption among forestry and other local officials, the scientific logging procedures were ignored [Ibid., p. 40]. The article continues to describe the actions by which the land, in essence, was denuded of all vegetation.

Selective logging and sustainable forestry have not been successful in the past; unfortunately, there is little hope that these scientific practices for the sound utilization of the forest resources can be successful in the future:

Corruption, commercial pressures, the high rate of return expected on capital, the ravages of heavy machinery all make sustainable logging a pipedream.

The tragedy of the rain forests is that they are being managed neither in the traditional manner, by hunters and shifting cultivators making their livings from the forests without destroying them, nor by strong state forest agencies or large commercial companies willing and able to adopt strategies for the long-term management of a sustainable resource [*New Scientist*, September 16, 1989, p. 43].

In a last-ditch effort to save the tropical forests, it has been suggested by numerous environmental groups that the industrialized nations should simply refuse to import tropical hardwoods from areas that have been improperly logged. This has been strenuously resisted both by the exporting countries and the importing companies.

The argument of the exporting countries is that this proposal is an attack upon their national sovereignty, upon their right to manage their own resources in their own way for their own interests. Delegates from those countries are occasionally willing to acknowledge that political corruption has led to the wasteful exploitation of some of those resources, but they maintain that the overall results have been beneficial to their countries, if not to the world. It is necessary to recognize, they say, that cutting the tropical rain forests does create rural jobs, increase export earnings and tax revenues, and provide the additional agricultural land needed for an expanding population.

"I worry about the greenhouse effect too," says one of the Brazilian delegates to the ITTO (International Timber Trade Organization) meeting. "But why is it the tropical forest countries that have to pay the price to try to do something about it? . . . Environmentalists are always talking about our moral duty, but our people can't live on moral duty" [*Far Eastern Economic Review*, January 12, 1989, p. 41].

Environmentalists from Western Europe, the United States, and Japan have already cut down their forests for economic development and to provide the land needed for agricultural use. Now they want to keep us from doing exactly the same thing [Verbal statement by a visiting faculty member from the Philippines].

The argument of the importing companies is that they do not cause the problem, and that they are merely buying commodity products at market prices and generating domestic employment and foreign exchange for the host countries, while providing needed products for retail and industrial consumers in their home countries.

Tropical Plywood Imports, Inc. (disguised company name) is an importing company. It was formed in Seattle, Washington by a local entrepreneur who has often been quoted as saying that he saw a niche in the U.S. plywood market that could be filled by importing meranti plywood from Indonesia. Meranti is a tropical hardwood very similar to mahogany; it is a strong, dense wood without growth rings that can be cut into very thin veneer and then laminated into plywood sheets that are ¼ inch thick. American softwoods such as Douglas fir and southern pine cannot be cut into such thin veneers because of the existence of the growth rings (the veneer would tear at the soft inner portion of those rings if it were cut in thin cross-sections). Consequently, all plywoods produced in the United States are a minimum of ⅜ inch thick. It would be possible to produce ¼ inch plywood from the strong and dense American hardwoods such as birch, maple, cherry, or walnut, but those woods are very expensive, and are reserved in this country for fine furniture.

The meranti plywood is ideal for concrete forms. It is much less costly than American plywood when used for this purpose, partially because it is thinner and uses less wood, partially because it comes from foreign mills with lower wage rates, and partially because it can more easily be sawed, drilled, and nailed without danger of splitting. Meranti plywood is also used in manufacturing kitchen cabinets and paneling travel trailers and mobile homes.

Tropical Plywood Imports, Inc. has grown very rapidly. It was founded in 1982 with approximately $50,000 in start-up capital, and sales the first year were under $2 million. In 1990 the company expects to sell $37.5 million worth of meranti plywood to lumber yards and industrial firms throughout the country. In an interview with the local newspaper, the founder of the company was quoted as saying that "cutting the meranti trees helps provide jobs and income for the Indonesian people, as well as a useable product for the American market. The meranti trees have to be at least 20 inches in diameter, and the timber is harvested in a selective logging method in which smaller trees are left to be cut 35 years from now. Environmentalists disagree with us, of course; they say that you should let the large trees stay there and rot."

At the conclusion of the interview, the founder of Tropical Plywood Imports admitted that he had never visited the logging sites in Indonesia where the meranti was being harvested, and that he was relying upon assurances from the concessionaire and government officials.

Class Assignment

The class assignment is divided into two separate parts:

1. Should the industrialized nations in North America, Europe, and Japan band together, and refuse to import tropical hardwoods in order to preserve the tropical forests? Be prepared to say why; don't just say "yes" or "no" and then stop.

2. Given that the industrialized nations have not as yet agreed to ban the importation of tropical hardwoods, should a company such as Tropical Plywood Imports, Inc. feel free to continue purchasing meranti plywood from a concessionaire in Indonesia?

Case 8-4

MUNICIPAL SOLID WASTE DISPOSAL

In the United States the average citizen throws away 1,840 pounds of household rubbish each year; that amounts to 230,000,000 tons annually. Companies, including retail shops, industrial firms, fast-food restaurants, wholesale distributors, health care facilities, governmental agencies, etc. dispose of another 628,000,000 tons. Together this residential and commercial trash is called municipal solid waste.

Municipal solid waste includes paper (50.6 percent), food (19.6 percent), glass (10.1 percent), metal (9.9 percent), wood (3.5 percent), textiles (3.0 percent), rubber (1.7 percent), and plastic (1.4 percent). Some of the items are large and bulky with a mixed content, such as automobiles, appliances, household and office furniture, industrial equipment, and building demolition debris. Other items are small and exceedingly numerous, such as 55 billion tin cans, 26 billion glass bottles, 16 billion disposable diapers, 2.0 billion disposable razors, 1.6 billion disposable pens, and 220 million automobile tires.

The United States, with its affluence and industry, leads the world in the generation of municipal solid waste, but other nations are not far behind and some are catching up rapidly. A typical person in New York City throws away 4.0 pounds of solid household trash each day, but Tokyo (3.0), Paris (2.4), Singapore (2.2), Hong Kong (2.0), Hamburg (1.9), and Rome (1.5) are in the running. Even cities thought to be in the developing or third world have numbers that seem to belie their poverty: Lahore (1.4), Jakarta (1.3), Manila (1.1), and Kano, Liberia (1.0).

Most of the waste, both household and commercial, has historically been sent to landfills. In the past these were often abandoned quarries, gravel pits, strip mines, swamps, and wetlands. The intent was to "fill in" the land, and make it usable for commercial or residential purposes. The trash was compacted, covered with earth, and allowed to settle for a number of years before any building was attempted. The problem, of course, was that rain and surface moisture continually seeped through the compacted trash, dissolved many chemical pollutants, and contaminated the ground water.

The next step was to build clay-lined pits, and then mound up the rubbish to encourage runoff and cover it with plastic to prevent seepage. Some of these pits are huge: the one now serving most of New York City is 3,000 acres (5 square miles) in extent, and the mound is expected to be 500 feet high when the pit is completely filled by the year 2000. It will be tall enough that a local entrepreneur has seriously proposed making this municipal dump into a ski resort by installing snow-making equipment, chair lifts, and a base lodge.

Most municipal dumps do not have such happy and innovative endings.

The clay linings and the plastic covers both tend to develop leaks over time, and chemical compounds thereby continue to contaminate the ground-water. It is now thought necessary to install perforated pipes above the clay lining to collect the seepage, drains and pumps below the lining to re-move contaminated groundwater, and treatment plants to concentrate the seepage and reduce the contami-nation. These and other problems have caused the available landfill capacity to drop dramatically since the late 1970s. From 1978 to 1988, 70 percent of the 14,000 landfills in the United States were closed. By 1993 about 50 percent of those re-maining will be closed. Some are to be closed because they will have reached capacity; others because it is impossible to bring them into compliance with the new and much more stringent environmental reg-ulations.

Very few new landfills will be opened to replace the old ones. From 1988 to 1993, for example, the State of New York was expected to shut down 83 of its landfills and open only three. Potential landfill operators, both pub-lic and private, pointed to the strict environmental codes as a major rea-son for the decline of landfill disposal for municipal solid waste. Another major reason was the lack of readily available sites anywhere near a major metropolitan area. No one wanted to see a new solid waste landfill built in his or her "backyard":

> Nobody wants dumps in their neigh-borhood. Rubbish doesn't look nice or smell nice. It attracts vermin, brings truck traffic, and employs garbagemen. I see a potential that eventually, even

at any cost, you won't be able to landfill your city's garbage either within the city or outside the state [Harry Perks, streets commissioner of Philadelphia, quoted in Anthony Marro (ed.), *Rush to Burn*, 1989, p. 44].

Given that there will be substantial opposition to new landfill sites, either close by in the metropolitan area or at some distance in a neighboring state, it is necessary to look at alternatives. The first alternative is by far the most attractive from an environmental viewpoint, but also the most difficult to put into practice in any meaningful way. It is the "reduce, reuse, recycle" attempt to substantially lessen the amount of material sent to a landfill for disposal.

Some of the waste stream can be reduced at the source. The most com-mon example is the paper, plastic, and cardboard packaging for food and consumer products which seems, to many people, to be excessive. Stores have tried selling these products in bulk, but with a notable lack of suc-cess. It is obvious that consumers like the convenience of the prepared and packaged items. Oranges, for exam-ple, can be purchased in bulk and squeezed for juice at home for 65 per-cent of the cost of the frozen concen-trate in cans, or 50 percent of the cost of the "ready-to-drink" mixture in cartons, yet raw oranges account for less than 5 percent of the total sale of orange products. This preference for convenience is expected to continue, given the increasing number of house-holds where both partners now work full-time.

Some of the waste stream can be reused at the home or, particularly, the store or factory. "Reuse" means to use the item once again in its original form for its original purpose, and often requires redesign to be effective. The disposable corrugated boxes made of paperboard in which packaged food and consumer products are now shipped from the factory to the warehouse and finally to the retail store, for example, can be redesigned to be permanent shipping containers made of composite plastic or fiberglass. These permanent shipping containers have to be returned from the store to the warehouse and then to the factory to be reused, but the delivery trucks are frequently empty on the way back and consequently the return often adds little cost. The problem is that it is difficult to find many other examples where product redesign leads so easily and naturally to waste stream reuse. Disposable paper diapers can be replaced by reusable cloth products, to cite another example, but few parents would claim that they are equally convenient, and washing the reusable cloth diapers just moves the pollution problem from a solid waste to a liquid waste category.

Finally, some of the waste stream can be recycled. "Recycled" means to use the material in the product once again either for its original or for a completely new purpose. Newsprint can be recycled into newsprint, or into wallboard, home insulation, charcoal briquettes, etc. Except for aluminum cans or glass bottles, however, there is little question that the recycled products are inferior in some respects, create pollution problems during the recycling, or both. Recycled newsprint, for example, has a much lower tensile strength than the original

paper made from wood pulp so that the newspaper presses must run much more slowly, and the black ink and short fibers from the recycled newsprint have to be recovered during the recycling process, dried, and then dumped back into the waste stream headed towards a landfill.

It is frequently estimated that the stream of municipal solid waste can be lessened by 10 percent by the "reduce" stage, 10 percent by the "reuse" stage, and 30 percent by the "recycle" stage. That is a *compound* reduction of 56.7 percent. Seattle, which has by far and away the most comprehensive waste reduce-reuse-recycle program of any American city, is now saving 30 percent of its waste stream. The city's goal by 1998 is to reach 60 percent through the use of extensive charges to family households, retail stores, and manufacturing plants for waste disposal, and through the use of economic incentives for waste recycling.

Technically, slightly over 80 percent of the solid municipal waste stream can be saved. Practically, however, the rates of 50 percent to 60 percent that the Japanese maintain in their cities is considered to be approaching realistic limits. Even the most avid recyclers agree that topping 60 percent to 70 percent will prove to be nearly impossible.

A sizable portion of our waste stream, 30 percent to 40 percent, is simply not recyclable, and will therefore continue to pose problems for our landfills [Statement of Allen Hirshkowitz, the director of Municipal Waste Research for INFORM, quoted in Anthony Marro (ed.), *Rush to Burn*, 1989, p. 145].

The conclusion of many experts is that—despite our best efforts to reduce the waste as manufacturers, reuse it as consumers, and recycle it as community members—we will continue to generate about 350,000,000 tons of municipal solid waste each year within the United States (230 million tons of household waste plus 630 million tons of manufacturing waste less the maximum reduce-reuse-recycle rate of 60 percent).

The question, of course, is what to do with 350,000,000 tons of solid municipal waste each year. There are two basic process alternatives, each with substantial though different problems, and then numerous geographic choices. Each process alternative, when combined with a geographic choice, has a different economic, political, and environmental cost. The two basic process alternatives are as follows:

1. Modern landfill. It is possible to construct a properly engineered landfill—that is, with a clay lining, a plastic cover, and a drainage pumping and pollution treatment station to recover and purify the inevitable seepage—to compact and store the municipal solid waste. This is the simplest of the two process alternatives. It is also the least costly. The problem is that it is by far and away the least certain; no one knows how long the clay lining and plastic cover will last before major leaks occur. Those major leaks may be beyond the capacity of the drainage system to recover, and groundwater supplies may be contaminated.

The nonrecyclable materials are put into the landfill without processing. These materials include small traces of heavy metals such as arsenic, cadmium, lead, mercury, and zinc that are used in many consumer and industrial products. They also include large amounts of halogenated hydrocarbons in which chlorine, bromine, fluorine, and iodine atoms have been added to hydrocarbon chains to produce solvents, paints, lubricants, plastics, and pesticides. They are often contaminated with pathogens such as bacteria, parasites, and viruses that are known to be harmful to humans. A simple butter or margarine tub, for example, is made of a plastic halogenated with chlorine, printed with an ink that contains cadmium, and—when it reaches the landfill—contaminated with all three types of pathogens. As is well known the margarine tube will not decay, but over time the chlorine and cadmium ions are water soluble, and the pathogens are water survivable.

Municipal solid waste used to be burned at landfills before it was compacted and covered with earth. This was done to reduce the volume, destroy the hydrocarbons, and kill the pathogens. Open burning, however, created extensive air pollution. It is possible to control the burning to very substantially reduce the air pollution. This leads to the second basic disposal alternative: modern combustion.

2. Modern combustion. It is also possible to construct a properly engineered incinerator—that is, with a continuous-feed, a high-temperature fire, and an emission control and acid neutralization station—to

burn much of the municipal solid waste. This was originally termed a "waste-to-energy" conversion process for the hot gases from the combustion chamber were led through the flues of a high-pressure boiler to make steam to generate electric power. It has been found, however, that it is much harder to neutralize the acids and recover the particles from the flue gases after heat has been extracted in the boiler, and consequently the generation of electric power has been greatly diminished as an objective of the process.

Three broad categories of pollutants are generated by burning municipal solid waste in a high-temperature fire: particulate matter that contains the heavy metals, acid gases that include the halogens, and dioxide emissions that are generated in the burning process itself. Unburned carbon or smoke is not a problem; hydrocarbons tend to be fully converted to carbon dioxide if the temperature in the combustion chamber is maintained at 600–650°C. with a proper air flow, and of course all pathogens are killed at that temperature.

The particulate matter comes in two types known as "bottom ash" and "fly ash"; both consist of small particles of unburned material, primarily metallic oxides. The bottom ash—which tends to be much larger in size—falls through the grates in the combustion chamber and can easily be collected. The fly ash is carried away by the flue gases and has to be collected by electrostatic precipitation or by air filtration. In electrostatic precipitation the particles in the flue gases

are given a positive electrical charge, and then collected on negatively charged plates from which they can be later scraped for disposal. In air filtration the flue gases are cooled and then passed through huge cloth bags somewhat similar to those in a vacuum cleaner.

Acid gases, the second main category of pollutants from a high-temperature fire, include sulfur dioxide, nitrogen dioxide, and the various halogen dioxides. They are neutralized by "scrubbers": a concentrated lime slurry is sprayed from the top of a tower onto the passing hot flue gases. The hot gases evaporate the water, leaving widely dispersed lime particles to neutralize the acids. The neutralized particles fall to the bottom of the tower, where they can be collected for disposal.

Dioxins, the third and most troublesome category of pollutants from a high temperature fire, are complex hydrocarbons that are formed either in the heat of the fire itself or in the cooling process as the flue gases are treated and dispersed. They have been linked to birth defects, miscarriages, cancers, neurological damages, and immune system disorders, but those harmful associations have never been conclusively proven. Some scientists consider dioxins the most dangerous substances ever produced in a laboratory; one drop in 10,000 gallons of water is contrary to Federal regulatory law. In 1982 it was found that dioxins had been illegally dumped in the town of Times Beach, Missouri. The entire population was evacuated, and the area quarantined until a plan could be agreed to as a solution. That solution was to build a special on-site incinerator, and over the next 10 years all buildings, along with all trees, shrubs, plants, roadways, and 135,000 tons of topsoil, will be burned at a heat of 4,000°F.

Other scientists believe that the dangers of dioxins have been greatly exaggerated. They contend that concentrated amounts undoubtedly produce biological harms to animal subjects such as mice and rats in laboratory experiments, but that humans would never encounter such high concentrations of the chemical even if living directly adjacent to a modern incinerator. It is now thought that further laboratory experimentation will not settle this dispute and that the only way to resolve it will be to build a modern incinerator and keep careful records that compare apparent harms to people within that area to members of an equivalent control group outside that area.

Modern incinerators can be designed to burn 500 to 3,000 tons of municipal solid waste per day, or 150,000 to 900,000 tons per year assuming a 300-day year. The typical citizen in the United States is responsible for 1.4 tons per year (230 million tons of household waste plus 630 million tons of manufacturing waste less the reduce-reuse-recycle rate of 60 percent = 350,000,000 million tons divided by 250,000,000 national population). Consequently, single combustion facilities can be designed to serve cities of 100,000 to 600,000 persons; multiple combustion facilities can be used to service larger population centers.

The problem is that modern combustion facilities reduce the volume of municipal solid waste by 90 percent, but they do not totally eliminate the volume. Ten percent by weight is left, in the form of metallic bottom and fly ash and neutralized acid solids. This material must be disposed of, primarily in engineered landfills, which may make it seem as if the municipal solid waste problem is circular and that we are now back at the starting point, but the volume is now 90 percent less, the halogenated hydrocarbons have been 99.9 percent eliminated, and the pathogens have been 100.0 percent destroyed. It should be easier to maintain the integrity of an engineered landfill containing only incinerated waste by-products because the size would be smaller and two of the harmful pollutants would be missing.

The alternative disposal methods—engineered landfills or high-temperature incinerators—have problems that are primarily technical in nature. No one is certain how long the linings and covers of the landfills will last, and no one is certain what the impact of the dioxins will be over time. The different geographic locations, however, have problems that are firstly political and then moral. No one wants either a landfill or an incinerator anywhere near his or her home, office, or business. Economic incentives can be offered to overcome at least part of that political resistance but—as will be readily apparent—there are moral problems in offering those incentives. The different geographical choices can be described very briefly:

1. Inner cities. The centers of many metropolitan areas have decayed over time. Land values are low. Unskilled labor is readily available. Highways and railroads tend to be underutilized. Either an engi-

neered landfill or a modern incinerator could be located here to serve the entire metropolitan area. Transportation costs would be low because the solid waste would move towards the center of a circle. A rough estimate of the cost of landfill disposal in the inner city is $45/ton; of incinerated disposal $75/ton, with an additional charge of $15/ton of incoming waste for the residual landfill of metallic ash and acidic solids. That is, to eliminate any misunderstanding about this latter charge, each ton of incoming waste will be incinerated and reduced to 200 pounds of metallic ash and acidic solids at a cost of $75; the 200 pounds (10 percent) that are left of the incoming ton can then be landfilled for an additional charge of $15. Remember, the $45 charge for complete landfill is for 2,000 pounds; the $15 charge for residual landfill is for only 200 pounds. The residual landfill is more expensive when compared to a full 2,000 pounds because metallic ash and acidic solids are concentrated pollutants, and have to be more carefully handled and compacted to avoid wind-blown dust, and then more carefully covered and monitored to prevent waterborne pollution.

2. Outer suburbs. The outer suburbs of many metropolitan areas, too far from the employment centers for all except the most dedicated of commuters, have medium land values and some unskilled labor from closing factories and abandoned farms. Roads, however, tend to be overutilized and would need to be modernized. Railroads often are nonexistent. Transportation costs are high, both to pay the capital costs of road improvement and to adjust to the longer routes (across the circle, not towards the center). A rough estimate of the costs of complete landfill disposal in the outer suburbs is $75/ton; of incinerated disposal $105/ton. The cost for the incinerated disposal does not include any charge for the landfill of the residual metallic ash and acidic solids; it is thought that these obviously toxic materials will have to be shipped elsewhere to make this proposal even marginally possible on a political basis.

3. Economically depressed regions. Within 500 to 700 miles of most major metropolitan areas are economically depressed regions that were previously dependent upon extractive industries such as coal or metal mining, forestry, or fishing. The anthracite regions of eastern Pennsylvania; the bituminous sections of West Virginia, Virginia, Kentucky, and southern Ohio; or the iron ore sources in northern Minnesota and Wisconsin are all examples of localities looking for revitalization. Land values are low. Skilled and unskilled workers are both available. Railroads are old, but serviceable with some repair. Highways are also old and unsuitable for heavy trucks. Transportation is the major cost differential for facilities located here. Complete landfill disposal is estimated at $105/ton; incinerated disposal is estimated at $135/ton, with an additional charge of $15/incoming

ton for the residual landfill disposal of the 200 pounds of metallic ash and the acidic solids. If one wanted to ship just the metallic ash and acidic solids from an incinerator located within a city for residual disposal here, the cost is estimated at $210/ton.

4. Sparsely populated areas. Within 1,000 to 2,000 miles of most major metropolitan areas are regions that have very limited populations due to the climate that makes agriculture almost impossible. Northern Maine, northern Quebec or Labrador, or the desert regions of New Mexico, Arizona, Utah, and Colorado are all examples. The desert regions have limited rainfall amounts, which makes the protection of seepages from either complete or residual landfills that much easier. Cross-country highways and railroads are modern and suitable, but both would have to be supplemented with new local lines or roads to the site. Land costs are low. Labor costs would be high, due to the need to move workers into the area. An estimate of costs for complete landfill disposal is $145/ton; for incineration disposal, $175/ton, with an extra $15/incoming ton for the residual landfill disposal of the ash and solids. Again, if one wanted to ship just the metallic ash and acidic solids from an incinerator at a different location for residual disposal here, the cost is estimated at $220/ton.

5. Foreign third world countries. Many third world countries are willing to accept municipal solid waste either for landfill or for incineration. Transportation costs are low because sea-going vessels or barges can be used, and the disposal sites will be close to the ports. It is assumed that both the landfill and incinerator facilities at those sites will be designed and built to meet U.S. specifications. It is also assumed that local workers will be employed at wages that would seem high to them, but low to U.S. employees, to operate those plants. Complete landfill disposal can be arranged at $75/ton, incineration disposal at $105/ton, but here there would be only a small or nonexistent charge for the residual disposal of the metallic ash and acidic solids. Both tend to be mixed with concrete or asphalt and used for building blocks or road bases abroad. Many third world countries suffer from a lack of sand or gravel, and the officials in some of those countries claim that there is very little water or air pollution once the toxic materials have been locked into a cement or asphalt binder. This is a practice that is illegal in the United States, Europe, and Japan, but that is widespread in many other parts of the world. The officials in those developing countries, however, are seldom willing to accept the waste products of an incinerator located in a different country; they want the investments and the jobs that come with the full operations in their own country.

Class Assignment

Assume that the governor of your state has asked you to be on a panel that must recommend a policy for the disposal of solid municipal wastes. Assume that your state is one of those on the eastern or western seaboards; that is, it does not have within its borders any economically deprived areas or sparsely populated regions. It does, however, have access to inexpensive sea transport to many foreign countries. What would you decide? That is, what alternative or alternatives would you select? What arguments would you use to convince others to accept your proposed solution to this ongoing problem of municipal solid waste disposal? For the purpose of this assignment accept the estimate that no more than 60 percent of the current waste stream can be reduced, reused, or recycled.

Case 8–5

MEDICAL MALPRACTICE: DOCTORS VERSUS LAWYERS

Medical malpractice is a massive problem within the United States and is getting worse. In 1987, $3.8 billion dollars were awarded in medical malpractice jury settlements, up from less than $700 million in 1974. 20 percent of all practicing physicians were sued for malpractice in 1987, up from fewer than 3 percent in 1974. 75 percent of those suits are currently settled out of court, often with only a token payment for the prior patient. 75 percent of the suits which reach the courtroom are decided in favor of the physician, with no payment for the patient. But, for the balance of the cases which do reach the courtroom and are settled in favor of the plaintiff—about 7,500 per year—the amounts awarded to the patient and his or her attorney are substantial, with an average of $506,000 each.

The amounts are large, and that is what drives the process. It costs the patient very little to sue, for patients can always find an attorney who is willing to take the case on a "contingency" basis, accepting a large percentage of the final settlement. A patient doesn't have to look very far to find those attorneys; they even advertise on television now.

But, the money is only part of the problem. The worst part is the emotional shock of being sued. You may have done your absolute best for a patient, but then weeks, months, or even years later, you receive legal documents formally accusing you of incompetence and carelessness. Sure, 75 percent of those suits are settled out of court, which is very cost effective for the insurance company but seems to admit guilt on the part of the physician. Sure, the insurance company wins 75 percent of the cases which get to court, but that means you have to sit there in the courtroom and listen to expert witnesses impugn your integrity and your competence. There has to be a better way [Statement of physician].

Many attorneys are also dissatisfied with the current means of recovering damages for medical malpractice, and strongly object to being portrayed as the villains, driven by greed and heartlessness, in medical malpractice.

> Malpractice does occur. It is not a fictionalized event to provide employment and income for attorneys. As with every other profession, some doctors do sloppy, incompetent work. When a plumber does sloppy, incompetent work you just find another plumber to fix the leaks. But, when a doctor does sloppy, incompetent work you may have major, major problems that last for the rest of your lifetime, or that of your child. When that happens, you certainly are entitled to compensation for the future medical costs you have to bear, and for any loss of income you may experience. But, you will find that the medical establishment and the insurance companies are arranged against you. You need an attorney who is willing to carry the costs just to work through the system [Statement of attorney].

Lastly, the major health care institutions are concerned about medical malpractice, partially because hospitals and clinics can also be sued for incompetence and neglect, but primarily because of the effect the potential for malpractice has upon total health care costs.

> The $3.8 billion dollars in jury awards is just the tip of the medical malpractice iceberg. You can get any estimate you want as to the cost of "defensive" medicine—the unneeded treatments and extra tests that are performed to protect physicians against the accusations of malpractice—but the amounts are huge. The lowest figure I've heard is $15.0 billion; the highest is $240 billion, about 35 percent of the total cost for health care in the United States.
>
> Let me give you just one example:

> myringotomy. Children are very susceptible to ear infections, which can lead to deafness. In myringotomy, a tiny plastic tube is inserted into the ear of a child to provide drainage. It doesn't hurt and it does relieve pressure but it is expensive. One million of these operations are performed each year, at an average cost of $1,000. Probably 95 percent of those operations are not needed, but if you don't do it and it falls in the 5 percent that is needed, you are automatically guilty of malpractice [Statement of health care consultant].

Medical malpractice is not a small problem. It is also, to the surprise of many, not a new one. In 1880, *The Medical Herald: A Monthly Journal of Medicine and Surgery* carried an article that is evidence both of the incidence of malpractice and of the frankness of speech during the previous century:

> The doctor, to be a successful practitioner and escape the penalties of the law, must bring to his practice ordinary skill and knowledge. He must possess the learning and experience of his profession, as laid down in the authorities of his day; and he must administer that knowledge with reasonable diligence, care, and skill. If he goes to his work thus armed with the experiences of the past, and uses his best judgment in new cases and in cases of doubt, he can have no fear of a contest with dishonest patients or knavish lawyers.
>
> He may (it is true) sometimes have to go into court at the suit of a miscreant, who finds it more to his taste to pursue the doctor for damages than to pay him for services, but such annoyances are incident to the best pursuits of life. The good and industrious are doomed in one way or another to support the bad and lazy. The lawyers who promote such suits are more to blame than the patients in whose names they are con-

ducted. Their clients are the mere machinery with which the dirty work of pettifogging is to be done, mere automatons that move through the courts at the debased will of impecunious knaves ... [all] for the purpose of filching money from doctors who may have accumulated a little property through service night and day in the cause of suffering humanity [Reuben T. Durrent, Esq., "Medical Malpractice—The Law Governing It," *The Medical Herald: A Monthly Journal of Medicine and Surgery*, 1880, quoted in the *1987 Report on Medical Liability*, Michigan State Medical Society, Lansing, Michigan, p. 17].

Despite the openly expressed concerns of Reuben T. Durrent, Esq., the incidence of legal claims for medical malpractice remained low until after World War II. It is not altogether an idealized portrait of that period to say that the family doctor was often also a family friend. House calls were still a practical necessity as many patients lacked the personal transportation needed to get to a doctor's office. A physician could still carry all of the diagnostic equipment needed, and most of the drugs that were available, in the traditional small black bag. With those limited resources, physicians were often unable to help many of their patients. But, patients and their families seemed to understand that; they expected the doctor's best efforts, and recognized that those best efforts might not inevitably be successful.

With the advent of the "wonder" drugs in the 1950s—primarily penicillin and other antibiotics—and the development of medical electronics during the 1960s, patients' expectations increased. At the same time, public respect for professionals such as doctors, attorneys, and government officials began to decline. It is not surprising that the first medical liability crisis occurred in the early 1970s, just at the time that *Marcus Welby, M.D.*—the flawless but fictional TV physician who cured every patient he ever saw and made lifelong friends with most of them—topped the Nielsen ratings. "That's the sort of care I want from my doctor" seemed to be the new attitude of the American public. But, of course, it was not available because it was fictional.

Most American physicians sincerely believe that excellent medical care is routinely available, and that it is generally provided in a humane, considerate manner. But, it cannot guarantee results. Patients die, or fail to recover, or suffer adverse consequences from the complex, and often painful, treatments. And, the friendly father figure who came to the home, dispensed drugs, prescribed rest, and reassured the family that all would be well in time, was now a technician, dressed in a starched white coat, who often seemed too hurried for full explanations or careful descriptions of what lay in store. Patients rebelled, and they sued.

The increase in malpractice suits can be attributed to a variety of factors that go considerably beyond the disenchantments and dissatisfactions of the regular patients. With health insurance and government funding, more people now have access to medical care. Technological advances have increased the chances of iatrogenic (medical-related) injury for those people. Care is being rendered for them in an increasing number of locations, by an increasing number of institutions, and by an increasing number of specialists. There are more actors, more settings, more procedures, *and* more risks of a bad outcome.

Patients sued for malpractice (a bad effort), though they often recovered for maloccurrence (a bad result). Almost all parties involved in malpractice litigation now admit that in many, if not most instances, there has been no negligent or unprofessional conduct. Instead, a blood clot develops during an operation, and the patient is paralyzed. Or, a baby is born slightly retarded, and the parents are devastated. Someone must be responsible, or some help must be provided, and the legal response was to file a tort.

Stated simply, a tort is an unjustified wrong committed by an individual that causes harm to another's person or property. Recovery of damages is then dependent upon proof that there was either an intentional or a negligent act. But intent and negligence are sometimes hard to prove, and our society has grown increasing sympathetic with an individual who has suffered an injury, whether caused by an intentional or negligent act or not. The net result, which has been documented in any number of reports over the past decade, is that both judges and juries have found ways to expand liability without adhering to traditional tort theory [Robben Fleming, *Report to Governor James Blanchard on the Subject of Health Care Provider Malpractice and Malpractice Insurance,* State of Michigan Printing Office, December 24, 1986, Lansing, Michigan, p. 2].

Our company has interviewed jurors after they rendered their decisions against our policyholders to determine what factors influenced their judgments. Frequently we are told they didn't believe the physician had committed malpractice, but that they felt sorry for the patient and decided to award insurance money to them as compensation for their unfortunate circumstances. The problem is that medical malpractice insurance dollars were intended to compensate people for injuries resulting from malpractice, not for unfortunate outcomes and circumstances [Letter from Michigan Physicians Mutual Liability Company published in the *Detroit Free Press,* December 19, 1988, p. A17].

One result of the increased payments for "unfortunate outcomes" is, of course, an increase in the premiums paid for medical malpractice insurance. The average premium for a general family practice increased from $4,500 in 1984 to $9,830 in 1986. The average premium for an obstetrical practice increased from $15,400 in 1984 to $37,780 in 1986. Premiums for some of the high-risk specialties, such as neurosurgery, came to over $100,000 in that year.

Alarmed by the growth in insurance premiums, and even more alarmed by the increasing reluctance of many physicians to treat high-risk patients, a number of states enacted tort reforms during the mid-1980s in an attempt to slow the increase in malpractice claims and jury awards. The tort reforms in Michigan were typical of those enacted throughout the country:

Noneconomic damages (that is, for pain and suffering) were limited to $225,000. Economic damages, however, continued to include loss of wages and cost of care for the balance of the person's disability, or life.

Plaintiffs had to deduct payments received from third parties [that is, from health care insurers for hospital stays, etc.] from the damage awards, and could no longer collect twice for the same occurrence.

Adults were prohibited from pursuing malpractice claims more than two years after the alleged malpractice occurrence, while minors had to commence a lawsuit before their 15th birthday.

Expert witnesses had to specialize in the same medical specialty as the defendant, and had to devote substantial time to the active clinical practice of that speciality; they could no longer be supported by court appearances.

It was felt that the tort reforms of the mid-1980s slowed the number of malpractice suits, but not the size of the awards. The premiums for malpractice insurance continued to rise. The costs of defensive medicine continued to escalate. And the dissatisfactions of the participants continued to be expressed:

If maloccurrence and malpractice continue to remain indistinguishable in our society, our efforts to tinker with the tort system will do little to prevent crises in the availability and cost of medical care. These reforms do not adequately address two major problems with our civil justice system: (1) true victims of malpractice most often wait years to recover damages, and (2) more than half of an award goes not to the victim, but to legal costs and attorney fees [Michigan State Medical Society, *1987 Report on Medical Liability*, p. 18].

It is true that the number of frivolous lawsuits filed by attorneys has decreased since the Legislature attempted to alleviate the crisis in 1986. The reduction may be the result of tort reform, or it may be just a low ebb in a familiar cycle, leaving even the reduced number much higher than it was 10 years ago.

But the underlying problem in our liability crisis, the archaic, antiquated and much abused tort system, has not been reformed enough to solve the crisis. A legal system that eats up over two-thirds of the insurance premium dollar through court costs and attorney fees is clearly not the best solution [Fred W. Bryant, M.D., Letter to the Editor, *Detroit Free Press*, December 10, 1988, p. 14A.].

As is true of almost all disputes that continue unabated over time, eventually each of the parties begins to attack the motives, character, and intent of the others. This has certainly happened in medical malpractice. Many doctors think that lawyers exploit the situation, for private gain. Many attorneys say that it is entirely the fault of the physicians, for failing to police their profession. Both blame the insurance companies, for inaccurate projections of their liabilities and insufficient returns on their investments. Hospitals blame doctors, attorneys, and insurers alike for much if not all of their escalating costs.

Many physicians now assume that if a testing technology is available, the doctor is legally obligated to use it, even if the clinical indications that the test is called for are minuscule. If your patient has a headache, you feel compelled to order a CT scan to compile a record useful in fighting a future malpractice claim because you know that the attorney in the courtroom will sarcastically ask you, "Even though Mr. James complained repeatedly about headache pain, you did not believe that it was necessary to employ modern diagnostic equipment, and preferred to rely upon your "professional" intuition [Statement of health care consultant].

The arguments between doctors, attorneys, insurance firms, and hospitals over who is basically to blame for the medical malpractice crisis have to a considerable extent neglected the impact of those squabbles upon one of the major participants in the system: the patient. A recent survey showed a definite impact upon the type and availability of care received by patients:

> The severity of the medical liability problem can be seen in the attitudes expressed by family practice physicians. Over 3 out of 4 rate medical liability as the most severe problem facing them today. Almost all report practicing more defensive medicine as a result of the problem. Over 3 out of 4 say they routinely order more tests, and over 2 out of 3 say they avoid high-risk patients. Nearly 3 out of 4 family practice physicians in the current study say that they believe women in Michigan are unable to get competent obstetrical care because of the medical liability problem [Martin Block, *Medical Liability Insurance and Family Practice*].

Five explicit proposals have been made to remedy or at least ameliorate the medical liability problem. These proposals are listed below, together with brief statements by the supporters and the opponents:

1. Establish arbitrators to review all cases before they come to court; only those with clear evidence of incompetence or neglect would be allowed to proceed.

   The problem is that "malpractice" used to mean negligence or error; now it just means an unfortunate occurrence. If a child is born with a withered arm, all the attorney has to do is get that baby before a jury, and he or she will win the award.

We need a trained arbitrator to eliminate that type of "sympathy" case when it involves absolutely no evidence of malpractice [Statement of physician].

The problem is that the trained arbitrator will have to be a physician, and physicians have never been willing to discipline other physicians. Doctors have historically been unwilling to admit that another doctor could be incompetent or inattentive. The result will be that only the most blatant examples of malpractice will ever be approved for trial [Statement of attorney].

2. Limit payments to attorneys to a "reasonable" amount per hour, and prohibit contingency fees where the attorney received a percentage of the award.

Can it really be that American doctors are such nincompoops that one in five does something dangerously negligent each year? Can it really be that doctors in major cities, where malpractice suits are most frequent, are nowhere near as proficient as doctors in small towns, where claims are infrequent? Logically, the increase in malpractice claims has to be related to the increase in numbers of lawyers in society. It is the big cities, after all, where those vultures roost. Canada and England and the balance of Western Europe prohibit contingency fees, and they have no medical malpractice problem. If we do the same thing, we will have the same result [Statement of physician].

If you limit the fee, you limit the right to sue. Medical malpractice cases are expensive to research and then to try. You need extensive preparation, for the details of each are different, and you have to have truly expert "expert" witnesses and they are expensive to bring to court. If you prohibit contingency fees, you prohibit most patients from ever having their day in court [Statement of attorney].

3. Remove the right to practice from physicians who are repeatedly sued, and found guilty of medical malpractice, in order to "clean up" the profession.

No one wants to defend incompetence in any field, particularly medicine. But doctors go through four years of medical school, a minimum of two years of internship, plus two to three years of residency in their speciality, and they have a requirement for continuing education. How do you establish that a person with that extent of training is incompetent? You can't just count up all of the times that a given person is in court; he or she may be the physician that takes the risky cases [Statement of physician].

In one study in Pennsylvania, it was found that 25 percent of the malpractice payments were caused by 1 percent of the practicing physicians. It is a pretty good bet that this 1 percent comprises a guided tour of the state's worst doctors. Why not get rid of them? Nationally, just 406 medical licenses were revoked in 1985, or one out of every 1,300 physicians in the country. I cannot believe that the other 1,299 are all competent, concerned, and current in their fields [Statement of attorney].

4. Provide a federal or state subsidy for malpractice insurance and in essence accept the current trend in public opinion towards payments for "medical maloccurrence."

If we are going to do this, then for goodness sake we should be honest and enact a full catastrophic health care bill. We should not reward just those patients and their attorneys who sue for malpractice. The attorneys won't like that. Now they get 40 percent to 50 percent of the maloccurrence awards, but that income stream will just plain stop with federal funding for catastrophic health care. Attorneys could still sue for malpractice, but there they will have to prove incompetence, not just elicit sympathy for the financial plight of the patient, and that is much harder to do [Statement of physician].

I think that some public support of malpractice insurance, combined with some increased stringency in licensing physicians, is the only way to solve the malpractice problem. The doctors won't like it. But, at some point they are going to have to recognize that the public good takes precedence over their private gain [Statement of attorney].

Class Assignment

Decide which of the four alternatives you would recommend if you were a member of the governor's staff, assigned to study the malpractice problem within your state. Be specific on the ethical principles that you would use to support your judgment.

REFERENCES

Bickel, Alexander, "The Uninhibited, Robust, and Wide Open First Amendment," in *Where Do You Draw the Line?*, Victor B. Cline (ed.), Brigham Young University Press, Provo, UT, 1974, pp. 63–78.

Christenson, Reo, "Without Redeeming Social Value?" in *Where Do You Draw the Line?*, Victor B. Cline (ed.), Brigham Young University Press, Provo, UT, 1974, pp. 309–316.

Cline, Victor, *Where Do You Draw the Line?*, Brigham Young University Press, Provo, UT, 1974.

Demac, Donna, "Limits of the Law," *Media and Values*, Media Action Research Center, Los Angeles, Fall 1985, p. 21.

Fowles, Jib, "The Craniology of the 20th Century: Research on Television Effects," *Television Quarterly*, 1984, pp. 30–45.

Freedman, Jonathan L., "Effect of Television Violence on Aggressiveness," *Psychological Bulletin: American Psychological Association*, 1984, pp. 227–246.

Friedrich-Cofer, Lynette, "Time for Research Is Past," *Media and Values*, Media Action Research Center, Los Angeles, Fall 1985, pp. 15–16.

Liebert, Robert M., Emily S. Davidson, and John M. Neale, "Aggression in Childhood: The Impact of Television," in *Where Do You Draw the Line?*, Victor B. Cline (ed.), Brigham Young University Press, Provo, UT, 1974, pp. 113–128.

Lynn, Barry W., "Piecing the Puzzle," *Media and Values*, Media Action Research Center, Los Angeles, Fall 1985, p. 9.

Siegel, Alberta, "The Desensitization of Children to TV Violence," in *Where Do You Draw the Line?*, Victor B. Cline (ed.), Brigham Young University Press, Provo, UT, 1974, pp. 129–146.

Singer, Dorothy, "Does Violent Television Produce Aggressive Children?" *Pediatric Annals*, December 1985, pp. 804–810.

Singer, Dorothy, "Caution: Television May Be Hazardous to a Child's Mental Health," *Developmental and Behavioral Pediatrics*, October 1989, pp. 259–261.

Singer, Dorothy, and Jerome Singer, "TV Violence: What's All the Fuss About?" *Television and Children*, Spring 1984, pp. 30–41.

Singer, Dorothy, and Jerome Singer, "Television Viewing and Aggressive Behavior in Preschool Children: A Field Study," *Annals New York Academy of Sciences*, 1989, pp. 289–303.

Social Research Unit and Broadcast Standards Department, *A Research Perspective on Television Violence*, American Broadcasting Companies, Inc., New York, 1983.

Wilson, James Q., "Violence, Pornography, and Social Justice," in *Where Do You Draw the Line?*, Victor B. Cline (ed.), Brigham Young University Press, Provo, UT, 1974, pp. 293–308.

NOTE: These books are references for Case 3–5, "Violence on Television and the Impact upon Children."

Index